D1154464

Cockpit

OF THE REVOLUTION

THE PRINCETON HISTORY
OF NEW JERSEY

Capture of General Charles Lee by the British, December 13, 1776.
(From a contemporary print)

Cockpit

OF THE REVOLUTION

THE WAR FOR INDEPENDENCE
IN NEW JERSEY

By Leonard Lundin

OCTAGON BOOKS

A DIVISION OF FARRAR, STRAUS AND GIROUX

New York   1972

Reprinted 1972
by special arrangement with Princeton University Press

OCTAGON BOOKS
A Division of Farrar, Straus & Giroux, Inc.
19 Union Square West
New York, N. Y. 10003

Library of Congress Catalog Card Number: 74-159210

ISBN 0-374-95143-8

Printed in U.S.A. by
NOBLE OFFSET PRINTERS, INC.
NEW YORK 3, N. Y.

INTRODUCTION

IN the second volume of the Princeton History of New Jersey, *Cockpit of the Revolution: The War for Independence in New Jersey*, Professor Leonard Lundin, maintains the high standard set by Dr. Wheaton J. Lane in *From Indian Trail to Iron Horse*. The reader moves through the fascinating pages with a sense of being a participant in the events described, of witnessing the marches of the British army or of Washington's troops, of being personally acquainted, not only with great military and political leaders, but even with minor characters. The volume brings one step nearer completion the design of a comprehensive and voluminous history of New Jersey, financed by Lloyd W. Smith, of Madison, and edited by the Department of History of Princeton University.

Professor Lundin gives a picture of conditions in the colony prior to the outbreak of war, separates the people into the hostile camps as Tories or Whigs, rewrites with a vivid pen the story of the vitally important campaigns which culminated at Princeton and Monmouth, pictures the alternating elation or despair of the patriots as the fortunes of war varied, analyzes the first state constitution, explains the injurious effects of partisan politics in the state during the Revolution, adds new and vivid details to the old story of burnings and pillaging, of raids and reprisals. In addition he presents for the first time a connected narrative of many troop movements and engagements, relatively unimportant in themselves, but affecting vitally the more decisive campaigns and the final outcome of the struggle. The chief political developments in the years from the Stamp Act to the Declaration of Independence have either been omitted or touched upon lightly, as they are to be treated fully in the third volume of the series, *The Path to Freedom*, by Professor Donald L. Kemmerer.

Professor Lundin stresses the economic causes of the Revolution and economic factors in dividing the people of the colony into Loyalists and Revolutionists, in harmony with the school of historical interpretation led by Charles Beard. He shows that the holders of lucrative colonial offices, the wealthy merchants, the great landholders as a class frowned on "rebellion" and aided the king during hostilities; while the ironmasters, whose profits had been cut down by governmental restrictions, went over to the patriot side. If, in throwing the pitiless light of historical investigation upon the careers of leaders on both sides, he dims the glamor which has long hovered about some of them, it is but the sacrifice which sentiment must make to truth.

If we are to understand the great movement which brought independence to the American people, students of history must give us more detailed studies of its origin and development in the different colonies and sections. Historians have been slow to recognize the fact that national history is founded on local history, and so have fallen into the error of making generalizations or sweeping statements upon insufficient evidence. We can no longer leave the field of local history to the antiquarian and the genealogist, who only too frequently sacrifice breadth of treatment and interpretation to insignificant details. The history which treats of a limited field or limited period should be a scholarly study, ready to be fitted into the great field of American history as a whole. This important service Professor Lundin has accomplished in admirable style for the American Revolution in New Jersey. Local in scope, his volume is national in its implications.

T. J. W.

PREFACE

NEW JERSEY has never been blessed with that genius for self-advertising so highly developed in some of its sister states, and its importance during the Revolution has received scant attention from historians trained in the tradition of New England or Virginia. Nevertheless, the chronicles of the state for those years of turmoil are of no little interest.

Insofar as the outcome of the American struggle for independence was decided at any one time and place, that decision occurred during the winter of 1776-1777 in the territory between the Delaware and the Hudson. Of the determining factors, Washington's daring and military skill and the corresponding blunders of British commanders were of first importance; but the attitude of Jerseymen themselves helped to weight the scales. So far as communications and strategy were concerned, New Jersey was virtually a bottleneck between the states lying to the east and to the south of it. Had the British succeeded, as they nearly did, in overrunning it entirely, intercourse between New England and the South would have been almost totally disrupted. An advance of fifty or sixty miles northwest of the farthest British outposts in New Jersey might have accomplished the same end which Germain vainly endeavored to achieve through the invasion from Canada in 1777. It is hardly too much to say that the fate of Morristown was more important for the outcome of the war than the fortunes of any other town in the thirteen states except Albany, and that the Watchung Mountains, of which probably few schoolboys outside New Jersey have heard, were of greater significance in the contest than was Breed's Hill.

This book, however, is not primarily a dissertation on the military and strategic aspects of the Revolution. Such topics appear only as a background for the picture the following chapters attempt to draw—the picture of a community caught in a struggle which it had done little to precipitate, of a small, bewildered, disunited province, narrowly provincial in outlook and interests, which suddenly found itself in the path of contending armies. In the reactions of New Jersey to the emergency we can perhaps find a truer picture of Revolutionary America than that afforded by New England, with its extraordinary degree of political consciousness, or Virginia, with its amazing crop of leaders. From the Hudson to the Delaware confusion, hesitancy, prejudice, and dissension were as general among the people as they are over the great public issues of today. Courage was not lacking, when obviously required, but conviction often was. Positive action was required of people who had not made up their minds.

As the unwelcome war thrust itself into the lives of Jerseymen, they showed themselves to be not particularly wise, most of them, or particularly foolish, not outstandingly heroic or notoriously craven, capable at times of great bravery or generosity, but relapsing more often into indifference, timidity, greed, and quarrelsomeness. They were, in other words, ordinary people; and ordinary people are not happy in extraordinary crises which they do not understand. Yet for year after year they and their leaders had to go on with the dull, dreary business of enduring and persevering, with the shadow of disaster never far from their doorsteps. Such men as Governor William Livingston, who bore with unflagging courage and energy the responsibility for administering this distracted state, deserve at least as high a place in the roster of Revolutionary heroes as the more colorful military men.

This volume has no pretensions to definitiveness: it is nothing more ambitious than a preliminary survey. To search out, read, and assimilate all the widely scattered materials relating to New Jersey during the War for Independence would be a task requiring many years of labor. As yet there exist no adequate special studies to lighten the burden, and local histories of the state are, with a few notable exceptions, unscholarly, unreliable, and often maddeningly uninformative upon precisely the points in which one is most interested. Many such studies as the monograph on New Jersey Loyalists by Miss E. Marie Becker of Freehold, in process of preparation as this volume goes to press, are needed before the story of the Revolutionary years can be fully understood and properly recounted.

The shortcomings of the present work are obvious. Various repositories or collections of source materials have been left untouched. Certain important topics—notably wartime finance and the actual quantitative military contribution of New Jersey—have received scant attention, either because information is unavailable or because I am not competent to deal with them adequately. My hope is that scholars and students who read this book will be less interested in censuring it for what it has not done than in pursuing the lines of investigation which it may suggest.

For such merits as this study may have I am indebted to the assistance of many persons, who bear, however, no responsibility for its defects. Professors Thomas Jefferson Wertenbaker and Clifton R. Hall of Princeton University were generous with help and criticism while the manuscript was in preparation. Dr. T. Walter Herbert of Berry College was responsible for some improvements in style. To Mr. Lloyd W. Smith, whose generosity makes possible this series of volumes, hearty thanks are due. In the course of my research I have had reason to be grateful to the Honorable Henry E. Pickersgill of Perth Amboy, who gave me access to his collection of manuscripts; to the cheerful and incredibly efficient Miss Dorothy Lucas of the New Jersey State Library; to Mr. Carlos E. Godfrey of the Public Record Office in Trenton; to Dr. Amandus Johnson of the American

Swedish Historical Museum; to Miss Edna Vosper and Mr. Randolph G. Adams of the William L. Clements Library; to the staff of the Library of Congress, in particular Mr. Donald Mugridge of the Manuscripts Division; to Miss Marion Cushman of the Rutgers University Library; to the staffs of the Princeton University Library (in particular Mr. George M. Peck), the John Carter Brown Library of Brown University (especially Mr. Lawrence C. Wroth), the Harvard College Library, the Stevens Institute Library, the New York Public Library, the Ridgway Library of the Philadelphia Library Company, and the Morristown Library; to the Massachusetts, New York, and New Jersey Historical Societies and the Historical Society of Pennsylvania; to the staff of the Morristown National Historical Park; and to the Council of Proprietors of the Eastern Division of New Jersey for access to records in the office of the surveyor general of Perth Amboy. Mr. William H. Richardson of Jersey City was prodigal of his time and his advice in a way that only those who know him personally can appreciate. Dr. Ransom E. Noble of Long Island University assisted generously in the preparation of the manuscript. Mr. and Mrs. Louis H. Bean of Arlington, Virginia, gave unstinted hospitality in the long weeks when I was working at the Library of Congress.

I cannot conclude these acknowledgments without a word of appreciation for the assistance of my parents. They have been unfailingly helpful and encouraging in all the stages of preparing this book; they furnished me with financial assistance when other means of support ran low; my father adapted for publication the Robertson sketch of New Brunswick; and my mother has given countless hours of intelligent and efficient work to typing, indexing, and other irksome duties.

Acknowledgments are due to the John Carter Brown Library for permission to reproduce parts of the Ebenezer David letters; to the William L. Clements Library for permission to publish the plan of Howe's winter cantonments and the map of the country about Morristown, both taken from the British Headquarters Maps; and to the following publishers or copyright owners for leave to quote from the books mentioned after their names: Dr. Amandus Johnson, *The Journal and Biography of Nicholas Collin*; Harald Elovson, of Lund University, Sweden, *Amerika i svensk litteratur*; the Yale University Press, *The Correspondence of General Thomas Gage*; the Society for Promoting Christian Knowledge (London), *Life and Letters of Charles Inglis*; Goodspeed's Book Shop, *History of the Arts of Design*, by William Dunlap; Jonathan Cape, Limited (London), *The Journal of Nicholas Creswell*; G. P. Putnam's Sons, *Literary History of the American Revolution*, by Moses Coit Tyler; J. B. Lippincott Company, *Glimpses of Colonial Society*, by W. J. Mills; Houghton Mifflin Company, *Builders of the Bay Colony*, by Samuel Eliot Morison, and *The Battles of Trenton and Princeton*, by William S. Stryker; Harper and Brothers, *American Economic History*, by Harold U. Faulkner; The Macmillan Company, *History of the United States*, by Edward Channing, and *Travels in the American Colonies*, by Newton D. Mereness; the Bobbs-Merrill Company, *George Washington Himself*, by John C. Fitzpatrick.

L. L.

A NOTE ON THE SOURCES

MATERIALS concerning New Jersey in the period of the American Revolution are widely scattered, and special phases of the subject are mentioned or discussed, often very briefly, in almost innumerable published works, as a glance at the footnotes in this volume will suggest. Under these circumstances it would be sheer pedantry to prepare a bibliography listing the multitude of sources from which the substance of this work has been drawn. Only a few of the most useful need be mentioned here. The most valuable printed materials are to be found in the *New Jersey Archives*; the *Proceedings* of the New Jersey Historical Society; *The Writings of George Washington*, edited by John C. Fitzpatrick and published by the United States George Washington Bicentennial Commission; the *Acts of the Council and General Assembly of the State of New-Jersey*, compiled by Peter Wilson and published in Trenton in 1784; the *Journal of the Votes & Proceedings of the Convention of the State of New Jersey*, published at Burlington in 1776 and reprinted in 1831; the *Votes and Proceedings of the General Assembly of the State of New-Jersey* for the war years; and *Selections from the Correspondence of the Executive of New Jersey, from 1776 to 1786*, published at Newark by order of the Legislature in 1848. (The last-named work regularizes spelling, punctuation, and occasionally grammar.)

Among manuscript collections richest in material dealing with the history of the state during the war are the Washington Papers in the Library of Congress, which contain hundreds of documents dealing with almost every phase of the struggle as it affected New Jersey and constitute an indispensable source; the collections in the Public Record Office and in Room 118 of the State Library in Trenton; the

Sparks Collection in the Harvard College Library; the William Livingston Papers in the Library of the Massachusetts Historical Society (not voluminous, but interesting); the Brunswick Papers in the Manuscripts Division of the New York Public Library; and the Von Jungkenn Manuscripts in the William L. Clements Library at the University of Michigan. Both of these last-named collections throw light on military aspects of the war as seen through German eyes, and occasionally furnish useful correctives to the views held by historians who have depended solely on sources in the English language. Doubtless the Clinton Papers, now also in the Clements Library, would be very valuable to the military historian; they were not available at the time when this study was in preparation.

Investigators of special topics touched upon in this book may find bibliographical help in the footnote references.

(The most common abbreviations in footnote references are as follows: *N.J.A.* for *New Jersey Archives*, *N.J.A.*, 2nd S., for *New Jersey Archives*, Second Series; *N.J.H.S.P.* for *Proceedings of the New Jersey Historical Society*; *N.J.H.S.P.*, 2nd S., for *Proceedings of the New Jersey Historical Society*, Second Series; *N.J.H.S.P.*, N.S., for *Proceedings of the New Jersey Historical Society*, New Series; S.P.G. transcripts, for Society for the Propagation of the Gospel in Foreign Parts, transcripts of correspondence, in Manuscripts Division, Library of Congress.)

CONTENTS

ILLUSTRATIONS

Cockpit

OF THE REVOLUTION

CHAPTER I ☼ *NEW JERSEY IN 1776*

TO a casual traveller journeying by land from New York to Philadelphia in the early 1770's, nothing in the smiling countryside through which he passed could have suggested the imminence of revolution or of bitter civil war. "The garden of America," as more than one visitor called the province of New Jersey,[1] seemed remote from the turmoils and contentions which result in armed violence. Charmed with this peaceful and idyllic region, Europeans compared its appearance to that of England, and wrote with approval of its fertile, well tilled fields, its prosperous orchards, its substantial stone houses, barns, and granaries.[2]

The kindly soil, as travellers might observe on all sides, afforded to the poor man an opportunity of achieving a modest prosperity through hard work. "Take this Province in the lump," said Governor Belcher in 1748, "it is the best country I have seen for men of middling fortunes, and for people who have to live by the sweat of their brows."[3] Thirty-eight years later, an observer well acquainted with New Jersey could still declare: "On the whole this is an excellent Country for the poorer and middling ranks of people: as with due Industry they may all earn a comfortable living and even advance themselves, tho' not so speedily as formerly."[4]

Yet in this apparently happy and thriving province the approaching war was to work such havoc and cause such

---

[1] *N.J.A.*, 2nd S., Vol. I, p. 432; Andrew Burnaby, *Travels through the Middle Settlements* (New York, 1904), pp. 110, 119; Newton D. Mereness, ed., *Travels in the American Colonies* (New York, 1916), p. 414; Marquis de Chastellux, *Travels in North-America* (Dublin, 1787), Vol. I, p. 169.

[2] Mereness, *op. cit.*, p. 414; Nicholas Creswell, *Journal, 1774-1777* (London, 1925), pp. 264-5; Count Axel Fersen, *Diary and Correspondence* (Boston, 1902), p. 48.

[3] *N.J.H.S.P.*, Vol VII, p. 102.

[4] John Rutherfurd, "Notes on the State of New Jersey" (1786), in *N.J.H.S.P.*, 2nd S., Vol. I, p. 87.

internal convulsions as were scarcely paralleled in any other part of America. It was not merely that the opposing armies, in their interminable campaigns, crossed and recrossed the territory between the Delaware and the Hudson, leaving in their train destruction and want: almost more baneful than these ravages were the civil dissensions which racked the entire state. Among the frontiersmen of the northwestern valleys, the rich merchants of Perth Amboy, and the simple farmers of the southwest, life became feverish and uncertain.

Civil discord divided families and estranged friends. Life-long neighbors plundered one another, drove one another from home, shot one another from ambush. Farmhouses and villages went up in flames. Fierce raiders swept suddenly out of the night upon sleeping communities and homesteads. Over the placid fields of Quaker farmers along the Delaware drifted the noise and smoke of violent naval cannonades; but the bellowing fury of royal battleships can scarcely have been more terrifying to the residents of this vicinity than the crackle of musket shots at daybreak in nearby Swedesborough as refugee Loyalists suddenly attacked the settlement to avenge their expulsion.

Why did peaceful, bucolic New Jersey fall prey in such measure to the disruptive forces of hatred and violence? Neither the dissolution of the normal pattern of life among the people nor the course of military operations can be properly understood without a somewhat familiar acquaintance with the geography and social conditions of the province. In the following survey of the New Jersey of 1776, with its sprawling and heterogeneous population, the observations must necessarily be rambling and connected chiefly by the loose thread of geographical juxtaposition. From them, however, we may be able to reconstruct with some fidelity the appearance of this small but surprisingly complex colony in the years immediately preceding independence.

To the visitor approaching from the city of New York by the most customary route, New Jersey presented in the eighteenth century a countenance less seamed, worn, and dingy, to be sure, than that which greets the traveller today, but one scarcely more alluring. The ridge of the Palisades, which rises from the Hudson River as a sheer cliff farther upstream, retreats somewhat from the edge of the water opposite the lower end of Manhattan Island, and decreases steadily in both height and steepness as it stretches southward. Separated from this wooded upland by a strip of salt marsh, and lying directly opposite the tip of the island on which nestled the small city of New York, there existed a century and a half ago a congeries of sand-hills known as Powles Hook. To this, the nearest point in New Jersey, plied the chief ferry from Manhattan. Unless the traveller happened to be a devotee of horse-racing, a sport for which a track had been laid out among the sand-hills of Powles Hook, there was nothing at the New Jersey terminus of the ferry to hold his interest.[5] Passing over the belt of tidal marsh, he crossed the ridge, here about a hundred feet high, near the top of which perched the Dutch village of Bergen, "a small ill built town" which offered little to charm or detain him.

West of the upland extended the valley of the Hackensack—a wide, flat expanse of dreary tidal meadows, interspersed with cedar swamps, and almost uninhabited. The American soldiers who marched through this territory during the war were obliged, even on the causeway which had been built across the marshes, to wade "half leg deep in mud and water," and made the acquaintance of those swarms of mosquitoes for which New Jersey has always been famous.[6] Through the soggy plain the wide Hackensack River mean-

[5] Charles H. Winfield, *History of the County of Hudson, New Jersey* (New York, 1874), pp. 279-80.

[6] "Campaign Journal of Algernon Roberts" in Sparks MSS. (Harvard College Library), 48; William A. Whitehead, *Contributions to the Early History of Perth Amboy* (New York, 1856), p. 287.

dered sluggishly; the Passaic, too, for its last few miles, flowed across the marshes before emptying into Newark Bay.

To the north, the area of the tidal meadows gradually narrowed, and, above the pleasant village of Hackensack,[7] gave place almost entirely to a gently undulating country more attractive to settlers. Here, in the upper valleys of the Hackensack and Saddle Rivers, there was a considerable farming population. The inhabitants, like those scattered along the Palisades ridge to the east and south, were chiefly of Dutch extraction, and retained many features of that peculiar culture of New Netherlands which Washington Irving was to satirize a few decades later.[8] Their churches and dwelling houses, one observer tells us, were mostly one story high and built of rough stone. "There is a peculiar neatness," he continues, "in the appearance of their dwellings, having an airy piazza supported by pillars in front, and their kitchens connected at the ends in the form of wings. The land is remarkably level, and the soil fertile, and being generally advantageously cultivated, the people appear to enjoy ease and happy competency. The furniture in their houses is of the most ordinary kind, and such as might be supposed to accord with the fashion of the days of Queen Ann. They despise the superfluities of life, and are ambitious to appear always neat and cleanly, and never to complain of an empty purse."[9]

In addition to the homes of these simple and thrifty farmers, Bergen County[10] contained a number of more pre-

---

[7] Andrew Hunter, MS. diary (Princeton University Library), Nov. 14, 1776.

[8] For example, William Livingston writes over a pseudonym to the *New Jersey Gazette* in 1777 about the "rural ladies" of Bergen County who "pride themselves in an incredible number of petticoats; which, like house-furniture, are displayed by way of ostentation, for many years before they are decreed to invest the fair bodies of the proprietors. Till that period they are never worn, but neatly piled up on each side of an immense escritoire, the top of which is decorated with a most capacious brass-clasped Bible, seldom read."— *N.J.A.*, 2nd S., Vol. I, p. 532.

[9] James Thacher, *A Military Journal* (Boston, 1823), p. 187.

[10] Including what has since been detached as Hudson County.

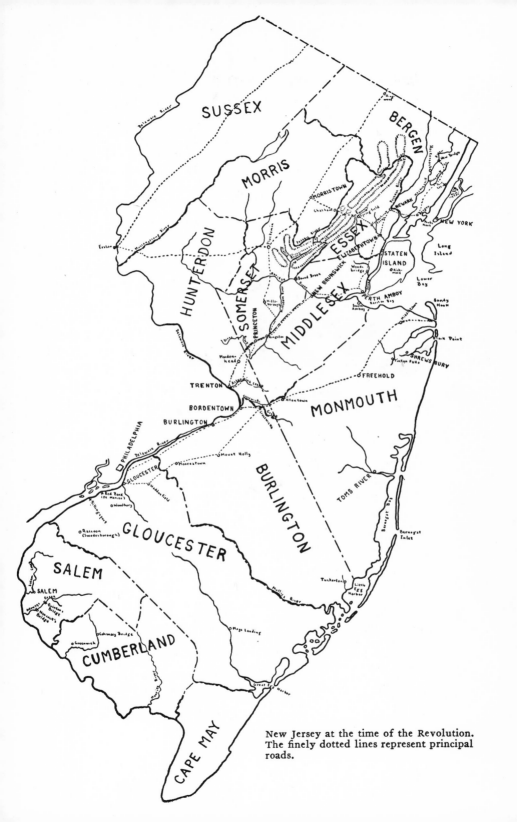

New Jersey at the time of the Revolution.
The finely dotted lines represent principal
roads.

tentious country residences and estates. Although there are probably few persons today to whom the name "Hoboken" connotes primarily either bucolic delights or sophisticated elegance, yet in the latter part of the eighteenth century both these attractions were united in the summer home at Castle Point or Hoboken belonging to William Bayard, merchant and landowner of New York City. Bayard's mansion was built on a hill above the river, now occupied by the Stevens Institute, and was surrounded by a prosperous farm with extensive gardens and orchards.[11] A good landing-place on the property led the owner in 1775 to encourage the opening of a ferry in competition with that at Powles Hook, a mile or so to the southward. So idyllic was the situation that the manager of the ferry, in advertising the opening of the enterprise, suggested that even those who were not planning to travel farther would find the excursion to Hoboken a delightful manner of spending a summer's day.[12]

Bayard, to be sure, was not so opulent as his neighbor, Arent Schuyler, whose broad acres were worked by fifty or sixty slaves, and who lived in the style of an English lord, even to the point of keeping two well stocked deer parks.[13] Yet the master of Hoboken was wealthy enough and prominent enough so that he felt obliged in the troubled early months of the Revolution to trim his political sails to the prevailing winds, in order not to forfeit his estate through ill-calculated zeal.

In the first instance he may have been impelled to this prudent course of conduct by a consciousness that he was not popular. For many years he had enlivened existence in his idyllic retreat by wrangling with his poorer neighbors over the apportionment of certain common lands in the vicinity.

[11] Winfield, *op. cit.*, p. 317; *N.J.A.*, 2nd S., Vol. I, p. 412 n.

[12] *ibid.*, pp. 279-80.

[13] "Journal of Isaac Bangs," in *N.J.H.S.P.*, Vol. VIII, pp. 120, 123-4; Aaron Lloyd, "Contributions to the Early History of the Reformed Dutch Church of Second River" in *N.J.H.S.P.*, 2nd S., Vol. IX, pp. 211-18.

In pursuing this dispute in the courts, Bayard enjoyed a great advantage in his superior financial resources, and succeeded, by means of his influence and prestige, in winning official support for his claims. This circumstance, we may well suppose, neither enhanced his popularity nor deepened the devotion to the royal government in the breasts of his opponents.[14]

Such protracted quarrelling over lands was a characteristic phase of neighborly relationships in Bergen County. The vicissitudes to which the colony of New Jersey had been subjected in its early years—the alternation between Dutch and English sovereignty and between royal and proprietary government—had created a series of legal tangles eminently suited to indulge the litigious bent of the American colonial mind. A legacy of interminable lawsuits which dragged themselves out through the seventeenth and eighteenth centuries served to poison social relationships throughout a considerable part of northeastern New Jersey.

To the annoying effect of this state of affairs one of Bayard's near neighbors could have borne eloquent testimony. In 1724, Archibald Kennedy, Sr., receiver-general and collector of customs in New York, had laid the foundation of both prosperity and trouble for himself by purchasing a tract of land at Horsimus, between Powles Hook and Hoboken. Possession of this farm was claimed also by the freeholders of Bergen township by a title dating back to 1668; and Kennedy's neighbors, believing that they were being kept from the rightful enjoyment of property which belonged to them in common, spared themselves no pains to make the newcomer aware of his unpopularity. Before he died in 1763, the receiver-general had grown accustomed to such incidents as finding his best apple trees girdled, or having a fine bull pushed into a well, a stallion pierced with a pitchfork, or a servant stoned. Resort to the courts had led

14 *N.J.A.*, Vol. X, pp. 153 *ff.*, 168 *ff.*, 188-91, 197.

to a verdict in favor of the freeholders; but when Kennedy threatened to appeal to England, litigation was allowed to lapse. "The plain people of Bergen could not think of contending with a crown officer in the British courts, and they remained quiet until a successful rebellion destroyed an appeal to the courts of the mother country."[15]

To this inheritance of unpopularity Kennedy's son, Archibald, a captain in the royal navy, succeeded in 1763, and he seems to have increased it by unneighborly acts.[16] Up to the time of the Revolution the heir of Horsimus continued to prosper in the face of widespread dislike. By an advantageous marriage, he came into possession of another fine estate, situated on high ground on the east bank of the Passaic, opposite Newark. The coming of the war, however, was to bring retribution. Upon the outbreak of hostilities, Kennedy retired to the country-seat on the Passaic, in the vain hope of withdrawing himself and his Loyalist sentiments from the notice of rebel committees. His neighbors, however, seized this long-awaited opportunity to make his life more disagreeable than ever; and before the end of the Revolution, having succeeded to a Scottish peerage, he shook from his feet the dust of New Jersey, leaving behind him forever his houses, farms, gardens, and fruitful orchards, his deer park, his seventy-foot-long greenhouse and tropical plants, his coach-house and stables.[17]

The Kennedy estate, situated in the rolling country along the Passaic, brings us to that belt of extensive cultivation and comparatively thick settlement which so many travellers saw and admired. It extended west and southwest from Bergen County between the shore and the double range of the Watchung Mountains which sweeps in a great arc from north of Pompton to Pluckemin. The level or gently undulating country between the hills and the sea has long

---

[15] Winfield, *op. cit.*, pp. 307-12.   [16] *ibid.*, p. 244.

[17] *ibid.*, pp. 312-13; Jones, *op. cit.*, pp. 119-20; Burnaby, *op. cit.*, p. 107. For Kennedy's part in the war, see p. 380.

since been transformed in large part into a region of smoking factories, busy urban centers, and areas of crowded, dreary habitations which for miles offend alike the eye and the humanity of the traveller; but in the eighteenth century the district was one of the most delightful in America. "I took a ride," writes a British army officer, "up the River, from Elizabeth-Town called Passaick, for twenty two Miles, and in my life I never saw, a more beautiful Country, its Banks are all clear, and houses at every 500 yards, on both sides of it."[18] Another British traveller of the period, making the same trip along the river bank to the Great Falls, where the Passaic breaks through the Second Mountain, speaks of the "rich country, interspersed with fine fields and gentlemen's estates."[19]

This flourishing agricultural region stretched southward through Essex and Middlesex Counties to the lower Raritan, on the farther side of which it soon divided into two branches. One of these followed the upper course of the river into Somerset County; the other, separated from it by the barren uplands of Rocky Hill and Sourland Mountain, bordered the main line of travel through Princeton and Trenton to Pennsylvania and included a belt in the northern part of Monmouth County about Freehold, Shrewsbury, and Middletown.[20] On the south, the farmlands were bounded by the "Pine Barrens" of southern New Jersey.

[18] Mereness, *op. cit.*, p. 413. By permission of The Macmillan Company, publishers.

[19] Burnaby, *op. cit.*, p. 106. See also Thacher, *op. cit.*, p. 187.

[20] An enthusiastic appreciation of part of this region is found in the diary kept by Philipp Waldeck, chaplain of a German regiment which was stationed during part of the war at Perth Amboy. He writes in 1777:

"The soil in New Jersey seems indeed to be thoroughly productive and fruitful, though not nearly so much so here on the sea as when one gets farther inland. In the strip of land Woodbridge-Spenton [Spanktown, i.e. Rahway] -Elizabeth-Town, through which we have travelled, certainly everything grows that is committed to the bosom of the earth. . . . In scarcely any other part of the world can one see orchards more beautiful, larger, laid out in

Throughout this agricultural territory, the most densely settled in the colony, there were no towns of any considerable size, although several of the villages were incorporated as municipalities. Elizabeth-Town was perhaps the most attractive center—"a very pretty place," according to the Baroness von Riedesel; "the most agreeable place imaginable" in the opinion of one of her compatriots.[21] It had a courthouse, an Anglican church, a Presbyterian meeting-house, barracks for troops, and between two and three hundred houses.[22] The dwellings, built at some distance from one another, were usually surrounded by gardens and orchards.[23] Among them were a number of fine residences, for Elizabeth-Town was the seat of a wealthy and cultured group of families quite disproportionate in number to the small size of the place. The homes of such men as the Daytons, the Ogdens, Elias Boudinot, William Livingston, and Cavalier Jouet—the last-named possessing a library worth £700—gave visible evidence of the profits obtainable from mercantile pursuits, land ownership, and the practice of law.[24]

A few miles away, another pleasant village, Newark, straggled agreeably along the road for nearly two miles. It

closer accordance with all rules of taste, and more richly planted than here in New Jersey. . . .

"When one stands on the height between Amboy and Woodbridge, . . . one has the bay behind him, and looks away in front over many kinds of blossoming fruit-trees. At the foot of the hill lie the scattered houses of Woodbridge. At a greater distance [are] farmhouses and country-seats, isolated and visible from afar because of their red stone. These houses, however, are surrounded not by artificially laid-out ornamental gardens, but by green spaces which belong to their pasture-lands. The interior finish of their houses is most important to them. It seems as if the owners of these earthly paradises had no taste for gardens of pleasure, and had wished to apply all their diligence to vegetable gardens and especially orchards. They would, indeed, deserve censure if they had wished to master and beautify through art that gracious Nature which has already lavished so many charms here."—Philipp Waldeck, *Diary of the American Revolution* (Philadelphia, 1907), pp. 30-1.

[21] Baroness von Riedesel, *Letters and Journals* (Albany, 1867), p. 164; Philipp Waldeck, *Diary of the American Revolution* (Philadelphia, 1907), p. 23.
[22] Burnaby, *op. cit.*, p. 105.   [23] Waldeck, *op. cit.*, p. 23.
[24] E. Alfred Jones, *The Loyalists of New Jersey* (Newark, 1927), p. 108.

contained an academy and some fine houses, but seems to have been less favored than Elizabeth-Town as a place of residence for opulent provincials.[25] Smaller than either of these towns, but enjoying a municipal corporation and the dignity of being one of the two capitals of the province was Perth Amboy, a village at the mouth of the Raritan River. In 1770, a resident clergyman calculated that it contained seventy houses and a population of about four hundred ninety.[26] The town was handsomely and regularly laid out on a rectangular plan, centering in a square where stood the locust-shaded market house of brick. A pretty Anglican church, a Presbyterian meeting-house—rarely used because of the few representatives of that denomination in the town —and barracks for three hundred men constituted the chief other architectural features.[27]

Although, owing to the proximity of New York, Perth Amboy had never achieved the commercial prosperity which its founders had envisioned for it, there was nevertheless enough coastal and foreign trade[28] to support a flourishing clique of mercantile families, united by intermarriage and exerting a powerful influence upon the government of the colony. The economic interests of this group were widespread. It constituted a considerable section of the Council of Proprietors of East Jersey, a body which had sought for years, against the determined opposition of many settlers, to enforce its claim to all lands in East Jersey which it had not deeded away. The members of the Perth Amboy Group

[25] Burnaby, *op. cit.*, p. 105; Thacher, *op. cit.*, p. 187.
[26] S.P.G. transcripts, Ser. B, Vol. 24, No. 280. See also Creswell, *op. cit.*, p. 242, and Burnaby, *op. cit.*, p. 105.
[27] Creswell, *op. cit.*, p. 242; S.P.G. transcripts, Ser. B, Vol. 24, No. 280; William Dunlap, *A History of the Rise and Progress of the Arts of Design in the United States* (Boston, 1918), Vol. I, p. 289; Letter of Governor Francis Bernard in Sparks MSS., 4, Vol. I, p. 27; Burnaby, *op. cit.*, p. 105.
[28] The exports consisted chiefly of boards, staves, shingles, and hoops, and the agricultural products (especially grain, flour, and bread) of the Raritan region for which Perth Amboy was the natural outlet. See Whitehead, *op. cit.*, p. 303, and *N.J.A.*, Vol. X, p. 454.

also possessed extensive tracts of land as individuals, and drew comfortable incomes from various other sources.[29]

The leading families of the town formed a social circle which, according to one witness, was "far superior to that of New York or Philadelphia."[30] Their mentality, opinions, and social customs were what might be expected from a group holding such privileges and vested interests as they had acquired. They were conservative and aristocratic in the highest degree. Surrounded by Negro slaves, they were completely severed by the barrier of race from those who did the humble work about them. We are told by a writer who grew up in Perth Amboy at the time of the Revolution: "Every house in my native place where any servants were to be seen, swarmed with black slaves—every house save one."[31]

It is significant of the pattern of life in Perth Amboy that, whereas the rest of northeastern New Jersey was inhabited largely by the democratic Presbyterians—who were chiefly descendants of New England Puritans—and by the spiritually similar Dutch Calvinists, with some admixture of Quakers, the residents of the capital were almost exclusively adherents of the Anglican Church—the communion of wealth, conservatism, and loyal obedience to authority.[32]

New Brunswick, the fourth of the chief towns of northeastern New Jersey, was less flourishing and less prepossessing than any of the three communities we have considered

[29] One of the most prominent of them, Philip Kearny, a lawyer with mercantile connections, drew up a will in 1770 which provided for the disposal of vast holdings of land, farms, and houses in and about Perth Amboy, Woodbridge, Barnegat, Philadelphia, Sussex County, and elsewhere. In addition to these, he left £5,500 in cash, £200 in English joint stocks, and a British Exchequer annuity. Such was the diversity of forms in which the wealth of the Perth Amboy coterie was embodied.—Lothrop Withrington and Henry F. Waters, "New Jersey Gleanings in England," in *N.J.H.S.P.*, 3rd S., Vol. V, pp. 4-7.

[30] Lorenzo Sabine, *Biographical Sketches of Loyalists of the American Revolution* (Boston, 1864, 2 vols.), Vol. II, p. 20.

[31] Dunlap, *op. cit.*, Vol. I, p. 288.

[32] Sparks MSS., 4, Vol. I, p. 27; S.P.G. transcripts, Ser. B, Part I, Nos. 265, 280.

so far. Situated at the head of sloop navigation on the
Raritan, it had enjoyed a brisk trade for some years; but
about 1760 it had entered upon a period of decline.[33] The
Anglican clergyman reported in 1764 that of the one hundred
and thirty families in the town, "many . . . I might say the
greatest Part, [are] but in indifferent Circumstances."
A few merchants still prospered, but the general appearance of the community was not one of wealth or even of
simple neatness. One traveller, who was apparently trying
to maintain a judicial impartiality, called it "a dismal
town, but pleasantly situated."[34] Even this advantage, however, was denied by a youth from Pennsylvania who wrote
bitterly of the "small town disagreeably situated upon the
W. side of the Rarinton and surrounded by the adjesent
hills in such a manner that it lies undiscovered till one has
almost entered the streets which in wet weather are almost
impasable not being paved and the water collecting in
them from the houses and adjesent hills." To make matters
worse, this disgruntled observer found the boatmen who
ferried his party across the river to be "a set of the most
stupid mortals living."[35] John Adams, more tolerant, admired
the beauty of the river, found some paved streets and "three
or four handsome houses," and mildly commended the
appearance of the stone barracks—though the last compli-
ment lost some of its savor through an immediately ensuing
comparison with the Boston jail.[36]

Ill-favored though it may have been in its streets, its
buildings, its trade, and its boatmen, New Brunswick found
abundant compensation in charms of a more personal, if

[33] This commercial stagnation seems to have preceded by a few years the
general business depression into which the colonies sank at the conclusion
of the French and Indian War.—Eliza S. M. Quincy, *Memoir of the Life of
Eliza S. M. Quincy* (Boston, 1861), p. 12.

[34] Mereness, *op. cit.*, p. 574. By permission of The Macmillan Company, publishers.

[35] Roberts, *Journal*, pp. 40-1.

[36] John Adams, *Works* (Boston, 1851), Vol. II, p. 355.

fleeting, order. The Rev. Andrew Burnaby, minister of the Church of England, who travelled through the American colonies in 1759 and 1760, noted that the town was "celebrated for the number of its beauties." And, gazing with an appreciative eye upon the buxom Dutch wenches, the reverend gentleman was forced to agree that, except for the fair inhabitants of Philadelphia, here were the handsomest women he had seen in America.[37]

Nor was the cultivation of the learned mind subordinated to that of the beautiful body. Queen's College, later to be known as Rutgers, had recently been founded by the Dutch Reformed Church, and was leading a struggling existence. Its continuance was to be seriously threatened by the disturbances of the Revolution; but already its roots had struck deep enough to enable it to weather the storm.

If New Brunswick itself lacked the prosperity and urbanity of Elizabeth-Town and Perth Amboy, its surrounding countryside, "exceedingly rich and beautiful," was in better case. The banks of the Raritan up to the hills near Bound Brook were "covered with gentlemen's houses." At one of these, Burnaby found "some good portraits of Vandyck, and several other small Dutch paintings."[38] With an institution of higher learning in an impoverished, unpaved town, and Vandycks in rural dwellings, the lower Raritan valley was no contemptible region. Evidently there were the beginnings of high cultural standards in what less than a century before had been a wilderness.

Two more towns in the lowland agricultural belt deserve brief mention before we pass on to a survey of other districts. Princeton, a village of about sixty houses scattered along a single street, boasted an imposing stone college building, Nassau Hall, and enjoyed some reputation as a "seat of Learning & Politeness,"[39] but otherwise could lay small

[37] Burnaby, *op. cit.*, p. 104.   [38] *ibid.*, p. 104.
[39] Letter of Dr. John Beàtty, Princeton, Aug. 31, 1772, in Princeton University Library MSS., AM 1594.

claim to distinction. "Very butifully Situated on a . . . high and seemingly healthy[40] piece of ground commanding an extencive prospect of a beautifull and fertil well inhabited country,"[41] the town was a convenient and agreeable stopping-place on the highroad between New York and Philadelphia.

Trenton, with something over a hundred houses, is almost invariably described by travellers of the period in the brief phrase, "a pretty village,"[42] though many of its houses were "mean and little."[43] Its chief importance was due to its location at the falls of the Delaware, and thus at the head of navigation for vessels of any considerable burden, though the falls were passable for the many flat-bottomed boats which carried five or six hundred bushels of wheat apiece from the upper Delaware to Philadelphia.[44] Besides its advantageous situation for general trade with the region to the north, Trenton enjoyed some industrial consequence, as the seat of two iron furnaces and steel works.[45]

Of a nature quite different from that of the region we have been observing was the territory to the north and northwest. Behind the double mountain barrier which marked the end of the coastal belt, settlement had advanced more slowly. Morris County, the strip of Essex beyond the mountains, and the northwestern part of Bergen County[46] presented geographical features which differed greatly from

[40] The Princeton physician writes in 1772 that the place is "not only Tolerable, but Intolerably healthy—What is the Consequence? The D^r must starve."—Letter of Dr. John Beatty, Princeton University Library MSS., AM 1594.

[41] Roberts, *Journal*, p. 40.

[42] Mereness, *op. cit.*, p. 413; Adams, *op. cit.*, Vol. II, p. 357; Claude Blanchard, *Journal* (Albany, 1876), pp. 134-5; Louis Philippe, Comte de Ségur, *Mémoires souvenirs et anecdotes* (Paris, 1859, 2 vols.), Vol. I, p. 202.

[43] *N.J.A.*, 2nd S., Vol. I, p. 432.

[44] Trenton Historical Society, *A History of Trenton 1679-1929* (Princeton, 1929, 2 vols.), Vol. I, p. 103.

[45] *ibid.*, p. 108.

[46] Now largely included in Passaic County.

those of the older areas of settlement. Along the valleys of
the upper Passaic, the Pequannock, the Ramapo, and other
streams there were frequently to be found level and fertile
lands, which broadened now and then into plains of considerable extent; but much of the surface of the region
consisted of rolling hills, frequently of considerable height.

Buried in these uplands was a lure which drew colonists
far sooner than they would have reached the district by the
ordinary expansion of agricultural settlement. The discovery of iron ore in Morris, Bergen, and Sussex Counties
led to a rapid mining development in the eighteenth century.
Furnaces were established at Hibernia, Ringwood, Mt.
Hope, Rockaway, Charlottenburg, Andover, and other
places. With some exceptions, British colonial policy forbade the manufacture of iron in the colonies beyond the bar
or bloom stage, and even slitting-mills for making nails were
prohibited. Although these mercantilist regulations were
sometimes evaded,[47] the restrictions were enough to prevent
as rapid an industrial development as might otherwise have
occurred. Nevertheless, despite occasional business difficulties, a fairly prosperous class of ironmasters grew up. One
historian thus describes their situation during the Revolution:

"As at the South the planters constituted an aristocracy
distinct from all the classes about them, so in the mountains
of New Jersey the iron masters were an aristocracy in more
respects than one. They were usually the largest landowners
of the region. They handled the money in circulation. They
occupied in most cases excellent houses, while their dependent tenants lived in very common dwellings. The cabins
of the woodchoppers, colliers, teamsters, miners and forge-
men were crazy affairs, usually occupied by a very migratory
population. These people lived 'from hand to mouth,' rarely
laying up any of their wages. The mansions of the iron
masters were often furnished with many costly luxuries, and

[47] Joseph Tuttle, "Hibernia Furnace," in *N.J.H.S.P.*, 2nd S., Vol. VI,
pp. 104-5; *N.J.A.*, Vol. X, p. 444.

it was not rare to find elegant equipages among their
adjuncts, and their owners were apt to be exclusive in their
social relations."[48]

Class-consciousness, indeed, was well marked among such
members of this iron aristocracy as the energetic John Jacob
Faesch, born in Switzerland, who came to New Jersey in
1764 and made a fortune in the iron industry. "Mr.
Faesch," we read, "was said to be skeptical in his religious
opinions, but one of the promptest supporters of the Rockaway church, giving as a reason for the apparent incon-
sistency that 'religion was a very good thing to keep the
lower classes in proper subordination!' "[49] In candor, however, it cannot be said that the ironmasters always displayed a
sense of *noblesse oblige* commensurate with their pretensions to class superiority, if one is to judge from the case of
Samuel Ford, the chief promoter of the Hibernia ironworks,
who, with Benjamin Cooper, one of his early associates,
diverted some of his abundant business energies to counter-
feiting operations.[50]

In Morris County, then, one of the earliest industrial
regions of America, there was foreshadowed even before

[48] Tuttle, *op. cit.*, p. 150. This description applies more particularly to conditions existing at the time when the industry was expanding under the
demands of the Revolution, and the wealth and prestige of the ironmasters
were growing rapidly in consequence; but there can be little doubt that it
also characterizes with fair accuracy the general state of affairs during the
preceding years. See also the description of Ringwood in Chastellux, *op. cit.*,
Vol. I, pp. 346-7. There is other testimony to a similar effect. In January 1781,
a detachment of the army marching southward to reduce some mutinous New
Jersey troops stopped at Ringwood, where all the field officers found lodgings
with Mrs. Erskine, widow of a recently deceased ironmaster. "We were
entertained," one of them writes, "with an elegant supper and excellent wine.
Mrs. Erskine is a sensible and accomplished woman, lives in a style of
affluence and fashion; everything indicates wealth, taste, and splendor; and
she takes pleasure in entertaining the friends of her late husband, with
generous hospitality."—Thacher, *op. cit.*, pp. 301-2.

[49] *N.J.H.S.P.*, 2nd S., Vol. I, p. 37. The authority for this statement is no
sinister Marxist commentator, but an eminent nineteenth century clergyman,
the Rev. Joseph F. Tuttle, D.D., president of Wabash College!

[50] Tuttle, *op. cit.*, pp. 153-4.

the Revolution a type of entrepreneur destined to become increasingly prominent in the development of American economic life during the following century. Energetic, able, adaptable, not greatly impeded by humanitarian or ethical scruples, he was ready to take an active part in the life of the country when the old British shackles that bound the American economy should be thrown off.

There were other inhabitants of this region besides iron-masters and their dependents. Abundant forests led to the establishment of at least one factory for the production of pearl-ashes.[51] A thin stream of farmers, finding the valleys fertile, trickled into them and was gradually changing the appearance of the country. Though the hills on either side were left untouched, the bottom lands were becoming pleasant and well cultivated places. Between the Rockaway River and Pompton, especially, one French traveller was "astonished at the degree of perfection to which agriculture is carried." His brief description of the farms of the Mande-ville brothers gives an interesting picture of the manner of life among the Dutch settlers who, with their customary eye for good farming land, had established themselves in large numbers in the vicinity of Pompton and Pequannock:[52]

"Their domains join each other. In each of them the manor is very simple and small, the barns alone are lofty and spacious. Always faithful to their national economy, they cultivate, reap, and sell, without augmenting either their houses or their enjoyments, content with living in a corner of their farm, and with being only the spectators of their own wealth."[53]

Not all the farms in northern New Jersey were so pros-perous, so well managed, or so well established. Pioneer conditions still persisted for numbers of poor settlers, who occupied one-room huts, slept on beds of dried leaves, and

[51] Jones, *op. cit.*, p. 228.
[52] Chastellux, *op. cit.*, Vol. I, p. 143; *N.J.H.S.P.*, 2nd S., Vol. I, p. 53.
[53] Chastellux, *op. cit.*, Vol. I, pp. 341-2.

were separated from civilization by miles of woodland.[54] In 1760 the Anglican minister of Newark made a journey across the mountains to Morris County. The inhabitants of those sections of Morris and Essex Counties near Horse Neck,[55] he reported, "are generally very poor, and can very hardly support their families, a very few in Morris County excepted. . . . The People of Horse Neck are extremely ignorant, few I believe are taught to read, and have no Minister of any denomination residing among them—The most of 'em are said to live on Lands not their own, but have built little Huts where they could find Bits of Land unoccupied by others, and there provide a poor maintenance for their wives and Children, all their Riches consist in Children of which they have commonly more than they know what to do with."[56]

In sharp contrast to such conditions were the comforts of Morristown, a village of some fifty houses, situated in the southern part of Morris County. The dwellings in this community were handsome and well built, and there was considerable quiet luxury among some of the inhabitants.

[54] Quincy, *op. cit.*, p. 26; "Auszug aus dem Journal des Marsches der Bourgoyneschen Armee, von Boston bis nach Virginen," Library of Congress MSS., Hessian Journals, Vol. II.

[55] Now Caldwell.

[56] S.P.G. transcripts, Ser. B, Vol. 24, No. 19. Many of the early inhabitants of Horse Neck, according to one historian, "paid little if any regard to law, human or divine. . . . When a certain Mr. Dean, a Separatist preacher, . . . made . . . excursions through this region to preach, they often treated him with much rudeness, even to profanity. They seemed to find pleasure in annoyance; and succeeded by their persistence in it, in more than one instance, in deciding new comers not to remain. In their intercourse with the Indians, they are described as 'corrupting and being corrupted,' 'depraved manners and spiritual degradation being thereby increased.' . . . It was far from uncommon to find men unable to write their own names. And men lived isolated in rude log huts, on mountain paths, by springs or anywhere, that some trifling advantage seemed to present itself. There were but few houses in this township that could keep out an ordinary storm. Books were rare and expensive, and often, where (as here) land was densely covered with timber, it was a struggle to provide even the simplest means of subsistence."—C. T. Berry, *An Historical Survey of the First Presbyterian Church, Caldwell, N.J.* (Newark, 1871), pp. 11-13.

Through its beautiful situation and "consequential look," Morristown wrung words of commendation even from a Southern belle who visited there in 1777, and who unbent sufficiently from her Virginian pride to describe it as "a very clever little village," though she dismissed the native inhabitants as "the errentest rusticks you ever beheld."[57]

Doubtless this description of their manners would have been warmly disputed by the Morristonians, for their town had some pretension to aristocratic dignity. Not far outside it stood Mt. Kemble, the pretentious estate of a retired merchant, Peter Kemble, whose son, Samuel, was continuing the family mercantile business at New Brunswick. Old Peter, a member of the New Jersey Council since 1745, the father-in-law of General Thomas Gage, and a close connection of the prominent New York families of Van Cortlandt, Schuyler, DeLancey, and Van Rensselaer, had created an estate worthy of his social prestige. The stony soil of his well cleared acres was cultivated by many slaves. His library delighted a Connecticut clergyman who visited it during the Revolution. Several subsidiary farms were rented out to tenants, and added to the income of the owner.[58] Among the hills of Morris County, Mt. Kemble stood as a proud outpost of the mercantile-landowning community of New York and East Jersey.

A few miles to the south, in the hills of northern Somerset County near Basking Ridge, was another showy establishment, based, however, on a less solid foundation of wealth. William Alexander, son of a prominent New York lawyer, possessed but mediocre attainments and a personality of no great charm or brilliance. The distinction which Nature had denied him he sought to achieve by superficial splendor. He

[57] Chastellux, *op. cit.*, Vol. I, p. 144. "Life in Morristown in 1777," in *N.J.H.S.P.*, Vol. LI, p. 151.

[58] Emory McClintock, *Topography of Washington's Camp of 1780 and Its Neighborhood* (Paper read before the Washington Association of New Jersey, Feb. 22, 1894), pp. 23-5.

wasted much time and money in England in a futile attempt
to induce Parliament to recognize his claim to the title of
Earl of Stirling. Disappointed in this endeavor, he returned
to America without abandoning his pretension; and the title
was almost universally accorded to him by courtesy here, so
that he is generally referred to in history as "Lord Stirling."
Empty title, however, did not suffice; for Alexander was
determined to shine with all the social luster of a genuine
earl. No railroad king of the nineteenth century, or Holly-
wood star of the twentieth, could have done more in proportion to the available means to import the most glamorous
trappings of the Old World. According to one unfriendly
critic, who may or may not have been telling the truth,
Stirling brought back with him from England "horses and
carriages, a valet de chambre, a butler, a steward, a friseur,
a cook, a coachman, and a mistress."[59] Be that as it may,
there can be no doubt of the pretentiousness of the large
estate which his lordship maintained in Somerset County.[60]

"Designed to imitate the residence of an English nobleman, it was unfinished when the war began. The stables,

[59] Thomas Jones, *History of New York during the Revolutionary War* (New
York, 1879, 2 vols.), Vol. II, p. 322.

[60] A partial list of the furnishings and other personal estate appertaining
to this residence, taken in execution and sold at auction in 1775 and 1776, has
been preserved. It indicates that the appointments of the Stirling household
were luxurious, and also reveals the fact that a number of the unfortunate
gentleman's prominent contemporaries (such as Elias and Elisha Boudinot,
Philip Livingston, and Jacob Ford) apparently attended the sales in the hope
of picking up a few bargains, and were not disappointed. Of greatest interest,
perhaps, in the long list of possessions sold is the library, which suggests the
selection of books an eighteenth century American gentleman, with agricultural, military and political leanings, might be expected to possess. It consisted of two hundred and seven volumes and a number of pamphlets, and
included Hume's and Smollett's histories of England; histories of France, the
French Settlements, Italy, and New Jersey; Montesquieu's *Spirit of Laws*;
Johnson's *Dictionary*; Sully's *Britain*; a number of volumes on husbandry,
gardening, and horsemanship; Robertson's astronomy; a military dictionary;
a volume of New York laws; and other items.—"Condition of the Vendue
held heare this day for the Sale of the goods & Chattles Lands & Tenements
of the Right Honora^b William Earl of Sterling," in Ford House, Morristown
National Historical Park, Morristown, N.J.

coach-houses and other offices, ornamented with cupolas and
gilded vanes, were built round a large paved court, behind
the mansion. The front with piazzas, opened on a fine lawn,
descending to a considerable stream called 'the Black River.'
A large hall extended through the center of the house. On one
side was a drawing-room, with painted walls and a stuccoed
ceiling."[61] The stables contained fine horses; there was a
park stocked with deer; and it is said—though not on best
authority—that skilled gardeners were hired to design a
rose garden and an Italian vineyard. The estate included
a large orchard of the choicest fruits; and so productive
was the farm that the mortgagee who foreclosed on the
property at about the beginning of the war reported in 1777
a clear annual profit of double the interest on £10,000.
During Stirling's occupancy of the country-seat, slaves were
at hand to perform the hard labor. When the owner and
his family travelled, it was in a coach drawn by four or six
horses and "ornamented with gilded coronets, and coats-of-
arms emblazoned on the panels."[62] By such ostentation the
pseudo-nobleman, "old and rather dull"[63] and more than
a little ridiculous, paraded his importance before the startled
gaze of the Somerset farmers.

Such a lavish mode of living was based upon the considerable property which Stirling had inherited from his
father, a surveyor-general for the East Jersey Proprietors,
and by the extensions of these holdings which he himself
had made. He was a member of the Council of Proprietors
of East Jersey, owned extensive tracts of land in the eight
northern counties of the state and in New York, and had an
interest in the Hibernia ironworks.[64] Unhappily, however,

[61] Quincy, *op cit.*, p. 23.
[62] *ibid.*, p. 24; McClintock, *op. cit.*, p. 29; W. Jay Mills, *Historic Houses
of New Jersey* (Philadelphia, 1902), p. 232; *N.J.A.*, 2nd S., Vol. I, p. 66;
Letter of Lucas von Beverhoudt, quoted in *N.J.H.S.P.*, N.S., Vol. IV, pp. 133-4.
[63] Chastellux, *op. cit.*, Vol. I, p. 118.
[64] Tuttle, *op. cit.*, pp. 160-1. Acts of General Assembly: Act of May 31, 1779,
to vest Stirling's estate in trustees.

his business acumen by no means equalled his ambitions, and by the outbreak of the war he was on the verge of bankruptcy.[65]

It was in Somerset County, near Pluckemin, that the double rampart of mountains enclosing Morris County disappeared. South of the range, and west of its termination, lay the valley of the upper Raritan and its principal tributary, the Millstone. Here was a productive and pleasant farming district, more open and level than the country north of the hills. Although it had not been under cultivation so long as the part of the valley below Bound Brook, it was now fairly well settled, chiefly by Dutch, with a considerable admixture of Germans, Scots, and others. Ever since the valley had been farmed, wheat had been one of its principal crops. Grist mills were numerous, and as early as 1748 Raritan Landing, a little above New Brunswick on the river, had been described as a "market for the most plentiful wheat country for its bigness in America."[66]

Towards the headwaters of the Raritan, in Hunterdon and Morris Counties, the land grew hillier, and settlement was not so dense, though the soil was still fertile. Here also was to be found the approximate limit of penetration by the Dutch, who gave place to colonies of Germans and others. The hills of Hunterdon, like those of Morris and Bergen Counties, were in some places rich in iron ore; and at Union there were furnaces and forges. Numerous farmers lived in the valleys,[67] especially in the southwestern section near Trenton, and Hunterdon County was growing in favor as a place of country-seats for the prosperous inhabitants of mercantile towns as far away as New York and Philadelphia.[68]

[65] See below, pp. 87-90.   [66] *N.J.H.S.P.*, 2nd S., Vol. V, p. 89.

[67] W. Jay Mills, ed., *Glimpses of Colonial Society and the Life at Princeton College* (Philadelphia, 1903), p. 142.

[68] The Rev. William Fraser to the S.P.G., Oct. 8, 1773, S.P.G. transcripts, Ser. B, Part I, No. 244.

Considered as a whole, Hunterdon had become the wealthiest county of New Jersey; but in some of its northern parts the stern influence of frontier conditions was still strongly felt.[69] The struggle to wrest from the wilderness a home and a living was even more general on the farther side of Musconetcong Mountain. Although the extensive territory then included in Sussex County (out of which Warren County has since been carved) had been in the process of settlement, especially along the Delaware, for more than three-quarters of a century, penetration had been slow, and most of the primeval forest lying back inland from the chief river was just beginning to yield to the axe and the plow. During the French and Indian War, the region had been severely devastated. With the cessation of hostilities, a new wave of pioneers had moved in, and it has been estimated—perhaps too liberally—that there were some 13,000 inhabitants in the county at the time of the Revolution.[70] As yet, however, the immigrants had built no towns of any consequence: Newtown, the county seat, was a mere village of twenty or thirty houses, partly surrounded by woods.[71]

The economic promise of the new county was rich and varied. As in the Raritan basin, the limestone soil of the Sussex valleys was excellent for raising many crops, particularly wheat, and the inhabitants were soon sending to Philadelphia and New York grain, flaxseed, cattle, hams, butter, and other farm products.[72] Iron ore of good quality had for some years past been supplying forges and furnaces at Andover and Oxford.[73] No less prized than iron by the

[69] S.P.G. transcripts, Ser. B, Part I, No. 237.

[70] The Rev. Thomas Chandler to S.P.G., Jan. 5, 1770, S.P.G. transcripts, Ser. B, Vol. 24, No. 97; *N.J.H.S.P.*, N.S., Vol. VI, pp. 134, 138; *N.J.A.*, 2nd S., Vol. I, p. 389 n.; James P. Snell, *History of Sussex and Warren Counties . . .* (Philadelphia, 1861), pp. 24, 30, 33.

[71] James Moody, *Narrative* (New York, 1865), pp. 23-4.

[72] The Rev. Uzal Ogden to S.P.G., July 8, 1771, S.P.G. transcripts, Ser. B, Vol. 24, No. 154.

[73] *N.J.A.*, 2nd S., Vol. I, p. 389 n.; Snell, *op. cit.*, p. 78.

mother country was a product yielded by the dense forests—
potash, which was manufactured in some quantities under
the encouragement of a bounty from the British government.[74] Nor did the wood of Sussex County have to be
burned in order to become valuable for export. Down the
streams which flowed briskly among the heavily timbered
hills into the Delaware, there floated a considerable quantity of lumber to swell the volume of one of Philadelphia's
most important exports.

As a result of this abundant and varied natural wealth,
the development of Sussex was proceeding apace when the
Revolution came. The consequent prosperity, however, was
very unevenly distributed. Far-sighted persons well supplied
with capital had early acquired from the Proprietors of
East or West Jersey huge tracts of the best land. As
population flowed in, these speculators rode the crest of the
rising land values, either by selling their property at a considerable advance, or, as seems to have been more often the
case, by retaining title to it and permitting tenants to clear
and cultivate it for them. Thus a large part of the profits
of development tended to flow out of the county into the
pockets of absentee landowners in Perth Amboy, New York,
or other coastal centers.[75]

In Sussex itself, the results were clearly evident. On the
one hand there were many prosperous farmers, such as the
descendants of the original Dutch settlers along the upper
Delaware, whose well cultivated fields were the admiration
of travellers;[76] the speculators or their agents who themselves
resided in the county; and many people who had been able
to obtain title to good land and pay off their indebtedness.

[74] Alexander Fraser, *Second Report of the Bureau of Archives for the
Province of Ontario* (Toronto, 1905), Vol. I, p. 604; *N.J.H.S.P.*, 2nd S., Vol. I,
p. 83.

[75] Fraser, *op. cit.*, Vol. I, pp. 600-3; Vol. II, pp. 1275-6; Snell, *op. cit.*, p. 33;
Benjamin B. Edsall, "Centennial Address" in *The First Sussex Centenary*
(Newark, 1853), p. 46.

[76] Chastellux, *op. cit.*, Vol. II, p. 312.

Side by side with these were to be found large numbers of hard-working tenants or debtors who found it difficult to get ahead—so difficult, indeed, that in the year 1765 the Provincial legislature was obliged to appropriate £200 to be used in buying grain for the more distressed inhabitants. In the opinion of an Anglican missionary who visited the district in 1770, the inhabitants were "all very poor, as the first Settlers of a new country generally are."[77] Though his generalization does not take account of the many exceptions, it does indicate what seemed to him to be the plight of the majority. No very keen insight is needed to suspect that such disparity between the interests of those who were developing the county by their labor and those who were reaping the profits from it added to the internal instability of Sussex when the Revolution broke out.

The territory we have surveyed so far comprises roughly the northern half of New Jersey. It was for the most part included in the old territorial division of East Jersey, which had ceased to have a separate existence in 1702. The region was characterized, as we have seen, by great variations in its topography, by diversity in the national origins of the population, and by striking differences in the economic interests and social conditions of the inhabitants. Should we seek, among all these dissimilar elements, for the type of man most characteristic of the region, we should undoubtedly have to decide upon the small farmer, cultivating his own ground, and achieving a modest degree of comfort. His simple and exacting mode of life gave him independence of character and manner. Visitors from Europe were agreeably impressed by the difference between the farmers and servants of New Jersey and the subordinate classes across the ocean. They admired "that modest pride of the independent man, who sees nothing above him but the laws, and who knows

[77] The Rev. Thos. Chandler, Elizabeth-Town, to S.P.G., Jan. 5, 1770, S.P.G. transcripts, Ser. B, Part I, No. 97; Edsall, *op. cit.*, pp. 45-6.

neither the vanity, nor the prejudices, nor the servility of our European societies."[78]

Such sturdy independence had, of course, its less agreeable connotations. Absence of servility frequently tended to become lack of courtesy, and self-sufficiency a narrow provincialism. The Marquis de Chastellux, who inspected the Moravian mill in Sussex County, mentions significantly that the proprietor showed him about with "an anxiety and respect more German than American."[79] The family of a New York merchant who moved to Basking Ridge during the war and lived there in very comfortable style found that their alien way of life aroused distrust and dislike among the neighboring country people. In the words of a daughter of the family:

"The lower classes in New Jersey did not enjoy the advantage of the common schools of New England; and they were too ignorant and selfish even to understand the peculiar hardships endured by those who were driven from their homes, and exposed to severe suffering for the same cause in which they were also engaged. Jealousy is often excited in ordinary minds by any degree of superiority. It was a common taunt among the most ignorant and uncivilized, that any article complained of was good enough for 'the Yorkers,' or for 'the Quality,' as they termed the exiles, whom they envied, even in their unhappy circumstances, for their superior advantages of education and manners."[80]

There is in these lines a definite suggestion of snobbery, which helps explain why the Somerset farmers were annoyed by the New York family; nevertheless it is not difficult to believe that in the less travelled districts of New Jersey in the eighteenth century prejudice and crude provincialism were not uncommon.[81]

---

[78] Ségur, *op. cit.*, Vol. I, p. 201. [79] Chastellux, *op. cit.*, Vol. II, p. 308.
[80] Quincy, *op. cit.*, p. 21.
[81] There were some less serious disadvantages of bucolic simplicity in New Jersey. French travellers during the Revolution learned through sad ex-

Between the northern and southern halves of New Jersey there existed a number of significant differences—geographical, historical, and social. In physical structure, the southern region is much simpler. Its general conformation is that of a plain, highest in the middle and lowest at the margins. South of the Navesink Highlands near Sandy Hook, the land seldom rises to a height greater than a hundred feet above sea level; and in the whole southern section of the state, including those Highlands, the total area higher than two hundred feet does not exceed fifteen square miles.[82]

The central part of this low-lying territory was occupied in the eighteenth century by the Pines, or Pine Barrens, a dense primeval forest into which the inroads of the wood-cutter had made but little progress by the time of the Revolution. Besides the pines which gave the district its name, there was a varied forest growth. One of the most common trees, the white cedar, was highly prized for boat-building, shingle-making, and other purposes.[83] It grew in swamps along the course of rivers and in isolated patches of varying size; the largest of these, the Great Cedar Swamp, stretched from Delaware Bay at the mouth of Denis Creek to the Atlantic at the mouth of the Tuckahoe, and cut off Cape May from the rest of the province. In many cases, we are told by a naturalist who visited the region a few years after the

perience that "cleanliness is not so well established as frankness." Some of them were distressed at being obliged to drink from the common convivial bowl when toasts were proposed at table, at having to sleep between sheets which all too evidently had served previous travellers, and at awakening in the night to discover "a new arrival coming to share without formalities one's bedding and one's bed." When protests were made against such practices, the hosts were usually willing to humor the idiosyncrasies of their guests.— Duc de Broglie, ed., "Deux Français aux États-Unis et dans la Nouvelle Espagne en 1782. Journal du Prince de Broglie et lettres du Comte de Ségur," in *Mélanges publiés par la Société des Bibliophiles François* (2e· Partie) (Paris, 1903), p. 50; Louis Philippe, Comte de Ségur, *Mémoires souvenirs et anecdotes* (Paris, 1859), pp. 201-12.

[82] Rollin D. Salisbury, *The Physical Geography of New Jersey* (Vol. IV of the Final Report of the State Geologist) (Trenton, 1898), pp. 54-7.

[83] Sydney G. Fisher, *The Quaker Colonies* (New Haven, 1920), pp. 143-6.

Revolution, the swamps were half a mile to a mile wide, and five or six miles long; they appeared to occupy the former channels of choked-up rivers, streams, lakes, or arms of the sea.

"The appearance they present to a stranger is singular— a front of tall and perfectly straight trunks, rising to the height of fifty or sixty feet, without a limb, and crowded in every direction, their tops so closely woven together as to shut out the day, spreading the gloom of a perpetual twilight below. On a nearer approach, they are found to rise out of the water, which, from the impregnation of the fallen leaves and roots of the cedars, is of the color of brandy. Amidst this bottom of congregated springs, the ruins of the former forest lie piled in every state of confusion. The roots, prostrate logs, and, in many places, the water, are covered with green, mantling moss, while an undergrowth of laurel, fifteen or twenty feet high, intersects every opening so completely, as to render a passage through laborious and harassing beyond description; at every step, you either sink to the knees, clamber over fallen timber, squeeze yourself through between the stubborn laurels, or plunge to the middle in ponds made by the uprooting of large trees, which the green moss concealed from observation. In calm weather, the silence of death reigns in these dreary regions; a few interrupted rays of light shoot across the gloom; and unless for the occasional hollow screams of the herons, and the melancholy chirping of one or two species of small birds, all is silence, solitude, and desolation. When a breeze rises, at first it sighs mournfully through the tops; but as the gale increases, the tall mast-like cedars wave like fishing-poles, and rubbing against each other, produce a variety of singular noises, that, with the help of a little imagination, resemble shrieks, groans, growling of bears, wolves, and such like comfortable music."[84]

---

[84] Alexander Wilson, *Wilson's American Ornithology* (Boston, 1840), p. 555.

In view of the abundance of this type of forest, it is small wonder that there were few habitations in the interior of the Pines region by 1776, except for the occasional huts of cedar-choppers who "mined" and cut the well preserved logs which had been accumulating in the ooze for thousands of years.[85] The discovery of extensive beds of bog-iron ore, however, had led to the establishment of furnaces at Batsto and Atsion, places easily accessible by water on the upper branches of the Mullica River.

The most thickly settled area in southern New Jersey, or West Jersey as it was usually called, was a strip of land along Delaware River and Bay and the streams flowing into them. In this district, which stretched from the vicinity of Bordentown on the north to the shore of Cumberland County on the south, and which was in few places more than twelve miles wide, the sand and clay soils of the interior blended to form a loam suitable for agriculture.[86] Here had grown up a class of farmers able to make a fairly comfortable living. Of greatest prominence among them were the Quakers, who had been enabled, by their original proprietary rights to the soil and by their policy of not marrying outside their own sect, to build up landed estates of very respectable size. The large farms had been worked in earlier times to a considerable extent by slaves; but the growing disapproval of slavery by the Society of Friends was having its effect by the time of the Revolution, and the Negroes seem to have been replaced in large measure by indentured servants.[87]

The wealthy landowners of West Jersey have been compared to the plantation aristocracy of the tobacco colonies;[88]

[85] New Jersey State Geological Survey, *Geology of the County of Cape May, New Jersey* (Trenton, 1857), pp. 57-65.

[86] Thomas F. Gordon, *A Gazetteer of the State of New Jersey* (Trenton, 1834), p. 2.

[87] See in *N.J.A.*, 2nd S., Vol. I, the large number of runaway white servants in West Jersey for which advertisements were published in the years 1775-1777.

[88] Francis B. Lee, *New Jersey as a Colony and as a State* (New York, 1902), Vol. I, pp. 187-8; Fisher, *op. cit.*, pp. 154-8.

but they lacked any such political power as that enjoyed by the Virginia planters. Remote, on their farms, from the business and tumult of the world, they could not compete with the active merchants and professional men of East Jersey for a determining influence on the conduct of government. Burlington, indeed, which had been the governmental center of West Jersey while the latter was a separate province, remained one of the two official capitals of the united colony of New Jersey after 1703, and the colonial legislature continued to hold its meeting alternately at Burlington and at Perth Amboy. Regardless of this official equality, however, the real center of power and influence was Perth Amboy, with its group of enterprising families which kept a secure hold upon governmental offices.

Life, too, was simpler and less sophisticated on the New Jersey farms than on the Southern plantations. We find an interesting description of conditions on the Delaware in the papers of a Swedish clergyman, Nicholas Collin, who had arrived from Europe in 1770 to take charge of the vanishing Swedish congregations in West Jersey. His account of the region, written in 1771, applies to life on both sides of the lower Delaware, in the former territory of New Sweden; but, since most of his time had been passed in Salem and Gloucester Counties, in New Jersey, it is safe to assume that this region furnished him with the opportunity for most of his observations. He remarked:

"The people are in general prosperous, . . . industrious, and careful in their management; the unreasonable and harmful prejudice that work does not become rich and honorable people, is unknown here. Many a man goes and plows who is the possessor of great wealth. . . . The empty vanity of wishing to make a show with titles and ill-paid but distinguished offices is scorned here, nor can it have any place in a colony if there be no court and few public offices. There is no nobility here. All are generally [considered] equally good. . . .

"In general the people live well, not with many dishes, but with good and nourishing food, particularly a good deal of meat. Many kinds of wines and liquors are used here. Tea, coffee, and chocolate are general. The wealthier farmers also for the most part have wine and punch in their houses. . . . Houses even in the country are now mostly built of brick, two stories high. Beautiful furniture, in [the form of] sideboards, chairs, and tables of walnut, good beds, etc., is used by many farmers. Thus the wealthier farmers are the same as the lesser country gentry with us;[89] at least most of them [are] like our petty squires. They use fine linen, [and] clothing of fine cloth . . . keep good riding horses, etc. . . .

"The earlier simplicity is still retained among the old people, especially in the country, where they clothe themselves very lightly in summer. Thus when one comes to [the home of] a man of wealth and reputation, one may meet the gentleman of the house with his oxen, and when one enters one finds the mistress and the young ladies barefooted at the coffee table. Indeed, many a woman has been courteous enough to bridle my horse and hold the stirrup."[90]

A few small but solidly-built and comfortable towns along the shore of the Delaware took care of the trade of this prosperous region. There was little direct foreign commerce, though Salem, the chief port, had at times a few sea-going vessels; but from every creek, cove, and village, small vessels and boats carried the products of the district to Philadelphia. Wheat, flour, bread, corn, beef, hides, bacon, cheese, butter, barrel-staves, cedar shingles, and bar iron were taken to the metropolis. In exchange, the traders brought back rum, sugar, and molasses from the West Indies; manufactured products from Great Britain; oil, wine, and salt from south-

[89] i.e. in Sweden.
[90] Nils Collin, "Berättelse om Nya Sverige," in *Personhistorisk Tidskrift* (Stockholm, 1925), Årg. XXVI, Häft 1-2, pp. 25-6.

ern Europe; tea and spices from the East; and indentured servants, in large part from Ireland.[91]

Prominent among the West Jersey towns which served as local centers for this trade was Burlington, a "pleasant village" of something over a hundred houses. Disappointed in its dream of growing into a great port, it was stagnating commercially and losing some of its young people through emigration.[92] Other villages were Bordentown and Gloucester, each probably with fewer than a hundred houses; Salem, about the size of Burlington;[93] Greenwich, near the mouth of Cohansey Creek; and, at the head of navigation on the same stream, Cohansey Bridge,[94] the county seat of Cumberland County.

Back of the strip of well cleared and fertile land on the Delaware, with its predominantly Quaker inhabitants, was a region in Salem, Gloucester, and Cumberland Counties where a more dispersed and diversified population was still struggling to subdue the wilderness. The boundaries of this district cannot be defined, for on the one side it merged into the old prosperous settlements, and on the other it lost itself gradually among the rude huts of the cedar-choppers scattered through the woods.

Here was a mixture of varied national elements. In the vicinity of Raccoon Creek and Oldman's Creek lived the descendants of the ancient colonists of New Sweden. Although many families in this group had forgotten their mother tongue, and although its use was fast disappearing among the younger generation, there were still many who understood it and spoke it occasionally. The Swedish Crown maintained a Lutheran clergyman, with headquarters at Sveaborg or Swedesborough, to care for the spiritual needs of the inhabitants and maintain the culture of their fathers;

[91] Israel Acrelius, *A History of New Sweden*, tr. by William M. Reynolds (Philadelphia, 1874), pp. 145-6.

[92] The Rev. Colin Campbell to the S.P.G., Jàn. 4, 1763, S.P.G. transcripts, Ser. B, Vol. 24, No. 67.

[93] Acrelius, *op. cit.*, pp. 144, 145.   [94] Now Bridgeton.

but Nicholas Collin, the hard-working pastor, poured forth
into his journal and letters his sorrow over the extent to
which Swedish virtues and traditions were disappearing.
Mingled with the Scandinavians, and mostly assimilated
to them, were some Dutch families whose ancestors had
settled on the Delaware when their nation conquered the
surrounding territory; and scattered through the district
were Protestant Irish, Germans, and, of course, many
Quakers of English stock.

Life among these settlers was not easy. Clearing away
woods and draining marshes for field and pasture, struggling
with a sandy soil, suffering from the ravages of fever and
dysentery in summer and from various ailments in the cold,
wet winter, the people, for the most part poor and isolated,
led an unenviable existence. A few had attained a considerable degree of prosperity; but as late as 1786, Collin
wrote of "the wild nature of the country, and the poverty of
the people, which to a large extent still continue."[95]

Harsh though their existence was, the inhabitants of this
backwoods district were not without their enjoyments. The
consolations of religion were of greater importance and more
varied nature here than in most other parts of the colony;
for in this poverty-stricken frontier region there was a more
diversified array of sects than could be found in any of the
wealthy towns. Quakers, Presbyterians, Lutherans, Anglicans, Moravians, Anabaptists, and Methodists, com-
peting for attention and converts, afforded one of the chief
means of diversion to the hard-working settlers. "Frivolous
people in this country," complains Pastor Collin, "run from
one sect to the other. . . . Independence is so rampant that
in all congregations several leave, if a pastor speaks the
truth without regard to persons, saying that he has pointed
them out." And again he writes bitterly of "some old women
who, I believe, could be converted and backslide again

[95] Nicholas Collin, *The Journal and Biography of Nicholas Collin* (ed. by
Amandus Johnson, Philadelphia, 1936), p. 296.

fifteen times a day," and who let themselves be baptized two or three times as they change denominations.[96]

For the most part, the preachers of the various sects preserved an appearance of mutual tolerance; but at times their latent animosities blazed forth in a manner which must have furnished more pleasurable excitement than spiritual edification to their flocks. The bitterness of the interdenominational and intradenominational squabbles which we can trace in the ecclesiastical records of this region suggests a general emotional instability in the populace—a condition doubtless due at least in part to the unremitting toil and lack of normal emotional release in their lives. We need not be surprised, then, at the fury and cruelty which, during the Revolution, were to characterize the civil war in this section, where on the face of things no such outbursts might have been expected. The repressions of the pioneer life were to find a fearful outlet.

It was not to be expected that the adverse conditions of existence should produce characters in which the gentler virtues predominated. Sexual relationships were frequently characterized by that crudity and informality so often found on the frontier.[97] The struggle for existence inevitably developed in many persons a grasping trait for which the term "business shrewdness" would be all too euphemistic. Collin records in his journal that an innkeeper of his congregation took advantage of his own sister's funeral in cold, wet weather to sell liquor during the church service to the funeral guests.[98] The clergyman's growing disgust with some characteristics of the people about him was expressed in a description of American character which he wrote in 1775. We must suppose his general conclusions were based chiefly on the actions of the men and women more immediately surrounding him, when he declared:

[96] Collin, *Journal*, p. 226; Collin, "Berättelse om Nya Sverige," p. 27
[97] Collin, *Journal*, pp. 234, 257, 260.   [98] *ibid.*, p. 229.

"The morals of the people are not of the best. . . . Self-interest is a prevailing passion, which often triumphs over friendship and kinship. To be sure, it does not often break out in theft, robbery, and murder, because no necessity compels one to take such risks; but fraud is all the more common in their dealings, and, far from being regarded with the proper aversion and contempt, it is called by many people cleverness and caution. . . . Manners and customs are simple and border on rudeness. . . . Politeness is regarded as affectation or servility. The unfeigned, cordial courtesy which is so pleasing among the humbler folk with us [in Sweden] is wanting here. Everything is cold and ugly."[99]

Between the main body of West Jersey and the settlements on Cape May a definite break was made by the marshes surrounding the Maurice River and by the Great Cedar Swamp, which, extending from Delaware Bay to the Atlantic, isolated the southern tip of the province. Communication by land between the two sections was difficult, since the roads, which throughout most of southern New Jersey were poor and best adapted for pack and saddle horses, were particularly bad in the marshes, and the journey was long.[100] When Collin travelled from Swedesborough to the Maurice River district in 1770—a journey which he had made only a month before—he "went astray in the wilderness a whole afternoon."[101]

Inadequate land transportation, however, worried the Cape May people but little, since their interests were largely maritime. Many of the seventeenth century settlers of the peninsula had come there to establish a base for whaling operations, and the sea-going tradition had remained an active force. Shipbuilding and piloting became natural occupations of the inhabitants. Lumber from the cedar swamps, corn from the farms, meat and hides from the cattle which

[99] Harald Elovson, *Amerika i Svensk Litteratur, 1750-1820: en studie i komparativ litteraturhistoria* (Lund, 1930), p. 222.
[100] Fisher, *op. cit.*, pp. 160-4.   [101] Collin, *Journal*, p. 213.

throve on the rich pasturage,[102] oysters from the neighboring beds, and oil and whalebone from the whale fishery were carried by water to Philadelphia, to Long Island and New England, or elsewhere.[103]

There was also a brisk trade with the West Indies; but no estimate of its extent can be made, since most of it was of a nature not to be entered on official records. John Hatton, the collector of customs in Cape May and the adjoining region, was an enterprising man who early came to a satisfactory working arrangement with the local traders. The American inspector of customs calls attention in 1769 to the curious fact that "every Vessell which entered with him [Hatton] from the West Indies was only in Ballast except 5. from April 1765 to May 1766, which was detected by the Man of War and Cutters, and what is still more remarkable he never entered any, but what belonged to noted Smugglers. . . . Since September 1767, three Vessels entered with M[r] Hatton from Guadaloupe and one from Dominico, all in Ballast, and he has not received a Shilling Duties during that Time.—Every Smuggler speaks well of him as a Collector."[104]

Hatton's personality, however, was violent and overbearing; perhaps it wore down the patience of his neighbors, or perhaps he demanded too large a share in the profits of their commercial enterprises. Whatever the reason, he came into violent collision with them in November 1770, when he was forcibly prevented from boarding a British vessel from which several pilot boats were busily unloading goods without the formality of a customs declaration. When, after his

[102] In May 1777, it was estimated that there were "in & about the Neighbourhood of Cape May New Jersey 30,000 head of Cattle of different kinds, & near as many sheep."—Captain Francis Wade to George Washington, May 1777, in Washington Papers (Library of Congress), Vol. 48.

[103] Fisher, *op. cit.*, pp. 160-4; Maurice Beesley, "Sketch of the Early History of the County of Cape May," in New Jersey State Geological Survey, *Geology of the County of Cape May* (Trenton, 1857), pp. 198-9.

[104] *N.J.A.*, Vol. X, p. 296.

repulse, he seized one of the boats, it was recaptured from him, and he, his son, and a Negro servant were roughly handled. The resentment of those with whose business Hatton had attempted to interfere was not appeased; and his son was later set upon in Philadelphia by a group of sailors, "tarr'd and feathered, put in the Pillory, dragged by a Rope through the Water and left in such a Condition that his Life was despaired of."[105]

These events led to further unpleasantness. Hatton broke completely with his former associates, complained to the commissioners of customs, and charged that the local magistrates at Cape May had connived at violent actions on the part of the smugglers. He declared that a group of Philadelphia merchants had made the Cape a center for contraband operations, that several thousands of pounds' worth of goods had recently been illegally landed, and that a wagon-load of them on the way to Philadelphia had actually passed by his door in broad daylight, under the escort of armed men who challenged him to seize them.[106]

The investigation which followed yielded no results. It is significant of the state of the British colonial administration at the time that, whereas the customs officials, who were in close contact with their superiors in England, zealously supported Hatton, Governor Franklin and his Council attempted to smooth matters over as quietly as possible. Wise governors had learned long since that it was advisable for them to modify unpopular policies of the imperial administration; and Franklin, we may suppose, had no desire to stir up a hornet's nest by any attempt to enforce customs regulations. Accordingly, Hatton's charges against the Cape May magistrates were heard and dismissed; the deputy secretary of the province wrote soothingly that "the Bulk of the People and all the Magistrates of whom he has complained, are Farmers, unacquainted with Trade, and accustomed to

[105] *ibid.*, p. 286.   [106] *ibid.*, p. 213.

a retired and peaceful Life"; and the governor's report bristled with righteous displeasure in deploring Hatton's "very unhappy violent Temper, sometimes bordering on Madness, so that it is impossible that he can live long in Quiet with his Neighbours."[107]

The Hatton affair casts an interesting light on the temper of the people of Cape May, and, incidentally, of many other places in America. So long as the imperial system remained a far-away abstraction, they were willing to tolerate it; but as soon as it threatened to interfere with their daily lives and occupations, it was to be ignored or, if necessary, resisted by violence. Governor Franklin was well aware of this; had British officialdom been possessed of his political shrewdness and tact, there would have been no American Revolution. But common sense was as completely absent from British administrative circles as was breadth of vision. John Hatton, obnoxious though he had proved himself to the people of Cape May, was retained as collector of customs. There was probably little trade for him to interfere with during the troubled years 1770-1776, but his meddling was never forgiven by the inhabitants of southern New Jersey. When the Revolution broke out, he was denounced by mobs and imprisoned in Philadelphia; his property was confiscated; and his wife was ill-treated.[108] The men of the southern counties, he learned too late, were bad people to antagonize.

Among the inhabitants of Cape May there appear to have been few social distinctions. Most of the colonists lived in one-story farmhouses, each consisting of a heavy timber framework built about a huge central fireplace and covered with rough, unpainted clapboards. A farm supplied its owner with food, and his sheep furnished the wool for his clothing. Beyond these things his wants or his means to indulge them were not great, for in the whole of Cape May County in

[107] *N.J.A.*, Vol. X, pp. 282, 289.   [108] Jones, *op. cit.*, pp. 92-3.

the years preceding the Revolution there were but two families which might properly be called wealthy.[109]

The settlements of this simple, enterprising, and none too gentle Cape May community stretched northward in patches to Great Egg Harbor, where the Great Cedar Swamp met the seashore. Between this point and Little Egg Harbor was a thinly settled region; and north of the marshes of the Mullica River extended the woods and shore of Monmouth County, sparsely inhabited except in the fertile northern section. The long stretches of barrier beach, covered in many places with red cedars, and innocent as yet of the fevered architectural eruptions of summer colonies, ran for miles in lonely and unspoiled grandeur.[110]

The few dwellings along the beaches were mostly the habitations of whalemen, a class of people which had first settled in this region nearly a century before. During the intercolonial wars, many of these seafaring men had found new sources of gain in privateering, and it is rumored that certain of them were not inclined to observe too sharply the distinction between privateering and open piracy.[111]

Most of the inhabitants of the coastal region, however, lived back of the inlets and marshes which lay behind the beaches. Such of the original settlers as had not been engaged in whaling had established themselves either near the salt marshes, which furnished excellent pasturage for horses and cattle, or along the navigable streams, where they could supply themselves with food by fishing and could enjoy ready access to water transportation for the lumber—chiefly cedar—which they had gone there to cut.[112] In the course of the eighteenth century, a considerable, though scattered,

[109] Lewis Townsend Stevens, *The History of Cape May County* (Cape May City, 1897), pp. 137-9.

[110] Philip V. Fithian, *Journal, 1775-1776* (Princeton, 1934), p. 252.

[111] John Clement, *Atlantic County* (Camden, N.J., 1880), p. 404; Fisher, *op. cit.*, pp. 163, 164, 196.

[112] Clement, *op. cit.*, p. 413; Leah Blackman, *History of Little Egg Harbor* (Camden, N.J., 1880), pp. 181-3.

population had grown up, interested principally in farming and lumbering. The soil, when cleared, produced good crops of rye and was favorable for orchards; horses and cattle throve so well on the salt pasturage that buyers were attracted from some distance; and hogs and sheep were easily raised. Thus agriculture prospered moderately, though the distance from the market did not encourage the production of a large surplus. A few clandestine salt works were constructed on the bay meadows, in violation of the British mercantilist prohibition, and the bog-iron works at Batsto and Atsion had not yet been driven out of business by competitors having access to ore supplies of higher quality and greater quantity.[113]

For the most part, until the Revolution suddenly thrust the shore villages into prominence as centers of privateering and blockade-running, the contacts of southeastern New Jersey with the outer world were scanty. Already, however, there was perceptible the first faint stirring of the movement destined in the course of the next century and a half to transform the entire seacoast of the state into a summer resort.

For a number of years, Pennsylvania had been aware of the attractions of the New Jersey shore as a vacation center for gunning, fishing, and general relaxation.[114] One Philadelphian who evidently passed part of the summer of 1775 at Black Point, at the mouth of the Shrewsbury River, in the company of Governor Penn and other persons, was sufficiently impressed by the experience to write two rhapsodies on the beauties of "Shrewsbury Vale," as he called the place. A few quotations from one of them will suggest that the author, Joseph Stansbury, was ahead of his time as a propagandist for the seashore as a vacation resort:

[113] Blackman, *op. cit.*, pp. 183-4; Alfred M. Heston, *South Jersey, a History 1664-1924* (New York & Chicago, 4 vols., 1924), Vol. I, pp. 216-17.
[114] Blackman, *op. cit.*, p. 189.

SHREWSBURY VALE

Let Poets the Beauties of Ida rehearse,
Of Paphos, of Tempe, which they never saw,
Make Venus, or Juno the Subject of Verse,
And Pictures of Gods and Goddesses draw:
      Tho' pompous their Diction
      'Tis all but mere Fiction,
The plain Truth at last will most clearly prevail,
      And even Apollo
      I'm sure to beat hollow
When singing the Beauties of Shrewsbury Vale.

What tho' the Musquetoes and Sand-flies abound,
And form a thick Cloud, intercepting the Sun;
Tho' Samphire and Sea-weed enamel the Ground,
And land-frogs and Land-crabs by Myriads run;
      Yet their Woodlands alone
      For these *Trifles* atone,
And yield rich Perfumes which Arabia excell,
      To their Cassia and Aloes
      Our Senses grow callous
When breathing the Fragrance of Shrewsbury Vale.

Hyegeia, the rosy-lipped Goddess of Health
From Cities and Palaces made her retreat,
And, turning her back upon Grandeur and Wealth,
Hath chosen *these Wilds* for her favorite Seat.
      Here Freedom attends her,
      And fair Peace befriends her,
Here Discord and Faction can never prevail;
      For Wealth, Titles, Place,
      Foul hearts with fair faces,
Are not to be met with in Shrewsbury Vale.[115]

[115] Manuscript volume of "Loyalist Rhapsodies, 1775-83" in Library of Congress.

With this final pleasant glimpse of the shore, we have completed our rambling tour of the New Jersey of 1776, and have gained some idea of what diverse types were included among its inhabitants.

That the life of the province was not so idyllic as it has sometimes been pictured is evident. Slaves, approximately ten thousand in a total population of some hundred and twenty thousand or hundred and fifty thousand, were held throughout the province, but chiefly in the middle and northern counties. They gave New Jersey the unenviable distinction, shortly after this time, of having a larger servile population than any other state north of Maryland except New York.[116] Although their treatment is reputed to have been not unkind in general, the provisions of criminal law dealing with them were harsh: in 1750 two Negroes convicted respectively of murder and of attempted murder had been burned alive in Perth Amboy.[117] The uneasiness in which a slaveholding class must always live in times of commotion is shown by the actions of the Shrewsbury Committee of Observation, which, in 1776, confiscated all arms in the possession of Negroes, whether free or bond, and restricted the movements of slaves.[118]

Slaves were not the only sufferers from a harsh labor system. That the lot of many indentured servants must have been hard is suggested by the large number of them who ran away in the years 1775-1777, when the disturbed state of the country seemed to promise a fair chance of escape.[119] The indenture system affected not only adults who knew what they were doing when they sold themselves into servitude for a period of years, but also children, who were bound out by their parents or guardians at early ages. A resident of

[116] Henry S. Cooley, *A Study of Slavery in New Jersey* (Baltimore, 1896), pp. 30-1.
[117] *ibid.*, p. 41; Whitehead, *op. cit.*, p. 319.
[118] *N.J.H.S.P.*, Vol. I, pp. 195, 196.
[119] See the many advertisements for runaways throughout *N.J.A.*, 2nd S., Vol. I.

Gloucester County advertises in 1775 for "an indented female child . . . very near 5 years of age," who is lost, and is suspected to have been taken away by her parents. A reward is offered to anyone who secures the family so that the parents may be convicted of the theft.[120] Included in the estate of another Gloucester County resident which is offered for sale a few months later are "the indentures of a bound girl, about nine years of age, to be disposed of for a small premium, to a good place."[121]

Much simpler to describe than social conditions is the political organization of the province at the outbreak of the Revolution. There was a royal governor. There was an Assembly, the members of which were elected by such freeholders as possessed one hundred acres of land each in their own right, or were worth £50 in real and personal estate; a representative elected to the Assembly was required to possess one thousand acres of land or to be worth £500 in real and personal estate. Finally, there was the Council of New Jersey, the members of which were appointed by the Crown on the recommendation of the governor.

It is interesting to note in passing that most of the key positions in the government were occupied by members of that coterie to which we have already referred earlier in the chapter as "the Perth Amboy Group." It would be an exhausting task to trace in detail the relationships and ramifications of this clique, composed for the most part of merchants, large landholders, and lawyers, living chiefly at Perth Amboy, but with branches elsewhere in the province and close connections with the DeLanceys, Rutherfurds, and other prominent New York families. A bewildering web of marriages knit the Johnstons, Skinners, Kearnys, and Parkers into a family unit which, with its friends, dominated not only the capital city but much of the life of the entire province as well.

[120] *N.J.A.*, Vol. XXI, p. 207.   [121] *N.J.A.*, 2nd S., Vol. I, p. 543.

It is significant that of the twelve members of the Council in 1775,[122] three were members of the Perth Amboy inner circle, and four others were closely connected by marriage and interest. Another member of the Group, John Smyth, was examiner in chancery, clerk of the court of common pleas of Middlesex County, and treasurer of East Jersey, having succeeded his wife's brother-in-law, Stephen Skinner, in the last-named capacity. Stephen Skinner's brother, Cortlandt, combined in his own person the important offices of attorney general of New Jersey and speaker of the Assembly, the latter position having been filled a few years previously by his mother's brother-in-law, Andrew Johnston. James Parker, brother-in-law of the Skinners, was not only a member of the Council, but held office as mayor of Perth Amboy at various times, as had his father before him.

Of even more dominating influence was the position of the Perth Amboy Group in the Council of Proprietors of East Jersey. The Proprietors held title in common to a million or more acres of unallotted lands in the province and also maintained a hotly disputed claim to the ownership of some of the best-cultivated territory of East Jersey. Of the twenty-one persons who attended meetings of the Council in the years 1775 and 1776, thirteen—probably fourteen—were members of the Group, or, like the De-Lanceys of New York, were closely connected with it by marriage.[123] The president of the Council, James Parker,

[122] *Peter Kemble, David Ogden, Lord Stirling, John Stevens,* Samuel Smith, *James Parker,* Frederick Smyth, Richard Stockton, *Stephen Skinner,* Daniel Coxe, *John Lawrence,* and Francis Hopkinson. The names italicized are those of members or connections of the Perth Amboy Group.

[123] The persons who attended these meetings were *James Parker, Cortlandt Skinner* (for himself and devisees of *Michael Kearny*), *Walter Rutherfurd, Henry Cuyler,* Joseph Sharp, *John L. Johnston* (executor of A. Johnston), Elias Bland (for himself and Mercy Mann), A. Sharp (for executor of Isaac Sharp), *Heathcote Johnston, Lord Stirling, John Stevens,* John Stevens, Jr., Elias Boudinot (for Lord Perth), *John Smyth* (for Colonel John Reid), *Stephen DeLancey,* William Burnet, Lewis Morris, J. Williams (for himself and Stephen Tallman), *David Ogden* (executor of Robert H. Morris), *Stephen*

had been for a number of years surveyor-general for the Proprietors—an office earlier held by his brother's father-in-law, James Alexander of New York. The vice-president—until he was compelled to flee to the British for protection early in 1776—was Parker's brother-in-law, Cortlandt Skinner.[124] The registrar was John Smyth, husband of a cousin of Skinner's.

Here, then, was a small but powerful coterie, firmly entrenched behind the British colonial system. It enjoyed economic prosperity, social prestige, and official favor. Some of its sons entered the royal army or navy; some of its daughters married men distinguished in those services. Its land claims, unpopular in the colony, were supported by the British government. Although it was closely identified with the Council, against which the Assembly had been struggling periodically for years, several of its members had seats in the Assembly itself. Their influence was exerted in favor of imperial policies, and they were mentioned with approval in governors' reports as "friends to Government."[125]

What stand would this group take when the unwelcome storm of the Revolution broke over it? What was to be its fate as a result of the war? These are among the questions which the following chapters will attempt to answer.

Skinner (as executor of A. Johnston), and *Oliver DeLancey*. The italicized names, to which that of the younger Stevens should probably be added, are those of members of the Perth Amboy Group, or connections of it.

[124] Minutes of the Council of Proprietors of the Eastern Division of New Jersey No. B (in office of surveyor-general at Perth Amboy).

[125] Letter-book of Francis Bernard (Sparks MSS., 4, Vol. I), pp. 146, 147.

CHAPTER II ✿ *THE BACKGROUND OF CIVIL DISCORD*

THE strangely compounded society which has been sketched in the foregoing pages was tense with serious internal strains. Conflicts of interest and growing new forces, held in check by the political and social organization of the colony, were ready to be released with explosive violence when the Revolution should remove imperial constraints. What happened in New Jersey during the years 1776-1783 was in large part determined by the division of the inhabitants into two hostile camps; and this cleavage between Whig and Tory cannot be fully understood without some reference to the social antagonisms created or inflamed during the immediately preceding decades. Once hostilities with England had broken out elsewhere in America, a number of special grievances, cherished by certain groups within the province, lent themselves readily to exploitation by the revolutionary movement, and aggravated the bitterness of partisan strife during the war.

It was of importance to the course of the Revolution in New Jersey that the province had a long and vigorous tradition of conflict between the more or less popular Assembly, on the one hand, and, on the other, the royal governor and the aristocratic Council with which he worked hand in glove. More than one historian has recounted the many occasions on which the Assembly stubbornly asserted its prerogatives and rights—or what it conceived to be its rights—against encroachment by the other two branches of the government. As early as 1739, Governor Lewis Morris had complained that the Assembly fancied itself "to have as much power as a British house of commons, and more," and prophesied darkly that if the pretensions of its members were suffered long to pass unnoticed, the aid of British Parliament might one day be required to persuade the legislators to entertain "juster sentiments of their duty and their true interest."[1]

With the passage of time, the Assembly grew ever more fixed in its determination to brook no undue interference from the representatives of the Crown, or from their henchmen. The crabbed and domineering Governor Morris passed from the scene, and was succeeded by Jonathan Belcher, who devoted himself chiefly to piety and good works, and had no taste for wrangling with the legislators. Belcher, in turn, was followed in 1758 by Francis Bernard, whose tact and political sagacity prevented serious conflicts between the authorities in Great Britain and the chosen representatives of the colonists. Indeed, Bernard's term of office marks a significant point in the political development of New Jersey. To all intents and purposes, the governor ceased to be merely an intermediary through whom the wishes of British officialdom were conveyed to the more or less docile colonists. He became instead a mediator between mother country and province, trying to explain the needs and desires of the colony to the bureaucrats at Westminster, and, if necessary, quietly ignoring his instructions, in order to let a necessary piece of legislation pass.

This change of policy was the more marked because the British government, needing the wholehearted cooperation of the colonies in preventing the French and Indian War, was obliged to loosen the reins of authority for the time being. As a result, Bernard could boast with justice in 1760 on retiring from office that, though he had found widespread mistrust of the government when he arrived in New Jersey, there had grown up during his short term "an harmony between the Several branches of the legislature that never was known before."[2]

[1] *The Papers of Lewis Morris, Governor of the Province of New Jersey, from 1738 to 1746* (Newark, 1852), p. 123.

[2] Bernard to Halifax, July 18, 1760 (Sparks MSS., 4, Vol. I, p. 266); same to same, Feb. 16, 1760, *ibid.*, p. 193.

The new harmony, however, had been purchased by concessions which the Assembly, having once tasted power, was loath to relinquish. When, at the conclusion of the war, the British authorities asserted once more their earlier theories of imperial relationships, and attempted to enforce them, the result was an increasingly sharp conflict with the colonists.

The last royal governor, William Franklin, succeeded with remarkable agility in balancing himself between the Assembly and the home government; but his political gymnastics could not avert or appreciably soften the clash between British bureaucrat and stubborn assemblyman. Again and again during his term of office the policies and wishes of the two antagonists proved to be irreconcilable. There had grown up in New Jersey, as elsewhere in America, a people whose way of life was different from any that the world had known before and inevitably rendered them impatient of the governmental ideas held by European statesmen. Nicholas Collin, the Swedish clergyman whose pronounced opinions on American customs have already been quoted, observed the phenomenon and commented upon it. With his European background and conservative turn of mind, he was unable to sympathize with the New World freedom, but his remarks are none the less interesting.

"The chief trait in the character of an American," writes the Swedesborough minister in 1775, "is an immoderate love of liberty, or rather license. . . . And this enthusiasm rules in the breasts of all from the highest to the lowest. Education, manner of life, religion, and government—all contribute to it. Parents exercise no authority over children, beyond letting them for the most part do what pleases them. Everyone can maintain himself without trouble, for here there is room enough, and wages are high. No one, therefore, knows oppression or dependence. All are equally good; birth, office, and merits do not make much distinction. Freedom of conscience is unlimited, without the least control by secular law, and church discipline means nothing. The

English method of government is in itself quite mild, and is all the less able, in this remote part of the empire, to exercise a reasonable strictness. The reins of government lie so slack that they seldom are noticed, and the hand that guides is never seen. The result of all this is that the people neither know nor will know of any control, and everyone regards himself as an independent prince. One can grow weary of continually hearing and reading about noble liberty. Many, as stupid as shameless, regard all other nations as slaves. Their imagination constantly sees apparitions coming to steal away that goddess of theirs. All the enterprises of the government arouse suspicion. The most reasonable regulations are invasions of their rights and liberties; light and necessary taxes, robbery and plunder; well-merited punishment, unheard-of tyranny."[3]

Between a people of such temperament and the determined ministers of George III, with their idea of a more closely integrated empire, the prospects for cooperation were not bright.

In the period following the French and Indian War, the irritability and suspiciousness of the colonists were aggravated by a general economic depression. This had originated in England, in part as a result of the industrial and agricultural revolutions,[4] and, spreading to America, was intensified by the commercial and fiscal policies introduced in the 1760's. In New Jersey the effects were felt with particular sharpness.

During the French and Indian War, the farmers in parts of the colony appear to have enjoyed an exceptional prosperity;[5] but after the conclusion of hostilities a reaction set in. The British troops, with their consuming power, were withdrawn; the West Indian market for grain was restricted

[3] Elovson, *op. cit.*, pp. 222-3.
[4] Harold U. Faulkner, *American Economic History* (New York, 1931), p. 157.
[5] The Rev. Colin Campbell, Dec. 26, 1761 (S.P.G. transcripts, Ser. B, Vol. 24, No. 65).

by new mercantilist regulations; and an increasing acreage of excellent wheat-producing land was brought under cultivation in Sussex County upon the removal of the Indian menace. The price of wheat fell,[6] and there developed, in the northern counties at least, a condition of acute agrarian distress. A perusal of the large number of bankruptcy and foreclosure announcements in the newspapers of the years 1765-1770 leaves no doubt as to the desperate condition of large numbers of farmers. A severe monetary stringency, to be discussed in the course of the following pages, made it impossible for hard-pressed agriculturists to meet their obligations, when a moderate amount of credit might have tided them over their difficulties. Repeated local crop failures added, in the districts where they occurred, to the troubles occasioned by the general prostration.[7] Another contributory cause of difficulty, though one of minor importance, was a level taxation relatively high for American standards.[8] This last burden was a consequence of the generous assistance furnished by New Jersey in the prosecution of the French and Indian War—an assistance which Governor Bernard readily acknowledged,[9] but which did not evoke any marked tenderness at Westminster in the following years when the needs of the province were under consideration.

Amidst all these accumulating woes, one fact was unpleasantly clear to many of the colonists: the stagnation of economic life was due in large part to recent elaborations of the British mercantile system. Although, as we have seen, New Jersey had little foreign commerce of its own, there

[6] See in the Lord Stirling Papers (New York Historical Society) for 1767 (Vol. III), an undated petition, addressed to Governor Franklin and asserting that "the price of Wheat and Other Grain within this and the Neighbouring Colonies, has of late greatly fallen arising Chiefly from the late Parliamentary Checks given to the foreign Trade formerly used from North America."

[7] The Rev. William Frazer, May 9, 1769 (S.P.G. transcripts, Ser. B, Part I, No. 239).

[8] ibid., Ser. B, Vol. 24, Nos. 62 and 63.

[9] See his letter-book, especially letter to Pitt, March 26, 1760 (Sparks MSS., 4, Vol. I, p. 201).

was a certain amount of exportation from Perth Amboy, and a large part of the province was economically tributary to Philadelphia, which carried on a brisk trade with the West Indies. Imperial legislation of the year 1764, particularly the Sugar Act and the ordinance adding lumber, an important item in the West Indian trade, to the list of "enumerated articles" exportable only to Great Britain, virtually ruined the busy commerce between the Middle Colonies and the French West Indies, and created great distress. The colonists believed, not without reason, that the new restrictions were intended to favor the planters of the British sugar islands at the expense of the inhabitants of the continental provinces, and resentment was keen.

This state of mind is clearly reflected in a letter written by Cortlandt Skinner of Perth Amboy in October 1765. As has already been pointed out, Skinner belonged to the mercantile-minded Perth Amboy Group which reaped great benefits from the British colonial system. He was in no sense a political malcontent, and when the Revolution came he was to be one of the most active New Jersey loyalists. Hence his disapproval of the governmental policies, and his forebodings for the future, possess exceptional interest.

"Everything here," he writes, "is in the greatest confusion, and the first of November is dreaded. The laws of trade had ruined the merchants, and drained the colonies of their silver. Little was left after paying the duties, to pay their debts in England. . . . Discontent was painted in every man's face, and the distress of the people very great, from an amazing scarcity of money, occasioned by the sudden stagnation of trade. At this time (and a more unlucky one could not have been chosen) the Stamp Law and the Mutiny Bill found their way through parliament.

"Upon those laws all restraints were broken through, and the papers will abundantly show you the violence and fury of the people. . . . It is hoped that with the new ministers will follow a change of measures, and that the interest of

Britain with respect to her colonies will be better understood, and the colonies relieved both from duties and stamps. . . . Taxes and a restraint on the West India trade are most likely to force the colonists into manufactures and put independence into their heads. They are in the high road to it now, and though 'tis true that they have not the strength to effect it, but must submit, yet 'tis laying the foundation for great trouble and expense to Britain, in keeping that by force which she might easily do without, and alienating a people which she might make her greatest prop and security."[10]

After repealing the Stamp Act, Parliament also modified the objectionable legislation affecting the West Indian trade and in a measure placated the merchants. But the damage that had been wrought in the lives of many colonists by the depression could not easily be undone, and the resentment aroused by British commercial policy was not entirely wiped out.

Whether the ironmasters whose furnaces and forges were scattered through various parts of New Jersey were seriously aggrieved by the British mercantilist legislation aimed at preventing the manufacture of finished iron goods in the colonies, it is difficult to say. High labor costs in America made competition with any kind of British manufactures difficult, even in the local market; and after the Revolution the iron industry which grew up under the stimulus of the war was to languish as foreign products invaded the country. Nevertheless, colonial foundries do appear to have competed with some success in fields not affected by legal restrictions.[11] It is not unreasonable to suppose that the industrial prohibitions irked some of the colonists who might have attempted to establish manufactures had they been permitted. The restriction of the iron industry was recalled in 1770 when the manifold iniquities of the British govern-

[10] Whitehead, *op. cit.*, pp. 102-3.   [11] Acrelius, *op. cit.*, p. 167.

ment were being reviewed by exasperated Jerseymen.[12] Certainly the act of 1764 which placed iron on the list of commodities which might be exported only to England aroused resentment, since, as John Dickinson of Pennsylvania pointed out, the great weight of the article limited the quantity which might be shipped on any one vessel, so that not half the product could be sent directly to England.[13] It is not without significance that, immediately upon the outbreak of the Revolution, numerous ironmasters in New Jersey entered with alacrity upon an expansion of their business and turned their attention to branches of the industry forbidden under British rule.

Even more unpopular among the people of New Jersey than the mercantile system was the policy of the imperial government in regard to paper money. In no way did British officialdom during the eighteenth century display more completely its incapacity to rule an empire than in its stupid handling of the problem of securing a medium of exchange for the colonists. This problem, says one outstanding economic historian, "had always been an important one in the colonies. No gold or silver mines existed; the colonists were poor and needed other kinds of wealth rather than money. . . . The West Indian trade was the source of specie, most of which was shipped to England in payment of manufactured goods. . . . With such a condition of affairs the expansion of domestic trade naturally led to the issue of paper money in the absence of uniform or sound coinage acts which would keep coins in the country as needed."[14] The difficulties were felt with particular sharpness in New Jersey, which had little direct commerce with regions from which specie could be obtained.

[12] *N.J.A.*, Vol. XXVII, p. 256.
[13] Mary Alice Hanna, "Trade of the Delaware District before the Revolution," in *Smith College Studies in History*, Vol. II (Northampton, 1917), p. 286.
[14] Faulkner, *op. cit.*, pp. 159-60. By permission of Harper & Brothers, publishers.

As a result of unfortunate experiments with paper money
which a number of the colonies had made, the British government entered upon a course of decisive restriction about
1740, making little distinction between provinces which had
offended badly through uncontrolled inflation and others
which, like New Jersey, had maintained the value of their
currency at a relatively high level. Throughout the admin-
istrations of Morris and Belcher, the Lords of Trade, who
directed British colonial policy, offered an increasing opposition to efforts on the part of the New Jersey Assembly to
issue paper money. Their objections were not lessened even
when a proposed measure attempted to secure the stability
of the currency issued, and they ignored the usefulness
which a loan office, such as was proposed in some of the
bills, would possess in New Jersey at a period when banking
facilities scarcely existed and were inadequate to the needs
of a growing province.[15]

During Bernard's governorship, however, the British authorities were obliged to modify their opposition to expansion of the circulating medium. The exigencies of the war
in America required that money be raised quickly for military purposes, by the issue of paper currency, if necessary,
without the delays entailed by referring measures to the
colonial administration across the Atlantic. Bernard himself
soon became converted to the colonists' point of view, and
explained to the Lords of Trade that the paper bills in
circulation were the only legal tender to be found in the
province, since English gold and silver could not be had in
quantity sufficient for a currency, and the foreign coins
commonly found were debarred by statute from being made
legal tender.[16]

Impressed less, it is probable, by Bernard's arguments
than by the necessities of the war, the British government
acquiesced in a series of emissions of legal-tender bills during

15 *N.J.A.*, Vol. VIII, Part II, p. 15.   16 *ibid.*, Vol. IX, pp. 135-6.

the struggle with France; these were redeemable in the period from 1757 to 1783. At the conclusion of hostilities, however, the general stiffening in the attitude of the home government towards the colonies extended to the issue of paper money. Sympathizing with the fears of British merchants, who dreaded an American inflation disastrous to creditors, the Lords of Trade in 1763 presented a long report to the King. It traced the pernicious effects of bills of credit, as shown in the history of the American provinces, but totally ignored the vital question, raised time and again by governors and assemblies, of how a satisfactory medium of exchange could be secured for the colonies. By a sweeping generalization which took no account of varying local conditions, this short-sighted and dogmatic document condemned in advance all attempts to make paper bills legal tender, however they might be restricted or secured. Parliament, it recommended, should set a date beyond which all bills then current as legal tender in the colonies, without fixed dates of redemption, should be demonetized.[17] Making all due allowances for official stupidity, it is difficult to escape the conclusion that those who wrote the report were not averse to seeing a contraction of the currency which would prove very profitable to British and American creditors at the expense of the large American debtor class. Parliament displayed its customary deference to the wishes of the administration, and the law demanded by the Lords of Trade was passed in 1764.

The effects of the new policy were soon felt in New Jersey. Instead of the gradual expansion of currency which a growing province would naturally require, the colony was subjected to a reduction in the supply of the circulating medium at the rate of £12,500 a year.[18] There is ample testimony concerning the effects of the ensuing deflation.[19]

[17] *ibid.*, pp. 406-14.   [18] *ibid.*, Vol. X, pp. 248-9.
[19] Mills, *Glimpses of Colonial Society* . . . , p. 142; S.P.G. transcripts, Ser. B, Part I, No. 231.

In agreement with others writing on the same subject, a resident of Hunterdon describes in the *New York Gazette* in 1770 what he believes to be "the Case of two Thirds of the People of this Province, and that of every degree more or less; they are in Want of Money; they are in Debt; and do not know how to extricate themselves; they are hard pressed by their Creditors, and cannot pay; they are sued, Judgments are obtained against them, they try to borrow, offer good Security for the money; but all in vain, there is no Money nor money lenders; Execution issues against them, a heavy Bill of Costs arises, the Sheriff levies, advertises and sells the Effects for one fourth or fifth part of their Value, not because the Effects are not wanted, but because there are really no Buyers who can furnish the Money; hence a Man possessed of an Estate worth £5,000 will have it torn from him, tho' all his Debts amount to but £100; a situation which will naturally make a man feel desperate."[20]

In an effort to find some means of supplying credit facilities to the afflicted farmers, the Assembly prepared another bill early in 1770, providing for an emission of paper money to be put into circulation through loans on real estate. Not only was the property of the borrower to be security in double the value of the loan: the whole county in which he lived was liable to make good any deficiency. Having thus done its utmost to give the money a proper backing, the legislators attempted to forestall any objections in Great Britain by not making it legal tender except in discharge of the mortgages for which it was originally borrowed. Governor Franklin sent the bill to England with his recommendation, and optimism concerning the beneficial effects to flow from the act was widespread in the colony. All the more crushing was the disappointment when news arrived in June that the act had been disallowed by the King in

[20] *N.J.A.*, Vol. XXVII, pp. 81-2.

Council. Apparently, the provision making the bills receivable in payment of the loans which they had originally constituted was construed in England, by strained interpretation, as making them legal tender; so the proposed law was vetoed on the ground that it violated the Parliamentary act of 1764.[21]

The general resentment aroused by this veto was reflected in the attitude of the Assembly, which, at its next meeting, flatly refused to make any further provision for the support of the British troops stationed in New Jersey. On expostulation by the governor, the legislators finally granted enough to keep the soldiers through the winter,[22] but a few months of brooding at home over their wrongs and conversing with their constituents put the Assemblymen into no mood for further concessions when they gathered at Burlington in March 1771. A long wrangle between them and the governor over the question of army supplies lasted until December, when Franklin, by expert political manipulation, succeeded in getting the requisite grant. At almost the same time, the home government withdrew its troops from New Jersey, and, through these mutual concessions, the tension subsided, on the surface at least. The paper-money issue lay dormant until early in 1775, when the British authorities, seeking to allay the rising storm of rebellion in the colonies, consented with ostentatious benevolence to the issue by New Jersey of £100,000 in bills of credit.[23]

The policies of the imperial administration which we have outlined unintentionally fostered a steadily sharpening class conflict in America. During the economic depression, the severity of which is in large part traceable to British legislation, the debtor class, as we have seen, suffered with particular intensity. As has often been the case in other crises, the victims did not clearly recognize the source of trouble, but struck out blindly at its nearest manifestations. They

[21] *ibid.*, Vol. X, p. 197.
[22] *ibid.*, p. 202.
[23] *ibid.*, pp. 549-50, 558.

observed the increasing number of lawsuits by which creditors deprived them of their property, noted the legal
expenses which they incurred in vainly contesting such suits,
and concluded that lawyers and creditors were in an unholy
alliance to rob the farmers of their prosperity. The prejudice
against the legal profession which had always been active or
latent in many of the colonies burst into flame under the
stimulus of general distress. The functions of the Sons of
Liberty in the '60's did not consist entirely, as we have
sometimes been led to believe, in direct action by patriotic
citizens against the enforcement of legal innovations like the
Stamp Act, while sympathetic lawyers seconded their vigorous tactics by arguments of constitutional law. Some of
the Sons of Liberty, at least, used the movement to further
their campaign against the encroachments of creditors and
lawyers. A minor but significant indication of this fact
occurred during the celebration which the Sons of Liberty
in Woodbridge held in honor of the King's birthday in
1766, in the midst of general rejoicing over the repeal of the
Stamp Act. Among the eighteen toasts drunk about the
Liberty Oak on this very festive occasion, two represent
indubitably, though in polite form suited to the occasion, the
attitude of the debtor class: "May the Gentlemen of the
Law prosecute their Business with moderation" and
"Peace and Happiness to those who treat their debtors with
Lenity."[24]

During the following years, these pious wishes were not
fulfilled; men of substance continued to foreclose mortgages
which they held, despite the pleas and threats of distressed
debtors.[25] In 1769 and 1770 occurred mob violence aimed

[24] *N.J.A.*, Vol. XXV, p. 144.
[25] For example, Walter Rutherfurd of New York, one of the East Jersey
Proprietors and the owner of considerable land in New Jersey, increased his
holdings by process of foreclosure during the period of distress. See in the
Rutherfurd Papers (New York Historical Society), Box 4, the interesting case
of Robert Martin of Woodbridge. During the boom times of 1761, Martin
had borrowed some money from Rutherfurd, giving a mortgage on his land,

directly at stopping the operation of the legal machinery which was bringing ruin to many a family. But there was another contributory cause of these riots, which must be mentioned before the disturbances are discussed.

In the previous chapter we have spoken of the Proprietors, who claimed title to the soil of New Jersey under royal grant. They were divided into two groups, corresponding to the ancient separation between East and West Jersey. The West Jersey Proprietors constituted a fairly democratic body, with their powers spread widely among the residents of the western district, so that apparently little antagonism existed between them and the rest of the community.[26]

In East Jersey, however, the Council of Proprietors was a much narrower clique of wealthy men, consisting in large part of members of the Perth Amboy Group and its New York connections. In the early days of the colony, the Proprietors had served a useful purpose, bringing settlers to the territory and in general fostering its development. It is difficult to see, on the other hand, that by the middle of the eighteenth century the heirs and successors of these men were performing any public service commensurate with the profits they reaped from their position. The area of unappropriated lands in their common possession at the outbreak of the Revolution was estimated at between a million and two

upon which he soon afterwards built a gristmill and sawmill and a dwelling house. Rutherford foreclosed in 1766, and, owing probably to the lack of money among other potential buyers, bid in the property himself for the amount of his debt. Martin evidently felt that his creditor was making rather too handsome a profit by receiving the mills and the house; for he refused to vacate the buildings until he was ejected, and thereafter, with the assistance of several neighbors, he took the house to pieces and carried it away. Rutherfurd brought suit for the house, but that he suspected a widespread sympathy for men in Martin's position is shown by the fact that in July 1768 he wrote to his agent, John Smyth of Perth Amboy: "After all I submit to you whether it will be prudent to carry on the Suits, you best know the Juries in that Part."

[26] Edgar J. Fisher, *New Jersey as a Royal Province* (New York, 1911), pp. 174-5.

million acres,[27] from which the Council surveyed and sold tracts to such persons as wished to purchase them.

In order to prevent "insiders" from buying up immense tracts and retaining for themselves the profits of appreciation in land values, a limit was placed on the quantity of lands which might be sold to a Proprietor.[28] Nevertheless, a number of these gentlemen succeeded in evading the intent of the restriction, and in building up handsome private domains in the back country.[29] Irrespective, however, of any special opportunities to obtain such individual holdings— the land being worth in many cases, as insiders might discover, considerably more than the flat price charged by the Council—the Proprietors as a Board received a tidy income from their sales. Before the Revolution, we are told, a twenty-fourth share in the proprietary rights was estimated to be worth from £1000 to £1200, New Jersey currency.[30]

The sizable income from the sale of lands was indeed lavish compensation to the Board of Proprietors for maintaining a sort of registry of deeds and surveying office; but the group was not without its troubles. For years large numbers of the inhabitants of New Jersey had refused to recognize the title of the Proprietors to the soil, but claimed for themselves full ownership of the lands they occupied, on the basis of purchase from the Indians or prior grants from royal authority. The confused legal issues of the dispute

[27] Fraser, *op. cit.*, Vol. II, p. 1236; *N.J.H.S.P.*, 2nd S., Vol. I.

[28] *ibid.*, Vol. II, p. 1242.

[29] Oliver DeLancey claimed from the Loyalist commissioners in 1784 compensation for confiscated estates in New Jersey to the extent of many thousand acres. Though some of his fellow Loyalists, when called upon to testify in support of his claim, indicated that his figures were overoptimistic, the commissioners estimated the value of his losses in New Jersey at over £11,000 sterling. (Fraser, *op. cit.*, Vol. II, pp. 1242, 1244.) Henry Cuyler, another Proprietor resident in New York but, like DeLancey, connected by marriage with the Perth Amboy Group, owned, at the time of his death shortly before the Revolution, 6,598 acres in Sussex and Somerset Counties, and held mortgages on other extensive tracts. (*ibid.*, p. 1275.) Cortlandt Skinner owned a thousand acres in Sussex County. (*ibid.*, p. 1239.)

[30] *ibid.*, pp. 1236, 1242.

are not pertinent to this discussion, and cannot be detailed here. It must suffice to remark that the legal advantage appears to have lain with the Proprietors, particularly since they had in general the support of the government—for reasons that are obvious when one considers the close identification between Proprietors and colonial officials. The lands in dispute, however, mostly in Monmouth and Essex Counties, included some of the oldest and most thriving settlements in the colony, whose inhabitants, largely of stubborn New England stock, were not inclined by temperament or tradition to bow their heads to authority. Nearly every attempt on the part of the Proprietors to collect their quitrents or secure other material acknowledgment of their rights had resulted in such disturbances as completely paralyzed the enforcement efforts of the authorities. Litigation intended to determine the matter once for all had been dragging on since 1745, but was still unfinished at the time of the Revolution.

The smoldering hostility to the Proprietors combined with the rising agitation against lawyers in 1769 and 1770 to produce startling explosions of popular sentiment. In December 1770, some of the miserably poor inhabitants of Horse Neck, on the western border of Essex County, bade defiance to the Proprietors and also, in the words of one unfriendly contemporary, "to the laws, government, and constitution of the county." When the authorities took action against two of the leaders, Newark, the county seat, was invaded on two occasions by a considerable crowd of protesters. On their second visit the intruders, about a hundred fifty in number, seem to have come with a vague notion of defending, by forcible action against lawyers if necessary, their claim to a title, based on purchase from the Indians, to the lands which they occupied and which were also claimed by the Proprietors. Interestingly enough under these circumstances, they called themselves "liberty boys" and carried a banner inscribed "Liberty and Property." There was a minor clash with the sheriff and his supporters when the officers attempted to take some of the leaders of the gathering into custody, but the demonstrators were not in a fighting mood and, despite the mild resistance, the arrests were made. After a considerable time, during which apparently little if any damage was done, the liberty boys sent a message to the court, demanding leave to present their grievances against two lawyers who had been retained by the "Indian purchasers" to sustain their claims against the Proprietors, and who were suspected of betraying, as a result of bribery, the cause in which they were engaged. The court refused to listen to such an unlawful assemblage, and admonished it to present its case some other day through two or three persons. The crowd dispersed; but late that night fire destroyed barns and outbuildings belonging to David Ogden, reputedly the most brilliant legal mind in New Jersey, who was one of the lawyers denounced by the crowd. When the charges against Ogden and another prominent lawyer, Elias Boudinot, were later presented to the court, they were dismissed in short order.[31]

At about the same time that these disturbances were taking place, similar troubles occurred in Monmouth County. There the agitation against the legal profession rose to such heights that a demonstration took place before the Monmouth County Court House at Freehold in July 1769, with the object of preventing lawyers from entering the building. The attempt failed; but in January 1770 a throng of rioters, armed with clubs and missiles, stormed the courthouse, drove out the attorneys and forced the court to close.[32]

Great excitement was aroused in the province by the Monmouth and Essex uprisings. Governor Franklin called a special meeting of the Assembly to consider the situation,

---

[31] The two conflicting contemporary accounts from which this account of the Essex County "riot" has been drawn are printed in *N.J.A.*, Vol. XXVII, pp. 53-6, 63-7.

[32] *N.J.A.*, Vol. X, pp. 148-9.

and the legislators hastened to record their abhorrence of the outrages. In well rounded phrases which carefully ignored the underlying causes of the difficulties, the Assembly declared:

"There are few but what have, or may have in future a lawful and honourable, and we think, the best Remedy, in their own Hands, against any Abuses from the Practitioners of the Law, an honest Care to fulfil Contracts; and a patriotic Spirit of Frugality and Industry, would soon make this evident."[33]

In the centers of the disturbances, trials of the rioters were held. A number of those indicted in Essex County in February 1770 pleaded guilty and "shewed strong Marks of Contrition"; they were fined, not too heavily. Three of the accused, however, despite overwhelming evidence against them, stubbornly pleaded not guilty, and were sentenced to heavy fines, and in two cases to short terms of imprisonment, from which they were later released when pardoned by the governor.[34] In Monmouth County, sympathy with the rioters was so general that no conviction of the defendants could be secured from the jury.[35]

The general state of affairs was such as justly to alarm the chief beneficiaries of the colonial system. Heretofore, they had been willing to join in popular protests against such generally disliked British legislation as the Stamp Act, or at least had observed such protests without serious misgivings. Now, however, the rising unrest was threatening the whole social and political structure of the province. The authority of the government had been flouted, and some of its functions interrupted. One of the most respectable classes in the community, the legal profession, was being savagely attacked. Destructive violence had been used against the property of an eminent citizen of the colony, of distinguished

[33] *ibid.*, p. 181.   [34] *ibid.*, Vol. XXVII, p. 78; Vol. X, pp. 187-8.
[35] *ibid.*, Vol. XXVII, p. 175; Richard S. Field, *The Provincial Courts of New Jersey* (New York, 1849), p. 172.

family. And there was indisputably a growing contempt among the populace for the vested rights of those established leaders, the Proprietors. The slogan "Liberty and Property," which was all very well when used to oppose Parliamentary taxation, was being turned against the hallowed privileges of the most securely entrenched class in the province. Evidently, the word "property" was acquiring new meanings as a result of the increasing talk about "natural rights." Property, it seemed, was not, in the eyes of the rude multitude, a matter of sacrosanct title embodied in ancient royal charters, but rather a result of work and use and derivation from "natural" owners, such as the Indians. With such dangerous doctrines in the air, the bases of society were in danger. More respect for authority was desirable, and the Assembly must not be encouraged to pursue too far its differences with the home authorities.

There is material for speculation in the explanation which General Thomas Gage wrote from New York in 1771 to Lord Hillsborough, Colonial Secretary in England, concerning the refusal of the New Jersey Assembly to grant provision for the British troops:

"I am told the Reason is, the present Assembly's being composed of more low People than was ever known in it, who are trying by popular Arts to make themselves of Consequence, telling the People they have been imposed on, and that the Gentlemen have given away their Money to supply the King's troops without Occasion; for that other Provinces had refused such Supplys, and they would incur no Prejudice in refusing. The better sort wish the Supplys granted, and would have it contested to the last; fearing if they yield, that all Influence over the common People will descend to those of the lowest Class: and I believe would not be displeased if the Province suffered Some Inconvenience from the Assembly's late Disobedience."[36]

[36] Edwin Carter Clarence, comp. and ed., *The Correspondence of General*

Royal officials in America with an eye to future promotion were not in the habit of gratuitously reminding their superiors at home of errors in imperial policy; and Gage may have been deliberately ignoring the effect of the paper-money controversy on the attitude of the Assembly and offering an explanation of its conduct which would be more soothing to bureaucratic ears. Nevertheless, being the son-in-law of Peter Kemble of Morristown, who was president of the New Jersey Council, Gage may have had good authority for his account of the uneasiness felt by "the better sort" for their power in the Assembly.

Although in all probability such forebodings were scarcely better justified than Governor Franklin's professed fears of anarchy and mob tyranny,[37] the suspicion of the dominant class that its prestige and power were threatened by the agitation against the British authorities was not wholly without foundation. By no means all the opponents of British imperial policy were in sympathy with the internal disturbances of 1769 and 1770; but the Essex and Monmouth rioters seem to have been warmly attached to the anti-Parliamentary cause. Of the three Essex County demonstrators whose names have come down to us as being most severely punished, two, David and John Dodd, rendered military service to the Americans during the Revolution,[38] and the third, Lewis Crane, an elderly man, died in July 1777, apparently at home, and thus, it would seem, at least not an active Tory.[39] A search of such of the old Monmouth County Court records as still exist at the courthouse fails to reveal the names of any of the persons indicted there for the rioting in 1770; but elsewhere we find interesting light

Thomas Gage and the Secretaries of State, 1763-1775 (New Haven, 1931), Vol. I, pp. 312-13.

[37] *N.J.A.*, Vol. X, p. 179.

[38] William S. Stryker, comp., *Official Register of the Officers and Men of New Jersey in the Revolutionary War* (Trenton, 1872), p. 574; *Genealogical Magazine of New Jersey*, Vol. IV, No. 1 (July 1928), p. 68.

[39] *Genealogical Magazine of New Jersey*, Vol. IV, No. 1, p. 67.

on the career of one of those implicated in the disturbances. Josiah Holmes, a justice of the peace at Shrewsbury, was removed from his office by the governor in March 1770 for aiding and countenancing the riotous proceedings at Freehold.[40] The clergyman of the Anglican church at Shrewsbury, of which Holmes had long been a warden, asserted in a letter of 1780 that his parishioner's conduct during the riots had been actuated by a thirst for popularity. His removal from office, the writer continued, had much chagrined Holmes, who "in his subsequent conduct became so violent, that the Vestry and myself thought it proper to reject him as Church-Warden. . . . At the very commencement of this Rebellion, he broke out, took the Lead as a Committee Man, and joining with a few Presbyterians who were in my Parish created all the Disturbance in his Power against me and my Congregation. He, about two years ago, took Possession of the Glebe, and continues to live on it with his Family."[41]

As early as 1770, then, an acute member of the dominant class might note sinister signs and portents in the political unrest of the province. We may suppose that the significance of the disturbances in Monmouth and Essex Counties was not forgotten when the events of the early '70's focused general attention on questions of continental rather than local importance. With the occurrences of the earlier years in mind, we can better understand why the royal cause found so many supporters in New Jersey in 1776, despite the general lack of sympathy for many of the Parliamentary pretensions which had precipitated the war. Few of the "Gentlemen," Governor Franklin wrote to the Earl of Dartmouth in July 1775, would be willing to draw their swords in support of taxation by Parliament, but many would fight to maintain the connection with Great Britain, as there was

---

[40] *N.J.A.*, Vol. XVIII, p. 172.

[41] S.P.G. transcripts, Ser. B, Vol. 24, No. 120; cf. also *N.J.A.*, Vol. X, pp. 600-1.

widespread dread that some of the leaders of the people were aiming to establish a republic.[42]

To conservative minds of the time the word "republic" connoted something dark and unknown, a nightmare state where the masses ruled unchecked by venerable authority; whereas the ancient British governmental system was a guarantee of social stability. Political turmoil was under all circumstances to be avoided. "A prostration of Law and Government," declared Daniel Coxe, member of the New Jersey Council, in a letter written in 1775,[43] "naturally opens the Door for the licentious and abandoned to exercise every malevolent Inclination—what then have men of Property not to fear and apprehend, and particularly those who happen and are known to differ in sentiment from the generality? . . . Those who are not for us are against us is the Cry, and Publick necessity calls for and will justify their Destruction, both Life & Property."

[42] *N.J.A.*, Vol. X, p. 653.   [43] *ibid.*, p. 654.

CHAPTER III ☼ *WHIG AND TORY*

HAVING had a mild foretaste of insurrection, many of the more substantial inhabitants of New Jersey were predisposed in 1775 and 1776 to look with apprehension and disfavor upon the growing revolutionary movement. Yet the internal conflicts, which in this small province became entangled with the general political issues of the day, by no means resulted in a division of sentiment strictly along class lines. As in most historic crises, both of the contending parties were recruited from all ranks of society. Many persons took sides as their interests obviously dictated. There were others whose habits of thought and sets of beliefs were so firmly fixed that no inducement or pressure led them to forsake the old loyalties. Still others firmly resisted the claims of the British government, even though this resistance aided in overthrowing the system under which they had enjoyed prosperity and security.

Bearing these reservations in mind, we can nevertheless observe certain well marked tendencies among the various social groups in New Jersey as the people gradually divided into Revolutionists and Loyalists. In the first place, it is not surprising to find that most of the persons in high office in the colony strongly supported the British authorities.

Governor William Franklin heads the list of Loyalists. Though a native American, and a son of the independent Benjamin, he had acquired through residence in England the outlook and prejudices of the governing class, and was a sincere believer in the ultimate beneficence of British rule for the colonies. He was an affable gentleman, handsome in appearance and engaging in conversation; an adept politician; and, insofar as his understanding went and his prejudices allowed, a true well-wisher of the colony he governed. As the state of affairs grew more turbulent in America year by year, and his attempts to soften the clash between imperial claims and colonial aspirations proved futile, he became seriously alarmed. In May 1775, he wrote to urge upon his superiors in England the advisability of calling a duly authorized congress in the colonies to discuss grievances with commissioners appointed by the King.

"For I am convinced," he declared, "that Matters are now carried so far that the Americans in general are disposed to run the Risk of a total Ruin rather than suffer a Taxation by any but their own immediate Representatives and that there is not the least Reason to expect they will ever, in this Instance, consent to acknowledge the Right, even if they should be obliged to submit to the Power of Parliament."[1]

Once more, however, Franklin's statesmanlike advice went unheeded by bureaucratic ears. The British authorities remained devoted to coercion rather than conciliation, and the unhappy governor continued his delicate policy of "Keeping up some Appearance of Government"[2] while endeavoring to avoid giving conspicuous offence to the revolutionary leaders. A Provincial Congress met in the summer of 1775, and gradually usurped the powers of the Assembly; local government passed into the hands of revolutionary Committees of Correspondence or of Observation; the more timid Loyalists fled to places of safety; but Franklin continued in his mansion at Perth Amboy. Deserted by some of his most trusted supporters, regarded with suspicion by the Assembly and with dislike by the revolutionaries, attacked— much to his surprise—even by the Council,[3] and lacking a single soldier in the barracks or a single warship in the harbor to sustain his authority, he could do little but watch while the government crumbled before his eyes; yet he stayed on. His was a somewhat apprehensive nature, and he had a dread of being "seized upon and led like a Bear through the Country to some Place of confinement in New

[1] *N.J.A.*, Vol. X, p. 595.
[2] *ibid.*, p. 658.
[3] *ibid.*, pp. 678-9.

England";[4] but he felt it his duty to remain at his post as long as he could maintain the least semblance of authority. He was determined to give the rebels no excuse for saying, as they had said in New Hampshire, that the old government had ceased to function with the governor's absence, and for replacing it formally by a new one.

In the tense state of the times, such a courageous and unsupported position could not be indefinitely maintained. In January 1776, Franklin was arrested by a detachment of the militia upon order of Lord Stirling, whom the governor had recently suspended from the Council for helping to organize the troops of the Provincial Congress. Upon intercession by the chief justice, Franklin was released again almost immediately; but thereafter his freedom depended entirely upon his inactivity.[5] By venturing on May 30 to issue a proclamation summoning the Assembly to meet the following month, he incurred the wrath of the Provincial Congress. That body voted him, on June 14, 1776, "an enemy to the liberties of his country"; and when the governor refused to sign a parole obliging him to remain quietly at Princeton, Bordentown, or Rancocas, he was brought before the Congress for examination. He refused to answer the questions put to him by a body whose authority he did not recognize and whose presumption he denounced. Though he was the personal representative of the King to whom the Provincial Congress still professed allegiance, he did not escape the indignity of an abusive speech by Dr. John Witherspoon, president of the college at Princeton, who wound up with a sarcastic allusion to the fallen dignitary's illegitimate birth.

Within a short time, Franklin was sent, as he had feared, into confinement in Connecticut; and there he languished month after month without being permitted to visit his

[4] *N.J.A.*, Vol. X, p. 658.   [5] *ibid.*, pp. 699-706.

dying wife.[6] In July 1778 he was exchanged, and went, an embittered man, to New York, where in the course of time he became president of the Board of Associated Loyalists. In this capacity, his name is associated with some of the cruel depredations committed upon the Whigs by the refugees during the years of ruthless civil warfare.

Next to the governor, doubtless the most prominent Loyalist in New Jersey was Cortlandt Skinner, whose name has already occurred several times in these pages. By the standards of his day, Skinner was a man of great wealth. His real estate and proprietary rights were valued by the Loyalist commissioners at almost £7,000 sterling; and his office of attorney-general of the province, though it carried a salary of only £18.15s. a year, was estimated to be responsible for at least three-fifths of a private practice which brought him £500 sterling annually.[7] Skinner's views were largely determined by his prominent position among the Proprietors and the mercantile-minded Perth Amboy Group. He deplored some of the Parliamentary legislation of the 1760's. If we are to judge from a letter he wrote in 1765, his ideal scheme of things for America was for the British government to remove restrictions on trade with the West Indies, to elim-

[6] *Journal of the Votes and Proceedings of the Convention of New Jersey. . . . 1776 . . .* (Burlington, 1776), pp. 11-14, 16-17, 22, 26. Ashbel Green, *The Life of Ashbel Green . . .* (New York, 1849), p. 61.

[7] Fraser, *op. cit.*, Vol. II, pp. 1238-9, 1256; *N.J.A.*, Vol. X, p. 51. An anonymous writer (probably Governor William Livingston) in the *Pennsylvania Evening Post*, Jan. 21, 1777, accuses Skinner of having been "a vendor of noli prosequies," and asserts that those who have bought them from him "are sensible there is no danger from the law while there is a shilling of hard money in the Jersies." (*N.J.A.*, 2nd S., Vol. I, p. 265.) It must be remembered, however, that the political journalism of the Revolution, as at other times of stress, was not characterized by an overfastidious regard for truth, and on the other side we have a warm tribute to Skinner's honesty by his brother-in-law, James Parker, who, after a visit to the British authorities in New York in 1778, wrote to a friend: "Skinner, a good officer, inattentive to his interests, has had much in his power without making the most of it. An intelligence office would have been a fine thing to anybody but him, he receives his money duely and spends it as certain." (Charles W. Parker, "Shipley: The Country Seat of a Jersey Loyalist," in *N.J.H.S.P.*, N.S., Vol. XVI, p. 128.)

inate the Indian menace by withdrawing British garrisons and French settlers from the western territory and leaving the aborigines in peace, and to let the colonies develop as separately governed agricultural communities—to the incidental enrichment, doubtless, of the merchants and the holders of undeveloped lands east of the Appalachians.[8]

Regret though he might such imperial policies as interfered with the realization of this ideal, Skinner was too conscious of the privileges his class enjoyed within the solid framework of the empire to desire a separation. In September 1775 he succeeded for the moment, by ambiguous utterances, in rescuing himself from embarrassment by an inquisitive Revolutionary committee;[9] but in December he incautiously expressed in a letter to a brother in the British army his conviction that the leaders of American resistance were planning an attempt to establish a republic, which would deluge the country in blood. "A few regiments and fleets to the different Provinces," he declared, "will set us right; at least bring us to our senses, and support the friends of Government."[10] This letter, intercepted by the Americans, was enough to brand the attorney general as a Tory; and he escaped to a British man-of-war only the day before his house was raided by provincial soldiers in search of him. So hasty was his departure that he left his wife and thirteen children behind.[11] Skinner's flight, however, by no means denoted the end of his connection with New Jersey. For years to come, his hand was felt in the well planned raids which British and Loyalist soldiers made upon the state. Though he was never again to set foot upon its soil in peace, he was to return briefly with the sword.

The dignitary of highest rank next to the governor was the chief justice, Frederick Smyth. He, too, was a Loyalist, though being a cautious man, he seems to have avoided, as far as possible, antagonizing the people. In 1777 he removed

8 Whitehead, *op. cit.*, p. 103.   10 Whitehead, *op. cit.*, p. 105.
9 Jones, *op. cit.*, p. 192.   11 *N.J.A.*, Vol. X, pp. 700, 706.

to the British lines, but his departure was preceded by a
friendly letter to John Stevens, treasurer of the Revolutionary state of New Jersey, expressing his warm appreciation for the civility with which he had been treated. Leaving
thus in a friendly rather than a vengeful spirit, he seems to
have taken no further part in the struggle, aside from being
appointed one of the commissioners sent out by the British
government on its ill-planned and ill-fated peace overture
of 1778.[12]

One of Smyth's two associates on the bench of the Supreme
Court was Richard Stockton, a prominent Whig, who will
be discussed in another connection. The third justice was the
same David Ogden who had been an object of resentment
on the part of the Horse Neck settlers in 1770. Ogden was
employed as counsel by the Board of Proprietors, and as
early as the time of the Stamp Act had adopted a cautious
attitude towards proposed measures of opposition to Parliamentary legislation. His disapproval of rebellious activities
increased as time went on, and early in 1776 his stand
became so obnoxious to the Whigs that he felt obliged to
flee to New York. He never returned to his home except for
the short period when British troops occupied Newark.
Either in a vain attempt to save his property from confiscation, or because of a genuine longing to go back peaceably to the surroundings where he had spent his life, Ogden
wrote a pathetic letter to a former friend in Elizabeth-Town
in July 1777, explaining that he had left Newark only
in order to obtain imperative medical treatment in New
York, expressing the hope that he might soon be able to
return, and complaining of the harsh treatment which his
property was undergoing. Except for a vague bemoaning
of "the present ruined and melancholy State of my Country,"
Ogden refrained in the letter from any expression of opinion
on political matters; and evidently the New Jersey authori-

[12] Frederick Smyth to John Stevens, 1777, in Stevens Papers, Stevens Institute, Hoboken; Jones, *op. cit.*, p. 202.

ties found no indication that his opinion had changed sufficiently to warrant his receiving favorable treatment.[13]

As Loyalists, Smyth and Ogden represented the predominant body of opinion not only on the supreme bench but in the Provincial Council, of which they were members. Among the twelve men comprising the latter body in 1775 (one of whom[14] resigned in that year because of age and infirmities, and soon died), only four became supporters of the Revolution. The others either openly shared the views of Smyth and Ogden or adopted an attitude of neutrality which leaned at times towards support of the royal cause.

Daniel Coxe, of Trenton,[15] was a descendant of one of the wealthiest and most influential families in New Jersey, his great-grandfather having been nominal governor and Chief Proprietor of West Jersey, and his grandfather speaker of the Assembly and justice of the Supreme Court. Although only a little over thirty years old at the time of the Revolution, Coxe had been admitted to the highest degree in the practice of the law, and enjoyed a professional income of £400 a year. From his proprietary ancestors he had inherited extensive landholdings: his property was to be found in six western counties from Sussex to Cape May, and in the province of New York. His position being what it was, he was naturally opposed to all revolutionary proceedings; but Governor Franklin later asserted that, although Coxe had never taken any oath to the insurgents, he had "made interest with some of the Rebels to let him remain quiet." When the British troops invaded New Jersey, however, the councilor seized the opportunity to leave his precarious position, and thereafter remained within the British lines, zealously supporting the authorities in the prosecution of the war.[16]

[13] *N.J.A.*, Vol. IX, p. 532; *N.J.A.*, 2nd S., Vol. I, p. 16 n.; Jones, *op. cit.*, pp. 157-8; David Ogden to John De Hart, July 20, 1777, in Public Record Office, Trenton.
[14] Samuel Smith.
[15] See end of Chap. II for his alarm at the unrest in the province.
[16] Jones, *op. cit.*, pp. 52-3.

Of equal Loyalist zeal was Stephen Skinner, younger brother of the attorney general, and a retired merchant. His holdings of real estate were so extensive that he later claimed £6,975 from the Loyalist commissioners in compensation for his losses. After a sensational robbery of the East Jersey Treasury in 1768, Skinner, the treasurer, had become intensely unpopular in the province, the Assembly first blaming his negligence for the misfortune and then charging him directly with the theft. So violent was the storm that he was obliged to resign in 1774, and legal steps were being taken to recover the value of the losses from him when the old form of government and all its pending operations disappeared in the turmoil of the Revolution. Skinner had received the warm support of Governor Franklin throughout his difficulties, and the attacks on him seem to have emanated from the popular as against the governmental faction in the Assembly; so it was but natural that when the time of decision came he should cleave unhesitatingly to the government which offered him and his class protection against the irresponsible multitude. By the people of Perth Amboy, who broke away but slowly from the domination of the leading families, he was elected, together with James Parker and Jonathan Deare, to the Provincial Congress in April 1775. He appears to have taken no steps to occupy the office, and early in 1776 fled, first to the vicinity of Newark, and then to Second River. In July he was arrested by the Revolutionary authorities, but was with the British by the time they occupied New Jersey, and remained with them thereafter.[17]

Besides these avowed Tories, there was another member of the Council whose Loyalist sentiments are scarcely open to doubt, though he was circumspect in expressing them. Peter Kemble, president of the Council, was over seventy years old when hostilities broke out, and so was unable to

[17] *ibid.*, pp. 196-8; Whitehead, *op. cit.*, pp. 111-12; Sabine, *op. cit.*, pp. 307-8.

take an active part in the struggle. He was well known, however, as a Tory, and in 1777 found himself in difficulties with the Council of Safety in consequence of a charge that he had been circulating some of Sir William Howe's procla-mations. In some way—either because of his advanced age or the professed revolutionary principles of his son Richard, who lived with him, or possibly through those means by which certain men of wealth and resourcefulness have been able to extricate themselves from embarrassments in all ages —the old man succeeded in escaping retaliatory measures, and continued living peacefully on his estate near Morris-town. We are told that he became popular with the American officers when the army was encamped in the neighborhood. Kemble and his son, says one historian, "were obviously carrying out the old and well tried system of English landed proprietors in troublous times, by which the owner and the heir took different sides, so as to secure the property against any contingency."[18]

Another councillor, James Parker of Perth Amboy, mer-chant, politician, and president of the Board of Proprietors, attempted, by avoiding commitments to either party, to escape finding himself on the losing side of the war. He was the author of an address to the governor by the Council in 1775 in which an almost complete absence of meaning was disguised by moving and impressive language. "We shall," it declared, "with all sincere loyalty to our most gracious Sovereign, and all due regard to the true welfare of the inhabitants of this Province, endeavor to prevent the mis-chiefs which our present state of affairs seems to threaten; and, by our zeal for the authority of the government on the one hand, and for the constitutional rights of the people on the other, aim at restoring that health of the political body—which every good subject must earnestly desire."[19]

[18] McClintock, *op. cit.*, p. 24.
[19] James Parker, *The Parker and Kearny Families of New Jersey* (Perth Amboy, 1925), pp. 13-15.

Such dignified sidestepping of the burning issues of the time was characteristic of Parker. He had enjoyed the safe honors of public office for years, and was to do so again after the dangers of the war were past; but in his country's crisis he sought to withdraw from all responsibility. When New Jersey seethed with unrest, the eminent merchant-politician resigned from the Council, and did nothing to assist Governor Franklin in his brave struggle to maintain royal authority; but he was careful to avoid taking the seat in the Provincial Congress to which he was elected in 1775. Finding the excited atmosphere of the seaboard towns unpropitious for his policy of inactivity, Parker retired with his family to an estate in Hunterdon County. Rather than take an oath of allegiance to the independent state of New Jersey, or openly support the authority of the British government, he permitted himself to be imprisoned for a time in 1777 by the Council of Safety, in retaliation for the kidnaping by the British of John Fell, a prominent Revolutionary leader of the state.[20]

There can be no question where Parker's sympathies lay in the struggle. Early in 1778, he paid a visit to New York on parole to negotiate with the British for Fell's release; and upon his return he wrote a long letter to an intimate friend, criticizing, from the point of view of a supporter, the military command in the city, and coming to the conclusion: "I think we are in a critical situation, but good conduct and activity would still do the business. . . . I wish L'd North and Sr Wm. Howe may meet with their deserts, the one for not giving the terms before drawing blood, as he says he always intended (this impeaches his humanity as well as his policy), the other for not making the most of his strength against the runaways; how much have they both to answer for."[21]

[20] *N.J.A.*, Vol. IX, p. 446 n.; *N.J.A.*, 2nd S., Vol. I, pp. 454 n., 455 n.
[21] *N.J.H.S.P.*, N.S., Vol. XVI, pp. 127-9.

We may well suppose that no word of these sentiments or of his desire to see the Loyalist volunteer troops with the British "all take the field and fight it out with the enemy," escaped Parker's lips during the occasions on which his family entertained John Stevens, treasurer of the state, at dinner, or called upon Governor Livingston;[22] for after his release in February 1778 he remained undisturbed until the close of the war. Upon the return of peace, he moved back to Perth Amboy, where he once more became mayor, and where, says a later commentator, he "was honored . . . as a man of ability and distinguished probity, and died full of years and honors."[23]

Of somewhat different flavor was the neutrality of the final member of the Council, John Lawrence of Burlington. As a high dignitary of the colony, a prominent lawyer, a former mayor of Burlington, and a good Episcopalian, he inclined in sympathy, at the beginning of the war, to the side of the constituted authorities. With his Quaker neighbors, however, he seems to have shared a horror of violence, and he remained quietly at home until events forced him to take an active part. Unlike Parker, he did not seek to hide himself from notice in the country; and, again unlike his colleague, he was willing to commit himself to a positive course of action if by so doing he could render what he considered public service. In December 1776, when the Hessians approached Burlington, Lawrence acted as a voluntary intermediary between the invaders and the American armed vessels in the river, and obtained an agreement that neither should harm the town. By a mistake or a change of mind on the American side, the truce was broken, and Burlington suffered a bombardment which drove the Hessians away. He accompanied them and seems to have assisted Count

---

[22] James Parker to John Stevens, June 1778, in Stevens Papers, Stevens Institute.

[23] *N.J.A.*, 2nd S., Vol. I, p. 455 n.; Parker, *The Parker and Kearny Families*, p. 14.

Donop, the most gentlemanly and humane of the Hessian commanders, in issuing "protections" to such Americans as would take the oath of allegiance to the King. We have a glimpse of his interceding for the release of an imprisoned Jerseyman, and another of his promising to use his influence to stop the "infamous practice" by which slaves were denouncing their masters as rebels and thereby obtaining their freedom. Finally, we see him on the panic-stricken night after the battle of Trenton, accompanying Donop's detachment in the capacity of guide and interpreter as the Hessians fled from Bordentown towards the safety of the main British lines. From this point, there is no further record of any activity on Lawrence's part. He soon fell into the hands of the Council of Safety, and was imprisoned for a time, but seems eventually to have taken the oath of allegiance to the Americans and remained more or less undisturbed at Burlington.[24]

Besides members of the Council and the Supreme Court, many other officials in the colony remained loyal to Great Britain during the Revolution. They included such men as John Smyth, who had succeeded Stephen Skinner as treasurer of East Jersey and who held other offices, and Isaac Ogden, sergeant of the Supreme Court in which his father was a judge. John Antill, secretary of the Supreme Court, surrogate, keeper of the records and clerk of the Council, had purchased his collection of offices for £2,900 sterling, and they yielded him an annual income of £600;[25] small wonder that this scion of a prominent Perth Amboy family looked sourly upon any movement to overturn the government! Appointees to positions peculiarly connected with the imperial system, such as collectors of the customs, were, of course, unwavering in their support of the British govern-

[24] *N.J.A.*, Vol. X, p. 302 n.; Margaret Morris, Journal (MS. copy in Sparks MSS., 48, No. 1), pp. 3-7, 26, 27; MS. "Evidence of Jnᵒ Pope concerning of John Lawrence Junʳ.," April 1, 1777, in Public Record Office, Trenton.
[25] Jones, *op. cit.*, p. 13.

ment.[26] The high sheriffs of the middle belt of counties (Middlesex, Monmouth, Hunterdon, Burlington and Gloucester) were Loyalists, as were a considerable number of judges and justices of the peace—substantial and conservative citizens who in most cases took an early stand against illegal or extralegal agitation.[27]

In addition to those in official position, many persons of wealth and prominence upheld British authority. Outstanding among them were, of course, a number of East Jersey Proprietors. Cortlandt and Stephen Skinner held Loyalist views heartily shared by the DeLanceys of New York and a number of other important Proprietors. Less uncompromising than these, some members of the Board attempted to preserve an attitude of neutrality. James Parker, their president, was joined in his inglorious retirement in Hunterdon County by Walter Rutherfurd of New York, who, like Parker, was treated by the Americans as a Tory for his refusal to swear allegiance to the new state, but who, too, survived the storm and lived to enjoy his possessions after the war.[28] Another member of the Perth Amboy Group, John Lewis Johnston, enjoyed a Loyalist pension, we are told, until his death in 1824; but he was present at the constitution of a rump Council of Proprietors, supposedly non-Loyalist, at Freehold in 1778.[29] It is impossible to determine how large a proportion of the Proprietors were open or secret Loyalists; but the departure of so many leaders into the British lines embarrassed the activities of the Board for some time.

A number of landowners adhered to the royal cause. Prominent among these was Joseph Barton, who had used his

[26] Jones, *op. cit.*, pp. 58, 92-3, 207-8.

[27] *ibid.*, pp. 20, 31-2, 45, 58, 74-5, 97, 215, 232-4, 241, 511-12; Fraser, *op. cit.*, Vol. I, pp. 504, 547-8; Vol. II, pp. 894-5; Sabine, *op. cit.*, Vol II, pp. 387-8, 465.

[28] *N.J.A.*, 2nd S., Vol. I, pp. 455-6 n.

[29] Jones, *op. cit.*, p. 107: Minutes of the Council of Proprietors of the Eastern Division of New Jersey No. B. (in office of Surveyor-General at Perth Amboy), pp. 195-6.

position as agent of the East Jersey Proprietors to carve out for himself a huge domain, mostly in Sussex County. The homestead farm on which Barton lived contained eight hundred twenty-two acres, and he owned in addition twenty-two parcels of land ranging in size from half an acre to eleven hundred acres. He had two gristmills on his farm, ran a potash-making establishment, and received an income not only as the agent of the Council of Proprietors, but also as the local representative of a wealthy New York speculator in lands, Henry Cuyler. Finally, as a member of the Assembly, Barton enjoyed outward recognition of his prestige and power. What had such a man to gain from a revolution? His prosperity had been favored by the colonial system; and there could be nothing but uncertainty for him in new political experiments. He retained his seat in the Assembly until the last, and, when the old government broke down, joined the British, was appointed lieutenant colonel in their forces, and raised over a hundred Loyalists to fight for King and country.[30]

Sussex County also contained many a man who, though he may not have enjoyed such possessions as Barton's, was, like James Moody, "a plain, contented farmer, settled on a large, fertile, pleasant, and well-improved farm of his own." The dismay and growing anger with which such a man greeted the Revolution is well described in Moody's account of himself:

"Clear of debt, and at ease in his possessions, he had seldom thought much of political or state questions; but he felt and knew he had every possible reason to be grateful for, and attached to, that glorious Constitution to which he owed his security. The first great uneasiness he ever felt, on account of the Public, was when, after the proceedings of the first Congress were known, he foresaw the imminent danger to which this Constitution was exposed; but he was

---

[30] Fraser, *op. cit.*, Vol. I, pp. 600-4; Vol. II, p. 1275.

completely miserable when, not long after, he saw it totally overturned. . . .

"Of the points in debate between the parent-state and his native country, he pretended not to be a competent judge: they were studiously so puzzled and perplexed, that he could come to no other conclusion, than that, however real or great the grievances of the Americans *might* be, rebellion was not the way to redress them. It required moreover but little skill to know, that rebellion is the foulest of all crimes; and that what was begun in wickedness must end in ruin. With this conviction strong upon his mind, he resolved, that there was no difficulty, danger, or distress, which, as an honest man, he ought not to undergo, rather than see his country thus disgraced and undone. . . .

"The general cry was, *Join or die!* Mr. Moody relished neither of these alternatives, and therefore remained on his farm, a silent, but not unconcerned, spectator of the black cloud that had been gathering, and was now ready to burst on his devoted head. It was in vain that he took every possible precaution, consistent with a good conscience, not to give offence. Some infatuated associations were very near consigning him to the latter of these alternatives, only because neither his judgment, nor his conscience, would suffer him to adopt the former. He was perpetually harassed by these Committees; and a party employed by them once actually assaulted his person, having first flourished their *tomahawks* over his head in the most insulting manner. Finding it impossible either to convince these associators, or to be convinced by them, any longer stay among them was useless; and an attempt made upon him soon after, rendered it impossible. On Sunday 28th March 1777, while he was walking in his grounds with his neighbor Mr. Hutcheson, he saw a number of armed men marching towards his house. He could have no doubt of their intention; and endeavoured to avoid them. They fired three different shots at him, but happily missed him, and he escaped. From this time, there-

Lieutenant James Moody, Loyalist fugitive, rescues a British prisoner from the Sussex County jail in the spring of 1780. This daring exploit, effected some seventy miles beyond the British lines by a party of seven men, is characteristic of the audacity of this New Jersey Tory. (Illustration from a contemporary print)

fore, he sought the earliest opportunity to take shelter behind the British lines; and set out for this purpose in April 1777. Seventy-three of his neighbors, all honest men, of the fairest and most respectable characters, accompanied him in this retreat. . . .

"They were, in general, men of some property; and, without a single exception, men of principle. They fought for what appeared to be the true interest of their country, as well as to regain their little plantations, and to live in peace under a constitution, which they knew by experience to be auspicious to their happiness."[31]

Such men, resentful of being harried from their homes for not joining in an agitation for which they saw no good reason, waged relentless war against their fellow countrymen who had not left them in peace.

Officials, Proprietors, and landowners were not the only types of Loyalists. Numerous merchants, however strongly they may have opposed the elaborations of the British mercantile system after 1763, became alarmed when the anti-Parliamentary movement threatened to detach America from the empire. They foresaw that such a separation would inevitably mean a complete disruption of trade, and that it would take some time for American commerce to adjust itself to new conditions. Rather than assist in such a radical change, these merchants preferred to take their chances inside the empire, whatever its flaws, and to seek reforms through peaceful methods. In this class of Loyalists were most of the merchants of the Perth Amboy Group, and such prosperous traders as William Dumayne and Thomas Gummersall, who, as partners, kept a store at Elizabeth-Town— reputedly one of the finest in New Jersey—with a branch at Morristown.[32] Samuel Kemble, a merchant at New Bruns-

---

[31] James Moody, *Narrative of the Exertions and Sufferings of Lieut. James Moody, in the Cause of Government since the Year 1776* . . . (New York, 1865), pp. 10-11, 13-14, 55.

[32] Fraser, *op. cit.*, Vol. I, pp. 254-7.

wick, was another type. That he had felt little sympathy with American methods of protest against Parliamentary legislation is indicated by his dealings in tea in January 1771, at a time when the import tax levied by the British government had rendered its use generally unpopular, and almost none of it was being imported into New York and Philadelphia. When hostilities broke out, Kemble joined the British, and, appropriately, acted as collector of the port of New York during the Revolution. He also prospered so well as agent for disposing of captured American vessels that a friend wrote in 1778: "For an unlucky man he is the most fortunate I know."[33]

Here, then, we have already an imposing array of respectability, property, and prestige in favor of the royal cause; but the list is not yet complete. Among the Loyalists were also a number of prosperous physicians—usually a conservative class—and not a few lawyers. One of the latter was Daniel Isaac Brown of Hackensack, possessor of a reputation "for giving advice which tended to promote suits which often proved unsuccessful, but produced fees for himself."[34] Another was Bernardus LaGrange of Raritan and New Brunswick, who had been reprimanded by the Assembly, during the anti-lawyer agitation of 1769, for charging exorbitant fees,[35] and had long been the object of widespread "hatred and aversion."[36] Knowledge that he was so unpopu-

[33] Ridgway Library (Philadelphia) MSS. Yi 2 7308 F 56; Edward Channing, *A History of the United States* (New York, 1926), Vol. III, p. 128 n.; *N.J.H.S.P.*, N.S., Vol. XVI, p. 129; McClintock, *op. cit.*, p. 24. He was a son of Peter Kemble, president of the New Jersey Council.

[34] Fraser, *op. cit.*, Vol. I, p. 543.   [35] Richard Field, *op. cit.*, p. 166.

[36] An anonymous writer in Monmouth County informed LaGrange in 1769:
"If thou comest this way, may God Almighty have Mercy on thee, for I am convinced the people have none, if the Lord does not turn their hearts from their present resolutions.

"I will let thee know what I heard the other day among a parcel of people, having met accidentally with 'em at the Mill at English town concerning you and some more of your brethren, thee especially they seemed to have the greatest grudge against: One of them said, He wished that fellow Legrange would come to Court this month, he should not escape from out a back

lar scarcely conduced to make him look with favor upon the general activities of rebel committees: the rift between him and his neighbors widened, and in June 1775 he was burned in effigy in New Brunswick by demonstrators.[37] LaGrange and Brown had other associates more deeply influenced by the traditionalism of their profession than by the new ideas which were turning many lawyers into ardent spokesmen for European revolutionary doctrines, modified to suit American conditions.

Such were some of the diverse types included among the Loyalists. The staunch Whigs presented an equally varied appearance. A minority of the Council threw its influence to the side of the revolutionists. The rebel councillor who cut the greatest figure in the public eye was William Alexander, self-styled Earl of Stirling, who became a member of Washington's staff. Local tradition has made him one of the chief Revolutionary heroes of New Jersey; but the unprejudiced

window as he did before; another of the company makes answer Damn him, I hear he is to come and act as King's Attorney; but that shall not screen the rascal, says he; Aye, says he, the lawyers has done that a purpose, that we might not disturb the villain; but if we catch him, we will Legrange him!

"I hearing the people expressing themselves in this manner I began to examine them what you had done unto them that enraged them so against you. Why, says one, he will bring down our heads & humble us. They say you egged up their Creditors to put their bonds in suit saying Monmouth people are all like to fail, and much more of the like nature. And, I inquired, if they cou'd prove their assertions against you, they say, yes they can, by some of their creditors; and will if you carry some action; but I could not learn against whom, or where the person lived.

"Yesterday I was in Upper Freehold among some Company, where I heard them resolve concerning you, much the same as above; wishing you might come to Court, for there were between seven and eight hundred of them ready to receive you. Nay, I have heard some of them declare solemnly they would use you as the informers were used at New York and Philadelphia. I know, they collected some money to purchase two barrels of Tar and have agreed with a man to haul it a Monday. And as far as I can learn it is for you. They intend to tar & feather you, and to cart you from the Court house to Vankirk's Mill & back again. . . .

"I can positively affirm if thou hadst dwelt in this County there would not been left one stone on another of your house ere now." Edwin Salter, *A History of Monmouth and Ocean Counties* . . . (Bayonne, N. J., 1890), pp. 93-4.

[37] Jones, *op. cit.*, p. 122.

student can find little in his conduct, civil or military, to warrant the veneration in which his name is so widely held.

Why Stirling broke away from most of his associates in the dominant clique of New Jersey and cast in his lot with the Revolutionaries is a mystery. He has left no record of profound thought or deeply felt convictions on political questions: At the time of the Stamp Act, for instance, his advice as a member of the Council to Governor Franklin had expressed no opinion at all on matters of principle, but had been based solely on considerations of expediency.[38] During a period when, in the colonies north of Maryland, a warm interest in the Church of England was almost invariably associated with support of imperial as against colonial pretensions, Stirling shared with Governor Franklin the honor of membership in the Society for the Propagation of the Gospel—the organization which was building up Anglican parishes on the inhospitable soil of the northern colonies and planting in each of its missionary clergymen a spokesman for constituted authority, civil as well as ecclesiastical.[39] In all his associations and his habits of life, indeed, so far as we can discover, the "titular Lord" gave evidence of thoroughgoing conservatism; and beside such dynamic personalities as William Livingston, the brilliant war governor, and John Witherspoon, the crusty Scotch president of the college at Princeton, he fades into a dull and uninteresting figure.

Unfriendly critics were not wanting to charge that his lordship's espousal of the rebel cause was due to very personal motives. Considerable though his original fortune had been, it proved inadequate to support both his costly efforts to secure confirmation of his title and his extravagant style of living. By 1776, a large part of his interest in the languishing Hibernia ironworks seems to have passed into the

[38] *N.J.A.*, Vol. IX, pp. 509-10.
[39] John Wolfe Lydekker, *The Life and Letters of Charles Inglis* (London, 1936), pp. 127, 151 n.

hands of New York merchants;[40] and in the years from
1775 to 1779 his misfortunes multiplied. At the outbreak
of hostilities, his entire property was mortgaged—doubly, in
some cases—and in 1775 and 1776 his pretentious estate in
Somerset County went on the block. By 1779, his affairs had
become so muddled that he obtained from the legislature the
passage of a bill to vest all his remaining property in trustees,
who were "to sell the same, or a sufficient Part thereof, for
the Discharge of his Debts, and to convey the Remainder, if
any there should be, to him."[41]

Under these circumstances, it is not surprising to find
contemporaries charging Stirling with having made the "desperate push" of joining the Americans in order "to get rid
of the Inconvenience of his legal obligations."[42] Whether
or not this accusation be true, we may suppose that his affection for the British government had not been increased by
the failure of his expensive efforts to have his title recognized. In any case, he accepted a commission in the Continental army, and in consequence was suspended from the
Council by Governor Franklin.

Whatever his motives may have been, Stirling was never
taken very seriously by the British. Jonathan Odell, the
bitter Tory satirist, who scarcely could find words venomous
enough to damn men like Livingston or Witherspoon, dismissed his lordship in four contemptuous lines:

> "What matters what of Stirling may become?
> The quintessence of whiskey, soul of rum;
> Fractious at nine, quite gay at twelve o'clock;
> From thence till bed-time stupid as a block."[43]

[40] Tuttle, *op. cit.*, pp. 160-1; *N.J.A.*, 2nd S., Vol. I, p. 13.

[41] *N.J.A.*, 2nd S., Vol. I, p. 13; *Acts of the General Assembly of the State
of New Jersey*, May 31, 1779; *Votes and Proceedings of the General Assembly
of the State of New Jersey*, May 7, May 10, May 18, 1779.

[42] B. F. Stevens, ed., *Facsimiles of Manuscripts in European Archives Relating
to America 1773-1783* . . . (London, 1889-1898, 25 vols.), Vol. XXIV, No. 2042.

[43] Moses Coit Tyler, *The Literary History of the American Revolution
1763-1783* (New York, 1897, 2 vols.), Vol. II, p. 120.

In the American army, too, there was an undercurrent of amusement at some of his weaknesses. He had a reputation for "liking the table and the bottle, full as much as becomes a Lord, but more than becomes a General";[44] and an officer who had attended one of the "sumptuous & elegant" entertainments which he delighted in giving was not above recounting a current anecdote:

"Being present at the execution of a soldier for desertion, the criminal at the gallows repeatedly cried out, 'the Lord have mercy on me'; his Lordship with warmth exclaimed, 'I won't, you rascal, I won't have mercy on you.' "[45]

Nevertheless, for all his weaknesses, Stirling was a useful man to the American cause. Having made his choice, he stayed faithfully in the service through the darkest hours of the war, for year after year of irksome duty, in the face of recurrent attacks of rheumatism which would lay him low for weeks. Sincerely devoted to Washington, he exposed the Conway Cabal; and though he might lose his temper with others, towards the commander-in-chief his manner was invariably respectful and considerate. One very amiable and uncommon trait in him was his lack of personal military ambition. The cheerful readiness with which he acquiesced in the assignment to others of commands to which he might have laid claim, while he remained in posts of lesser importance, must have been comforting to his chief, harassed year after year by the complaints and recriminations of officers who seemed to value their own advancement and prestige above the general good of their cause. Hence, though Stirling's military record may be for the most part one of failures and misadventures, his courage, faithfulness and unselfishness were unchanging, and were perhaps what the Americans needed more than they did ability or enterprise.[46]

---

[44] Chastellux, *op. cit.*, Vol. I, p. 117.   [45] Thacher, *op. cit.*, p. 246.
[46] *ibid.*, pp. 245-6; Chastellux, *op. cit.*, pp. 117-19; Stirling to Washington, Dec. 9, 1779, and March 19, 1780, in Washington Papers, Vols. 129 and 130.

Stirling's brother-in-law, John Stevens, was another member of the Council who actively aided the Revolution. Though a resident of Rocky Hill, he belonged to the Perth Amboy Group and the Council of Proprietors, and had been a merchant until his retirement in 1761. Since that date he had occupied himself with the management of his extensive landed estates and his copper mines at Rocky Hill, and had been active in public life. As a member of the Assembly in the decade before 1761, Stevens enjoyed the confidence and esteem of the governors: Bernard referred to him in 1758, in a letter written to the Lords of Trade, as "a Gentleman of greatest Consequence to the Support of the Government & by no means to be spared out of the Assembly at Present." In the ensuing years, however, despite his appointment to the Council in 1762, he had developed ideas different from those of many of his associates, and had strongly opposed the Stamp Act; now, in the summer of 1776, he exchanged his seat in the Council for the vice-presidency of the Revolutionary legislature, and he soon became the state treasurer.[47]

The two other councillors who sympathized with the Revolution were both lawyers, and both young enough to be affected by the libertarian intellectual currents which were sweeping through their profession. Richard Stockton, forty-six years old in 1776, was comfortably settled on an estate in Princeton at the outbreak of hostilities. As early as 1765 he had argued that Parliament had no authority over the American colonies, and in 1774 he had sent Lord Dartmouth a draft of a plan for a self-governing America retaining allegiance to the Crown. It was quite in accord with the developing course of his views that Stockton took his seat in the Constitutional Congress in June 1776 in time to assist in the passage of the Declaration of Independence.[48]

Francis Hopkinson, seven years younger than Stockton, had but recently joined the Council. Although he resided

[47] *ibid.*, p. 335 n.; Sparks MSS., 4, Vol. I, p. 147.
[48] *N.J.A.*, Vol. X, pp. 427-9 n.

at Bordentown, he was connected almost as closely with Pennsylvania and Delaware as with New Jersey; but the province in which he lived was eager to acknowledge and employ his talents. Already the intellectual and literary power which this gifted lawyer was to exercise in the interest of the Revolution had been revealed; and in June 1776 he was chosen by the Provincial Congress of New Jersey as a delegate to attend the Continental Congress at the critical juncture when the question of independence was to be decided.[49]

Many lesser officials of the province joined in resisting the attempts to enforce British authority. Sheriffs, assembly-men, county judges, and justices of the peace placed themselves at the head of the opposition to the measures of Parliament, and in so doing maintained their leadership among the people.

The mercantile class, too, was by no means wholly devoted to the royal cause. Such traders as Andrew Sinnickson of Salem County, the richest and most prominent of the Swedish descendants in New Jersey, Thomas Brown, the slave-dealer of Pamrapaugh in Bergen County, the Neilsons and Schuurmans of New Brunswick, and John Burrowes, the "Corn King" of Middletown Point, took vigorous part in the struggle on the American side.[50] They must have had frequent occasion to reflect that Heaven favors the virtuous; for, whereas their more cautious Loyalist colleagues in many cases suffered heavy losses from confiscations of their property, merchants who remained with the Americans frequently found time amidst their patriotic duties to make very acceptable profits as prices rose and a scarcity of goods began to be generally felt.

49 N.J.A., Vol. X, pp. 427-8 n.

50 Collin, Journal, pp. 277-8; N.J.A., 2nd S., Vol. I, p. 313 n.; Mills, Historic Houses, pp. 76, 175-6; Jones, op. cit., pp. 152-3; Rutgers Alumni Monthly, Vol. I, No. 9, p. 255; James Neilson Papers in Rutgers University Library; Richard Wynkoop, Schuremans of New Jersey (New York, 1902), pp. 27-8, 39.

One group in the province which economic considerations unmistakably commanded to cast in its lot with the Revolutionary cause was that of the ironmasters. With the restrictions of British mercantilism removed, an artificial protection from foreign competition afforded by the difficulties of commerce with Europe, and an expanding market created by the needs of the American army, there was every prospect of large and speedy profits for the ironmaster who may have long been chafing under the British yoke. One historian remarks of Jacob Ford of Morristown: "As a man of business, and more especially as an extensive manufacturer of iron, his grievance against the policy of the mother country was not alone sentimental, it was decidedly practical, since his material interests were seriously involved."[51]

It is not surprising, then, that as the sudden expansion of the industry gets under way, we find on the Revolutionary side the names of ironmasters such as Ford, John Jacob Faesch, Samuel Ogden, Stephen Crane, Lord Stirling, and Robert Erskine.[52] Nevertheless, despite the clear command of personal interest to this class to join the movement for independence, we find some who remained loyal to the Crown. Among them were John Allen, owner of the Union Ironworks in Hunterdon County; the proprietors of the Andover Works in Sussex County; Nicholas Hoffman, who had large interests at Boonton; and certain persons like William Dumayne and David Ogden, Jr., who combined mercantile pursuits with investments in iron.[53]

Without a very long and difficult investigation, it would be unwise to hazard a guess as to what proportion of the

[51] Andrew M. Sherman, *Historic Morristown, New Jersey: The Story of Its First Century* (Morristown, 1905), p. 153.

[52] The Scotch manager of extensive mines at Ringwood owned by an English company.

[53] *N.J.H.S.P.*, 2nd S., Vol. I, pp. 36-7; Hamilton Schuyler, *A History of St. Michael's Church, Trenton* (Princeton, 1926), p. 103; Fraser, *op. cit.*, Vol. I, pp. 140, 255, 528; *N.J.A.*, 2nd S., Vol. I, pp. 114 n., 122 n.; Jones, *op. cit.*, p. 160; Trenton Historical Society, *op. cit.*, Vol. I, p. 144; *N.J.H.S.P.*, Vol. VII, p. 76.

discontented debtors and anti-Proprietary settlers actively
aided the American side during the Revolution. It may be
significant that Essex County, the chief seat of unrest about
1770, was also the most energetically Revolutionary section
of the province. To many farmers whose property was mortgaged or held on lease, the Revolution offered—or seemed
to offer—a welcome chance to free themselves at least temporarily from the demands of creditors. During the war, for
instance, the numerous mortgages and leases, mostly on
farms in Sussex County, which were held by the Loyalist,
Joseph Barton, for the heirs of Henry Cuyler, were "destroyed by the Rebels," while the occupants continued in
possession of the property.[54]

The support of the war by some of the poorer and more
discontented elements in the colony, however, should not be
construed as an indication that the Revolution in New Jersey
constituted in any sense a revolt of the masses against the
aristocracy. Class distinctions, though not so rigid as in
Europe, were too essential and accepted a part of American
society to be easily altered or ignored,[55] and men looked for
leadership to the class which had always furnished it. The
chief figures of the Revolution belonged for the most part
to prosperous and prominent families, though they included
few members of the small clique which enjoyed the choicest
plums of the colonial system. Resistance to the British government was led by those to whom the encroachments of Parliament appeared as an anachronistic attempt to check the
natural expansion and prosperity of a growing people, and,
perhaps, as a threat to their own security and potential
power. Probably few tears were shed in the province when

[54] Fraser, *op. cit.*, Vol. II, p. 1275.
[55] Among some of the farmers there was a latent, though not violent, anti-
aristocratic sentiment. See, for example, the controversy about fox-hunting
which raged in the columns of the *Pennsylvania Gazette* in January and
February 1770, after the publication of a letter from "A Jersey Farmer"
protesting the damages wrought by the "haughty gentry" of Philadelphia
who rode over farmers' fields.

numerous members of the Perth Amboy Group cut off their own political heads by joining the British forces; but there is evidence that strong efforts were made at first by the Revolutionary organizations to enlist the aid of these established leaders. Cortlandt Skinner later informed the Loyalist commissioners that he had been approached in August 1775, by representatives of the Provincial Congress with the offer of an army rank of major general or "the Govnt. of the Province or any station within it upon his own terms."[56] Democratic enthusiasm was far from general among the legislators and statesmen of the Revolution. Not many of them resembled Abraham Clark of Essex County, signer of the Declaration of Independence, who was a steady advocate of popular measures, and whose long and effective attacks upon the expensive intricacies of the law earned him the title of "Poor Man's Counselor."[57]

"At all times, indeed," as an upperclass Pennsylvania Whig of the period remarks, "licentious, levelling principles are much to the general taste";[58] but what anti-aristocratic sentiment existed in New Jersey trailed along in the wake of the Revolution, seizing what advantages it could but exerting little influence on the course of events.

Of outstanding importance in the Revolutionary party were lawyers, particularly young ones. They were probably in closer touch with European thought than any other class in the community, and it was largely through them that the ideas of the eighteenth century philosophers filtered into America and were embodied in the philosophical justifications of the American cause. The roster of Revolutionary statesmen in New Jersey includes the names of numerous

[56] Fraser, *op. cit.*, pp. 1234-5.

[57] *N.J.A.*, 2nd S., Vol. I, p. 527 n.; *N.J.H.S.P.*, 2nd S., Vol. I, pp. 150-1.

[58] Alexander Graydon, *Memoirs of His Own Time* (Philadelphia, 1846), p. 134. In the other camp, James Moody also hinted that the Revolution was largely supported by "multitudes who, with little property, and perhaps still less principle, are always disposed, and always eager for a change."—Moody, *op. cit.*, p. 13.

comparatively young legal practitioners like Richard Stockton, Francis Hopkinson, William Paterson, Elias Boudinot, David Brearley, and Jonathan Dickinson Sergeant.

Older than these men,[59] but similarly affected by the intellectual trends of the time, was William Livingston, the first governor of the independent state of New Jersey. He was endowed by nature with the ability to penetrate and expose pompous shams, and with a biting wit that few of his contemporaries could match. For some years, he had been a thorn in the flesh of conservatives. As editor of the *Independent Reflector*, a short-lived but zestful periodical, he had vigorously attacked the attempts of the Anglican clergy to extend and consolidate their influence in America. That Livingston, born lover of controversy and hater of pretentiousness, should be found on the side of the dissentient party upon the outbreak of the Revolution, was but to be expected. His sarcastic comments on imperial dignitaries, no less than his stern treatment of Loyalists, made the British regard him with venomous dislike. "Pernicious Caitiff" was one of the milder terms applied to him, and the Tory publicists, Rivington and Odell, groped with raging helplessness for more satisfying epithets. In the war of words, the New Jersey governor was more than a match for any opponent, and much of his controversial writing still makes amusing reading today—something which cannot be said of the virulent outpourings of his opponents.[60]

Although he had of late years met heavy financial reverses, which had compelled him to move to the comparatively inexpensive Elizabeth-Town, Livingston enjoyed before the

[59] He was fifty-three years old in 1776.
[60] *N.J.A.*, 2nd S., Vol. II, pp. 30-1; Mills, *op. cit.*, p. 109; Lucius Q. C. Elmer, *The Constitution and Government of the Province and State of New Jersey ...* (Newark, 1872), pp. 56-61; James Rivington to William Eden, March 27, 1780, in B. F. Stevens, ed., *Facsimiles of Manuscripts in European Archives Relating to America 1773-1783* (London, 1889-1898, 25 vols.), Vol. VII, No. 725; Sir Henry Clinton to Livingston, April 10, 1779, and Livingston to Clinton, April 15, 1779, in Livingston Papers (Massachusetts Historical Society), Box 2.

Revolution the social prestige of belonging to one of the most prominent New York families. No such background, however, aided some of the younger lawyers who found in the debates and the political activities of the Revolution a sudden and unexpected opportunity to attain public distinction. William Paterson became attorney general of the state during the war, and was able by 1783 to move into the fine residence in New Brunswick formerly owned by Bernardus LaGrange, the prosperous and unpopular Tory lawyer; but in 1775 he was supplementing a languishing law practice by keeping store on the upper Raritan.[61] In 1769, while but a poor young law student, he had written to a friend:

"I shall leave Princeton in the Spring, but to what corner of the Globe I know not. To live at ease, and pass through life without much noise and bustle is all for which I care or wish."[62]

Had it not been for the Revolution, with its shaking up of the social organization and its opportunities for new talents, such a modest future might well have fallen to the lot, not only of this young man, but of numerous of his contemporaries who likewise rose to prominence.

The ferment of thought in the intellectual classes was nowhere better illustrated than at the College of New Jersey, in Princeton. The Rev. Dr. John Witherspoon, president of the institution, had brought with him from Scotland a full measure of his nation's intellectual independence, and was called by John Adams "as high a son of liberty as any man in America."[63] His keen mind, wide learning, remarkable oratorical gifts, and tireless energy made him one of the most useful and respected public figures of the time. Among the students at his college, the influence of his personality

[61] William Paterson, MS. Life of William Paterson (in Princeton University Library, Austin Scott Papers), Chap. XIII, p. 37, Chap. XV, pp. 6-7.

[62] Mills, *Glimpses of Colonial Society*, p. 66. By permission of J. B. Lippincott Company, publishers.

[63] John Adams, *Works*, Vol. II, p. 356.

and ideas was marked. In 1763 and 1764, the annual Commencement exercises which lasted through most of a long day had been enlivened by such entertainment as "a Beautiful Harangue on the Advantages of *Health*," and debates in Latin and English on topics like "The Light of Reason alone does not afford sufficient motives to Virtue." By 1766, such innocuous subjects were suddenly replaced in large part by fervent orations on "Liberty" and "Patriotism." Commencement programs of the following decade display a wealth of speeches and poems denouncing arbitrary power, praising "The Rising Glory of America," contemning luxury (in the interest of the non-importation agreements), and making much of "natural law" which binds kings and nations and obliges subjects to defend their liberties against the illegal acts of their rulers.

The students carried their Whig principles to the point of dressing only in American-made cloth at Commencement, though this policy seems to have been hard to follow, owing to the difficulty of procuring material. Further, in 1770, the collegians publicly burned a copy of a letter written by New York merchants to a committee at Philadelphia, announcing their intention of ordering goods from Great Britain in violation of the non-importation agreement.[64] There were other exciting concomitants of patriotism. A letter written by a Princeton student in 1774 tells how the defense of liberty afforded an agreeable occasion to break the dull routine of college life:

"Last week to show our patriotism, we gathered all the Steward's Winter Store of Tea, and all the Students had in College and having made a fire in the Campus, we there burn't near a dozen pound, tolled the bell, and made many spirited resolves.—But this was not all. Poor! M^r. Hutchinson's Effigy shared the Same fate with the Tea, having a Tea

[64] *N.J.A.*, Vol. XXVII, pp. 203, 209, 586 n.; Princeton University Library MSS., AM 9641.

Cannister tyed about his Neck—This is the only entertaining News I have at Present."[65]

By May 1775 the students had formed a military company —of which all the members, it appears, as befitted their position as gentlemen, were officers.[66] The tumults of the day had penetrated the halls of learning, and Minerva was being rudely jostled aside by Mars.

One more or less intellectual class was sharply divided in its sentiments by the Revolution. The clergy in New Jersey, as elsewhere in America, generally took sides according to denominations. The Presbyterian ministers, who had not lost the Covenanter tradition, supported the American cause with but few exceptions, and some of them were among the most forceful advocates of independence. British observers tended to regard the Calvinists as the chief fomenters of trouble, and laid plans for curbing their influence when the struggle was over.

"I could never have believed," one of Lord Dartmouth's representatives wrote him from New York in November 1776, "but from ocular Demonstration and other indisputable Evidence, that so many warm Teachers could have been found any where for public Inflammation, or that these could so universally have forgotten, that some of the first Principles of their Profession are Peace, Love, and Good will towards all men. . . . The War is . . . at the Bottom very much a religious War; and every one looks to the Establishment of his own Party upon the Issue of it. And indeed, upon the Issue, some one Party ought to predominate, were it only for the Conservation of Peace. It is perhaps impossible to keep the ecclesiastical Polity out of the Settlement, without endangering the Permanency of the civil. There will never be a fairer Opportunity, nor a juster Right, to fix the Constitution of America in all respects

[65] Charles Clinton Beatty, Nassau Hall, Jan. 31, 1774, to the Rev. Enoch Green (Princeton University Library MSS., AM 1591).
[66] Same to Betsy Beatty, May 28, 1775 (*ibid.*, AM 9641).

agreeable to the Interests and Constitution of Great Britain, than upon the Conclusion of this War, which there is every Reason to believe will end, after a little more Perseverance and Firmness, according to the just Wishes and Expectations of our King and Country."

Which denomination the writer thought should be the beneficiary of this salutary settlement imposed from above, he did not say, but he reminded his lordship significantly that Calvinists had "a pretty strong Inclination to every sort of Democracy."[67] A few months later his feelings had become much stronger. "When the war is over," runs a letter written in April 1777, "there must be a great Reform established, ecclesiastical as well as civil; for, though it has not been much considered at Home, Presbyterianism is really at the Bottom of this whole Conspiracy, has supplied it with Vigor, and will never rest, till something is decided upon it."[68]

If the importance of Presbyterianism as a revolutionary force was somewhat exaggerated by a visitor fresh from England and unused to the general freedom of American life and speech, no historian can deny the tremendous effectiveness of the clergy of this denomination in inculcating and upholding ideals of independence. In this they were ably seconded by the ministers of the Dutch Reformed Church, likewise imbued with the stiff-neck spirit of Calvinism. Though the Dutch clergy in New Jersey produced no figures comparable to Witherspoon or the Rev. Jacob Green of Hanover, probable author of the State constitution, it did bring to the fore men of high caliber and wide influence. Such were Jacob Hardenbergh, parson of Raritan, and later head of Rutgers College, whose political activity in behalf of the Revolution was tireless; William Jackson, of Bergen, who defiantly preached Whig sermons to a churchful of luke-

[67] Ambrose Serle to Lord Dartmouth, Nov. 8, 1776, in Stevens, *op. cit.*, Vol. XXIV, No. 2045.
[68] Serle to Dartmouth, April 25, 1777, *ibid.*, No. 2057.

warm or Tory parishioners within the reach of the British garrison at New York; and Dominie Romeyn of Hackensack, who did much to sustain the morale of his Whig congregation in a Loyalist county.[69]

In sharp contrast to the activity of these denominations was the attitude of the Episcopalians. For some years there had been considerable ill-feeling between the Anglican clergy and the leaders of the dissenting sects, particularly the Presbyterians. The Episcopalian ministers had long agitated in favor of having an American bishopric established, in order to strengthen the position of the Church in the colonies. The Dissenters, however, with inherited memories of the persecutions their forbears had suffered in England at the hands of the state church, and with a disquieting object lesson in the intolerance of the Established Church in Virginia and the Carolinas,[70] resisted by every means in their power this proposal to increase the prestige and official power of the Church of England in the new land.

So violent did the controversy become that public opinion grew almost hysterical, and the Anglicans increased general irritation by their unwise tactics. Instead of attempting to conciliate hostile opinion, they emphasized their loyalty to the King and the British government, accused the Dissenters of republican principles, and exaggerated the beneficial effect which the naming of an American bishop would have on the growth of the Church in the colonies. They disdained to conceal from the public such sentiments as those which one "missionary," the Rev. Charles Inglis, wrote privately to the S.P.G. at the time of the Stamp Act disorders:

"If the Interest of the Church of England in America had been made a National Concern from the Beginning, by this Time, a general Submission in the Colonies to the

[69] *N.J.A.*, 2nd S., Vol. II, p. 116 n., Vol. III, pp. 441-3. 583-5; Winfield, *op. cit.*, pp. 385-6; the Rev. Solomon Freligh to the Rev. D. Romeyn, Feb. 6, 1784, in Ford House MSS., Morristown Historical National Park.
[70] George Otto Trevelyan, *The American Revolution* (New York & London, 4 vols., 1899-1914), Vol. III, pp. 290-1.

Mother Country, in every Thing not sinful, might have been expected."[71]

All this flouting of colonial apprehensions was bad enough. To make matters worse in a country which was strongly unclerical in its attitude, the Anglican clergy in New Jersey petitioned the governor in 1760 to deprive justices of the peace of the right to perform marriages; and, when the governor professed lack of authority for such a step, they carried their appeal to the Lords of Trade in 1765, through the Bishop of London.[72] Nothing seems to have come of the attempt; but the mere fact that it was made at such a time is an interesting revelation of the slight importance which the clergyman attached to American opinion, and of their complete dependence on British authority. A circumstance which further alienated the Anglican ministers in New Jersey from the American point of view was the fact that most of them, owing to the small size of their congregations, depended for their support chiefly on the British Society for the Propagation of the Gospel in Foreign Parts. Their material as well as their moral sustenance came from across the sea.

Given this background, and the fact that the ordination oath of Anglican clergymen acknowledged the supremacy of the King and promised conformity to the doctrines, discipline, and worship of the Church of England, there could be little doubt as to the stand this group would take in the Revolution. Before independence was declared, ministers frequently preached sermons "calculated as much as the Times would permit, to mitigate the general Infatuation," or to "inculcate the principle of peace, order and good government," and occasionally received unwelcome attentions from the Sons of Liberty for their pains.[73]

[71] Lydekker, *op. cit.*, pp. 52, 54.   [72] *N.J.A.*, Vol. IX, p. 504.
[73] S.P.G. transcripts, Ser. B, Part I, No. 245; *ibid.*, Ser. B, Vol. 24, No. 308.

After July 1776, when it became impossible to perform the liturgy with its prayers for the King, the Royal Family, and the High Court of Parliament, virtually all the Anglican clergymen preferred closing the churches to altering the form of service. In New Jersey only one minister of the denomination, Robert Blackwell, S.P.G. missionary at Gloucester, Waterford, and Greenwich, definitely joined the Americans; another, Abraham Beach of New Brunswick, reopened his church in the course of the war, omitting the objectionable prayers from the service.[74] Uzal Ogden, of Sussex County, fled at first to New York, but later returned to his parish, where he confined himself to preaching and practical ministrations, and made no attempt to use the liturgy. In 1779, he wrote a respectful and admiring letter to Washington, wishing him victory. No hint of these political sentiments, however, creeps into the clergyman's reports to the S.P.G., and he was considered by his fellow-clergymen in New York to be "strictly loyal."[75]

With these exceptions, all the Anglican ministers in New Jersey seem to have adhered faithfully to the Crown. From their number the British cause was furnished with one of its most talented satirists, the Rev. Jonathan Odell of Burlington. The influence of such ministers led a great proportion of the members of the Church of England to join the Loyalists—a fact not surprising since the generally conservative atmosphere of the Church before the Revolution appealed primarily to those persons who, for temperamental or other reasons, would naturally be attracted to the Loyalist camp when hostilities began.

One other denomination deserves mention because of its positive stand in the Revolution and because of the large

[74] *ibid.*, Nos. 148, 310; Samuel Alexander, *Princeton College in the Eighteenth Century* (New York, 1872), p. 121.

[75] S.P.G. transcripts, Ser. B, Part I, Nos. 159, 160, 161, 162; letter from Uzal Ogden to Washington, July 16, 1779, in Washington Papers (Library of Congress), Vol. 112; Lydekker, *op. cit.*, p. 194.

number of its adherents. The Quakers, who enjoyed a preponderant influence in several of the southwestern counties and were numerous elsewhere in the province, were traditionally opposed to violence. Furthermore, their sect had enjoyed in the past a considerable degree of protection from British authorities against the persecutions of other denominations in America, and was not unmindful of its debt. Although the Society of Friends held doctrines which were somewhat revolutionary in a social sense, and were not without political implications, its members had never committed themselves to a definite political philosophy, and their policy had always been to work within the framework of the established government. They sought by testimony and persuasion to convert the world to their point of view without political overturns; and, insofar as they could not succeed in this endeavor, they withdrew as far as possible into the life of their own communion. Finally, the Quakers in the Delaware colonies comprised some of the most prosperous merchants and farmers of the region, and shared the conservative views of many other members of these classes.

A meeting of representatives of the Quakers of Pennsylvania and New Jersey, held at Philadelphia in January 1775, considered the troubled state of the times and declared:

"The Divine principle of grace and truth which we profess leads all who attend to its dictates to demean themselves as peaceable subjects, and to discountenance and avoid every measure tending to excite disaffection to the King, as supreme Magistrate, or to the legal authority of his government. . . . The late political writings and addresses to the people . . . [are] not only contrary to the nature and precepts of the Gospel, but destructive of the peace and harmony of civil society, [and] disqualify men in these times of difficulty for the wise and judicious consideration and promoting of such measures as would be most effectual for reconciling differences, or obtaining the redress of grievances. . . .

"We are, therefore, incited by a sincere concern for the peace and welfare of our country publicly to declare against every usurpation of power and authority, in opposition to the laws and government, and against all combinations, insurrections and illegal assemblies; and as we are restrained from them by the conscientious discharge of our duty to Almighty God, 'by whom Kings reign and princes decree justice,' we hope thro' his assistance and favour to be enabled to maintain our testimony against any requisitions which may be made of us, inconsistent with our religious principles, and the fidelity we owe to the King and his government, as by law established."[76]

Such an uncompromising stand subjected many Quakers to persecution. After the Declaration of Independence was an established fact and the revolutionary governments were in actual operation, there was no longer a good reason why an essentially non-political group like the Friends should persist in public avowal of fidelity to the King, particularly since many of the Society were not hostile to the idea of independent American states. Accordingly, the Loyalist sentiments were allowed to lapse, but the Quakers stood firm in their refusal to fight in the war, or to violate their scruples against swearing by taking oaths of allegiance to the new government.

Besides those who early took a decided stand for or against the proceedings of the Whigs, there was a large section of the population which had no fixed ideas, but could be moved in either direction by the course of events. The energetic measures of the various local committees, in examining recalcitrants, fining them, boycotting them, or subjecting them to less dignified punishments, produced an appearance of unanimity that did not correspond to the mixed

[76] *N.J.A.*, Vol. XXXI, pp. 68-9.

sentiments or weak convictions of many inhabitants. Thomas Randolph of Quibbletown, for instance, was tarred and feathered and paraded on a wagon about the town in December 1775 for reviling and opposing the continental and provincial revolutionary bodies; and was compelled to offer a public apology and promise better conduct for the future. Probably he held his tongue thereafter; but we may doubt that this treatment produced a true conversion in him, despite the assurance of the newspaper account that "the whole was conducted with that regularity and decorum that ought to be observed in all public punishments."[77] There were many persons who, in the words of a young man of New Brunswick, "when they have on their Regimentals, are pretended Whigs; but as soon as they put them off are detestable Tories."[78]

During the early months of the struggle, a number of fundamentally conservative men accepted election to congresses and committees, on the theory that, as Governor Franklin said: "It is, perhaps best that Gentlemen of Property and Sense should mix among these People, as they may be a means of preventing their going into some Extravagances."[79] The extravagances, however, grew more and more radical. Soon those persons who, like Isaac Ogden of Elizabeth-Town,[80] attempted to exercise a moderating influence on the Whigs while they disgusted their more strait-laced friends by demagogic attempts to retain their popularity,[81] were obliged to declare themselves unequivocally.

It was, of course, the Declaration of Independence which finally determined the position of many persons. There were not a few anti-ministerialists who shrank from the thought of a complete break with Great Britain, and sent to the

[77] *N.J.A.*, Vol. XXXI, pp. 235-6.
[78] R. Beatty, New Brunswick, Dec. 1775, to the Rev. Enoch Green (Princeton University Library MSS., AM 1601).
[79] *N.J.A.*, Vol. X, p. 604.
[80] Son of the Supreme Court Justice, David Ogden.
[81] Jones, *op. cit.*, pp. 161-3.

Provincial Congress petitions urging that this final step be avoided. To the great good fortune of the advocates of independence, an event occurred in the summer of 1776 which strongly influenced public opinion. According to a recent biographer of Washington, the "Tory Plot" discovered in New York was apparently nothing more than an attempt on the part of Thomas Hickey, a member of Washington's guard, to enlist men for service with the British, to act when Sir William Howe arrived in New York. Hickey was convicted by court-martial of sedition and mutiny and holding a treacherous correspondence with the enemy, and was executed.[82] At once the story spread through the provinces, with the wildest exaggerations. Abraham Clark writes from Elizabeth-Town, on June 26, about the "Hellish Plot at New York. This Plot," he remarks with relish to his correspondent, "I expect you will be informed of by the Papers soon, it was to Assassinate Gen^{rl} Washington, blow up the Magazine, Spike up the Guns, take up Kings bridge and take Arms to destroy all they met, I hear they have found 1,100 already to have been in the Plot. You cannot conceive the effect it hath upon the Inhabitants, many were Luke warm before, but now Anxious for Spirited measures. . . . The discovery of the Plot may be reckoned Among the many Signal interpositions of a kind Providence in our favour and call for our most grateful Acknowledgments of it. As it is thought Independency will take place next Week, this Plot will give it efficacy; no Scheme could have been Devised better for that Purpose, It will Unite our Friends, discover, or at least discourage our Foes."[83]

The worthy Mr. Clark was doubtless giving undue credit to divine intervention. When so astute a man and so able a politician was circulating a tale of a plot with eleven hundred

[82] George Fitzpatrick, *George Washington Himself: A Common-Sense Biography Written from His Manuscripts* (Indianapolis, 1933), pp. 232-3.
[83] Abraham Clark to Colonel Elias Dayton, Elizabeth-Town, June 26, 1776 (Sparks MSS. 49, Vol. II, p. 159).

conspirators, there is ground for suspicion that Providence was being consciously aided by a very efficient propaganda machine.

Tory plot or no Tory plot, there were persons whose old loyalties and ways of thinking were so strong that the Declaration of Independence drove them, sometimes with heavy hearts, into the ranks of the Loyalists. Even among those who rendered lip-service to the new government, there was much faintness of conviction and fear of British punishment. But the extent to which acquiescence in the Revolution was a mere matter of expediency did not become clear until the dark months at the end of 1776 when the British military machine swept across New Jersey, driving the ragged American troops before it. In the summer of that year, when our story opens, the newly independent state bristled with warlike activity, and the dominance of revolutionary sentiment was unquestioned.

CHAPTER IV ✲ *THE WAR COMES TO NEW JERSEY*

UNDER the blazing sun of early July, all northeastern New Jersey was astir with feverish preparations to meet the British invader. Watchers on the shore, at the end of the anxious month of June 1776, had seen a British fleet of more than a hundred sail, bearing General Howe's army from Halifax, drop anchor off Sandy Hook and, after halting a few days, proceed up the Narrows to land its troops on Staten Island. This imposing display of royal power was known to be but the forerunner of a still greater fleet, under the command of Howe's brother the Admiral, bringing more British troops and the first of the dreaded Hessians. Looking across the narrow waters of Staten Island Sound, the inhabitants of the New Jersey shore from Perth Amboy to Constable's Hook could plainly discern the soldiers in their bright uniforms parading with military precision and throwing up fortifications on the island. Militia were hastily pouring into Perth Amboy, and others were on their way there. In the same town, preparations were being made by order of General Washington, commander at New York, to form a "Flying Camp," a mobile force ready to meet and oppose the British wherever they might land.

Encouraged by the visible evidence of royal succor near at hand, large numbers of persons who had been forced into a sullen acquiescence in the proceedings of the revolutionists were planning to give active aid to the delivering army. The impetus of the rebels' initial successes in overturning the government was spent. Now there was to be a real test of forces, and the crisis would determine whether the insurgents could keep and consolidate their gains.

So far, the Revolutionary party had swept all before it. It was helped by the prestige of American arms, which throughout the first year of the war had remained high. The expedition to Canada, it is true, had failed, but not without casting some glory upon the small, ill-equipped army which had battled valiantly in a northern winter, far from home. The British government, having started out contemptuously to crush a rebellion in New England, now found itself with a full-sized continental war on its hands, and was preparing to attack the strategic center of the colonies with an array of forces flattering, if alarming, in magnitude.

Within New Jersey, all imperial authority had long since disappeared. Government by Provincial Congress and local Revolutionary Committees had been in operation for well over a year. Recalcitrant individuals or districts had been brought sternly into line.[1] Since May 1775 the political organization of the province had been based upon an "Association" or social compact, adopted by the Provincial Congress, circulated by the local Revolutionary Committees, signed by the inhabitants, either voluntarily or under duress, and aimed at supporting the new de facto governing bodies, local, provincial, and continental.[2] By the summer of 1776, the old colonial Assembly was but a memory. Governor Franklin had been packed off, amidst insult, to imprisonment in Connecticut, there, no doubt, to meditate upon the follies of bureaucrats, the ingratitude of peoples, and the sad lot of the broad-minded conservative in times of stress.

[1] The freeholders of the town of Shrewsbury in Monmouth County had declined, in Jan. 1775, to choose themselves a Committee of Inspection, for fear such action might "prove a means of disturbing that peace and quietness which had hitherto subsisted in the township and which they were extremely desirous and would continue to use their utmost endeavours to preserve." In consequence, however, of this decision, the conservative farmers of Shrewsbury had found themselves so disturbed in their peace and quietness by their neighbors in Freehold and elsewhere that four months later they capitulated to the universal movement, set up a Committee to supervise the carrying out of the measures of the revolutionists, and elected delegates to the Provincial Congress.—N.J.A., Vol. X, pp. 533, 559, 600-1; Vol. XXXI, pp. 45-6.

[2] N.J.A., Vol. X, pp. 639-41.

This deportation of the King's representative snapped the last link that bound New Jersey to a colonial status. The Revolutionary leaders now prepared to take steps towards the formal avowal of that independence which had been the subject of a flood of petitions, favorable and unfavorable, pouring in upon them for some time past. On June 22, they elected five delegates to the Continental Congress, with instructions to join with the representatives of the other colonies in declaring independence, should that step seem necessary.[3] Two days later, a committee was appointed to draw up a frame of government; and on July 2, while the Declaration of Independence was still being discussed in Philadelphia, the new constitution of New Jersey was adopted. According to this document, all civil authority under the King of Great Britain was necessarily at an end, though the possibility of a reconciliation was expressly admitted. The instrument called for the election of a new Assembly and Legislative Council during the following month; after these bodies had met and chosen a governor, the new state would be officially launched on its independent existence, even though the constitution still designated it by the old term "colony."[4]

[3] Journal of the Convention, pp. 9, 11, 14, 15, 18, 22-5, 30; *N.J.A.*, 2nd S., Vol. I, pp. 130-1.

As early as June 15, Jonathan Sergeant wrote to John Adams from Burlington:

"Dear Sir:—*Jacta est alea*. We are passing the Rubicon, and our delegates in Congress, on the first of July, will vote plump."—*Life and Works of John Adams*, Vol. III, p. 55 n.

Abraham Clark wrote to Col. Elias Dayton on June 26:

"We have in Our Provincial Congress a set of firm, and well disposed Members, Determined on Spirited measures. Upon the Question for a New form of Government in this Province We had but 4 Who Voted Against it & upwards of 50 for it. And as to there Sentiments on the Capital Point to be Settled At Phil^a. Next Monday you may Judge of them by the Members they have Elected."—Sparks MSS. 49, Vol. II. The "capital point" was, of course, independence, and the members were the militant revolutionists, Clark, Stockton, Hopkinson, Witherspoon, and Hart.

[4] Journal of the Convention, pp. 26, 35, 36, 80-5.

Thus, for New Jersey, open avowal of independence, which finally drove many waverers to the royal side and increased the bitterness of the Tories, coincided in time with the first appearance of war as a grim reality. Until the arrival of General Howe's army, actual violence in the province, except for the rough handling of Tories, had been desultory and confined to the seacoast. In May 1776, some British men-of-war lying in Delaware Bay had landed men from boats near Greenwich and taken away twenty or thirty head of cattle. The incident had no importance, aside from furnishing excitement to the local militia, who chased away the invaders and captured from them a musket and five dead cows which had been left on the shore in the hurried retreat to the ships.[5]

More agreeable, because more profitable, than such an affair was the occasional brush with the enemy necessitated by a privateering venture. In this type of enterprise the inhabitants of the New Jersey shore had had considerable experience, and they lost little time in resuming their activities after the outbreak of war. As early as January 1776, a ship from England laden with supplies for the British army in Boston was boarded at Sandy Hook and brought into Elizabeth-Town, to be sold, with its cargo, at public auction.[6] The chief privateering center of New Jersey, however, and one of the principal ones of the continent, was to be Little Egg Harbor, which was peculiarly suited to this purpose by its remoteness and its difficult approaches. Seizure of British vessels distressed by weather had begun as early as October 1775.[7] By June 1776, two privateers were unloading rich booty at the Harbor, and the inlet had begun that brief career as a base for maritime depredations

[5] Peter Force, ed., *American Archives, Fifth Series* . . . (Washington, 1848, 1851, 1853) (hereafter abbreviated as *Am. Arch.*, 5th S.), Vol. I, p. 469; *N.J.A.*, 2nd S., Vol. I, pp. 96-8.

[6] *N.J.A.*, 2nd S., Vol. I, pp. 25-6, 68.

[7] *N.J.A.*, Vol. XXXI, pp. 210-14. For the incident of the *Viper's* tender see letters and depositions in Room 118, State Library, Trenton.

which lifted it from obscurity to notoriety and eventually
called forth reprisals by the enraged British.[8]

Although these incidents had brought some of the excitement of war to New Jersey, they had not brought bloodshed.
The first casualties which occurred in the state, aside from
the unfortunate Greenwich cows, seem to have taken place
at Cape May. On June 29, 1776, Captain Montgomery
of the brig *Nancy*, bound from St. Croix and St. Thomas for
Philadelphia, and hotly pursued by six British men-of-war,
ran his vessel ashore on Cape May, and, under cover of a
fog, succeeded in removing a large part of the cargo, consisting chiefly of powder and arms for the Continental Congress.
When the fog lifted and it was seen that boats from the
men-of-war were coming to board the brig, Montgomery
opened a quantity of gunpowder in the cabin and wrapped
fifty pounds of it in the mainsail, among the folds of which
he started a fire; then he abandoned ship. The crews of the
boats boarded the *Nancy* and took possession of her with
three cheers. In a short time, however, "the fire took the
desired effect, and blew the pirates forty or fifty yards into
the air," much to the gratification of the observers on the
beach, who diverted themselves for the next few days by
counting the corpses and "the great number of limbs floating
and driven ashore." Meanwhile, some of the local inhabitants, with men from two small American war vessels,
mounted a gun on shore, and exchanged shots with the
British. During the cannonade, one American, an officer
on a Continental warship, was killed, and a boy was
wounded.[9]

Such was New Jersey's initiation into the violence of
war, which it came to know all too familiarly in the six
ensuing years. This first round left the score in favor of the
Americans; but everyone knew that there was more serious
work ahead. General Howe's force, which appeared off

[8] *N.J.A.,* 2nd S., Vol. I, pp. 110-11.   [9] *Am. Arch.,* 5th S., Vol. I, p. 14.

Sandy Hook on the day the *Nancy* blew up, carried a far more immediate and inexorable menace to the state than any number of prowling commerce-destroyers.

Though New Jersey was alarmed by the proximity of the British, it was not lacking in martial ardor. Ever since the battle of Lexington, the inhabitants had been forming themselves into military companies. The comfortable Dutch farmer of the Raritan valley forsook his plow and his pipe long enough to drill himself in army exercises; the student at Princeton went through his military evolutions with zest; and in November 1775, Philip Fithian describes the state of things among the marshes and peaceful farms of the southwestern counties:

"Battalions of Militia & Minute-Men embodying—Drums & Fifes rattling—Military Language in every Mouth—Numbers who a few Days ago were plain Countrymen have now clothed themselves in martial Forms—Powdered Hair sharp pinched Beavers—Uniform in Dress with their Battalion—Swords on their Thighs—& stern in the Art of War—Resolved, in steady manly Firmness, to support & establish American Liberty, or die in Battle!"[10]

In this spirit the three battalions first raised by the Provincial Congress for the Continental service had set out for the north. They were an undisciplined lot, who sang while on sentry duty, fired their muskets at will merely to enjoy the noise, and had a tendency to argue with their officers; but they were out to defend liberty, and would willingly pause in their march to tar and feather a Tory who impugned their motives.[11] On their way to take service under Schuyler in the northern part of New York state, some of the troops had stopped long enough in Perth Amboy in the spring of 1776 to begin throwing up entrenchments;[12] but they had

[10] Above, p. 99; *N.J.H.S.P.*, 2nd S., Vol. I, p. 32; *N.J.A.*, Vol. XXXI, p. 139; Philip Fithian, *Journal, 1775-76* (Princeton, 1934), p. 131.
[11] *N.J.H.S.P.*, Vol. II, pp. 99, 100, 135, 137.
[12] *ibid.*, p. 101; Whitehead, *Early History of Perth Amboy*, pp. 328-9.

been ordered on before the fortifications of the town were completed; and, when the British threat became actual in July, it was militiamen who first appeared in the little capital to protect it against possible attack.

Much of the available force of militia, however, had been drawn off to defend the city of New York, which seemed to both the Continental and the New Jersey Provincial Congresses to be in the most immediate danger of attack.[13] Scarcely had the Jerseymen arrived in New York when they began to clamor to return. The sight of British troops boldly moving about with nothing but a narrow strip of water barring them from the farms and villages of Essex and Middlesex Counties had struck the inhabitants with alarm.[14] Although Washington believed that Howe would do nothing until the arrival of his brother's fleet with reinforcements,[15] the fears of the dwellers along the shore that they were being left unprotected in the face of an imminent invasion, while their own militia were detained in New York, increased daily.[16] These apprehensions were communicated to the men on duty, who began to worry about their families and friends.

Internal dangers, as well as external ones, occasioned the anxiety of the New Jersey troops to be where they could protect their homes. In more than one neighborhood, long-repressed Loyalists were making active preparations to assist the British in bringing the province back to its allegiance. On June 26, the Provincial Congress had been obliged to order a detachment of militia to apprehend a number of Tories in Hunterdon County who had resorted to open violence in opposition to the Revolutionists. At the same time, the legislators had decreed the arrest of several active

[13] Journal of the Convention, pp. 21-2, 27, 32, 77-9; *N.J.A.*, 2nd S., Vol. I, pp. 126-9; Abraham Clark to Elias Dayton, June 26, 1776, in Sparks MSS. (Harvard University Library), 49, Vol. II.
[14] *Am. Arch.*, 5th S., Vol. I, p. 42.   [16] Fithian, *Journal, 1775-76*, p. 186.
[15] *ibid.*, pp. 17-18.

Loyalists in Monmouth County.[17] In the latter region, disaffection to the new government was too widespread to be
quelled by a few arrests; indeed, all the efforts of the authorities throughout the years of the war could not tranquillize
the district. By the beginning of July, numbers of Tories
had taken up arms, and were assembling in the cedar swamps.
So alarming did the situation become that the Provincial
Congress dispatched four hundred of the militia to suppress
the incipient counterrebellion. The troops found little difficulty in dispersing the armed Tories, who seem to have numbered scarcely more than a hundred; but dispersion was not
conquest, and sullen hatred of the upstart government continued to smolder underground.[18]

A particularly annoying source of trouble to the American
authorities was the town of Shrewsbury. Local Revolutionary leaders blamed the "malign influence of our late Attorney-General [Cortlandt Skinner] and his execrable junto"
for the reactionary attitude of the community. Whatever
the cause, the more prosperous and influential farmers had
from the first used all their efforts to block the progress of
revolution. The Committee of Observation which they
finally elected, under pressure from neighboring communities, was, in the opinion of unsympathetic observers, such
"as you may justly suppose a disaffected majority would
naturally constitute." The extensive shoreline included
within the boundaries of the town facilitated communication
with British vessels offshore, and the prosperous farmers
were an ideal source of provisions for the newly arrived
royal forces. After General Howe's appearance in the vicinity, a number of active Loyalists from New York established
themselves in Shrewsbury and kept up a regular communication service between the British vessels and the city, so

[17] Journal of the Convention, pp. 28-9.
[18] *Am. Arch.*, 5th S., Vol. I, pp. 2, 37; *N.J.A.*, 2nd S., Vol. I, p. 138; Journal
of the Convention, pp. 27, 28, 32, 34, 36.

that the invaders were well posted on the activities of the American army.

According to one observer, these emissaries from New York also "secretly laboured to deceive the lower set of people, the higher being almost all [already] disaffected" to the Revolutionary government; but such propaganda was scarcely needed in a district where the reactionaries were operating almost unchecked. The colonel of the militia at Shrewsbury resigned his commission in despair, "making great complaints of the backwardness, 'to say no worse,' as he expresses himself, of his people; 'so few of whom,' he tells us, 'are ready to turn out (hiding themselves and deserting their houses) whenever he marches to defend the shores,' that he is discouraged." Even Whigs were afraid to do guard duty in the neighborhood, fearing to be betrayed into the hands of British landing parties by the unfriendly inhabitants. One militia captain was told by people dwelling along the Deal shore that "they did by no means thank him for guarding them, and that they would much rather have the Regulars than the Yankees there."[19]

Some of the Loyalists, more impatient than others, or, as their political antagonists grimly remarked, "finding the country too hot for them," joined the royal forces for actual military service. Before the British fleet had been off the coast a week, sixty men arrived from the vicinity of Shrewsbury and Upper Freehold, and General Howe was cheered with accounts of five hundred more of their neighbors ready to follow them. Although no such widespread exodus actually took place at this time, both British and Americans knew that, whenever the royal standard should be set up in New Jersey, many supporters would flock to it, ready to strike a blow for the ancient form of government.[20]

[19] *Am. Arch.*, 5th S., Vol. I, pp. 602, 603, 1534, 1535; *Selections from the Correspondence of the Executive of New Jersey, from 1776 to 1786* (Newark, 1848) (hereafter abbreviated as *N.J. Exec. Corr.*), p. 7.

[20] *Am. Arch.*, 5th S., Vol. I, pp. 38, 106, 602, 603, 1534; *Journal of the Con-*

Nor was Monmouth County the only district where the proximity of the British army and fleet roused the dispirited Tories to activity. From Perth Amboy, according to one report, forty-eight men had crossed to Staten Island to join their fellow-townsman, Cortlandt Skinner, whom Governor Franklin, after being arrested in June, had commissioned major general of the loyal militia of New Jersey, *in absentia*. It was known that there were many zealous Loyalists still left in the capital, including some of the former officers of government; and General Washington feared that unless steps were taken to check them they might work mischief.[21]

Thus, within a very few weeks, the apparent security of the Revolutionary government in New Jersey was badly shaken. Faced by the plottings of embittered Tories at home and by a powerful army on their borders, many citizens fell into panic. Not only was a large part of the militia absent in New York, but such as remained at home, in close proximity to the invader, were inadequately supplied with ammunition. Probably to forestall a direct refusal of the Monmouth militia to leave their disturbed county, the Provincial Congress voted on July 2 that men from that quarter should not be subject to a general summons to New York. Three days later, Washington released from the city most of the New Jersey militia quartered there. At least two battalions, composed in part of men from the southwestern counties, remained with the commander-in-chief; the rest of the troops were not all discharged, but were mostly transferred to the command of William Livingston, brigadier general of the New Jersey militia, with a suggestion that they be posted along the shore opposite Staten Island, to ease the fears

vention, pp. 41-2, MS. "Examn. of Prisoners at Haddonfield Burlington County," in Public Record Office, Trenton.

[21] *Am. Arch.*, 5th S., Vol. I, p. 200; Fraser, *op. cit.*, p. 1235; Whitehead, *Perth Amboy*, p. 329.

of the inhabitants and prevent communication with the enemy.[22]

At the same time, Washington reiterated to Livingston his suspicion that the Loyalists in Perth Amboy might engage in correspondence with Howe, and attempt to stir up disaffection to the new government through the province. Accordingly, he suggested that former royal officials and others known to be British sympathizers "should be removed with all expedition to less dangerous places," and that further precautions should be taken to prevent intercourse with the island.[23] A similar recommendation was made to General Heard of the militia, who, on the next day (July 6), caused a number of the leading citizens of Perth Amboy to be arrested.[24]

General Livingston, who at first had charge of the prisoners, was much relieved when they were transferred to the custody of the Provincial Congress at Trenton. In view of his close social connections with the former ruling coterie of the province, it was not a little embarrassing to have on his hands a man like John Smyth, until recently the treasurer of East Jersey, for whose integrity he still retained a high respect. Passions had not yet been exacerbated to the point at which all kindly recollections of the past were forgotten; and Livingston, who, as governor, could a few years later address a former friend with cold contempt because of his political views, was in the summer of 1776 still close enough to his former associates to seek and obtain Washington's grudging consent for Smyth's release on parole. The other prisoners were permitted to reside at various places in the

---

[22] *Am. Arch.*, 5th S., Vol. I, pp. 2, 17, 18, 37; Journal of the Convention, p. 35; *N.J.H.S.P.*, 3rd S., Vol. VI, p. 82; Fithian, *Journal, 1775-76*, pp. 190 *ff*.

[23] *Am. Arch.*, 5th S., Vol. I, p. 17.

[24] *Am. Arch.*, 5th S., Vol. I, pp. 17, 38. Those arrested were John Smyth, Philip and Michael Kearny, William Hick, Thomas Skinner, Dr. John Lawrence (not the member of the Council), Captain Turnbull, Johnstone Fairholme, and Isaac Bunnell or Bonnell.

interior of the province, under pledge not to go more than six miles from these points without permission.[25]

During the summer, further efforts were made to check or forestall dangerous activities on the part of Loyalists. The Provincial Congress—which on the eighteenth day of July changed its name to the Convention of the State of New Jersey—established as a qualification for serving in the Assembly or Council an oath or affirmation abjuring allegiance to George III and promising loyalty to the new government. Within a few days thereafter, a law was adopted defining treason and retaining the ancient penalties for it; and on August 2 the Convention passed a resolution for sequestering the estates of all individuals who had left home to join the enemy.[26] Meanwhile, the rounding-up of Loyalists became a systematic procedure, and militiamen now entered for short periods specifically into the "Tory-hunt service."[27] The families of refugees like Cortlandt Skinner were required to move from Perth Amboy to the interior of the state, and persons of dubious Revolutionary zeal were placed on parole not to assist the enemy or travel about the country. Guards were finally posted all along the Shrewsbury and Middletown shores, and the supine Shrewsbury Committee of Observation was supplanted in its police functions by a small delegation from the County Committee of Monmouth, which began to inquire into the reasons for the presence of so many New Yorkers in Shrewsbury. To hinder the British from being supplied with fresh meat by their friends on shore, the Convention ordered that livestock on

[25] Jones, *op. cit.*, pp. 120, 197; *Am. Arch.*, 5th S., Vol. I, pp. 38, 39; Journal of the Convention, p. 47.

[26] Journal of the Convention, p. 45; *N.J.A.*, 2nd S., Vol. I, pp. 152, 162-3.

[27] "August 20: 1776 Recd. of Capt. Jacob Ten Eyck The Sum of 35£ 4s. 9d. in full of Capt. Vroom Company in the Tory hunt Service for Six Days Recd. in Behalf of Said Peter Vroom by me

John Vroom"

—Ten Eyck Papers, Rutgers University Library

the beaches and in the adjacent meadows, especially in Monmouth County, be driven back from the sea.[28]

All these precautions, however, could have but a temporary effect. No measures, however severe, designed to suppress Loyalist sentiment could remain in force if New Jersey succumbed to British invasion; and the question whether that invasion could be prevented occupied the minds of Whig and Tory alike. To the leaders of the American army, of course, the defense of New Jersey was of secondary importance. Their attention was fixed upon keeping the British as long as possible away from Manhattan Island, which the Continental Congress wished to have vigorously defended. Possession of this point was of the greatest importance to the royal forces, as its capture would leave them in control of both ends of the Hudson River route to Canada. Could that line of communication once be secured by a chain of British posts, New England, the birthplace and storm center of the rebellion, would be cut off from the rest of the colonies; and, with the circulation between the two parts of the American body politic thus stopped, strangulation would be swift and sure.

Yet even amidst his rather pitiful preparations to contest with the overpowering British fleet and army possession of the low-lying island of Manhattan, Washington did not forget the situation of New Jersey. Powles Hook, as one of the essential points for defending the mouth of the Hudson, was fortified during the summer of 1776 at the same time as the other approaches to New York, and the works were kept constantly garrisoned.[29] Moreover, it was evident that the King's forces would attempt at some time to supply

[28] For paroles: Journal of the Convention, pp. 50, 63; Jonathan Odell's parole is in the Princeton University Library MSS., AM 9211; cf. also letter of Odell in S.P.G. transcripts, Ser. B, Vol. 24, No. 147. For removal of women and families from Perth Amboy: Jones, op. cit., p. 191. For arrests, and affairs in Monmouth County and Bergen Neck: Am. Arch., 5th S., Vol. I, pp. 120, 1534-5; N.J. Exec. Corr., pp. 7-8; Journal of the Convention, p. 55.

[29] Winfield, op. cit., pp. 137-8, 140.

themselves with provisions from the rich agricultural region in the valleys of the Passaic and the Raritan; and the fertile, level country of New Jersey between the hills and the pine barrens would be the natural highway to Philadelphia for the British army in case Howe wished to seize the American capital either before or after taking possession of New York. In view of these circumstances, Washington and the Continental Congress had been making preparations since the beginning of June to establish a Flying Camp, composed of ten thousand militiamen from Pennsylvania, Maryland, and Delaware, which would protect New Jersey and the country to the southward from any invasion from the northeast, and would be mobile enough to dispute any surprise landing of the royal troops in force. A spot near Perth Amboy was chosen as the site for the Flying Camp, and at this town Brigadier General Hugh Mercer, the commander of the new organization, took up headquarters during the second week in July.

For the time being, the troops from west of the Delaware not having arrived, General Mercer's force consisted of about twelve hundred New Jersey militiamen returned from New York and stationed at Perth Amboy and the Blazing Star Ferry a few miles to the north. A body of about three hundred of the militia, mostly from Morris County, was posted on Bergen Neck to watch the enemy and the inhabitants, and there were a few guards at the ferries over the Hackensack and Passaic Rivers; but these troops, though under Mercer's command, were somewhat too remote to be counted as part of the Flying Camp proper.[30]

The spirit of the defenders was none too happy. Far from being satisfied when released from New York and allowed to take post in their own state, they were no sooner established in New Jersey than they began importuning their leaders for permission to go home. It was harvest time, and

[30] *Am. Arch.*, 5th S., Vol. I, pp. 120, 140.

the hot, dry weather of that July made the farmers anxious to get in their crops. As yet, the British had shown no signs of moving, and if the militia sat about waiting for the enemy to act, their harvests would spoil and they would be reduced to great distress during the ensuing year. So urgent did their pleas become that Mercer first permitted a small draught from each company to be discharged, and then released the others, for the period of the harvest, as fast as they were relieved by the Pennsylvania militia. By July 20, all the New Jersey troops, except those stationed east of the Hudson, had been temporarily excused from service to gather their harvest.[31]

The response of the Pennsylvanians to the crisis in New Jersey had been prompt and wholehearted. On July 5, the Continental Congress voted that all the Associated Militia of Pennsylvania (except those of three western counties) who could be furnished with arms and accoutrements should be requested to march directly to New Jersey, there to continue in service until the regular Flying Camp should be assembled to relieve them, and that such of the Pennsylvania troops of the Continental line as were still west of the Delaware should depart for New Brunswick at once. On that same day, the rifle battalion maintained by the state of Pennsylvania left for the front, and within a little over a week two thousand of the militia had crossed the Delaware.[32]

Even while the composition of Mercer's force was thus changing, the general considered the possibility of surprising the British by an attack on Staten Island, where the fortifications were not yet formidable. He had already taken the precaution of having the boats and canoes along the shore secured under guard, and so could obtain means of transport without difficulty. By the evening of July 18, he was ready to make the attempt, and marched the Continental troops and riflemen under his command to the mouth of Thomp-

[31] *ibid.*, pp. 140, 172, 370, 470.   [32] *ibid.*, pp. 34, 350, 1565-6.

son's Creek; but first adverse wind and tide and then a high gale made the crossing impossible that night. This failure meant an indefinite postponement of the venture, since the British would doubtless have been informed of the movement, and would henceforth be on their guard.[33] Such was the first in a long series of unsuccessful endeavors made by the Americans throughout the war to accomplish a perpetually tempting military objective: the surprise of all or an important part of the royal forces on Staten Island. Though not all these enterprises were to be such flat failures as the first, not one of them was to achieve results commensurate with the effort involved in it. From now on, for the duration of the war, Staten Island was enemy territory. To the inhabitants of New Jersey it was a perpetual threat, a reservoir of destruction which more than once overflowed their land. Yet nothing could be done to remove the menace or to punish the marauders adequately. Beyond that little belt of water separating the island from the mainland, American arms and American strategy remained powerless to effect anything of consequence.

In projecting the raid, Mercer had endeavored to use his inadequate force as an offensive weapon. The events of the summer made the Flying Camp nearly useless even for purposes of defense. As a military organization, it scarcely passed beyond the stage of the theoretical. Subordinate in importance to the main army under Washington, it was time and again subjected to a drain of its men to the northward. So fluctuating was its composition that it never achieved cohesion or form. It was fortunate for the Americans that the British concentrated their first offensive upon the east side of the Hudson, and so met with a more stubborn resistance than could have been offered by the disorganized and shifting force about Perth Amboy. As early as July 16, the Continental Congress resolved "That General Washington

[33] *Am. Arch.,* 5th S., Vol. I, pp. 120, 140, 328, 443.

be desired to call to his assistance, at New-York, two thousand of the men who have marched into New Jersey to form the Flying-Camp; and that the Convention of New-Jersey be requested immediately to supply their places with an equal number of the Militia of that State." Two days later, the Convention complied with this request by voting the desired levy of militia. It appealed to its constituents for prompt cooperation in filling the Flying Camp, and closed its address with a solemn admonition:

"Remember, the hour is approaching, which will, in all human probability, decide the fate of America—which will either ensure your title to the rank of freemen, or debase you to the lowest class of slaves. Life, liberty, and property, all await the issue of the present struggle. Arise, then, and exert yourselves!"[34]

Despite this exhortation, the militia arose only lethargically; and how far it could be depended upon to exert itself, no commander at that time could be sure. Its members were inexperienced in war, and, like all untrained troops, subject to panic.[35] Nor was the uncertain quality of the men the only source of anxiety to the military leaders. Quite as disturbing was an acute shortage of ammunition. An appeal to the Continental Congress by the president of the New Jersey Provincial Congress early in July, and another by General Livingston to Washington at the same time, led to some improvement in the situation; but there was so little ammunition to be had that by the middle of the month leaden weights were being collected from all possible sources in both Pennsylvania and New Jersey to be made into balls.[36]

Raw recruits, inadequately supplied with the implements of war and vacillating between extremes of overconfidence and panic, were no heartening materials out of which to build a force able to oppose the landing of well drilled

[34] Journal of the Convention, pp. 89-91.   [36] ibid., pp. 37-9, 327, 346, 369.
[35] Am. Arch., 5th S., Vol. I, p. 38.

British and Hessian troops furnished with the best equipment that the richest government in the world could buy. But Mercer's difficulties did not end here. Even of such undependable soldiers as he had, a quite inadequate number was at his disposal. Recruits for the Flying Camp appeared with exasperating slowness. To be sure, the Pennsylvanians had risen to the occasion with admirable speed, sending regiment after regiment of Associators until Philadelphia was, as Abraham Clark wrote, "almost Striped of Inhabitants." But these men were mostly stopgaps—militiamen serving for short terms—and both regular troops for the Flying Camp and temporary supplies from states other than Pennsylvania were hopelessly tardy in appearing. As late as August 4, Mercer wrote with anxiety to the commander-in-chief that only 274 rank and file properly belonging to the Flying Camp had joined him. As for the two thousand militia which the New Jersey Convention on July 18 had so warmly exhorted to turn out, not one of them was in service when the month of August opened.

Washington grew worried, and on the eighth of the month wrote to urge upon the Convention "the absolute necessity of adopting some immediate and effective measures for completing the troops voted." Of the thirty-three hundred men who were to be raised by the resolution of June 14, he pointed out, only 1458 were on duty—in New York, we may suppose[37]—and, as the harvest was over and the militia had promised most cheerfully to return if necessary, he hoped they could be called back into service.[38] Spurred to action by this appeal, the legislature reorganized the militia system of the state on August 11, dividing all able-bodied men between the ages of sixteen and fifty into two classes, to serve alternately for periods of a month, the first to march

---

[37] These 1458 men, we must assume, were the ones left at New York, for, as we have seen, all the others of the original draft had been dismissed.

[38] *Am. Arch.*, 5th S., Vol. I, pp. 674, 750; *N.J. Exec. Corr.*, p. 8; Letter of Abraham Clark, Aug. 1, 1776, in Sparks MS., 49, Vol. II, p. 168.

to the Flying Camp immediately.[39] This new plan coincided with a momentary increase of military zeal in New Jersey which produced visible, though temporary, improvement. Within a week, there were nine regiments of New Jersey militia serving under Mercer's command from South Amboy to Fort Lee, and the general's whole force of well over five thousand men began to include also troops from Delaware and Maryland.[40]

It was high time for these reinforcements. Washington's army in New York, weakened by sickness and by the non-appearance of new levies, was being strengthened at the expense of the Flying Camp. In the early part of August, Mercer forwarded to his chief over two thousand men, and arrangements were made to send more if necessary.[41] Moreover, the Pennsylvania Associators, who had arrived with great goodwill and confidence,[42] were beginning to lose their enthusiasm. Even before the advent of the New Jersey militia to replace them, many of the troops from across the Delaware grew discontented and began to leave for home. They found their term of service longer than they had expected. On August 4 Mercer wrote that it was with the greatest difficulty that the officers prevented desertions "not of men singly, but by companies." Matters became worse day by day, and it was not long before the dissatisfied soldiers began to depart in bodies. The troops which remained grew "very abusive to their officers," and the work of fortifying points along the shore, which had been started when the New Jersey militia were first on duty, proceeded at a slow pace. The officers had more than they could do even to keep their men at their posts. The Chevalier de Kermorvan, a French engineer in charge of erecting the fortifications at Perth Amboy, was in despair.

[39] Journal of the Convention, pp. 92-6.
[40] Am. Arch., 5th S., Vol. I, pp. 909, 1079-80.
[41] ibid., pp. 894, 908, 963-4.
[42] ibid., p. 499.

The Americans, he wrote to a member of Congress, "do not dig trenches until they see the enemy upon them. Thus patience is required, and I have needed a good deal of it to let them work against my will at a battery that I have made. They have never been willing to do as I told them, and so the work is imperfect."[43]

It was not until August was well advanced that the entrenchments in the town were fairly well completed. Meanwhile, so alarming did the "Cowardly infamous Spirit of Desertion" become that the New Jersey Convention, acting upon an appeal from Mercer, forbade anyone belonging to or coming from the army in New Jersey to use any of the ferries or travel through the state without a pass signed by one of the principal officers, and directed the apprehension of all persons violating this regulation. Thereupon the soldiers began to plead nonexistent illnesses in an attempt to secure discharges.[44]

Such defections were by no means universal, and they are not difficult to understand. The Associators, usually young and unacquainted with military service, started off on an adventure which soon lost all its glamor. The weather was hot, and the unaccustomed marching through a country parched and dusty from a long drought was fatiguing. Although the troops found the ordinary inhabitants of New Jersey in general friendly and hospitable, "supplying us in as plentious a manner as their circumstances would admit of," they got along less agreeably with the innkeepers, whom they regarded as extortionate and insolent. Arrived at their destination, the marchers frequently had the greatest difficulty in finding proper quarters, since all the towns of north-

[43] *Am. Arch.*, 5th S., Vol. I, pp. 750, 834, 885, 894, 909-10; Letter of the Chevalier de Kermorvan, Aug. 12, 1776, in manuscripts of Ridgway Library, Philadelphia, Yi 2 7260 F 35.

[44] *Am. Arch.*, 5th S., Vol. I, p. 885; Mercer to Washington, Aug. 7, 1776, in Washington Papers (Library of Congress), Vol. 32; Algernon Roberts, *Campaign Journal*, in Sparks MSS., 48, p. 42; orders for Aug. 27, 1776, in Orderly Book, Am. 617, in Hist. Soc. of Pennsylvania.

eastern New Jersey were crowded with soldiers, and tents were scarce.

Algernon Roberts, an Associator who arrived at Perth Amboy with his company in August, was obliged to take quarters in a house the two small rooms of which had to accommodate thirty-three soldiers in addition to the owner's family of six. He describes his plight, however, with humorous resignation. The hostess, he tells us, was "one of these Philosophers that think all happiness consists in gratifying our inclinations tho at the expense of many a pair of shoes which she lost in the dirt about the floor which did not appear to be clean'd since the house was built tho as they saying is its an ill wind that blows nobody good this dirt being dry made our lodgings soft and dusty tho not very cleanly."

There were even less agreeable experiences for some of the Pennsylvania troops. Such as were ordered to Bergen went, says Roberts, "with much reluctance as we had the most unfavourable accounts of that part of the country which in many parts we found true for we had not marched many miles before we came to a salt marsh that exhibited a frightfull appearance and extended as far as the eye could see." Splashing along through this waste, knee-deep in mud and water, or sitting idly in the unpleasant village of Bergen while swarms of mosquitoes devoured them, the unhappy Associators longed for the hills of Pennsylvania, and received "with in expressable joy" orders to return home.[45] Small wonder, then, that some of the less hardy spirits, shrinking from such new and manifold discomforts, slipped away without the formality of obtaining leave![46]

[45] Roberts, *op. cit.*, pp. 40, 41, 43. Fithian, *Journal, 1775-76*, pp. 196-8.
[46] Satisfaction over the departure of the Associators for home was by no means one-sided. General Livingston writes to a friend on Aug. 29, lamenting the lack of discipline among the New Jersey militia. "And the worst men," he adds, "(was there a degree above the superlative) would still be pejorated, by having been fellow soldiers with that discipline-hating, good-living loving, 'to eternal fame damned,' coxcombical crew we lately had here from Philadelphia."—*Am. Arch.*, 5th S., Vol. I, p. 1210.

The contagion of discontent spread to the New Jersey militiamen serving in the Flying Camp. They complained that they had been frequently summoned to duty but had as yet received no pay. The general dissatisfaction made men unwilling to turn out, and through the practice of monthly rotation in service the number actually under arms steadily diminished. Matthias Williamson, in accepting a commission as brigadier general on September 15, wrote gloomily to the new governor of New Jersey, William Livingston, that he feared the state forces would "dwindle away to a mere nothing in three or four relieves more," unless some steps were taken to improve the morale.[47] No such improvement, however, was possible in the confusion of that hectic summer. Travelling through northeastern New Jersey early in September, John Adams found the public houses, taverns, and roadsides swarming with straggling, loitering officers and men, whose undisciplined appearance and air of careless dissipation made a highly unfavorable impression upon him.[48]

If the crowding and confusion of the Flying Camp were disagreeable to the troops, conditions were still more distasteful to the inhabitants. Long before a single enemy soldier had set foot upon the soil of New Jersey, the state had begun to suffer the ravages of war at the hands of its own defenders. The mere presence of such a number of undisciplined soldiers packed into small towns from which many of the inhabitants had fled, either to or away from the British, was enough to ensure a widespread abuse and destruction of property. What made matters worse was the absence of a smoothly functioning machine to care for the elementary needs of the soldiers.[49] Such an indispensable

[47] *N.J. Exec. Corr.*, pp. 9-10.   [48] John Adams, *op. cit.*, Vol. III, p. 75.
[49] General Livingston informs a correspondent that in addition to his other functions as commander of the encampment of New Jersey militia at Elizabeth-Town Point, he has to do "the proper business of Quartermasters, Colonels, Commissaries, and I know not what."—*Am. Arch.*, 5th S., Vol. I, p. 1210.

article as fuel for cooking the rations was not provided in adequate quantities, and in consequence the vicinity of the encampments was soon stripped of fences and other portable objects of wood which could be burned. This was a serious matter in a farming region, as the removal of fences laid open the pastures and grainfields of the farmers to destruction. In August, Roberts mourned over "the forlorn state" of the country about Perth Amboy, "which now exibeted an appearance meloncholly beyond description."[50] Two months later, Abraham Clark, distressed by the burnt fences and ravaged cornfields of Elizabeth-Town, wrote to a friend: "We have not had the enemy among us, but Staten-Island hath not suffered from the British troops scarcely the tenth part of the damage this town hath from the Militia."[51]

All things considered, the late summer was turning into a gloomy season indeed. From any rational point of view, the American prospects were dark, and astute New Jersey leaders did not deceive themselves. In a confidential letter written on August 6, Abraham Clark declared to a friend:

"As to my title, I know not yet whether it will be honourable or dishonourable: the issue of the war must settle it. Perhaps our Congress will be exalted on a high gallows. . . . I assure you, sir, I see—I feel, the danger we are in. I am far from exulting in our imaginary happiness; nothing short of the almighty power of God can save us. It is not in our numbers, our union, our valour, I dare trust. I think an interposing Providence hath been evident in all the events that necessarily led us to what we are—I mean independent States; but for what purpose, whether to make us a great empire, or to make our ruin more complete, the issue only can determine."[52]

Meanwhile, the activities of the British forces indicated that they had little doubt as to the purpose which Provi-

[50] Roberts, *op. cit.*, p. 42; *Am. Arch.*, 5th S., Vol. II, pp. 365-6.
[51] *Am. Arch.*, 5th S., Vol. II, p. 1249.   [52] *ibid.*, Vol. I, p. 786.

dence had in mind. They went about their preparations with calm deliberation, and retaliated vigorously for any liberties taken by the rebels. On July 26, they bombarded Perth Amboy briskly for an hour, killing one man and wounding two others, after the Americans had had the temerity to fire upon some shallops bound for Prince's Bay with the King's troops aboard. Some weeks later, a party of Pennsylvania riflemen who shot from the trees of Bergen Point at English soldiers parading on the island were showered with twelve-pound balls, which, though they did no harm, bore a threat of vengeance to come.[53]

Indeed, the army of the King was in fine fettle, and anxious to begin execution upon the despised rebels. The troops, reported Ambrose Serle, a representative of Lord Dartmouth, on July 25, "show the utmost Ardor to attack the Rebels. I am sometimes [afraid] the Soldiers hold them too cheap. A certain Degree of Disdain it may be right to indulge; but an Excess of it, in the case of an obstinate Resistance (which, from the numbers of the Rebels, amounting to near 30,000, is not improbable), would occasion a Disappointment, that might end in Despair."[54]

Serle's misgivings were prophetic, as the next year was to show; but they found no justification in the first paralyzing blow struck at the rebels. On August 27, General Howe, with twenty thousand British and Hessian troops (some of them brought by his brother, the admiral, who had finally arrived), advanced upon the American fortifications on Long Island and overwhelmed the defenders. The New Jersey militia serving with Washington, who helped bear the brunt of the action, shared in their commander's praise for the resolution and bravery of the troops, and most of them lived to escape from Long Island to Manhattan with the

[53] *Am. Arch.*, 5th S., Vol. II, p. 599; "Journal of a Pennsylvania Soldier," in New York Public Library *Bulletin* I, Vol. VIII, p. 548.

[54] Serle to Dartmouth, July 25, 1776, in Stevens, *Facsimiles*, Vol. XXIV, No. 2040.

rest of the battered American army two days later.[55] After tedious weeks of waiting in New York, where heat, cramped, insanitary quarters, and poor diet had caused widespread sickness, and after a further period of outdoor duty on Long Island in heavy rains,[56] the men were sadly disappointed by the fiasco. Their spirits were depressed still lower when Washington retreated to the northern end of Manhattan Island without defending the city or attempting to avenge his defeat. He was afraid the British might sail up the East River and land a force in his rear, and he thought it would be in the highest degree unwise to hazard the prospects of his army in another general engagement with the victorious enemy. His opinion was confirmed when two of his brigades, attempting to hinder the landing of the British on Manhattan Island at Kipp's Bay on September 15, were seized with panic and fled ignominiously. Nevertheless, men grumbled over the retreat. "The Lads wish to fight," reports a New Jersey chaplain in his journal; and murmurings of discontent became quite audible. A corporal in a company of the New Jersey militia was sentenced by court-martial to receive thirty-nine lashes for "speaking disrespectfully and villifying the Commander in Chief." It was not until the skirmish at Harlem Heights on September 16 that the morale of the soldiers was in some measure restored.[57]

Some redistribution of the Flying Camp was rendered necessary by the British occupation of New York. It was now quite possible that Howe's army might enter New Jersey from some point on the Hudson above the city; moreover, as long as a sizable American garrison remained at Fort Washington on the upper end of Manhattan Island, it seemed advisable to support it by a strong encampment on

[55] George Washington, *Writings*, John C. Fitzpatrick, ed. (Washington, 1932— ?), Vol. VI, p. 21.

[56] Fithian, *Journal, 1775-76*, pp. 196, 197, 198, 209, 214, 220, *et passim*; Philip Fithian, *Letters to His Wife* (Vineland, N.J., 1932), p. 19.

[57] Fithian, *Journal, 1775-76*, pp. 231, 235, 236; Washington, *op. cit.*, Vol. VI, pp. 36-7.

the New Jersey bank of the river. Accordingly, on September 3, the commander-in-chief ordered Mercer to detach a force under "an officer of note, Authority and influence," with a skilful engineer, to lay out suitable works across the Hudson from Fort Washington. Mercer sent General Ewing with a command of fifteen hundred men. Before the month was out, Fort Lee, with its smaller outwork, Fort Constitution, was frowning from the top of the steep Palisades, and General Greene was on the spot with a command over four thousand strong.[58]

Scarcely was this new defense post established on the west bank of the river, however, before another one a few miles to the south of it was abandoned, and the first piece of New Jersey soil fell into the hands of the British army. The post at Powles Hook was garrisoned by a regiment of Continental troops from Connecticut under Colonel Durkee and by one of New Jersey militia from Middlesex under Colonel John Duychinck. On September 15, this garrison received the attention of three large British vessels sailing up the Hudson to assist their land forces in the capture of New York by bombarding the center of Manhattan Island. In passing Powles Hook, the ships kept near the New Jersey shore, and raked the entire promontory. Their fire did no worse harm than killing a horse, and was briskly returned by a company of American artillery. The little garrison was not the primary object of assault that day, and it waited for hours in suspense while the hostile vessels turned their cannon against the island across the river. The attack on New York was the most exciting military episode which had yet been witnessed from New Jersey, and to Ambrose Serle, safe aboard a British ship down the bay, the spectacle was a noble one. "Removing from one's Thoughts," he says, "the melancholy Seriousness of the Business, the Hills, Woods,

58 Washington, *op. cit.*, Vol. VI, pp. 9-10, 17-18, 33; *Am. Arch.*, 5th S., Vol. II, pp. 607-8.

Town, River, Ships, and Pillars of Smoke, illuminated by a brilliant Morning, formed the finest Landscape that the Imagination can conceive.''[59] The inexperienced Americans at Powles Hook, however, were impressed in a less agreeable manner, and they were thoroughly dismayed when, before the day was over, they saw the British flag raised over Fort George, and when later a rescue party brought over some American soldiers who had been trapped in the city.

An event of the following day completed the demoralization of the little garrison. One of the British ships, which had anchored about three miles upstream, returned past the fort and cannonaded it again. Although no damage was done to the American position, the New Jersey militia, unnerved by the excitement of the past twenty-four hours, were stricken with panic, and Colonel Duychinck was obliged to retreat with them to Bergen, leaving only the three hundred men from Connecticut at the river post.[60]

Mercer was incensed by this behavior, which he called "scandalous," and complained to Washington that at all the posts it was difficult to hold the militia to their duty.[61] Soon, however, he was obliged to imitate the spontaneous action of the militiamen. The position of Powles Hook was very dangerous so long as the British had control of the neighboring waters. It was nearly an island, low-lying and exposed to bombardment from the river; and there was but one way of retreat from it through the surrounding marshes. Should the British land a force somewhere else along the shore and cut off this line of retirement, the garrison would be hopelessly trapped. On the other hand, the battery stationed at the Hook had proved powerless to inflict serious damage upon the ships passing up and down the river; so, with New York in the hands of the King's troops, there was little reason for risking a garrison any longer on the peninsula. On

[59] Serle to Dartmouth, Sept. 25, 1776, in Stevens, *Facsimiles*, Vol. XXIV, No. 2043.

[60] *N.J.A.*, 2nd S., Vol. I, pp. 224-6.   [61] *Am. Arch.*, 5th S., Vol. II, p. 367.

September 22, therefore, the defenders of the post received orders to remove their artillery, stores, and baggage, and be ready to retreat. During that same morning, a considerable force of the royal troops embarked in flat-bottomed boats from the New York shore, and four ships hoisted sail and stood towards the Hook; but the vessels soon came to anchor again, such of the boats as had pushed off returned to shore, and the attack was postponed.

The Americans made full use of their interval of grace. By early afternoon of September 23, everything of value had been removed from the Hook, and the garrison abandoned the post and moved to Bergen. Immediately thereafter, four British ships dropped anchor near the shore around the Hook, a fleet of boats and floating batteries crossed the river, and, after bombarding the empty works vigorously, the royal forces landed and took possession.[62]

The campaign on New Jersey soil had opened—and had opened with a characteristic incident. As was to occur again and again, Howe had caught an American force at a disadvantage, and, by a brisk effort, might have trapped it. Instead, he mysteriously delayed his attack, and his enemy improved the respite to slip through his grasp. This was the basic theme of Howe's campaign of 1776, repeated with variations until the battle of Trenton brought a change. The people of New Jersey, fortunately, could not at this time foresee the melancholy recurrences—a more and more ragged and dispirited American army receding, receding before the triumphant enemy, perpetually in danger and apparently on the brink of destruction, permitted as by a miracle to slip away again, only to be overtaken by another crisis. At the moment, all that could be seen was the royal standard planted once more on the soil of New Jersey, and an untrained, disorganized force preparing to meet the victorious legions of the King.

[62] *N.J.A.*, 2nd S., Vol. I, pp. 204, 227-9.

CHAPTER V ✥ *THE CRISIS OF THE WAR*

FOR almost two months after the fall of Powles Hook, New Jersey remained comparatively quiet. All the efforts of the British forces were concentrated upon a clumsy pursuit of Washington's army in Westchester County, New York; and the Flying Camp, consisting of some six thousand men scattered from Perth Amboy to Fort Lee,[1] was left in peace. An occasional Tory-hunt helped to break the monotony of life in the overcrowded garrisions,[2] and an attack upon Staten Island by part of Mercer's forces during the night of October 17 yielded some much needed military experience as well as a handful of British and Hessian prisoners.[3] For the most part, however, interest centered in the news from across the Hudson, where Howe's army, like a fat and inefficient bully with no stomach for his work, sparred with the impudent American force, an undersized but agile adversary.

When, after some weeks of inconclusive maneuvering and fighting, the British troops at the beginning of November withdrew to Dobbs Ferry and Manhattan Island, the situation grew more menacing to the defenders of New Jersey. Washington warned Governor Livingston that Howe would probably detach a force to invade the state, and requested that the militia be put upon the best possible footing. He also sent Lord Stirling across the Hudson with eight regiments of infantry, which were divided between Rahway and New Brunswick, in order to impede any sudden advance by the British upon Philadelphia. Soon the American commander-in-chief himself followed Stirling with about

[1] A general return of the men under Mercer's command on Oct. 8, 1776, lists 6548 officers and privates, of whom 570 were sick and 103 deserted. *Am. Arch.*, 5th S., Vol. II, pp. 941-2.
[2] *N.J.A.*, 2nd S., Vol. I, p. 232.   [3] *Am. Arch.*, 5th S., Vol. II, pp. 1073, 1093.

five thousand men, and set up his headquarters at Hackensack.[4]

By this move, Washington showed that he understood Howe's purpose in changing the area of operations. Abandoning the half-hearted attempt to come to decisive grips with the Americans in the rough terrain of Westchester County, the British commander was now centering his attention upon the twin strongholds of Fort Washington and Fort Lee, which rose on either side of the Hudson. These fortifications had now demonstrated their inability to prevent British shipping from ascending the river, and Washington was inclined to withdraw from its dangerous isolation on the upper end of Manhattan Island the garrison of the fort named after him. Major General Nathanael Greene, however, who had been posted in Bergen County off and on since September, and who was now in command of both forts, availed himself of the discretionary power given by his chief, and resolved to defend Fort Washington vigorously. The garrison, instead of being removed, was reinforced from the Flying Camp; and when Washington arrived in the vicinity in the middle of the month, he found preparations for defense on the part of the Americans, and for attack on the part of the British, so far advanced that evacuation of the post seemed inadvisable. To withdraw again without trying conclusions with the enemy would be bad for American morale; and Howe, with his superiority on the water, might fall with devasting effect upon the retiring garrison when only part of it had crossed the river. On November 16, Hessian and British troops launched a hard assault upon Fort Washington, and in a few hours

[4] George Washington, *The Writings of George Washington* . . . , John C. Fitzpatrick, ed. (Washington, 1932—?), Vol. VI, pp. 243-4, 254, 255-6; *Am. Arch.*, 5th S., Vol. III, p. 750.

the stronghold surrendered, with a loss of about twenty-six hundred prisoners.[5]

This severe blow, following upon a whole season of misfortune, greatly discouraged Washington. He saw with alarm the precarious situation to which he was being reduced as his army moldered away by desertions, expiration of enlistments, and losses in battle, and the states delayed replenishing their quotas. In ten days, he informed his brother on November 19, there would not be more than two thousand men west of the Hudson, belonging to fixed and established regiments, to oppose the entire British army.

Among these men, morale was none too high. Repeated misfortunes had brought discouragement; and widespread sickness added to the general dejection. The surgeons, wrote General Greene from Fort Lee on October 10, were without medicines, and nothing was more depressing to the spirits of the men who were yet well than the miserable condition of the sick. "They exhibit a spectacle shocking to human feelings," he declared, "and as the knowledge of their distress spreads through the country, will prove an insurmountable obstacle to the recruiting the new army." The General Hospital was unable to accommodate more than half the invalids; the rest were without care. "Many hundreds are now in this condition," Greene continued, "and die daily for want of proper assistance; by which means the army is robbed of many valuable men, at a time when a reinforcement is so exceedingly necessary. Both officers and men join in one general complaint, and are greatly disgusted at this evil, which has prevailed so long."[6]

Small wonder that Washington began to feel that the odds against him were almost insuperable! "I am worried almost to death with the retrograde Motions of things," he admitted privately, "and I solemnly protest that a pecuniary reward

[5] Henry B. Carrington, *Battles of the American Revolution* (New York, etc., 1876), p. 247; Washington, *Writings*, Vol. VI, p. 244.
[6] *Am. Arch.*, 5th S., Vol. II, pp. 973-4.

of 21,000 £ a year would not induce me to undergo what I do."[7]

Nevertheless, discouraging though the prospects might be, the struggle must go on. Livestock, grain, wagons, and other property of possible use to an army must be carried back from the New Jersey lowlands into the hills, that they might not fall prey to the royal troops, who had plundered outrageously in their excursions east of the Hudson.[8] General Greene, who had remained in New Jersey during the attack upon Fort Washington, had for some days past been preparing to oppose any advance of the British west of the river. From Perth Amboy he summoned Mercer, now his subordinate in command, to the zone of more immediate danger; and he nearly drained the Flying Camp of troops to guard the landing places along the Palisades.[9]

After the loss of Fort Washington, however, Fort Lee was as useless to the Americans as Powles Hook had been two months earlier. Moreover, the garrison was in almost equal danger of being trapped by a surprise landing of the British; for the Hackensack River and its tributary, Overpeck Creek, which cut off retreat less than two miles back of the fort, were bridged at very few points. Under these circumstances, Washington planned to abandon the post, and ordered Greene to remove to places of greater security west of the Passaic all stores not considered necessary for its immediate defense.[10] Speed was essential, for the British might be expected at any moment. If they occupied the stronghold before its cannon, ammunition, and large quantities of military stores were removed, they would gain another consider-

[7] Washington, *Writings*, Vol. VI, pp. 245-6.

[8] *ibid.*, Vol. VI, pp. 254, 256; *N.J.A.*, 2nd S., Vol. I, pp. 230-1; Stephen Kemble, *Journal*, in *Collections of the New-York Historical Society*, 1883, pp. 96, 97, 98; *Am. Arch.*, 5th S., Vol. III, pp. 629-30.

[9] *Am. Arch.*, 5th S., Vol. III, p. 629; Washington, *Writings*, Vol. VI, pp. 293-4.

[10] Washington, *Writings*, Vol. VI, p. 293; William Gordon, *The History of the Rise, Progress, and Establishment, of the Independence of the United States of America* (hereafter abbreviated as Gordon, *Am. Rev.*) 4 vols. (London, 1788), Vol. II, p. 346.

Landing of the British under Cornwallis, November 20, 1776, at the foot of the Palisades. (Contemporary drawing, probably by Lord Rawdon, an engineer on the staff of Cornwallis)

able advantage over the Americans; but if they took an empty fort, the victory would be as barren as the capture of Powles Hook. By November 18, Greene had the removal operations in full swing. Powder and ammunition, the most valuable articles, were carted off, and a beginning was made of taking away the other stores. At this critical juncture, however, disorganization and inefficiency paralyzed the work. Throughout the war, the operations of the American army were cursed by the haphazard character of its auxiliary services; and this occasion was no exception. Greene could not find enough wagons to move the stores rapidly. In vain he tried to procure boats to convey the freight down Overpeck Creek and the Hackensack and up the Passaic to Newark: he was unable even to learn how many boats were available.[11] While his assistants dawdled, his scanty margin of time was wasted.

For once, Howe did not give his opponents leisure to complete their plans. At daybreak on November 20, a large force under Lord Cornwallis debarked unobserved at the foot of the Palisades a few miles north of Fort Lee, ascended a difficult and little-used path to the top of the cliffs, and advanced upon the American post. Receiving news that the enemy were approaching, Greene sent posthaste to Hackensack for Washington; but when the commander-in-chief arrived he had little choice of action. The garrison at Fort Lee consisted of between two and three thousand effective men, most of them, as Greene himself declared, "irregular and undisciplined." Cornwallis had a force of at least four thousand regular troops, and some reports placed the number considerably higher. If the soldiers stationed at Fort Lee were to escape the fate of their comrades across the river, there was no course open to them but a swift retreat.

The order was given, and the Americans streamed off in confusion, taking what baggage they could, but leaving

[11] *Am. Arch.*, 5th S., Vol. III, p. 751.

behind them a great quantity of tents, cannon, and miscellaneous stores. So short was the time for escape that, according to the British, the kettles of the garrison were still boiling over the fires when the captors entered the fort. For so large a body of troops the only practicable route of retreat was by way of the New Bridge, which crossed the river two or three miles above the village of Hackensack and was over six miles from the fort. Somewhat to the surprise of the Americans, the British had not seized this point, and most of the retreating soldiers, under Washington, crossed the river there. Others were ferried to the town of Hackensack from the junction of the river with Overpeck Creek; still others, after crossing the creek on a milldam and making their way through the marshes to the river opposite the town, were picked up there.[12]

Having reassembled his scattered followers at Hackensack and at the New Bridge, Washington considered his position. The prospect was by no means pleasing. His force was posted on a flat plain, hemmed in on the east by the Hackensack and on the west by the Passaic and Saddle Rivers—a situation very similar to that from which Greene's men had just escaped, except that in this open country the superior British forces could operate to even greater advantage. There was not an entrenching tool in the entire American army, and a number of its valuable pieces of artillery were now in the hands of the enemy. What was worse, the men,

[12] Greene later characterized the enemy's publication of the cannon and stores captured at Fort Lee as "a grand falsehood," and asserted that "not an article of military stores was left there, or nothing worth mentioning" (*Am. Arch.* 5th S., Vol. III, p. 1342). The weight of evidence, however, both British and American, and even of one of Washington's official letters, is against him. *Am. Arch.*, 5th S., Vol. III, pp. 663-4, 1071, 1291-2; Thomas Glyn, *Ensign Glyns Journal in the American Service with the Detachment of 1,000 Men of the Guards commanded by Brigadier General Mathew in 1776* (MS. in Princeton University Library), pp. 26-7; Andrew Hunter, MS. Diary (Princeton University Library), Nov. 20, 1776; *N.J.A.*, 2nd S., Vol. I, pp. 314-15; George Washington, *Writings*, Vol. VI, pp. 295-6; "Journal of a Pennsylvania Soldier," in New York Public Library *Bulletin*, Vol. VIII, pp. 548-9; Stephen Kemble, *Journal*, in *Collections of the New-York Historical Society*, 1883, p. 101.

as Washington noted with concern, were "much broken and dispirited," not only because of their constant defeats, but because many of them had lost their tents and baggage in the hasty departure from Fort Lee. To add a final touch of despondency, the weather, which throughout the fall had been the finest in the memory of men for that season, had changed just as the British crossed the Hudson; and now the chilling, gloomy rains of early winter were beginning.[18]

Under the circumstances, it would have been hopeless to risk an engagement before the American forces had been strengthened. Accordingly, Washington determined to move at once from his dangerous position, and on November 21 his discouraged army plodded away over miry roads, through a cold downpour, to Acquackanonck Bridge.[14] From here their soggy march took them to Newark, where they halted a few days while the outposts at Elizabeth-Town and Perth Amboy were gathered in and Washington waited for the New Jersey militia to rally to his assistance. The farmers of the state, however, weary of being called out to service, preferred sitting by their comfortable firesides to joining a handful of bedraggled troops against a well trained and apparently invincible army. Almost no recruits came in from the countryside; and, finding the enemy slowly approaching Newark, Washington gathered his followers again and moved on to New Brunswick.

Here another depressing event took place. The gloomy month of November came to an end, and with it expired the term of service of two brigades of the Flying Camp—those from Maryland and New Jersey. Only a short distance away, Cornwallis was approaching; but nothing could induce the released soldiers to stay with their commander in his hour of danger. Off they marched, and others whose terms were not out deserted in great numbers. Washington, fearing that

[18] Washington, *Writings*, Vol. VI, pp. 295-6, 297-8; Kemble, *Journal*, p. 101; *Am. Arch.*, 5th S., Vol. III, p. 1071.
[14] Now Belleville.

his destruction of the bridge over the shallow Raritan would not long delay the enemy, who were cannonading him from the opposite shore, resumed his march. With his pitiably small army—now reduced to fewer than four thousand men, including militia—he fell back through Princeton to Trenton, where he arrived on December 2.[15]

During this dismal retreat, the lack of military ardor in New Jersey was a bitter disappointment to the commander-in-chief. On November 21, he wrote to the governor, urging that the militia be called together to replace those troops of the Flying Camp whose service was expiring, and to help stop the progress of the enemy. Livingston replied by ordering out all the militia of the counties north of Monmouth and Burlington, to join the Continental army for a period not exceeding six weeks; and the state legislature voted to raise four battalions to serve until the first of April. The response of the inhabitants, however, was far from spirited. Brigadier General Matthias Williamson, who stationed himself at Morristown to collect the militia after the eastern part of the state had fallen into the hands of the British, reported on December 8 that no more than twenty men from Newark, or fifty from all Essex County, had joined him, and that not a soul had appeared from Acquackanonck. From Sussex County, Colonel Symmes had arrived, but his following was "inconsiderable." In Morris County alone, chiefly owing to the efforts of Colonel Jacob Ford, Jr., a fair turn-out had been secured, so that an "appearance of defence" was maintained.[16]

Such listlessness angered General Greene, who declared that the people of New Jersey were behaving "scurvily" and did not deserve the freedom for which the army was fight-

[15] Andrew Hunter, MS. Diary (in Princeton University Library), Nov. 20, Nov. 22, 1776; *N.J.A.*, 2nd S., Vol. I, pp. 273-4; Washington, *Writings*, Vol. VI, pp. 312-13, 320, 321-2, 324-5, 331-2, 337; *Am. Arch.*, 5th S., Vol. III, pp. 1071-2.
[16] Washington, *Writings*, Vol. VI, pp. 302-3; *Am. Arch.*, 5th S., Vol. III, pp. 869-70, 1120.

ing.[17] Washington, too, was disappointed, and was inclined to lay part of the blame for the backwardness of the militia upon Governor Livingston or General Williamson.[18] These gentlemen, however, were probably quite justified in asserting that they had used their best efforts to rouse the citizenry. Their lot was by no means enviable. Even such militiamen as appeared for service were not above squabbling with one another; and the stubborn, often petty individualism of the farmer in arms further complicated the already great troubles of the harassed leaders, both now and in the ensuing years.[19]

Wherever the fault for the defection of New Jersey might lie, it was obvious that the failure of the state to assist the army had produced a grave crisis. "If the Militia of this State," Washington wrote to John Hancock on December 5, "had step'd forth in Season, (and timely notice they had) we might have prevented the Enemy's crossing the Hackensack, although (without some previous notice of the time, and place) it was impossible to have done this at No. River. We might with equal probability of success have made a stand at Brunswick on the Raritan; but as both these Rivers were fordable (in a variety of places knee deep only) it required many Men to defend the passes, and these we had not."

Nevertheless, the general found some partial excuse for the delinquencies of New Jersey, and laid upon the military system the chief blame for the existing state of affairs. In his opinion, had a sizable permanent army been maintained from the beginning of hostilities, and the citizenry excused from duty, the situation would have been much better. "In such case the Militia, who have been Harassed and tired by repeated calls upon them, and Farming, and Manufactures in a Manner suspended would, upon any emergency have run with Alacrity to Arms, whereas the cry now is, they may

[17] *Am. Arch.*, 5th S., Vol. III, p. 1072.
[18] Washington, *Writings*, Vol. VI, pp. 320-1, 347.
[19] *Am. Arch.*, 5th S., Vol. III, pp. 1120, 1121; *N.J. Exec. Corr.*, pp. 18-20.

as well be ruined one way as another, and with difficulty are obtaind. . . . When danger is a little remov'd from them, they will not turn out at all. When it comes home to them, the well affected, instead of flying to Arms to defend themselves, are busily employed in removing their Family's and Effects, while the disaffected are concerting measures to make their submission, and spread terror and dismay all around."[20]

Although New Jersey had failed Washington so signally, and only a few of its citizens appeared in arms at Trenton to join him, Pennsylvania was not yet so demoralized. At the Delaware, the slender American army received a welcome reinforcement of about two thousand militiamen, some from Philadelphia and some from the German settlements in Pennsylvania and Maryland. He dispatched the first arrivals, as well as twelve hundred other men under General Greene, to Princeton, to strengthen Lord Stirling and General Stephen, whom he had left behind with about twelve hundred men as a covering party.[21]

On the way to the Delaware, Washington had sent a subordinate ahead to collect boats, and so was able, immediately upon his arrival, to begin moving across the river the baggage and military supplies brought with the army or stored in the town. This task in great measure accomplished, he faced about on December 7 and started back towards Princeton. Though his plans were vague, he intended to act according to circumstances and hoped he would be joined by a reinforcement under Major General Charles Lee, which he had summoned from across the Hudson some time before.[22]

On the same day that Washington started back towards Princeton the British army was set in motion towards the same point. Cornwallis, who had been detained in New Brunswick for some days by General Howe's order, was joined by his superior in person on December 6; and the

[20] Washington, *Writings*, Vol. VI, pp. 331-3.
[21] *ibid.*, Vol. VI, pp. 331, 333, 337 ; *Am. Arch.*, 5th S., Vol. III, p. 1072.
[22] Washington, *Writings*, Vol. VI, pp. 319-20, 321, 324-5, 330-4.

next morning the royal force, moving in two columns some distance apart, set off in the direction of the Delaware. The British advanced very slowly, while flanking parties scoured the patches of woodland and brush along the route to chase away any lurking bands of rebels. This caution was justified, for one careless group of British scouts was surrounded and killed in a thicket during the day's march; but the Americans could not hope seriously to check Howe's progress by any such annoyance. In consequence, Washington was met on the road by the news that General Greene was falling back from Princeton in order not to be surrounded; and the whole American force retreated to Trenton, where it began crossing the river.[23]

The transfer of the army was not quite completed on the following day when, at about two o'clock in the afternoon, the British vanguard, which had been somewhat delayed in repairing a broken-down bridge over Stony Brook, arrived at the outskirts of Trenton. Some of the inhabitants, delighted by the prospect of seeing their fellow countrymen fall into the hands of the invaders, hastened out and urged the British to move quickly and capture such of the American soldiers as had not yet embarked. But General Howe was cautious, and halted the entire army except for a detachment of light infantry and Hessian Jägers. Accompanied only by this small force and by Cornwallis and three adjutants, he rode through Trenton to the meadow which separated the village from the river. His wariness proved to be well justified. Scarcely had the King's soldiers appeared in the open when they were raked by a withering fire from the American batteries planted on the opposite shore of the Delaware. The infantry and Jägers fled to the shelter of the little wooded valley of Assanpink Creek a short distance to the left; but before they reached this refuge they had lost thirteen men. Howe

[23] *ibid.*, Vol. VI, pp. 324-5, 335-6; *Am. Arch.*, 5th S., Vol. III, pp. 1107-8; Journal of Capt. Fr. von Münchhausen, in Brunswick Papers, Vol. II, Bancroft Collection, New York Public Library, Dec. 5-8, 1776.

himself, with his four officers, remained on the field for some time, riding about, reconnoitering, and calmly ignoring the cannon balls which buried themselves in the earth all around him. One of his adjutants was bruised by a stone thrown up by a projectile striking the ground near him, and the same officer's horse lost a leg from another ball; but the general coolly finished his survey before returning to the village. As a parting remembrance, the Americans fired a shot which struck so near him that he was showered with dirt.[24]

The British commander's courage and self-possession were not equalled at this juncture by his enterprise. He brought his troops quietly into Trenton; but beyond this point he found progress "impracticable." Washington had swept this part of the river clean of boats, and Cornwallis was immediately dispatched, with four regiments, as far upstream as Coryell's Ferry,[25] under instructions to cross the river by the ferry or by means of such boats as he could procure. Here again, however, the British found that the Americans had been ahead of them, and Cornwallis retired, disappointed, to Pennington. A few days later, a detachment of four hundred Hessians under Colonel von Donop was sent down the river to Burlington to find means of crossing; but this expedition, too, was unsuccessful.[26]

There can be little doubt that an energetic commander, determined to press his advantage to the utmost, could have hit upon some method of passing the stream. The sour remark of one Loyalist, that Howe, in advancing to the Delaware, had calculated "with greatest accuracy, the exact time necessary for his enemy to escape,"[27] was unfair; but the commander laid himself open to justifiable criticism by his failure to continue the pursuit. It is scarcely credible that

---

[24] Münchhausen, Journal, Dec. 8, 1776.   [25] Now Lambertville.
[26] Münchhausen, op. cit., Dec. 8, 9, 11, 1776.
[27] [Joseph Galloway] Letters to a Nobleman, on the Conduct of the War in the Middle Colonies (London, 1780), p. 49.

within a few days, in a region so widely Loyalist in sentiment as New Jersey, the collection of watercraft and their removal to the other side of the Delaware, as ordered by Washington, could have been thoroughly performed. Joseph Galloway, a Pennsylvania Loyalist who accompanied the royal forces to Trenton, later assured the House of Commons that he had heard there were in a millpond, a short distance from the town, two boats able to carry fifty or sixty men apiece. Whether or not this statement be true—for Galloway on occasion took great liberties with facts—there is little reason to question his assertion that there were 48,000 feet of boards in Trenton, with a quantity of iron, from which pontoons, boats, or rafts might have been constructed.[28] The important place of lumber and iron in the river trade of western New Jersey, and the existence of wooden buildings and blacksmith shops in Trenton make it certain that, had Howe been anxious to follow Washington, he could easily have found the materials out of which some makeshift craft might have been hastily built. The American force was too weak to guard the whole stretch of the river effectively against a landing by superior numbers. Yet Howe, after the fruitless expeditions of Cornwallis and von Donop, made no further efforts to cross.

The British commander's inertia on the bank of the Delaware, however, is of a piece with his entire conduct after the battle of Long Island. His strange lack of energy did not escape the caustic and frequently unfair comment of his enemies, and it has puzzled historians ever since. During the campaign in New Jersey, he gave repeated examples of unsoldierly slothfulness. Powles Hook, as we have already noted, was occupied only after the Americans had been allowed ample time to evacuate it. If the British were not quite so considerate of the garrison at Fort Lee, at least they

[28] Joseph Galloway, *The Examination of Joseph Galloway, Esq: Late Speaker of the House of Assembly of Pennsylvania, before the House of Commons, in a Committee on the American Papers* (London, 1780), p. 41.

did not cut off its retreat by seizing the New Bridge, over the Hackensack, as they might easily have done. It was five days after the American army had crossed the Passaic River at Acquackanonck Bridge on November 21 before the British passed over the same stream. From Acquackanonck to Newark, a distance of only nine miles, the royal troops took two days, and Washington had ample time to effect his retreat. The American commander, whose own activity was never deterred by weather conditions, supposed that the heavy rains must be responsible for the sluggishness of the British advance.[29]

Nothing was done to outflank the slowly retiring Americans. One of Howe's adversaries in England pointed out a few years later that it would have been easy to send a detachment from Staten Island up the Raritan to New Brunswick to intercept Washington and, by putting him between two fires, complete his destruction.[30] His omission to perform this obvious maneuver was also criticized in the privacy of a diary by one of his own subordinates.[31] On the American side, Thomas Paine, a good revolutionist, a good deist, and a soldier in the retreating force, could see no explanation for this "great errour in generalship" but "some providential control" interfering with the progress of British arms, which he identified with "the power of hell."[32]

At New Brunswick the Americans enjoyed another breathing spell before the slow-moving Cornwallis once more threatened them. After leaving that town on December 1, they had six days to move their stores across the Delaware before the British force, detained at the Raritan by Howe's order, was allowed to resume its march towards the Delaware. Again Washington, who courted destruction by lin-

29 Glyn, *Journal*, pp. 28, 29; Washington, *Writings*, Vol. VI, p. 310.
30 [Israel Mauduit] *Three Letters to Lieutenant-General Sir William Howe, with an Appendix* (London, 1781), p. 38.
31 Kemble, *Journal*, p. 105.
32 *The American Crisis*, No. 1, quoted in *Am. Arch.*, 5th S., Vol. III, p. 1292.

gering in New Jersey until all hope of reinforcement was gone and the enemy were at last almost upon him, could find no explanation for their delay other than the old one of rainy weather.[33]

After Howe's failure in managing the American war had become apparent, the recriminations against him in England for this delay in New Brunswick were almost more violent than for any other phase of his activity—or inactivity. Joseph Galloway scathingly quoted a letter alleged to have been written by the American General Weedon, to the effect "that General Howe had a mortgage on the rebel army for some time, but had not yet foreclosed."[34] Obviously, Galloway shared this view, and harbored dark suspicions as to the reasons for the leniency. Others joined in the attack, and a controversy was opened which has continued down to the present.[35]

The explanations given by Howe and Cornwallis for loitering at New Brunswick when an energetic push might have trapped Washington's force against the Delaware and destroyed it, or at least inflicted irreparable damage upon it, seem extraordinarily feeble. In the first place, Howe declared that the Americans' destruction of the bridge at New Brunswick saved them from being "cut to pieces" by their pursuers.[36] But the condition of the bridge, as Cornwallis himself admitted under examination by the House of Commons, delayed the British only a small part of the time they

[33] *Am. Arch.*, 5th S., Vol. III, p. 1070.

[34] Galloway, *Letters to a Nobleman*, p. 49 n.

[35] An example is this scathing indictment by an officer of Howe's army:

"Thus to suffer the shattered remains of the rebel troops, a set of naked dispirited fugitives, encumbered with baggage, to run a race of ninety miles, and outstrip the flower of the British army, three times their number, appears to be an omission, not to give it another name, without example. . . .

"In the catalogue of military errors and misconduct, I will venture to assert, this appears so singular that it almost stands without example:—yet this march was extolled in the public papers, and drew applause from the deceived and credulous multitude."—[Capt. Hall] *The History of the Civil War in America. By an officer of the Army*, 2nd. ed. (London, 1780), pp. 221-3.

[36] *N.J.A.*, 2nd S., Vol. I, p. 367.

lingered at the Raritan by order of their commander. Cornwallis, in turn, said he had understood it to be Howe's order
that he should remain at New Brunswick; but he voluntarily
assumed a share of the responsibility for the delay, and
declared:

"Had I seen, that I could have struck a material stroke,
by moving forward, I certainly should have taken it upon
me to have done it."

Since Washington, however, had obtained such a good
start, Cornwallis did not see "any great object" for a further
pursuit of him:

"We arrived at Brunswic the night of the first of December. We had marched that day twenty miles, through exceeding bad roads. We subsisted only on the flour we found in the
country; and as the troops had been constantly marching,
ever since their first entrance into the Jerseys, they had no
time to bake their flour; the artillery horses, and baggage
horses of the army were quite tired; that sufficiently proves,
that we were not in a good condition to undertake a long
march. . . . If the enemy could not have passed at Trenton,
they might have marched down the east side of the Delaware. . . . We wanted reinforcement, in order to leave
troops for the communication between Brunswic and Amboy.
It was likewise necessary to pay some attention to a considerable body of troops, then passing the north river, under
General Lee."[37]

It requires no particularly keen critical sense to observe
a trace of disingenuousness in these explanations. It is obviously false, for instance, that the British troops had been
"constantly marching ever since their first entrance into the
Jerseys," unless their officers had kept them walking around
and around their quarters. Moreover, Cornwallis was forced
to admit upon further questioning that his troops were suffi-

[37] Sir William Howe, *Observations upon . . . Letters to a Nobleman* (London, 1781), pp. 65-6.

ciently rested to have left New Brunswick before they did.
One finds it difficult to see why it should have been considered a disadvantage to the British had Washington been
forced to move "down the east side of the Delaware," into
a peninsula from which he could never hope to escape, and
where he would be exposed to attack from the sea and from
Delaware Bay. As for the communication between New
Brunswick and Perth Amboy, if it was at all threatened in
a province where the inhabitants were hastening in throngs
to the British with offers of assistance, it could easily have
been secured by using the three thousand men who on December 1 sailed from New York under the unwilling General
Clinton to conquer Rhode Island. Finally, the movement
of the American force under Lee, though it excited some
speculation, was ignored with impunity when the British
troops finally did set out for the Delaware.

We are forced to conclude that Cornwallis was deliberately giving the investigators a false explanation of the
delay at New Brunswick, and was trying to shield his former
superior from too harsh a censure for his conduct. What,
then, were the real causes of Howe's strange procrastination?
The assumption of incompetence cannot be maintained in
view of his earlier military record and of his achievements
at the battles of Long Island and Brandywine Creek. An
explanation much favored by writers of some years ago—
that Howe's luxurious and notoriously loose style of living
sapped his vitality and called down upon him a species of
divine judgment in the form of military irresolution—was
more impressive in the nineteenth century than in this less
didactic age. The so-called art of war does not demand the
noblest human qualities; and debauchery is not necessarily
incompatible with successful generalship. Channing's suggestion that the professional officers and soldiers of the British
army "had no desire to endure the hardships of winter cam-

paigning, or to see hostilities come to a sudden termination"[38] does not adequately meet the case for the period of the autumn and open early winter of 1776.

According to one recent biographer of Washington, Cornwallis, somewhat surprised to find the Americans receding before him, pushed forward warily and occupied much more territory than had been included in his original plans. He was cautious about pressing his adversary too closely, for "the British general was well aware of Washington's ability, though some Americans of a later generation seem not to be."[39] In this connection, however, it is necessary to remember that by the winter of 1776, the American commander-in-chief had given few evidences of outstanding military ability, and that his recent career was marked by a series of failures which, though they may not have been attributable to him, tended to undermine confidence in him even in some American circles, and were by no means calculated to overawe his veteran antagonists. Furthermore, it is highly improbable that the British, whose intelligence service functioned with admirable efficiency throughout the war, and who had many friends in New Jersey, could remain unaware of the demoralized state of the American army during its retreat, particularly since British prisoners being exchanged seem to have passed freely through the American lines and could observe the facts.[40]

In the face of these objections to the "caution" theory, the historian who has made the most searching investigation into Howe's conduct comes to a very similar conclusion. Despite the successes of the British in the campaign of 1776, he asserts, their commander had become more pessimistic as the year wore on. He believed that another campaign would be

[38] Edward Channing, *A History of the United States* (New York, 1926-1927), Vol. III, p. 232. By permission of The Macmillan Company, publishers.
[39] John C. Fitzpatrick, *George Washington Himself: A Common-Sense Biography Written from His Manuscripts* (Indianapolis, 1933), p. 269. Used by special permission of the publishers, The Bobbs-Merrill Company.
[40] Washington, *Writings*, Vol. VI, p. 327.

necessary to finish the war, and thought that America would need to be subdued by a piecemeal occupation spreading gradually over the continent. Hence, when the revelations of Washington's weakness invited him to extend his lines for the winter beyond the area embraced in his original plans, it was with hesitation that he took advantage of the unexpected possibilities.[41]

A stimulating theory, which was shadowed forth in the writings of Joseph Galloway and of the contemporary British historian, Charles Stedman, who freely plagiarized him, has been most elaborately worked out by a recent biographer of Howe.[42] According to it, the British commander-in-chief, who belonged to the Whig party, was from political convictions not anxious to annihilate American resistance. His family, too, was closely associated with the history of the colonies, and he himself possessed a high regard for the Americans. Hence he placed more hope in his function as one of the commissioners for conciliation appointed by the King than in his military capacity. What he wished to do, rather than utterly to crush and embitter the Americans, was to overawe them by a show of force, and thereby induce them to submit voluntarily to his plan of conciliation.[43]

Even if the biographer, carried away by enthusiasm for his theory, can be accused of placing a strained interpretation upon a number of Howe's utterances, the idea appears to be fundamentally reasonable, particularly when modified by some of the other explanations. Howe was an easy-going and good-natured soldier schooled in the eighteenth century military tradition of slow and ponderous movement. With winter coming on and the attractions of a season in New York to beckon him—not always with too chaste a lure—he would be much more inclined to let the shattered and feeble

[41] Troyer S. Anderson, *The Command of the Howe Brothers during the American Revolution* (New York and London, 1936), pp. 183-4, 204-6, 208-9.
[42] Bellamy Partridge, *Sir Billy Howe* (London, New York, Toronto, 1932).
[43] *ibid.*, pp. 101-2.

American army fall to pieces of its own helplessness, dragging its cause with it into oblivion, than to allow it a heroic
end in battle. If pursued vigorously, it might dodge into the
mountains and escape; on the other hand if, left alone, it
should not disintegrate during the winter, then a soundly
posted British force, not too dangerously extended, would
be in a good position to resume activity in the spring.

Certainly all appearances at the close of 1776 sanctioned
such an analysis of the situation. Washington himself nearly
despaired, and the cause of the Revolutionists seemed almost
forsaken. Had it not been for Howe's fatal error in exagger-
ating the extent of the disruptive forces, underestimating
Washington's boldness under the spur of necessity, and care-
lessly cantoning the royal troops in a scattered and vulnerable chain of posts, the story of the winter and of America
might have been quite different. Defection from the Revolutionary cause, so widespread in New Jersey and rapidly pene-
trating other parts of the country, must inevitably have
grown in strength had the victorious army maintained its
conquests, and might well have undone the work of the past
year and a half, and swept the upstart governments out of
power.

General Alexander McDougall, who was in Morristown
in the middle of December and could watch the progress of
demoralization even in that last stronghold of rebellious zeal
in the state, cherished no optimistic illusions as to the future.
"When I anticipate the bad consequences that will result
to the common cause from the submission of this State," he
wrote to Washington on December 22, "it renders me almost
unfit for any business."[44]

If General Howe had not made the one mistake in disposing of his troops for the winter, those very Loyalists like
Galloway who were soon crying out at his weakness and
indecision might have been hailing him instead as a states-

---

[44] *Am. Arch.*, 5th S., Vol. III, p. 1365.

manlike victor who knew how to combine firmness with moderation. Once the crisis was past and the battles of Trenton and Princeton had restored confidence in American arms, the unique opportunity for realizing Howe's policy was forever gone. But the British general's very failure made it impossible for him to explain his policy to a world which has no sympathy for unsuccessful theories; and he and his subordinates were driven to flimsy excuses which have satisfied no one.

All this, of course, is mere conjecture; but there is no doubt that the state of New Jersey was almost as completely cowed by the deliberate and nearly bloodless advance of the royal army as it would have been had Washington's force been crushed in fierce battle. As Howe's troops penetrated farther from the Hudson, the whole countryside fell into the greatest alarm and confusion. People whose homes lay in the path of the invader hastened to remove themselves and their portable property out of the reach of the British and Hessian troops, whose evil reputation preceded them. In Newark, even the Puritan Sabbath, heretofore faithfully observed by the stern Presbyterians, did not check the frantic bustle of the inhabitants as they carried their goods to places of greater security.[45] In Evesham, "there was a great to Do Moveing of Goods and talk of hideing of Earthly treasure."[46] At Princeton, the College of New Jersey was hastily disbanded by the "deeply afflicted" President Witherspoon, who bade farewell to his students "in a very affecting manner," doubtless wondering whether he should ever teach there again in peace and honor, or whether he should hang as a traitor before the institution reopened.[47] When the British were reported to be approaching Princeton and Trenton, inhabitants of those towns were roused from their beds in the middle of the night to flee; and the ferry houses on the Dela-

---

[45] Hunter, Diary, Nov. 24, 1776.   [46] N.J.H.S.P., Vol. LII, p. 224.
[47] "A Campaign Journal, Nov. 29, 1776, to May 6, 1777," in *Princeton Standard*, New Series, Vol. III, No. 18 (May 1, 1863).

ware were so crowded with frightened civilians and sick and wounded soldiers, all waiting for a chance to cross to Pennsylvania and safety, that to one impressionable young girl the scene looked like the Day of Judgment.[48]

The state legislature fled from Princeton to Trenton and thence to Burlington; soon it broke up and its members did what they could for their own safety.[49] The speaker of the Assembly, John Hart, found his prosperous home in Hopewell ravaged by marauders, his wife dead, and his children driven to the wilds of Sourland Mountain, where he, too, was obliged to take refuge among the rocks for several weeks.[50] Government by the Revolutionary authorities virtually ceased to function. On December 22, General McDougall wrote from Morristown:

"This State is totally deranged, without Government, or officers, civil or military, in it, that will act with any spirit. Many of them have gone to the enemy for protection, others are out of the State, and the few that remain are mostly indecisive in their conduct."[51]

As the prestige of the Revolution fell in New Jersey, the Tories began to assert themselves, and were joined in their protestations of loyalty by countless of their fellow citizens who had not hitherto shown any marked affection for King or Parliament. As early as the beginning of October, some of the warier inhabitants had begun to suspect which way the wind was about to blow, and to trim their canvas accordingly. Stephen Kemble, son of Peter Kemble of Morristown and deputy adjutant-general in the British army, notes in his journal under date of October 7:

"My brother Bob. came last night from Jersey, having with another Gentleman found means to pass the Guard at

[48] Samuel Miller, *The Life of Samuel Miller* . . . (Philadelphia, 1869), p. 147.
[49] William S. Stryker, *The Battles of Trenton and Princeton* (Boston and New York, 1898), p. 13.
[50] *N.J.H.S.P.*, N.S., Vol. X, p. 380.   [51] *Am. Arch.*, 5th S., Vol. III, pp. 1364-5.

the Highlands near the Light House; says that some of the most Intelligent People of Jersey are struck with the Progress we have made, and that they think more justly of the Cause of Government, but that the Ignorant and more extensive part of the Province are in their false error, and still believe the King's Arms have not made that Progress they really have."[52]

After the campaign in Westchester and the fall of Forts Washington and Lee, great numbers of Jerseymen, who could scarcely fail to be "struck" by such progress, began ostentatiously to think more justly of the cause of government. Every mile that the royal troops advanced into the country swelled the number of persons who eagerly renounced their false error. Prudent men of property like William Bayard of Hoboken, who had found it expedient to run and double with the hares when the hares were flourishing under the summer sun, now joined the hounds and were soon baying in full pursuit of their former friends.[53]

General Howe did his utmost to encourage this movement. He offered a free pardon to those who had taken up arms against their sovereign, provided they subscribed an oath of allegiance to the King; and to such persons he issued "protections" which forbade his followers to molest them in person, family, or property. Anxious to save their possessions from the ravages of the victorious soldiers, great numbers of Jerseymen took the oath—over twenty-seven hundred before the winter was over, according to Howe.[54]

Surrender to what seemed inevitable defeat was not confined to the rank and file: some who had been most active in the Revolution, finding themselves in the power of the British, renounced their political past. Such were two members of the Legislature, Henry Garritse of Essex and John Covenhoven of Monmouth; the latter at least was carried

[52] Kemble, *Journal*, p. 92.   [53] *N.J.A.*, 2nd S., Vol. I, p. 412 n.
[54] Howe to Germain, March 25, 1777: MSS. Colonial Office, London: Class 5, Vol. 177, p. 127 (transcript in MSS. Division, Library of Congress).

off to New York by Tories, and made his recantation while a prisoner.[55] Samuel Tucker of Trenton, a leading spirit of the subversive movement for years, president of the Provincial Congress at the time the state constitution was adopted, second judge of the new Supreme Court, and one of the responsible Treasury officials, left Trenton on the day it passed from American into British possession. He remained out of the clutches of the enemy for several days; then, worried by the condition of his sick wife, who was imploring him to return home, he attempted to comply with her plea. On the way he was captured by a roving band of Tories, and was held in confinement for three days, during which time he learned that most of the private valuables and the public money which he had concealed from the British had been found and confiscated. In an effort to recover as large a part of these losses as he could, and to live peaceably at home, Tucker took a protection from Howe. This action was a grievous error. He never saw his phaeton, horse, cows, silver plate, or money again, and such of his mortgages and bonds as he recovered were picked up at Princeton after the British left. On the other hand, by compromising his principles, he lost his reputation, and was forced by general disapproval to retire from public life.[56]

Tucker's defection was serious enough; but an even more distressing one occurred at the same time. Richard Stockton, brilliant lawyer and signer of the Declaration of Independence, was taken prisoner at the home of John Covenhoven in Monmouth County at the same time as his host. While in captivity, he was subjected to such brutal treatment that the Continental Congress protested; and under the harsh pressure he signed Howe's Declaration and promised to refrain from

[55] *Votes and Proceedings of the General Assembly of the State of New Jersey*, Feb. 11 and March 4, 1777.

[56] *N.J.A.*, Vol. X, pp. 270 n.-272 n.; following MSS. in Room 118, State Library, Trenton: Tucker to John Hart, Jan. 20 and Feb. 4, 1777; affidavit by Tucker, Feb. 15, 1777; affidavits by Randle Mitchell and Samuel Abbott, Feb. 14, 1777.

further intermeddling in public affairs. Upon his release, his action became known, and he was "much spoken against for his conduct." Although he signed in December 1777 the oaths of abjuration and allegiance prescribed by the Legislature, he was never again active in political matters. Whether, despite his previous record of service, he would have been forced by public resentment to remain in retirement like Tucker cannot be determined, for he was condemned to inactivity by shattered health up to his death from cancer in 1781.[57]

To aid this widespread return to the old allegiance, British propaganda was not wanting. It did not stop with the negative policy of issuing delusive "protections" against plundering. At least one royal commissary at Pennington is said to have dispensed a large quantity of pork to the "Poor & protected Inhabitants."[58] Such benevolence was an agreeable surprise to the people of New Jersey. From the commander of the victorious army they had nothing to expect but a stone; instead, he gave them bread. What was more, he gave them circuses, for his well drilled and resplendently uniformed troops contrasted strikingly in appearance with the tattered rebels. Howe well knew that the joining of mag-

[57] Edmund C. Burnett, ed., Letters of Members of the Continental Congress, 8 vols. (Washington, 1931-1936), Vol. II, p. 243 and n.; N.J.A., Vol. X, p. 430 n. Until recently, the story of Stockton's temporary apostasy has been either unknown or suppressed, but the evidence quoted by Burnett seems conclusive. There can be no doubt as to the authenticity of Stockton's signature to the oaths of abjuration and allegiance, Dec. 22, 1777, still preserved in the Public Record Office in Trenton. Taking these oaths may have been merely a routine method of revoking adherence to Howe's Declaration. Nevertheless, one cannot help wondering why, if there was no widespread disapproval, perhaps even distrust, of Stockton, they were required of a man whose health had been critically impaired, probably as a result of his harsh treatment while in captivity. It was not until two years later (Nov. 8, 1779) that Dr. Benjamin Rush could write: "Our worthy friend Mr. Stockton continues to mend. All his physicians agree now in pronouncing his recovery complete." (Princeton University Library MSS., AM 1255.) Soon after this the cancer was discovered which resulted in his death.

[58] Philemon Dickinson to George Washington, Yardly's Farms, Dec. 24, 1776, in Washington Papers (Library of Congress), Vol. 38.

nanimity to dazzling achievement has always been an effective policy, and he cannot be blamed if he thought it was succeeding admirably in New Jersey. Everyone else agreed with him.

Many who had fled upon the first approach of the British now openly accepted the changed situation by returning with their families to their homes.[59] Loyalist farmers, rejoicing at the advent of the King's army, hastened to it with offers of assistance, placed their wagons at its disposal for the transportation of stores, and busied themselves gathering provisions for the troops. The country people gladly sold their cattle and produce to feed the soldiers: at Bordentown, for instance, a "very considerable magazine" of provisions was collected during the few days the British were there.[60]

The cooperation of the inhabitants with the army did not stop with such measures. From the beginning of November, when it became clear that New Jersey was to be invaded, Loyalists had been forming associations to join the British as fighters upon their arrival. Cortlandt Skinner, who had received from Howe a commission as brigadier general with authority to raise in the state five battalions of five hundred privates each, under the command of "gentlemen of the country," was joined by several hundred recruits in November and December, though his force never amounted to half the number provided for in his commission. Many Tories who did not care to enlist for extended service were nevertheless willing to assist the British army as loyal militia for the time being, and to avenge themselves upon their Whig neighbors for their long persecution. Receiving arms and ammunition from the royal forces, they set to work with a will disarming the Whigs and settling old grudges.[61]

[59] Waldeck, *Tagebuch*, p. 25.
[60] Fraser, *op. cit.*, Vol. I, pp. 561, 649-50; Galloway, *Examination*, pp. 18-19; Stryker, *Trenton and Princeton*, pp. 343-4.
[61] *Am. Arch.*, 5th S., Vol. III, pp. 601, 1169, 1174; Howe, *Observations*, p. 52; Jones, *op. cit.*, p. 32. An example of the malicious triumph with which many of the repressed Tories began to assert themselves at this time is found in

The collapse of Revolutionary prestige extended beyond the areas occupied by the British troops. From Monmouth and Sussex Counties, lying to either side of Howe's line of march, recruits streamed in to join the conquerors, and many a fat pig and cow from a prosperous Monmouth farm found its way into the pots of the King's soldiers.[62] Several prominent Loyalists[63] were appointed commissioners under Lord and General Howe, to administer the oath of allegiance to the King, and give protections to the people of Monmouth. In pursuance of their instructions, they posted public notices commanding all able-bodied inhabitants between the ages of sixteen and fifty who were capable of bearing arms to assemble at Freehold on December 30 to take the oath; fur-

a deposition taken for the Council of Safety some months later (now in the Public Record Office, Trenton):

"Personaly apeared before me Joseph Lawrence Esqr one of the Justics of the County of monmouth in the state of New jersey Catherine Cox of full age and was Sworne on the Holy Envenglis of Allmity god and Disposeth and said that She was at Wm Dansors on the 22th Day of December last and Jacob Dansor came thear and Asked her what Does the whiges think now & let you father go and take apertickson [a protection] and go about and let his tung run as I have heard him and I will inform against him and after Some talk he Said you Seem to [chawe ?] about yor father who the D—l is your father and he Sd he would Say as much about his owne father and the sd. Daseor said their is old Chamberlin I am the one that will give in his Estate for he had it all yet but he wont hav it long and he was a Dam-d fooll and Den[ied ?] his owne hand ritten and would lye and when the milisha called for his Sun he consealed him and if he wanst to know whearin he was a lyer let him come to me and I let him know and if he wont Come to me I go him and the Sad Danser said thears old [Cahail ?] I will turne hangman for him my self. and said it was in his power to have ropes about five or Six of their Necks and she toald him if it lays in your power I belive you would Do it he said no I Doant want to hurt anybodey but I have authoury to Do it and it must be Dun and he Said he had a pertiction this three Mounths agon but Swour he dare not Showe it for fear that his Neighbours would kill him that the whiges would all be glad to rune to the Toreys for pertictions and She toald him that none would Come to him and he Said would all be glad to Come to him yet and forther this Deponant Says Not

Sworn before me this 13th Day   Catherine Cox
of April 1777
Jos Lawrence Justus"

[62] Jones, op. cit., p. 32; Fraser, op. cit., pp. 649-50.
[63] John Taylor of Middletown, John Lawrence and his son Elisha, of Upper Freehold, and John Wardell of Shrewsbury.

ther, they ordered the county militia to assemble in arms for the support of the Crown.[64]

In the other direction, the invaders seem to have penetrated no farther northward into Bergen County than the New Bridge, but the whole region up to Tappan in the state of New York became enemy country for any American with a Revolutionary record. Armed by the munificence of their royal master, the triumphant Bergen Tories scoured the countryside, disarming, abusing, and plundering the Whig minority. Their recruiting parties moved freely about Hackensack, Paramus, and Tappan, and even approached Ringwood.[65]

At the opposite end of the state, along the lower Delaware, there was no such violent reversal of conditions; but the prosperous Quakers maintained an attitude of cold aloofness from the Revolutionary movement,[66] and the back-country settlers, who had for the most part been zealous supporters of the new state, split into two hostile parties as the more timid ones deserted the apparently hopeless cause. "Many concealed themselves in the woods," writes Pastor Collin of Swedesborough, "or within their houses; other people were forced to carry arms; others offered opposition and refused to go. The people were afraid to visit the church, because the authorities took the opportunity to get both horses and men."[67]

In the districts actually occupied by the British, the situation appeared even more hopeless for the Whigs. The conquering troops, one of their officers tells us, were filled with confidence and pleasant expectations, "the whole Jerseys seeming to submit to the British Government, & to give

[64] Depositions of David Forman, April 14, 1777, and of Abraham Hendricks, April 5, 1777, in Public Record Office, State House, Trenton.

[65] *Am. Arch.*, 5th S., Vol. III, pp. 833, 1169, 1174; Fraser, *op. cit.*, p. 561.

[66] *Am. Arch.*, 5th S., Vol. III, p. 1342; also broadside issued by a "Meeting for Sufferings, held in Philadelphia, for Pennsylvania and New Jersey," Dec. 20, 1776.

[67] Collin, *Journal*, pp. 236-7.

every possible assistance to the Kings Troops."[68] Most of the irreconcilables had fled from the state, and those inhabitants who remained at home intended to get along excellently with the invaders. So cordial were the relations between the citizens of Trenton and their military guests that General Philemon Dickinson of the New Jersey militia had great difficulty in finding a spy who would take the risk of visiting the town.[69]

All things considered, it is not difficult to understand why Washington privately expressed the opinion, in a letter to his brother, that "the Conduct of the Jerseys has been most Infamous."[70] Nevertheless, he still believed, as he wrote to General Heath, that "the defection of the people in the lower part of Jersey, has been as much owing to the want of an Army to look the Enemy in the face, as to any other cause"; and he hoped to strengthen his force enough to be able to return to New Jersey and keep the British from having things all their own way. Unless he recrossed the Delaware he had no hope of being able to keep the enemy for very long on the east side: "it is next to impossible," he said, "to guard a shore for sixty miles, with less than half the enemy's numbers; when by force or stratagem they may suddenly attempt a passage in many different places." The only hope of saving Philadelphia, in his opinion, lay in the speedy arrival of Major General Charles Lee with reinforcements.[71]

Day followed day, however, and still there was no sign of Lee. Washington had written to him from Hackensack on November 21, explaining the need of preserving "an Appearance of an Army" to oppose the enemy's main force in New Jersey, and urging him to cross from the east side of the Hudson to join forces with him. This initial summons was followed by further and more pressing ones as the

[68] Glyn, *Journal*, p. 31.
[69] Trenton Hist. Soc., *History of Trenton*, Vol. I, p. 120.
[70] Washington, *Writings*, Vol. VI, p. 397.   [71] *ibid.*, Vol. VI, pp. 346, 393.

expected force failed to appear. Lee, however, waited days before he started, and then proceeded at a snail's pace. Although he offered various excuses for his procrastination, the fact was that he had no real intention of joining Washington. He well knew, and indeed heartily shared, the opinion held by many persons, in both British and American circles, that he was Washington's superior in military skill, as he undoubtedly was in experience, having held a commission as lieutenant colonel in the British army and seen some service on the European continent. The prestige of the commander-in-chief was badly diminished by the recent disasters of the army, especially at Fort Washington, and Lee saw an opportunity to supplant him as the savior of America by winning some brilliantly contrasting successes. His plan, as he informed General Heath on December 9, was nothing less than "to reconquer (if I may so express myself) the Jerseys."[72]

To the urgent messages from Washington, Lee did not always reply; when he did, he explained in a kindly, almost paternal manner the advantages of harrying the British on the flank and rear. Such a policy was indeed not bad in itself: Lee's force encouraged the militia and caused the enemy some anxiety; but, as Washington pointed out in a desperate appeal on December 10, a diversion in the rear was of little value if there was nothing to oppose the British in front, and the utmost exertions that could be made by both forces combined would barely suffice to save Philadelphia. Still Lee answered evasively; and Washington wrote him with well merited asperity on December 14:

"I have so frequently mentioned our Situation, and the necessity of your Aid, that it is painfull to me to add a Word upon the Subject. Let me once more request and entreat you to march immediately."[73]

[72] *Am. Arch.*, 5th S., Vol. III, p. 1138.
[73] Washington, *Writings*, Vol. VI, pp. 336 n., 340-1, 370; Münchhausen. Journal, Dec. 10, Dec. 11, 1776.

Even before Washington penned these lines, however, they were rendered superfluous by the obliging action of a British officer who had never seen the American commander and certainly had no idea of the service he was rendering him. On the morning of December 13 a detachment of thirty British light dragoons under one Lieutenant Colonel Harcourt, patrolling at a greater distance from its lines than was its custom, discovered that General Lee was staying in a house near Basking Ridge, at some distance from the body of his troops, and with no protection between him and the enemy but a couple of pickets who were overpowered before they could give an alarm. The house was surrounded by the dragoons, and its distinguished occupant was forced to surrender, by a threat of setting fire to the building. Lee was whisked away on horseback to the British lines, where his delusions of grandeur wilted rapidly. He was refused parole, on the ground that as a rebel and a deserter from the British service he had forfeited his life; he was not permitted to write; and he was kept constantly under surveillance.[74] Before long, he was packed off to New York, where he did considerable service—probably unintentional—to the Americans by giving unsound advice to General Howe.

The capture of Lee was a stroke of good fortune for Washington, for it released the troops which had been tied up in New Jersey, and which now marched without delay, under the command of Major General Sullivan, to join the main army. To most Americans, however, the loss of the conceited general appeared to be a severe blow to their cause, for they had accepted him at his own valuation. The British were jubilant. *"Victoria!"* exulted a Hessian adjutant of General Howe in his journal. "We have got our hands on General Lee, the only rebel general we had to fear."[75]

[74] Münchhausen, Journal, Dec. 13, Dec. 14; Glyn, *Journal*, pp. 32-3.
[75] Münchhausen, Journal, Dec. 13, 1776.

In the opinion of such men, this final misfortune of the Americans, following upon a whole season of reverses, might well lead to the collapse of the rebellion. Already British officials were regarding victory as assured, and beginning to ponder upon what should be done to keep the rebellious colonists in order when the last sparks of their resistance were extinguished. "Upon the whole," reported Ambrose Serle, on November 26, "it does not seem a sanguine Opinion to those upon the spot, who know the Disposition and Resources of this People, that the Heart of the Rebellion is now really broken, and that a vigorous and continued Exertion of our Force will shortly reduce this Country to Subjection, if not to Reason. Perhaps, some new Arrangements in colonial Polity must be drawn out *at Home* to preserve that Dependence, which has already been so dearly purchased."[76]

A week later the same observer was happy to acquaint Dartmouth with a report, which he thought well substantiated, that the American General Putnam had declared:

"We all think that our Cause is nearly ruined; that as our Army is just disbanding, because their Time mostly expires on the 1st of December, and the King's Troops are severely pushing us, we shall not be able to get another together; and that, if we could, they could make no sort of Resistance, in the plain Country to the Southward, against such an Army as is brought against us."[77]

This promising state of affairs seemed to justify Howe's decision of December 12 to put his troops into winter quarters. What was the use of chasing the miserable American army when it was disintegrating of its own accord, its only good general had been captured, and the entire population seemed to be fast losing confidence in it? All that was necessary was to maintain a hold upon the territory already

[76] Serle to Dartmouth, Nov. 26, 1776, in Stevens, *Facsimiles*, Vol. XXIV, No. 2046.
[77] Same to same, *ibid.*, No. 2048.

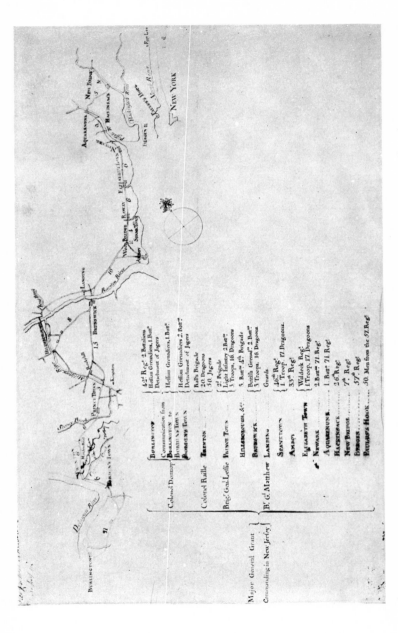

"The chain, I own, is rather too extensive." Howe's distribution of his troops in New Jersey for winter quarters, December 1776. Reproduced by permission of the William L. Clements Library.

occupied, to keep the inhabitants from relapsing into "false error," and time would destroy the rebels. So Howe and Cornwallis rode light-heartedly back to New York, leaving a chain of garrisons from Bordentown to Powles Hook. On the map, this line of posts looks tenuous and insecure; and Howe had some qualms about it.

"The chain, I own, is rather too extensive," he wrote to Lord George Germain on December 20, "but I was induced to occupy Burlington, to cover the county of Monmouth, in which there are many loyal inhabitants, and trusting to the general submission of the country to the southward of this chain, and to the strength of the corps placed in the advanced posts, I conclude the troops will be in perfect security. Lord Cornwallis having desired to return to Britain, the command in Jersey is given to Major-general Grant, in whose approved good conduct I place the greatest confidence."[78]

Neither the recipient nor the writer of this letter was aware of certain inaccuracies contained in it. Burlington was not occupied by royal troops for more than a few hours before they had to leave it; Howe's trust in the submission of southern New Jersey was somewhat too great; and before long it became evident that the security of the troops was not quite perfect. Lord Cornwallis, too, was obliged to restrain for some time his desire to go home.

For the present, however, Howe's description of affairs seemed correct enough. Major General James Grant made his headquarters at New Brunswick, and his troops were distributed among the numerous posts. The normal position of the Hessians in the royal line was at the left, and accordingly they were given the same relative place in the cantonments. Although this meant assigning them to the three most dangerous posts in the chain—Burlington, Bordentown, and Trenton—they had displayed such bravery and dependability during the campaign, particularly at the storming of

[78] *N.J.A.*, 2nd S., Vol. I, p. 368.

Fort Washington, that Howe saw no good reason for insulting them by placing them at points less exposed. Three regiments of Hessian infantry were stationed at Trenton under
Colonel Rall, and three battalions of Hessian grenadiers, a
company of Hessian Jägers, the Forty-Second Regiment, and
a company of British light infantry were quartered at Bordentown, Mansfield Square, and the Black Horse Tavern[79]
under the able Colonel von Donop. The latter had general
oversight of the Hessian troops from Black Horse to Trenton, who numbered, according to Howe, more than three
thousand men. The commander-in-chief gave orders that
Rall should erect "such field Works as may be necessary for
the security of his Quarters," and that patrols of light horse
flanked by infantry should be "constantly made from the
different Quarters." With these dispositions made, Howe
apparently felt that all steps necessary for safety had been
taken, and he turned willingly to the matter of having a
pleasant winter in New York.[80]

Lord Cornwallis, whose tastes did not coincide with those
of his superior, declined the delights of the American city
in favor of a visit home. He would come back in the spring,
wrote one of Howe's adjutants, "if there is another campaign, which we doubt." Certainly there would not be
another, continued the commentator, unless the American
Congress could keep its people in arms through promises of
assistance from a French fleet and a French and Spanish
army. Should it not succeed in this, there would unquestion-
ably be peace; for "the short but conquering campaign and
the capture of their best general, on whom they most depended, depresses the rebels mightily."[81]

[79] Now Columbus.

[80] Stryker, *Trenton and Princeton*, pp. 46-7; Sir William Howe, *The Narrative of Lieut. Gen. Sir William Howe* . . . (London, 1781), pp. 7-9; Howe,
Observations, p. 68; Glyn, *Journal*, p. 32.

[81] Münchhausen, Journal, Dec. 26, 1776.

Such were the pleasing prospects that filled the minds of the British high command. If the Hessians, crowded uncomfortably into the homes of Quaker farmers to whom they were obviously as unwelcome as American soldiers, or going about their duties with increasingly nervous uncertainty whether they might be picked off by concealed civilian snipers, felt less happy about the situation, their uneasiness never communicated itself to General Howe. He remained ignorant of three important facts: the incompetence of Colonel Rall to defend an exposed outpost like Trenton; Washington's hitherto unrevealed military ability and occasional audacity; and the growing resentment among the New Jersey population over the rapacity and licentiousness of the royal troops.

The honeymoon between the conquering army and the overawed inhabitants was soon over. Howe later declared: "My principal object in so great an extension of the cantonments was to afford protection to the inhabitants, that they might experience the difference between his majesty's government, and that to which they were subject by the rebel leaders."[82] A marked difference was indeed experienced by the inhabitants, but its only effect was to make them wish heartily that the rebel leaders might return.

On June 29, before a man had debarked from Howe's fleet, lying off Sandy Hook, the commander had forbidden plundering by any of his men, on pain of instant execution.[83] From the very beginning, however, this prohibition was a dead letter: Manhattan Island and Westchester County were mercilessly pillaged. The march of the British baggage column, according to Stephen Kemble, deputy adjutant general of the army, was "marked by the Licentiousness of the Troops, who committed every species of Rapine and plunder." He found the conduct of the Hessians particularly

---

[82] Howe, *Narrative*, p. 9.
[83] *Collections of the New-York Historical Society*, 1883, p. 383.

outrageous, and, as a former inhabitant of New Jersey, and one who still had relatives and friends in that state, he shuddered at the thought of its fate when he heard the army was to be sent there.[84]

Kemble's forebodings were more than justified. To be sure, the British officers issued more admonitions against ravaging the countryside. The day after he landed in New Jersey, Cornwallis gave out the following order:

"As the Inhabitants of this Country are in general well affected to Government, Earl Cornwallis expects the Commanding Officers of Brigades and Corps will exert themselves to prevent plundering amongst the Troops."[85] This instruction was much less drastic in tone than Howe's ruling of five months before; and the next order on the subject, promulgated by Howe on December 14 as the army was going into winter quarters, was even milder, partaking of the nature of an entreaty rather than of a command:

"The Commander-in-Chief calls upon the Commanding Officers to exert themselves in preserving the greatest Regularity and strictest Discipline in their respective Quarters, particularly attending to the Protection of the Inhabitants and their Property in their several Districts."[86]

Whether Howe's tone was threatening or pleading, however, it was equally ineffective in curbing the ravages of his followers. One inhabitant of Princeton wrote bitterly:

"Gen¹. How has made no other use of these good and kind orders, but only to serve us as Joab served Amasa when he took him fast by his beard with his right hand to Kiss him, while with the Other he Smote him in the fifth Rib and shed out his bowels to the ground, so here Gen¹. How had fast hold of us by the beard of conquest with one hand to kiss us with his good orders while, with his Cruel bad orders he

[84] Kemble, *Journal*, pp. 96, 97-8, 102.   [85] Glyn, *Journal*, p. 27.
[86] *Collections of the New-York Historical Society*, 1883, p. 425.

gave us a Mortal Blow and shed out our bowels to ye ground by their Insults Roberys & Plunderings."[87]

Upon crossing the Passaic River, the invaders found themselves in a promised land, where everything they could desire was theirs for the taking. They wasted little time in exploiting the golden opportunity. Many a page has been written to show that the Hessians were worse than the British, or the British worse than the Hessians; whatever may have been the case, the two in combination brought ruin and misery to a prosperous countryside. The chief demand of the army was for livestock and agricultural produce to feed the troops. These it seized with little formality and frequently with no compensation; but this was only the beginning. When the troops came to a community like Elizabeth-Town, where the homes of such prosperous Whigs as Mayor Isaac Woodruff and William Peartree Smith stood at their mercy, they held high carnival. Silver plate, jewelry, clothing, trinkets, horses, wines, books, surgical instruments, warming-pans, miscellaneous household furnishings, even such strange items as plaster-of-Paris busts with carved pedestals, a "Large Mahogany Case of Wax Works," and a marble slab disappeared before the greed of the conquerors. General Erskine, according to one reliable authority, had his room in Newark "furnished from a neighboring house with mahogany chairs and tables, a considerable part of which was taken away with his baggage when he went to Elizabeth Town." His subalterns followed this enlightening example, and what the officers left the common soldiers took.

No home was too wealthy or too humble to be visited by the ravaging hordes. Long and detailed lists of the depredations were compiled under oath shortly after the war, and, even allowing for exaggerations and falsifications, a reading of them today causes the imagination to reel. It is possible

[87] Varnum Lansing Collins, ed., *A Brief Narrative of the Ravages of the British and Hessians at Princeton in 1776-77* (Princeton, 1906), p. 27.

to understand what the soldiers might want of the countless scarlet cloaks, gold sleeve-buttons, silver knee-buckles, velvet and buckskin breeches, broadcloth coats, swanskin waistcoats, and linen shirts that they appropriated; but of what use to them, one asks, were damask napkins, tablecloths, pillowcases, cambric aprons, shifts, silk bonnets, lace handkerchiefs, bombazine gowns, and quilted petticoats?[88]

Some of these more delicate articles, we may suppose, went to the crowds of women who followed the army and who, though notoriously lacking in refinement of manner, were willing helpers in the work of removing property from its former owners. The manner in which the soldiers and their fair assistants operated while pillaging is well indicated by one man's account of what he saw at Piscataway:

"The men of the village had retired on the approach of the enemy. Some women and children were left. I heard their lamentations as the soldiers carried off their furniture, scattered the feathers of beds to the winds, and piled up looking-glasses, with frying-pans in the same heap, by the roadside. The soldier would place a female camp follower as a guard upon the spoil, while he returned to add to the treasure."[89]

Depredations were not confined to the removal of such portables as took the fancy of the invaders. Widespread destruction was caused by the routine activities of the army. After using up such firewood as the inhabitants had stored up for their own use during the winter, the troops burned the loose planks and timber in the possession of carpenters, pried boards off shops, outhouses, and even dwelling houses, cut down fruit trees for fuel, and finally brought in the fences from the countryside surrounding the garrisons.

[88] See the lists of depredations committed by the British troops and their followers, now preserved in the State Library at Trenton, and the report of the committee of Congress appointed to inquire into the conduct of the enemy (printed in the *Pennsylvania Evening Post*, April 24 and 26 and May 10, 1777, and reprinted in *N.J.A.*, 2nd S., Vol. I, pp. 347-53 and 362-7).

[89] Dunlap, *op. cit.*, Vol. I, pp. 202-3.

By accident or design, a number of houses and gristmills burned down, and it did not go unremarked that these misfortunes usually happened to the property of prominent Revolutionists.[90] Such extreme instances of revenge, however, were sporadic rather than systematic. General Howe was still wedded to his policy of conciliation, and it was only after the cold-blooded Sir Henry Clinton, more realistic than Howe and far less good-natured, assumed command of the British forces in the summer of 1778 that a system of deliberate, wholesale destruction and terrorism was inaugurated.

Nevertheless, it was, of course, the active Whigs who suffered most during the last two months of the year 1776. A tribe of informers grew up, who pointed out to the British authorities such men as had borne arms against the King or had held office under the Revolutionary government. These disclosures afforded a fine pretext for declaring estates forfeited, seizing them, and destroying what could not be used. Even goods which had been left in the keeping of friends by fugitive Whigs could not escape the prying eyes of those who worked with the tireless and uncanny efficiency of hatred.[91]

Although recalcitrant Whigs were singled out as objects for the most conspicuous vengeance, they were by no means the only victims of the ravages. Anyone possessing desirable property was liable to be robbed of it, and to be abused in the bargain. Peaceful Quakers fared as badly as bellicose Presbyterians. A written "protection" was of no value to its holder: the Hessians could not read it, and the British paid no attention to it. Good Loyalists were pillaged as mercilessly as ardent rebels. With a certain malicious satisfaction, the Whigs circulated the story of one Nutman, " a remarkable Tory" of Newark, "who met the British troops with huzzas

---

[90] Collins, *Brief Narrative*, pp. 3-6; Cornelius C. Vermeule, "Some Revolutionary Incidents in the Raritan Valley," in *N.J.H.S.P.*, N.S., Vol. VI, pp. 76-8.
[91] Collins, *Brief Narrative*, p. 14.

of joy," but who was stripped by them of everything, even his shoes.[92]

Naturally, the Tories were almost beside themselves with anger. For long they had suffered every kind of indignity at the hands of the Whigs; and now, when they might reasonably expect at last to enjoy security and the spectacle of just vengeance visited upon their persecuting neighbors, they found themselves as greatly menaced in their property by the delivering army as ever they had been by the rebels. From this time on, Loyalist distrust of Howe grew steadily; before many years it was to ripen into bitter enmity and cause him some bad hours.[93]

Robbery and destruction of property were accompanied by violence directed against individuals. Concerning the personal abuse of the inhabitants by the royal soldiers, however, it is safe to make only the most general assertions. Every war multiplies instances of the brutality of which human nature is capable; and every war, too, produces its own crop of atrocity stories fabricated for the purpose of inflaming public opinion. In the period of the American Revolution there were no such highly organized propaganda machines as those which, during the World War, fed the flames of public hysteria with deliberately invented tales of cruelty and horror. But there were skilful psychologists among the leaders and publishers on both sides, many of whom, we may suppose, would not hesitate, in their enthu-

[92] Collins, *Brief Narrative*, pp. 10, 13-14; *N.J.A.*, 2nd S., Vol. I, p. 351; *N.J. H.S.P.*, N.S., Vol. XV, p. 511; Hall, *op. cit.*, p. 251.

[93] Joseph Galloway, the Philadelphia Loyalist, was with the British in New Jersey at this time (*N.J.A.*, 2nd S., Vol. II, p. 30), and was observing the abuses to which he testified before the House of Commons in 1780. (Galloway, *Examination*, pp. 43-4.) Another Loyalist from the same city, Joseph Stansbury, has left a bitter attack on Howe in verse, in the course of which he discusses the "protections":

> "This magical Mantle o'er Property thrown,
> Secur'd it from all sorts of Thieves—but his own!"

—"Gen¹. Howe vindicated by R. R.," in volume of "Loyalist Rhapsodies," MSS. Division, Library of Congress.

siasm for their cause, to accept and spread diligently rumors
of inhumanity which sober investigation might have proved
to be baseless fictions.

At the present time, it would be a hopeless task to investigate the countless stories which circulated and were believed about the atrocious conduct of the British and Hessian
troops in New Jersey. Reports of heartless abuses inflicted
upon old people and invalids and, of course, tales dealing
with the perennially effective theme of rape, gained widespread credence, though it is perhaps significant that most
of those which have been preserved are third- or fourth-hand
accounts, and very few come from the victims themselves
or from eyewitnesses. Such cases as the widely publicized
one of the sixteen (or seven) young women of Hopewell
(or Pennington) who fled to Sourland Mountain to escape
the lust of the soldiery, but were found and brought back
to camp, may be authentic; but the indefiniteness and variations of the narratives inspire reasonable doubt. All that
it is safe to conclude at present is that the occupied province
suffered such violence as might well be expected from ill-
disciplined troops during a brutal age. Restraints upon their
excesses were lax; for among both officers and men the contemptuous opinion was widespread that the Americans were
a people made bold by too much prosperity and had forfeited all rights by rebelling against their appointed sovereign.[94]

Under these circumstances, it was but natural that such
of the inhabitants as were not confirmed Loyalists quickly
developed a thorough dislike for the British. They might
not be willing to join the organized American forces, whose
cause still looked hopeless as they lingered on the far side
of the protecting Delaware; but there was no harm in picking

[94] Trevelyan, *op. cit.*, pp. 29-35; *N.J.A.*, 2nd S., Vol. I, pp. 210, 347-53, 362-7;
Am. Arch., 5th S., Vol. III, pp. 1188, 1376; Gordon, *Am. Rev.*, Vol II, pp. 414-15;
Münchhausen, Journal, Dec. 7, 1776; Ashbel Green, *The Life of Ashbel Green*
. . . (New York, 1849), p. 136.

off an occasional British or Hessian soldier from the bushes when it could be done with safety and secrecy. Such desultory action might not be very effective; but it eased pent-up feelings, and conveyed to the invaders the unfavorable sentiments which their conduct had inspired among the people. So, singly and in combination, the New Jersey farmers began to go out hunting regulars. Washington was in error when he wrote on December 16 that the British patrols, however small, did not "meet with the least interruption" from the inhabitants of the state.[95] His opponents received a quite different impression. Two days before the American commander passed this judgment, a Hessian officer wrote in his diary:

"It is now very hard to travel in Jersey. The peasant *canaille* meet our people singly and in groups without weapons, but have their muskets lying hidden in some nearby bushes, ditch, or the like; when they think they can achieve their purpose successfully and see one person or only a few who belong to our army, they shoot at their heads, then throw their muskets away again at once, and act as if they knew nothing about it."[96]

To the professional soldiers from across the Atlantic, such conduct was as monstrous and unethical as it was incomprehensible. War was a game, played according to accepted rules between gentlemen with their pawns, the common soldiers. Under any circumstances, the British and Hessian officers looked with scorn upon the American farmers, shopkeepers, artisans, and men of similarly ignoble callings who had temporarily interrupted their normal lives to become military leaders. Such a proceeding seemed highly irregular and distinctly ludicrous to the gentlemen from overseas. But they were totally unable to conceive how the common peasants should dare to resent the invasion of their land

[95] Washington, *Writings*, Vol. VI, p. 342.
[96] Münchhausen, Journal, Dec. 14, 1776.

by foreigners, and to express this resentment by firing at will upon regular troops. The idea of patriotism, as distinct from loyalty to a ruler, and as implying a conscious partici- pation by the common man in determining the destinies of his country, was completely foreign to the European pro- fessionals. Not only did they not agree with the idea: it never even penetrated their consciousness. One may search in vain, in the voluminous correspondence and diaries of the Hessian officers, for any faintest indication that they knew what the Americans were fighting for, or realized that the Whigs had any case at all, however fantastic.[97]

The Americans were rebels; and that label placed them as completely beyond serious consideration or respect as certain equally facile labels place their bearers beyond the con- sideration of the rigidly conservative today. Time and experience made no alteration in the closed minds of the royal officers. Throughout the war they continued to write with the same honest indignation and bewilderment about the reprehensible guerrilla warfare of the farmers. For the most part, the common soldiers accepted the standards of their superiors as blindly as the common man of any age accepts the standards of those above him in the social scale. If a British or Hessian soldier began to doubt the validity of these attitudes, he probably ended by deserting to the Amer- icans. If he did not, he shared the anger of his officers at the infamous practices of native snipers, and avenged himself wholeheartedly when an unfortunate irregular fell into his hands.

In an attempt to put an end to guerrilla warfare, General Howe issued a drastic order on December 12, as he sent his troops into winter quarters:

"Small, straggling Parties, not dressed like Soldiers and without Officers, not being admissible in War, [persons]

[97] Colonel von Donop was perhaps an exception to this generalization. He seems to have had some respect for the Americans, and treated them not without kindness on occasion.

who presume to molest or fire upon Soldiers or peaceable Inhabitants of the Country, will be immediately hanged without Trial, as Assassins."[98]

But this blustering order had no effect. As Howe rode back to New York from Trenton a day or so later, the light dragoons who were beating the country surrounding his route came upon five farmers with muskets lying in wait for him in a ditch. Upon being discovered, they fired at the dragoons and ran away; but they were no match in fleetness for their mounted pursuers, and all were caught. Two were wounded, and all would have been killed by the infuriated dragoons had their commander not prevented it.[99]

It would have required more than the capture of an occasional farmer to enable General Howe to put an end to this desultory warfare. In issuing his order of December 12, he was contending against the growing resistance of America, which became more stubborn, if scarcely more effective, as people began to realize what was implied in conquest by the military machine sent over by the British bureaucracy. From now on, with increasing frequency, the irregular fighters of New Jersey cooperated with parties of militia and detachments of the Continental army in making life miserable for the royal soldiers.

This alteration of behavior on the part of the inhabitants was one indication of an important change in the nature of the campaign. When the King's troops turned back disappointed from Coryell's Ferry and Burlington and Howe decided to go into winter quarters, the British offensive was over. From that time on, the Americans took the initiative. They did it in a feeble, uncoordinated, haphazard way, closing in on the enemy from numerous separated points, necessarily without carefully preconcerted plans and frequently in ignorance of one another's movements, but with

[98] *Collections of the New-York Historical Society*, 1883, p. 429.
[99] Münchhausen, Journal, Dec. 26, 1776.

a persistence which finally bore fruit in Washington's brilliant stroke at Trenton.

The offensive in all its manifestations was by no means entirely of Washington's planning. Until the middle of December, he still believed that Howe would try to push to Philadelphia. He therefore distributed his forces at strategic points along the Delaware, admonished them to keep a sharp eye out for the British, gave careful instructions to guide them in case the enemy should effect a landing and compel them to retreat, worried about the watercraft along the river, sent a spy to Trenton to see if the British were building any boats, and had scouting parties constantly out in an attempt to discover Howe's plans. Not until the fourteenth of the month did he begin to speak more optimistically of effecting "an important stroke" which would give to American affairs "a more pleasing aspect than they now have."[100]

It was in the northern part of the state that the first thunderclouds began to loom up menacingly over the British and to dart occasional destructive bolts into their cantonments. During the early part of December, the northern counties swarmed with a variety of detached military commands, which showed a general inclination to disregard the orders given them, but otherwise had little in common.

In the first place, there were the New Jersey militia, assembled at Morristown in numbers fluctuating between seven hundred and a thousand, who made periodic descents into the lowlands to carry off with equal enthusiasm cattle, sheep, and Tories. Secondly, there was the force, approximately twenty-seven hundred strong, under the languidly moving General Lee, who planned to augment his corps with the militia and to make an independent attack upon the British flank. Lee's soldiers were abruptly removed from

[100] Washington, *Writings*, Vol. VI, pp. 349, 350, 358-64, 366, 371, 373; *Am. Arch.*, 5th S., Vol. III, pp. 1151, 1152.

New Jersey after December 13, when their commander was captured and replaced by the energetic Sullivan; but they did not leave before their presence had stiffened the spirit of resistance in Morris County and instilled into the minds of the British and Hessians a nervous uncertainty as to what danger might be lurking behind the hills.

Up in the northwestern corner of the state a third body of troops under General Gates passed through Sussex County on its way from Ticonderoga to joint the main army. This force did not immediately affect the military situation in New Jersey; but a detachment of three more regiments from the Northern army, which Gates had expected to unite with his command at Sussex Court House, was diverted to Morristown by order of the ambitious Lee. Although these regiments, numbering about five hundred twenty men in all, did not arrive in Morristown until five days after Lee had been captured, they were held there as firmly as if he had been on the spot to take them over. Brigadier General McDougall, who chanced to be in town at that time, took it upon himself, with the approval of Brigadier General Heath and in disobedience to Washington's instructions, to detain them in order to sustain the faltering morale of the militia, who were discouraged by the departure of Lee's troops, and to assist in checking a threatened British invasion of Morris County.[101]

In counselling this disregard of orders, Heath, though the soul of loyalty, was committing his second breach of instructions within the month. Ordered by Washington on December 7 to advance towards Morristown, he had started off from Peekskill with alacrity, accompanied by five or six hundred men. When he crossed the Hudson, however, he found the Whigs of Bergen County and the adjoining part of New York state in such distress from the pillagings and persecutions of their Tory neighbors that he decided to stop

[101] *Am. Arch.*, 5th S., Vol. III, pp. 1122, 1190, 1260, 1278, 1296, 1297, 1298.

long enough to restore order. So, while Washington was writing to him that he should hasten on to join Lee at Pitts- town, Heath on December 14 swooped down upon Hacken- sack, captured the five British soldiers who constituted the garrison of that place, arrested some fifty Loyalists, and took possession of arms and a considerable quantity of stores collected there for the use of the Tories. The acquisi- tions were rapidly removed to a place of safety; and, hearing that British forces were advancing upon him from two direc- tions, Heath fell back on the sixteenth to Paramus, where he remained for some days, not daring to proceed westward lest the British should move up the Hudson and attack the weakened garrisons of the forts in the Highlands, and un- willing to retreat so far from the centers of Loyalist activity that he could not occasionally extend a chastening hand over them.[102]

Just before retiring to Paramus, Heath was joined by the sixth of the independent little American armies which were operating in northern New Jersey during those confused weeks. General George Clinton, with six hundred of the New York militia, exceeded the terms of the cautious instructions issued to him by the New York Committee of Safety and moved down to the support of Heath. From the combined force of both commanders a detachment of five hundred men was sent out on the night of December 19 to the vicinity of Bergen Woods, where it captured twenty-three men of a newly raised Loyalist regiment.[103]

In such an uncoordinated and opportunist fashion, the American counteroffensive began. Washington approved the alterations in his plans made by Heath and McDougall, and probably recognized that the prompt action of these

[102] *ibid.,* pp. 1169, 1234-5; Washington, *Writings,* Vol. VI, pp. 335, 371, 373; William Heath, *Heath's Memoirs of the American War, Reprinted from the Original Edition of 1798* (New York, 1904), pp. 108, 109, 110, 112.

[103] *Am. Arch.,* 5th S., Vol. III, pp. 1157-8, 1261-2, 1344, 1347; Heath, *op. cit.,* p. 113.

officers in meeting the crisis according to their own best judgment had saved Morris County from submitting to the British like the rest of the state. McDougall moved forward a few miles to Chatham to support the New Jersey militia, who had made that place their base and were operating against the British below the mountains. At Springfield they so annoyed Leslie's brigade, which was passing through the town, that General Grant thought of stationing two regiments at that place "to bring the People to their senses."[104] The Americans had hit upon the secret of successful fighting by a force inferior to its opponents in numbers, equipment, and training, but operating upon home ground. Their strategy of making sudden raids from all quarters and then withdrawing to inaccessible regions was eventually to wear out the British and drive them from the state. Washington's victory at Trenton was but one spectacular incident in a long series of harassments by regular and irregular fighters.

To such devices the geography of New Jersey was admirably suited. The British troops, scattered in a long chain of posts extending through flat country and separated from one another by miles of lonely road frequently bordered by woods and thickets, were an easy prey. Small bodies of Americans lay in wait for isolated parties or made lightning raids, and then retreated to the hills where no punitive expedition dared follow them without running the risk of being trapped. When Lord George Germain, the Colonial Secretary, wrote to General Howe from London on January 14, 1777, to express his satisfaction that the troops had "so fair a prospect of extensive and good winter cantonments," events had already rendered his remarks singularly inappropriate. Far more to the point was the foreboding

---

[104] *Am. Arch.,* 5th S., Vol. III, pp. 1260-1, 1277, 1296, 1297, 1298, 1313, 1315; Stryker, *Trenton and Princeton,* pp. 330-1.

of a Hessian captain on December 14, that the winter quarters would be "uneasy."[105]

How thoroughly uneasy became painfully clear as the month of December wore on. Patrols and dragoons bearing dispatches from one post to another were intercepted; a train of eight baggage-wagons was captured; and livestock which the British commissaries had gathered by purchase or plunder was stolen away from under their noses. An adjutant of General Howe's estimated on December 11 that the commissariat had lost seven hundred head of oxen and some thousand sheep and hogs to the roving patrols of the enemy. On that very night a company of militia drove off from Woodbridge, at the very center of the British lines, four hundred more cattle and two hundred sheep which had been collected there for the use of the royal army.[106] The first joyous days when the inhabitants of New Jersey could be plundered with impunity were over; and jaunts through the country lost their charm if one was liable to become a target for rebel sharpshooters hidden in the bushes.[107]

Beyond any doubt, the most uncomfortable spot in all the long string of Howe's cantonments was Trenton. Its position exposed it on all sides to annoyance from the enemy, and its

[105] Great Britain. Historical Manuscripts Commission, *Report on the Manuscripts of Mrs. Stopford-Sackville, of Drayton House, Northamptonshire*, Vol. II (Hereford, 1910), pp. 2, 56; Münchhausen, Journal, Dec. 14, 1776.

[106] Münchhausen, Journal, Dec. 11; Otis G. Hammond, ed., *Letters and Papers of Major-General John Sullivan, Continental Army* (Collections of the New Hampshire Historical Society), Vol. I (Concord, N.H., 1930), p. 303.

[107] What is probably one of the most stilted letters of condolence ever written was sent by Colonel William Harcourt to Admiral Geary from New Brunswick on Dec. 18:

"It is with infinite reluctance I find myself under the very disagreeable necessity of communicating to you an event which must, I am persuaded, give you the utmost concern. Cornet Geary having been ordered to advance with a party some miles into the country to procure intelligence of the enemy's situation, was upon his return from that duty fired upon by a party of the Rebels, who had concealed themselves on each side of the road by which he proposed to have passed. Unfortunately a ball took place, which in one moment deprived you of a son, and the regiment of an officer, whose loss cannot be sufficiently lamented."—*Am. Arch.*, 5th S., Vol. III, p. 1277.

commander, Colonel Rall, made few dispositions for its defense. Although troubled by the constant attacks made upon his men whenever they left the town, he seems to have had little fear that the American farmers could do any serious harm to him should they assault the main force in Trenton; and, despite urgent recommendations from other officers, he failed to raise any fortifications. The reason he gave to his immediate superior, Colonel von Donop, for this neglect was a strange one: that the task was impossible because he was menaced by the enemy in all directions! Nevertheless, though he built no redoubts, he was insistent enough upon having his soldiers do guard, picket, and patrol duty; and, since there were not enough of them adequately to man the posts of danger, they were soon worn out.[108]

The Americans did their best to increase these discomforts. Whenever as many as six or eight Hessians showed themselves outside the town on the river side, they were greeted with a cannonade from the western bank of the Delaware, and even smaller scouting parties might expect to be peppered with shots from both cannon and muskets. Groups of as many as seventy Americans boldly crossed the river in full view of the Hessians, and, on one occasion at least, chased away a sergeant and six men on picket duty scarcely more than a musketshot from the village. Any attempt by Rall's men to attack one of these parties was the signal for a violent cannonade under cover of which the Americans withdrew in safety.

The detachment which guarded the drawbridge over Crosswicks Creek, by which the garrisons at Trenton and Bordentown remained in communication with each other, was in a particularly unenviable situation, for the post was surrounded by thickets in which, as one officer expressed it, "the rebels could sneak about like thieves" and from which they could shoot down sentinels without warning. A guard

---

[108] Stryker, *Trenton and Princeton*, pp. 99-108, 332.

of one hundred men was maintained constantly at this spot, and changed every forty-eight hours; such members of the detachment as were not immediately on duty had to sleep all in the same house, without undressing or even removing their cartridge pouches, in order that they might be able to rush to arms at a moment's notice. It is no wonder that one of Rall's subalterns wrote in his diary: "We have not slept one night in peace since we came to this place."[109]

Even more disagreeable was the lot of any soldier sent out on patrol duty. Parties of Americans reported to be as large as one hundred fifty men were constantly prowling about the countryside, and Rall's correspondence with von Donop is full of reports of dragoons being killed or captured or having their horses shot while patrolling or foraging or carrying messages. Rall declared his position was too exposed, and asked General Leslie at Princeton to post a few troops at Maidenhead[110] to keep the communication open. His request was not granted, and on December 20 two dragoons carrying letters from Trenton to Princeton were waylaid. One of them was killed; the other made his escape back to Trenton. Now thoroughly alarmed, and anxious to impress his superiors with the gravity of the situation, the colonel sent the letters off again, this time under an escort of a hundred men and a piece of artillery, and accompanied them by a renewed plea that at least two hundred men be stationed at Maidenhead.

General Grant, to whom the request was forwarded, was displeased by Rall's spectacular gesture; to von Donop he expressed the opinion that "it was making much more of the rebels than they deserve." He declared himself unable to send troops to Maidenhead, because of Howe's disapproval of the place as a post; and the best suggestion he could make

[109] *ibid.*, pp. 104, 323-4, 326; Münchhausen, Journal, Dec. 9; Von Jungkenn MSS. (William L. Clements Library, University of Michigan), 1:26; Trevelyan, *op. cit.*, Vol. III, p. 91; *N.J.A.*, 2nd S., Vol. I, pp. 432-3.
[110] Now Lawrenceville.

was that patrols from Trenton and Princeton should meet at the hamlet at fixed times. To Colonel Rall, who he apparently decided had a bad case of nerves, Grant wrote soothingly:

"I am sorry to hear your Brigade has been fatigued or alarmed. You may be assured that the rebel army in Pennsylvania which has been joined by Lee's Corps, Gates and Arnolds does not exceed eight thousand men who have neither shoes nor stockings, are in fact almost naked, dying of cold, without blankets and very ill supplied with Provisions. On this Side of the Delaware they have not three hundred men. These stroll about in small parties, under the command of subaltern officers none of them above the rank of Captain, and their principal object is to pick up some of our Light Dragoons."[111]

This stupid answer can have brought small comfort to Rall. He had as little respect as Grant for the American army, and felt no fear of being successfully attacked by it. What worried him was precisely the matter of having his dragoons "picked up" by strolling parties—a point which Grant brushed lightly aside as though there were an inexhaustible supply of horsemen and a few more or less made no difference.

If Rall, who remained safely in Trenton, was so disturbed by the activities of the prowling Americans, it is not difficult to imagine the state of mind into which the Hessian troops fell as they brooded upon the perils threatening them. It made no difference to them if the enemy who picked them up were no higher in rank than captains: they preferred not to be picked up at all. With their nerves drawn taut by severe duty, uncomfortable sleep, and the constant threat from the American batteries across the river, they exaggerated the dangers from the roving rebels. The light

[111] Stryker, *op. cit.*, pp. 108, 326, 329-35. By permission of the publishers, Houghton Mifflin Company.

dragoons, lamented one officer, "were so frightened when they were to patrol that hardly any of them were willing to venture it without infantry, for they never went out patrolling without being fired upon, or having one wounded or even shot dead."[112]

Such a spirit was by no means a desirable one for a body of troops holding so important a position as Trenton. Among the many factors which entered into Washington's victory of December 26, not the least important was the constant harrying tactics of the militia and irregulars, which succeeded in unnerving Rall's soldiers until they were no longer the formidable antagonists they had been at Fort Washington.

On the southern as well as the northern flank, the royal army was not without its troubles. Colonel von Donop kept his eye fixed wistfully upon the comfortable town of Burlington; but he was obliged to admire its charms from a distance. He had learned that the men on the American fleet of row-galleys which patrolled the Delaware were not to be trifled with. Their vessels were equipped with good-sized cannon, and, on the one occasion when he had tried to occupy Burlington, they had quickly driven his troops out by an energetic cannonade. So he settled down unwillingly in Bordentown, crowded his men into the inadequate quarters obtainable there, at Mansfield Square, and about the Black Horse Tavern a few miles away, and waited impatiently for a battalion of heavy artillery to come up. Once he had that, he might be able to occupy Burlington and raise some batteries during the night; and thereafter he could give the impudent galleymen as good a dose of ball and shot as they sent. But in the meantime he could be only an impotent spectator while the crews of the vessels, suspicious of Burlington's Revolutionary zeal, paid frequent visits to the town, browbeat the inhabitants in repeated

[112] Von Jungkenn MSS. 1:26.

searches for Tories or Hessians, and arrested persons who had openly welcomed the royal troops.[113]

Von Donop was showered by all manner of rumors concerning an American force alleged to be advancing from the southward under General Putnam. There were three thousand of the rebels; there were four thousand; there were five hundred; there were a thousand, with two thousand more in the rear to support them, and a thousand or so more about to join them from Pennsylvania by way of Dunk's Ferry. By December 21, the menacing army actually put in an appearance at Mount Holly. It consisted of four or five hundred men, mostly of the Pennsylvania militia, who had been sent across the river under Colonel Samuel Griffin, and a few hundred militiamen from the southern counties of New Jersey, who had joined the detachment. On December 22, these troops drove away the Hessian picket from a bridge over Rancocas Creek; but that night they retired to Mount Holly, and after a brush with von Donop's men the next day, continued their retreat to Moorestown and later recrossed the Delaware. The American threat from the south had been easily repulsed; but it had annoyed the Hessians once more, and had served the purpose—quite without design—of drawing von Donop away from Bordentown, so that he was in no position to support Rall's brigade when Washington attacked it.[114]

Yet all these minor affairs, destructive though they might be of the peace and the morale of the King's troops, could not in themselves accomplish any important military purpose. On December 18, to be sure, General Grant ordered

[113] Münchhausen, Journal, Dec. 12; Margaret Morris, Journal (MS. copy in Sparks MSS., Harvard University Library, 48, No. 1), pp. 3-7, 8-10; Stryker, *Trenton and Princeton*, p. 333.

[114] Stryker, *Trenton and Princeton*, pp. 69-70, 74, 318-20, 324-5, 333, 335-6, 337, 340; *Am. Arch.*, 5th S., Vol. III, pp. 1360, 1427; William A. Slaughter, "Battle of Iron Works Hill, at Mt. Holly, New Jersey, December, 1776," in *N.J.H.S.P.*, N.S., Vol. IV, pp. 22-30; Margaret Morris, MS. copy of Journal, pp. 15-16.

that nothing belonging to the army—not even an officer with permission to depart from quarters—should leave New Brunswick without an escort;[115] but there was no reason to expect that the British would abandon New Jersey merely because it had become such an unpleasant place in which to live. If they were to be prevented from continuing their journey to Philadelphia after the weather became more favorable, some drastic move must be made while the widely-scattered state of their forces offered an urgent invitation to attack.

The condition of the American army, as well as that of the British, called for prompt and decisive action. On December 22, Washington had with him encamped along the Delaware only 4707 rank and file fit for duty; there were, in addition, not quite three thousand more on command, most of whom could be called in for a general operation. The troops looked like a collection of scarecrows, "many of 'em," Washington wrote, "being entirely naked and most so thinly clad as to be unfit for service." Someone made the bitter jest that if the war continued through the winter the British soldiers would be demoralized by the appearance of their enemies; "for as they never fought with naked men the novelty of it will terrify them and make them retreat faster than they advanced."[116]

Even this unprepossessing crew would soon be gone. The term of service of most of the soldiers would expire with the year, and Washington faced the prospect of being left with almost no force but militia, who, as he said, "come in you cannot tell how, go, you cannot tell when; and act, you cannot tell where; consume your Provisions, exhaust your Stores, and leave you at last in a critical moment."[117] At this very juncture, the militia were acting in a characteris-

[115] Glyn, *Journal*, p. 33.
[116] *Am. Arch.*, 5th S., Vol. III, pp. 1401-2; Washington, *Writings*, Vol. VI, p. 381; Margaret Morris, MS. copy of Journal, pp. 15-16.
[117] Washington, *Writings*, Vol. VI, p. 403.

tically disconcerting manner. Party after party of them, without informing Washington's staff of their intentions, crossed the river into New Jersey; and Colonel Joseph Reed, surprised and annoyed, informed the commander-in-chief that probably nothing more would be seen of them.[118]

Washington believed that Howe was merely waiting for the freezing of the Delaware and the dissolution of the American army to resume his advance upon Philadelphia, and he informed his brother quite frankly on December 18:

"In a word my dear Sir, if every nerve is not strain'd to recruit the New Army with all possible expedition, I think the game is pretty near up."[119]

In New Jersey, all the advantages which had been won in recent days seemed in danger of being lost. The three brigades which McDougall had held at Morristown with such favorable effect upon the spirit of the people would soon be released from service. General Heath, fearing that Howe might make a sudden move up the Hudson, returned with his troops to Peekskill on December 22 and December 23. By this movement, Clinton's force of New York militia at Paramus was left too much exposed to a swift advance of the enemy, so it drew back to Ramapough, where it soon began to disintegrate as the men, lacking a commissary to supply them with provisions, chose desertion in preference to starvation. While the American defenses of Morris County were thus crumbling, a rumor spread that the British were about to invade that district in three divisions, proceeding from New Brunswick, Elizabeth-Town, and Newark.[120]

General Howe's proclamation of pardon of November 30 had fixed a limit of sixty days within which the rebellious Whigs could recant their errors. It was obvious that, unless the American army did something to revive its prestige, the

[118] *Am. Arch.*, 5th S., Vol. III, p. 1182.

[119] Washington, *Writings*, Vol. VI, pp. 346, 398.

[120] Washington, *Writings*, Vol. VI, pp. 366, 383, 385; Heath, *op. cit.*, p. 114; *Am. Arch.*, 5th S., Vol. III, pp. 1347, 1365, 1378.

end of the period of grace would see a large number, who had waited as long as they dared for a change in the state of affairs, make their submissions to the conqueror. The gravity of the situation was evident, and Washington was in full accord with Colonel Joseph Reed, who declared to him in a frank and earnest letter written from Bristol on December 23:

"We are all of opinion, my dear General, that something must be attempted to revive our expiring credit, give our cause some degree of reputation, and prevent a total depreciation of the Continental money, which is coming in very fast—that even a failure cannot be more fatal than to remain in our present situation. In short, some enterprise must be undertaken in our present circumstances, or we must give up the cause."[121]

Such was the atmosphere of desperate determination in which Washington swiftly and secretly began to make arrangements for a threefold attack upon the Hessians. It was the critical throw of the game, and on its success or failure turned the fate of the Revolution.

[121] *Am. Arch.*, 5th S., Vol. III, p. 1361.

CHAPTER VI ☼ *WASHINGTON TAKES THE OFFENSIVE*

Scarce had Aurora's blush tinged eastern skies,
And cast her purple blaze on mortal eyes,
When Washington, though least expected near,
Opened a fire upon the Hessians' rear.[1]

SO sang, a number of years after the war, a "Revolutionary Soldier" who celebrated his country's history in limping prose and verse. If he was one of the men in Washington's army during the attack upon Trenton, his memory is demonstrably as bad as his poetry. On the morning of December 26, 1776, Aurora's blush blazed upon no mortal eye in New Jersey, for dawn came in the midst of a driving storm of snow and rain which had been raging nearly all night. It was miserable weather for the second holiday of the Christmas season which Colonel Rall and some of his officers were observing with as close an approximation to German cheer as the dull village of Trenton afforded.

After having passed a festive evening on December 25, the jovial colonel, it seemed, was intending to begin the following day with the not unaccustomed luxury of a long morning sleep. His chief subordinate, Major von Dechow, was apparently in a similarly relaxed holiday mood, for he ordered that the regular early morning patrol of artillery from the center of the village to the doctor's house near the lower ferry should be omitted. Even the Jäger post stationed at General Dickinson's house some distance from the village up the river road caught the pleasant infection of the season and confined its patrolling to a detachment of three men which at five o'clock went a short distance up the river. After all, it was a holiday; and in such blustering weather what

[1] Benjamin Eggleston, *The Wars of America* . . . (Baltimore, 1839), p. 239.

was there to fear from the half-naked Continentals huddling beyond the swirling Delaware and its drifting cakes of ice?[2]

A timorous character, to be sure, might have grounds for slight uneasiness. During the festivities on the evening of December 25, the servant at the house where Colonel Rall was enjoying himself had been troubled by a Loyalist freshly arrived from Pennsylvania, who insisted upon seeing the commander. Failing in this purpose, the visitor had scribbled a note to Rall, who had thrust it unread into his pocket and thus spared himself the distress of learning that the Americans were preparing to descend upon him. Earlier in the evening, the Christmas atmosphere had been more roughly jarred when a picket of sixteen men stationed just outside the town on the Pennington road was fired upon by a wandering party of Americans. The attackers, however, withdrew quickly into the woods, leaving no trace, and Rall dismissed the affair as of no importance. He increased the size of the picket to twenty-five men and put it in charge of a competent though conceited young officer, Lieutenant Andreas Wiederhold; and, after making this arrangement, he postponed until morning all investigation of the attack. "Colonel Rall did not even send out a cavalry patrol," writes Wiederhold, "in order to reconnoiter the neighborhood at a distance, [but] laid himself in bed and slept until, the next morning, everything was in confusion."[3]

The young lieutenant made up as best he could for the negligence of his superior by posting a number of sentinels and sending out occasional patrols to cover the territory assigned to him. It was a relief when the night at the lonely outpost was over and the last of the reconnoitering parties, which had made its rounds since daybreak, returned to report that all was quiet. Wiederhold drank a cup of coffee and, bad

[2] William S. Stryker, *The Battles of Trenton and Princeton* (Boston and New York, 1898), pp. 122-5, 133, 139-40, 145-6, 420-1.

[3] Letter of Lieut. Andreas Wiederhold, April 15, 1777, in Von Jungkenn MSS., Clements Library, 1:31.

though the weather was, prepared to refresh himself after the long vigil by taking a walk in the open air. As he stepped to the door, he was startled to see a force of American soldiers emerging from the woods a hundred fifty paces away.[4] This, though the surprised officer did not yet know it, was the dire moment to which all the disturbances of recent days had been but a prelude. Upon Rall's worn and uneasy troops the desperate American army was about to hurl itself in a supreme effort.

Throughout that long, cold night, Glover's regiment of Marblehead fishermen had battled the swift current of the Delaware, the floating cakes of ice, the high wind, and the driving snow to transport Washington's force—perhaps twenty-four hundred strong—with its horses and artillery from Pennsylvania to New Jersey. Chilled and weary, but grimly determined, the Americans had begun their advance from McConkey's Ferry at about four in the morning; and at eight o'clock, marching in two columns along the river road and the Pennington road, they arrived at the Hessian outposts.

The men who had passed so disagreeable a night were in no mood for trifling. Fiercely they swept back into the town Wiederhold's little picket and two other outlying detachments stationed nearby. Before the Hessians had time to organize any resistance, the American forces deployed across the road leading to Princeton and New Brunswick, and, extending themselves to the bank of Assanpink Creek, cut off retreat to the northward. At almost the same time, the column on the river road, commanded by General Sullivan, bore down upon the Jäger outpost, and drove this detachment back to Trenton and across the one bridge spanning Assanpink Creek at the southern end of the village. After a sharp fight in the town, part of Sullivan's force crossed the bridge and set up a battery of artillery on the heights beyond

4 *ibid.*

the creek, where it effectually intercepted any retreat along the road to Burlington.[5]

Meanwhile the Hessians in the town were thrown into the greatest confusion. Aroused from sleep after the fighting had begun, Rall attempted to assemble his troops; but, even as they were forming, a battery of American artillery which had been placed at the northern end of the village began to rake the two principal streets. Rall's men, demoralized by the strain of the recent weeks and by the suddenness of the assault, responded but halfheartedly to their commander's call to advance; and the Americans, in a fierce charge, captured the only two Hessian cannon which had been brought into play and forced the enemy out of the village to the low grounds bordering Assanpink Creek.

From this point the Hessians made a desperate counter-attack upon the village; but the American marksmen, now sheltered in houses and behind fences, shot through the flying snow and rain and the drifting smoke of battle with deadly effect upon their exposed enemy. Rall ordered his men to retreat to an orchard near the creek; but before this movement was completed he fell from his horse, mortally wounded.

With their commander removed from action and their force nearly encircled by Americans who were in a position to wipe it out if it should try to struggle through the high waters of the creek, the field officers of the von Lossberg and Rall regiments had no choice but to surrender. At almost the same time, the third regiment, that of Knyphausen, which had been fighting at the southern end of the village, was captured while making a vain attempt to escape across the Assanpink.[6] The short battle was over, and one of the most important British outposts had fallen with but feeble resistance into the hands of the despised Americans.

[5] Stryker, *op. cit.*, pp. 130-52, 163-4, 166-8.
[6] Stryker, *op. cit.*, pp. 153-93; Wiederhold, *op. cit.*

More than nine hundred Hessians, officers and men, were made prisoners either at the surrender or in a later search of the village; and one hundred six had been killed or wounded in the engagement. Only about four hundred of the garrison escaped capture. Some of these had been stationed south of Assanpink Creek at the time of the battle; others fled over the bridge before the Americans took possession of it, or waded across the stream. In contrast, the losses of the Americans, according to Washington, were "very inconsiderable, not more than a private or two killed" and a few men wounded. The cost of their victory did not become apparent until after the chilled and exhausted troops had returned to the Pennsylvania shore; on the next day, it is said, over a thousand of them were reported unfit for duty.[7]

Owing to the unfavorable weather conditions, the Americans had not been able to carry out Washington's plan in its entirety. It had been his intention that General Ewing should cross the Delaware at Trenton lower ferry to cut off any retreat down the river, and that Colonel Cadwalader, with a force of Pennsylvania militia, should pass over at Bristol, and surprise von Donop at Mount Holly. Ewing, however, was held completely inactive by the difficulty of getting across the partly frozen stream; and Cadwalader, having actually ferried over some of his troops, was obliged to take them back to Pennsylvania because he could not land his cannon over the rough ice piled along the New Jersey shore.[8]

The first intimation of the battle reached the Hessian troops stationed below Trenton at ten in the morning, when four inhabitants of the recaptured town came galloping through the storm to the picket guarding the drawbridge over Crosswicks Creek. The startling news which they brought was hastily sent on to von Donop, and within an hour it was

[7] Washington, *Writings*, Vol. VI, pp. 443-4; Stryker, *op. cit.*, pp. 207-8, 427-8.
[8] Washington, *Writings*, Vol. VI, pp. 443-4.

confirmed by the first of the fugitives from the shattered regiments. Von Donop, whose principal force still lingered at Mount Holly, was too far away to make an immediate attack upon Washington even had he been so inclined; and he was by no means anxious to engage the victorious army. Rumor placed the number of the Americans in Trenton at ten or twelve thousand; and the Hessian commander, reflecting upon his scanty supply of ammunition, thought much less of how he could avenge the honor of his countrymen than of how he could withdraw his own troops to a place of greater safety. After moving to Allentown so hastily on December 27 that he had to abandon twenty of his sick and wounded and a supply of rations at Bordentown, he was summoned to Princeton with all his men by General Leslie, the next day, to resist an American attack which a baseless report said was impending.[9]

By his one bold stroke, Washington had cleared the entire shore of the Delaware of the enemy; but he dared not remain in Trenton. The hostile detachments nearby under Leslie and von Donop were too great a threat for his small and weakened army. Not only were his men worn out by the exertion and exposure of the attack: many of them, according to Colonel Reed, had aggravated their incapacity by refreshing themselves too freely with the "great Quantities of Spirituous Liquors" found in Trenton. Christmas cheer had been the ruin of Rall; and it might well be the ruin of his captors if they stayed long on the spot. On the very day of the battle, therefore, the American army carried back to Pennsylvania its booty of cannon, arms, ammunition, and baggage, as well as all the prisoners who were not too badly wounded to be transported. The village of Trenton, which had seen so much stirring military activity of late, was left for a brief spell to an unwonted civilian peace.[10]

[9] Von Jungkenn MSS., 1:26; Stryker, *op. cit.*, pp. 235-6, 398-400, 424-5.
[10] Stryker, *op. cit.*, pp. 206-7.

Great was the chagrin of the British army over the blow struck on the Delaware. General Howe prepared for Lord George Germain a thoroughly misleading account of the affair, which reached the comforting conclusion:

"This misfortune seems to have proceeded from Col. Rall's quitting his post, and advancing to the attack, instead of defending the village."[11]

Upon Rall and his subordinate, Major von Dechow, both of whom quickly died of wounds received in the engagement, their fellow officers of the royal service heaped bitter blame for the defeat. "Lucky is he," declared one Hessian, "that by his death he has escaped having to answer for much!" Von Donop, who on December 27 tempered his criticism of his comrade's failure to retreat by adding words of commendation for his "splendid courage," changed his tone within two days:

"Colonel Rall was to have been buried with his Lieutenant Colonel [Major von Dechow] yesterday. I am very well satisfied, because they would have been compelled to appear before a Court Martial, the former to explain his general conduct and the latter why he did not go out in the morning with Rall's patrol."[12]

Such also was the opinion prevailing among the Hessian officers conducting an official investigation of the Trenton affair a few years later. The verdict of this court of inquiry breathes not a word of criticism of Howe's overambitious system of cantonments, or of General Grant's smug and stupid inactivity in the face of increasing aggressiveness on the part of the Americans. As it was with the Hessians, so apparently it was with the British. Sir Henry Clinton might harbor critical thoughts about Howe's tenuous chain of winter quarters, and might lay upon General Grant severe

[11] *N.J.A.*, 2nd S., Vol. I, p. 369.
[12] Stryker, *op. cit.*, pp. 400, 427 (by permission of the publishers, Houghton Mifflin Company); Letter of Col. Johann Friedrich von Cochenhausen, March 17, 1777, in Von Jungkenn MSS., 1:29.

blame for the course of events; Howe's deputy adjutant general, Stephen Kemble, might censure in the privacy of his journal the unwise dispositions of his chief; but probably most of the officers, British and Hessian, agreed at least publicly with Cornwallis when he testified before the House of Commons:

"Human prudence could not foresee the fatal event of the surrender of Colonel Rhall's brigade. . . . The misfortune at Trenton was owing entirely to the imprudence and negligence of the commanding Officer."[13]

Although it was easy enough thus to cast the entire responsibility for the military reverse upon one who could no longer defend himself, the royal forces were alarmed by the turn of events and conscious of their exposed situation. Leslie's and von Donop's brigades, crowded into Princeton, were augmented by most of Grant's force from New Brunswick and by three British regiments drawn in from Hillsborough. Lord Cornwallis, on the point of sailing for England, was sent hastily into New Jersey to take charge of the army and repeat his former successes.

Pending his arrival, all precautions were taken to prevent the Americans from effecting any more surprises. A British regiment was sent forward to Maidenhead to reinforce the light infantry which had been stationed there, and a Hessian regiment, with posts at Stony Brook and Eight Mile Run,[14] maintained communication with the main body of the army. Two redoubts were thrown up on the south side of Princeton, and a strong guard was placed on the Allentown road after it became known that a rebel force had crossed the lower Delaware and was advancing northward. Wandering American snipers caused such annoyance by firing upon the British outposts after nightfall that finally, on the night of January 1, the Trenton road for some distance

---

[13] Kemble, *op. cit.*, p. 105; Howe, *Observations*, p. 68; Stryker, *op. cit.*, pp. 224, 402, 411, 414, 417, 422, 427.
[14] Now Shipetaukin Creek.

beyond Princeton was kept lighted by a row of bonfires. In the expectation of an attack by the Continentals, the soldiers at Princeton were required to lie on their arms several nights, and the constant strain and the overcrowding began to fatigue them just as similar conditions had wearied Rall's brigade at Trenton.[15]

Any relaxation of vigilance was likely to mean a minor disaster. Thus on one occasion a party of British dragoons accompanying a commissary who was collecting forage near Princeton were careless enough to let themselves become separated from their weapons while they devoted themselves to the pleasant business of "attacking and Conquering a Parcel of Mince Pyes." Before they knew what had happened, they were surrounded by a detachment of American light horse under Colonel Joseph Reed, and were whisked off, with the commissary, to inglorious captivity.[16]

A new American advance had begun on December 27, when Colonel Cadwalader, under the impression that Washington was still in New Jersey, crossed the Delaware near Bristol with about fifteen hundred men. After landing, he learned that his superior had returned to Pennsylvania; but, hearing that von Donop's force had also withdrawn from the vicinity, he spent a night in Burlington and then proceeded cautiously to Bordentown. On December 29 he moved on to Crosswicks, and General Mifflin occupied Bordentown with a force of some sixteen hundred Pennsylvania militiamen who had been crossing the river and assembling at Burlington for three days.[17]

The new recruits were filled with that optimism which has so often been a blessing to the American people, and so often a curse, since it has frequently been substituted for a

[15] Glyn, *Journal*, p. 36; Von Jungkenn MSS., 1:26; Collins, *Brief Narrative*, p. 31; Stryker, *op. cit.*, pp. 238-9, 247, 249-50, 434.

[16] Collins, *Brief Narrative*, p. 30.

[17] Stryker, *op. cit.*, pp. 239-43, 253; Washington, *Writings*, Vol. VI, pp. 451-2.

willingness to face unpleasant facts and to make careful preparations for dealing effectively with a difficult situation. The Pennsylvania soldiers talked lightly of "engaging the English as a verry triffling affair nothing [being] so easy as to drive them over the north river," according to one skeptical inhabitant of Burlington who was favored with their opinions.[18]

Washington, always a realist, was not so overconfident; but he made plans to recross the Delaware, and wrote to Heath on December 28 with something less than his usual conservatism of expression:

"I think a fair Opportunity is offered of driving the Enemy entirely from, or at least to, the extremity of the province of Jersey."[19]

There is not sufficient evidence to prove the assertion of a recent biographer that the American commander planned from the beginning to move his army to Morristown.[20] Indeed, he informed John Hancock on January 7 that only the fatigue and complaints of the militia had induced him to go to that place, and that, as the situation was "by no means favorable to our Views," he hoped to move elsewhere before long.[21] Doubtless he intended to form a junction somewhere with the Continental troops and militia then stationed in Morris County, whom he ordered to harass the enemy on flank and rear; and the idea of effecting a combination of forces somewhere in New Jersey was also implied in his instructions to Heath to move to his support by way of Hackensack with a detachment of New England militia. In view, however, of the uncertain military prospects for the immediate future, Washington must have had several alternative plans in mind when he entered New Jersey, and there is no reason to doubt that he was frank in informing the Continental Congress on December 29 that his purpose was

18 Morris, Journal, pp. 17-18.   19 Washington, *Writings*, Vol. VI, p. 448.
20 Fitzpatrick, *op. cit.*, pp. 282-4.
21 Washington, *Writings*, Vol. VI, pp. 477-8.

to "pursue the Enemy in their retreat, try to beat up more of their Quarters, and, in a word, in every instance [to] adopt such measures as the exigency of our affairs and our situation will justify."[22]

On December 30, Washington crossed to Trenton once more; his men followed during the course of that day and the next; and on January 1 Cadwalader's and Mifflin's forces were summoned to join the main army. By the earnest entreaties of several officers and the promise of a ten-dollar bounty, a considerable number of the New England troops whose enlistments expired with the year had been induced to remain for another six weeks; so Washington had at his disposal a total of some five thousand men, consisting mostly of inexperienced recruits, but with a kernel of seasoned veterans.[23]

He needed every soldier he could retain or procure to meet the threat of the enemy. On the evening of January 1, Cornwallis arrived in Princeton; the next morning he set out for Trenton, intent upon crushing the impudent rebels. Of the eight thousand troops at his disposal, he took with him all but the three regiments of the Fourth Brigade, under the command of Colonel Mawhood, which had been drawn into Princeton from Hillsborough and which were left behind as a rear guard until the following morning. At Maidenhead, Cornwallis left another brigade, the Second, under the command of General Leslie, but as he continued on his way to Trenton he is estimated to have had at least five thousand five hundred experienced soldiers to match against Washington's five thousand ill-coordinated and, in great part, untried fighters.

Such men as the American commander possessed, however, he disposed of in a manner to obtain the maximum effectiveness from them. As the British slowly advanced beyond Maidenhead, hampered in their progress by the

[22] Washington, *Writings*, Vol. VI, pp. 447-52.
[23] Stryker, *op. cit.*, pp. 246, 253-6, 435-6.

mud with which the midwinter thaw had filled the road, they soon fell in with the first American skirmishers. From then on, they were fired upon from every place of concealment which the retiring Pennsylvania riflemen and other snipers could find. At Shabakunk Creek, where the American detachments took shelter in a thick wood bordering the south side of the stream, the British were exposed to so severe a fusillade that they were brought up short in confusion. While their artillery raked the woods, part of their column was reformed in order of battle, and a considerable interval of time was consumed before their army swept across the creek, only to find that the enemy had already withdrawn. Thus fighting and retreating again and again, the American advanced detachments slowly fell back to the outskirts of Trenton. Here, behind some earthworks hastily constructed at a small ravine, four pieces of artillery and a body of infantry, consisting principally of a Virginia regiment, kept Cornwallis at bay for some time. Eventually, the overwhelming superiority of the British column forced the defenders to retreat through the village and across the bridge to the high ground behind the Assanpink, where Washington had drawn up his whole force in a strong position, well protected by earthworks at important points.[24]

The short winter afternoon was now at an end, and the weary British troops, though their casualties had been few, had had enough of fighting for one day. Some halfhearted attempts to cross the Assanpink met with such firm resistance from the American artillery that it was evident the rebels would retreat no farther. Cornwallis could see no good reason for launching an assault upon Washington's position in the dark with his exhausted soldiers, when the morning would find them refreshed and would bring reinforcements from the rear. So the British army settled down to recruit

[24] Glyn, *Journal*, p. 36; Stryker, *op. cit.*, pp. 248, 250-1, 254-64; Thomas Jefferson Wertenbaker, "The Battle of Princeton," in *The Princeton Battle Monument* (Princeton, 1922), pp. 59-63.

its energy by a good night's rest, while the American batteries hurled an occasional ineffectual cannon ball into the
town to disturb the peace of the newcomers.[25]

For the American troops, many of whom had been doing
as hard duty as the British that day, there was no rest.
At a council of war held during the evening, it was decided—
on whose initiative, it is now impossible to be certain—to
steal off by a back road to Princeton, surprise the garrison
there, and, if possible, capture the lightly guarded stores
and the military chest at New Brunswick. The move was
quite in line with Washington's consistent policy of avoiding
general engagements and striking swiftly at exposed points.
The care he had taken to prevent a large-scale battle that
day suggests that he had already planned to lure the main
British force to Trenton and then to dodge away behind it—
a type of maneuver in which he has had few superiors in
history.

What is surprising is that Cornwallis should not have
foreseen and forestalled the move. The British headquarters
maps, which seem to have been at least as good during the
war as those at Washington's disposal, plainly show the
roads which the Americans took in their fairly direct march
to Princeton; and it is nearly incredible that Cornwallis
should not have been aware of the possibility of Washington's slipping off towards the center of the long line of
British posts. By this time the rebel commander had learned
the fundamental strategy which he had to follow to win
the war: to harass the enemy at every possible point, but
never to give them the opportunity of crushing his army.
The King's generals, on the other hand, seem at no time
during the contest to have fully grasped the vital importance of making every exertion to bring the Americans to a
general engagement. Certainly, up to now, they had not

[25] Münchhausen, Journal, Jan. 3, 1777; Stryker, *op. cit.*, pp. 265-9; Wertenbaker, *op. cit.*, pp. 63-4.

learned to appreciate either Washington's energy or his ability—developed by painful experience during the campaign of 1776—to judge a military situation. Apparently Cornwallis thought that night either that the Americans would be too tired to move away or that their commander was too stupid to see his hopeless situation in the face of a superior army, and would still be on hand in the morning to be dispatched at leisure.

This was one of the greatest of the many errors which Cornwallis committed during the course of the war. His failure to pursue Washington vigorously during the earlier part of the campaign may be attributed to Howe's policy of gradual demoralization. Now, however, the situation was entirely changed, and his neglect of the opportunity to crush Washington on January 2 can be called nothing less than a blunder of the first magnitude. When Cornwallis awakened in the morning, Washington was far away, and soon the distant boom of guns announced what he was doing.

A fortunate drop in temperature had frozen the mud and made it possible for the Americans to move towards Princeton in the night with some speed, over roads roughly paralleling the main highway. Three of the heaviest cannon and most of the baggage were sent off to Burlington; and before the convoy reached that town, it had been joined by a good many more soldiers than were needed for the escort—about a thousand, according to one account. These men, members of the Pennsylvania militia, had become terrified on the march from Trenton, and had bolted. The valor which had been so easily donned to impress the quiet people of Burlington disappeared rapidly in the presence of actual cannonading and during the furtive nocturnal retreat to a mysterious destination.[26]

A few men from the American force were left at the creek to keep the fires burning brightly, throw up more

26 Stryker, *op. cit.*, pp. 274, 438; Morris, Journal, pp. 20-1.

earthworks with ostentatious noise, and otherwise create the deceptive effect of feverish preparations to resist an attack on the morrow. With the rest of his tired soldiers trudging along silently, and his cannon running on wheels muffled in rags and rope, Washington set out for the point where he was least expected.

Quietly the army marched through the night; and, just at sunrise, it reached the Quaker meeting house near Stony Brook, about two miles from Princeton. From this point a detachment under General Mercer was sent to continue along the road beside the stream. The party had instructions to break down the bridge where the main highway crossed the brook, in order to cut off retreat by the regiments stationed at Princeton should they attempt to withdraw, and in order to check any pursuit which Cornwallis might make from Trenton after discovering his adversary's move. The rest of the army filed off to the right on a road which ran to Princeton along a course south of the main highway.

Already, however, it was too late to catch all the troops which had been stationed in the town. The Fortieth Regiment had been left to guard the village; but as the Americans were dividing their forces at the Meeting House, Colonel Mawhood, with the Seventeenth and the Fifty-Fifth Regiments and a few other odd troops, including fifty light horse, had just started off for Trenton along the highway. His party had crossed Stony Brook and was ascending the hill on the other side when, looking back across the ravine, the horsemen caught sight of part of Washington's main force moving towards Princeton. Unaware of the size of the attacking force, contemptuous of the military abilities of the Americans, and anxious to assist the Fortieth Regiment, now exposed to surprise, Mawhood wheeled his men about and quickly retraced part of his route, with the intention of heading off the enemy by establishing himself on a hill close to which the attacking column must pass before entering the town.[27]

Meanwhile, Mercer, hidden in the wooded ravine of Stony Brook from the sight of the British, had learned of their presence and their retirement; and he turned away from the valley road to ascend a nearby height and observe the situation. This movement and his further oblique advance towards the head of the main American column, which he wished to support, brought his detachment into close proximity to the hostile force under Mawhood. To meet the new danger, the British colonel was obliged to divide his command: the greater part of the Fifty-Fifth Regiment he detached to assist the Fortieth in coming from the village; with the rest of his force he attacked Mercer's brigade. The first clash was sharp; and, after meeting the initial assault firmly, the weary Americans soon gave way under the fire of two British fieldpieces and a bayonet charge from Mawhood's men, still fresh from a night's sleep. The retreat became a rout. Mercer and several of his officers were either killed or mortally wounded; the two cannon of the brigade were captured by the British and turned upon the retreating men, increasing their confusion.

Upon the first reinforcements hastening up from the main American column—Cadwalader's Pennsylvania militia—the disorganized fugitives flung themselves. Demoralized by this incident and by a hot fire of grapeshot from the British, the newcomers soon caught the infection and fell back in confusion. Washington appeared on the scene and exposed himself boldly to the hostile fire in an attempt to restore order; but his expostulations were in vain. For several minutes, all attempts to reorganize the American line were fruitless, and it looked as if the small but efficient force

[27] [Capt. Hall] *The History of the Civil War in America. By an Officer of the Army*, 2nd ed. (London, 1780), pp. 258-60; Wertenbaker, *op. cit.*, pp. 65-78.

under Mawhood were about to defeat piecemeal a hostile army overwhelmingly superior to it in numbers. The advance guard of the Americans, consisting of some six hundred men under Sullivan, apparently was some distance ahead of the rest of the army, and was stalemated by the Fifty-Fifth Regiment, which from a wood on a hill between the battle-field and the town threatened to fall upon Sullivan from behind if he should turn about and move to support Mercer's detachment. The rear of Washington's force was out of range of action at the beginning of the battle and required some time to get to a place where it could participate.

In this moment of crisis, a few infantrymen and a small battery of artillery from Philadelphia held the victorious British in check until the Pennsylvania riflemen and veteran New England troops could be brought out on the battlefield. Once the American line was formed and charged upon the enemy under Washington in person, the fate of Mawhood's little detachment was sealed. The British commander, in imminent danger of being outflanked and surrounded, with-drew his men gradually and for some time in good order; but eventually his regiment broke and fled in confusion. Many of the fugitives were captured; but a determined stand by the British light horse checked the hot pursuit by the Americans until a large number of Mawhood's infantry had crossed Stony Brook and removed themselves to a safe distance from the victors.

The Fortieth and Fifty-Fifth Regiments, cut off from Mawhood's fleeing force, offered some resistance at a small ravine southwest of Princeton, but were soon dislodged. Some of the men made good their escape to Somerset Court House and New Brunswick; others were captured in flight; and one body of troops, which attempted to make a desperate last stand in Nassau Hall, the large stone college building in Princeton, was soon forced to surrender when the Americans began a cannonade against their shelter.[28]

Washington had hoped to press on to New Brunswick and capture the great collection of stores deposited there under a weak guard; but his men were too fatigued to make the further effort, and all he could do was to march them to a place of greater safety. He seized some of the scanty stores available in Princeton—a supply of blankets was perhaps the most welcome discovery—set fire to a magazine of hay, and then moved on through Kingston and Rocky Hill to Somerset Court House.[29] The detachment which he had sent back to break down the bridge over Stony Brook completed its task barely in time to check the British troops hastening up from Maidenhead and Trenton, and there was an exchange of cannon shots between the new arrivals and the departing Americans. The British, however, after wading through the icy, waist-deep waters of Stony Brook, waited for a cautious interval before they occupied the village their adversaries had left.[30]

The Americans crossed the Millstone River at Kingston, broke the bridge behind them to halt pursuit, and proceeded northward along the road following the right bank of the river. After two strenuous days and an exhausting night,

[28] Wertenbaker, *op. cit.*, pp. 87-111, 118; *N.J.A.*, 2nd S., Vol. I, pp. 254, 259-61; Hall, *op. cit.*, pp. 262-3; Stryker, *op. cit.*, pp. 292, 439-40, 451; Collins, *op. cit.*, p. 33; Washington, *Writings*, Vol. VI, p. 469. Like the battle of Trenton, the affair at Princeton had been short and sharp; and here again the number of killed and wounded was low in proportion to the number of prisoners taken. Accounts of the casualties vary widely: the *New York Gazette* reported, for instance, that the American loss was over four hundred killed and wounded, whereas an American estimate set the number at sixty. Probably Washington's army suffered thirty or forty fatalities as a result of the engagement; the number of wounded cannot be satisfactorily determined. According to the official British returns, the royal troops lost in the battle two hundred officers and men "missing"—which we may interpret as "captured"—eighteen killed, and fifty-eight wounded. These figures are probably rather low for all three categories, but there is too much conflict among the estimates to permit any reliable conclusions.

[29] Now Millstone.

[30] Wertenbaker, *op. cit.*, pp. 112-14; Hall, *op. cit.*, p. 264; Collins, *op. cit.*, pp. 35-6.

they were nearing the end of their endurance, and had no taste for more fighting. A party of British horse, which hastened down the road west of the Millstone and arrived at one end of a bridge just as the American van reached the other end, found no disposition in their adversaries to join battle. Instead, Washington had the bridge broken up to prevent a clash, and the horsemen rejoined their own army without having accomplished anything.[31]

At dusk, the Americans reached Somerset Court House, some fifteen miles from Princeton. Scarcely an hour before, a party of a hundred British troops, stationed in the town to guard the baggage of the Fourth Brigade, had abandoned the place in company with some fugitives from Princeton, taking with them their twenty baggage-wagons. Their withdrawal was made in the face of a detachment of some four hundred of the New Jersey militia, who ventured nothing more than an ineffectual demand for surrender, and permitted the enemy to depart unmolested when they showed fight.[32]

Great had been the consternation aroused at both Trenton and New Brunswick by news of the engagement at Princeton. At the former British headquarters on the Raritan, Brigadier General Matthews received word that the enemy were in full march towards his post. Hastily assembling his small garrison and a regiment which had arrived the day before, he marched them out to the high grounds that commanded the town, and prepared to delay the Americans as long as possible. Simultaneously, all available wagons were pressed into service to transport across the bridge at Raritan Landing, two miles upstream, as many of the stores as could be moved before the enemy should come up and render it necessary to retreat across the river and burn the bridge. Hour after hour passed, bringing only British fugitives and no Americans; but still the soldiers remained alert at their

---

[31] Stryker, *op. cit.*, p. 441.   [32] *ibid.*; Hall, *op. cit.*, p. 267.

posts and the procession of wagons rattled endlessly through the streets of New Brunswick, up the river road, and across the bridge.[33]

At Trenton, Cornwallis was thrown into a similar panic when the distant thunder of artillery a little after daybreak revealed the whereabouts of the elusive Washington. Not only the three regiments at Princeton, but also the men and stores and the military chest of £70,000 at New Brunswick were in imminent peril. The advanced corps was marched with all possible speed to the place of combat; but like General Leslie, who had started back from Maidenhead without waiting for orders upon hearing the firing, it reached Princeton too late to be of any assistance to Mawhood. When the British arrived they found the Americans gone from the town, the magazines burning, and the wounded of both armies already removed into the houses near the scene of the engagement.

Cornwallis himself soon appeared in Princeton with the rest of his force. He was still worried about the safety of New Brunswick; and so, after some inadequate provisions had been distributed, and certain of the soldiers had done what they could to leave a final unpleasant impression in the minds of the inhabitants, the army moved on in the late afternoon towards the Raritan. There was a delay at Kingston to repair the broken bridge; then the march continued. It was eighteen long miles from Princeton to New Brunswick; and the weary troops, who had had little to eat for two days, had rested but indifferently the night before, and had hastened all the way from Trenton or Maidenhead, plodded along all through the cold, dark night. Progress was slow, for the marching soldiers were often brought to a halt by stoppages of the cumbersome baggage-wagons, scattered everywhere through the disorderly column. At such times the exhausted men sank to the ground and were at once asleep;

[33] Hall, *op. cit.*, pp. 264-5.

only by the greatest efforts could they be aroused and brought to their feet when the column moved on again. Arriving finally at New Brunswick at about daybreak, and finding the place still in the hands of friends, they were obliged to remain in order of battle on the heights outside the town for several hours, until it became evident that no attack was impending; then at last they were sent into quarters.[34]

To such a humiliating experience the proud royal army had been brought by the despised rebels who, but a few weeks before, had been fleeing before it in apparently hopeless defeat. The easy self-confidence of the King's troops was badly shaken. Officers like Mawhood, who embodied the bravery, mental rigidity, and harsh intolerance of the professional militarist, never learned to feel either respect or consideration for the American rabble; but over many of the rank and file the successes of the enemy cast a deep gloom and a feeling of apprehension.

Responsibility for the turn of events was too obvious to be successfully concealed. Washington's exploit was freely accorded by members of the British army "a place amongst distinguished military achievements" and was owned to be "worthy of a better cause";[35] but it was too apparent that he had been assisted by the same sort of negligence on the part of Cornwallis and his subordinates which had handicapped British policy from the beginning of the campaign.

"Had our Light Dragoons patroled the Allens Town Road during the Night of the 2ᵈ," wrote one British ensign in his journal, "the Enemys movement round the Left of Lord Cornwallis s Corps could not have taken place without our notice."[36]

Before the war was over, a book written by a subordinate officer had appeared in London which openly asserted that

[34] Hall, *op. cit.*, pp. 263-4, 266-7 ; Von Jungkenn MSS., 1 :26 ; Glyn, *Journal*, pp. 38-9 ; Collins, *op. cit.*, p. 17 ; Washington, *Writings*, Vol. VI, p. 470.
[35] Hall, *op. cit.*, pp. 257-8.   [36] Glyn, *Journal*, p. 38.

the nocturnal departure of the Americans from the Assanpink had been observed and reported to headquarters by the British sentries, but that the report had been disregarded.[37]

Officially, however, the engagement at Princeton was treated as a minor affair significant only as a demonstration of British valor at its best. General Howe publicly congratulated Mawhood and his men. The *New York Gazette and Weekly Mercury*, the chief propaganda sheet for the royal cause, carried a brief and distorted account which gave the impression that the Seventeenth Regiment, singlehanded, had put the whole American army to flight, and mentioned only as an afterthought that the British had also withdrawn.[38]

Cornwallis himself brazened the matter out with the false cheerfulness and glib misrepresentation of one not unaccustomed to glossing over his own errors. He had to account somehow to his superiors for the fact that Washington had moved from Pennsylvania to Somerset Court House and thence back of the mountains to Morristown, where he was in such a strategic position for striking a blow in any direction that the entire British force in New Jersey was necessarily drawn together into the small district between New Brunswick and Perth Amboy. For this misfortune, Colonel Rall, now conveniently silenced forever, was an admirable scapegoat. In a letter written to Lord George Germain on January 8, which passed over with studied casualness the points needing explanation, Cornwallis remarked:

"The unlucky affair of Raal's brigade has given me a winter campaign. Washington is with about 7,000 men in Morristown, our quarters were too much exposed and it was necessary to assemble our troops; that is now done, and all is safe: he cannot subsist long where he is. I should imagine

[37] Hall, *op. cit.*, p. 258.
[38] *N.J.A.*, 2nd S., Vol. I, pp. 253-4 ; Glyn, *Journal*, p. 40.

that he means to repass the Delaware at Alexandria, the season of the year will make it difficult for us to follow him, but the march alone will destroy his army."[39]

Washington, however, made shift to feed his troops at Morristown, and Cornwallis was not given the opportunity either of pursuing him to the Delaware or of sitting comfortably and watching while the long-prophesied disintegration of the American army took place. Indeed, the British commander had troubles enough at home to take up his attention, and his chief preoccupation at first was to prevent a repetition of the distressing incidents at Trenton and Princeton. Fully impressed now with the disagreeable propensity of the rebels for striking at dawn, Cornwallis ordered on January 4 that the garrison at New Brunswick was to assemble at the alarm posts daily half an hour before daybreak, and to remain under arms until sunrise. "Lord Cornwallis," the order continued, "is thoroughly sensible of the great fatigue which the Troops have suffered, yet he flatters himself, if a glorious Opportunity should happen of attacking the Enemy, they will exert themselves upon that occasion, not thinking an unexpected March a hardship."[40]

It was perhaps as well for Cornwallis that this question remained an academic one; for many of his men, in particular the German auxiliaries, craved glory and exertion less than peace and safety. The fate of Rall's soldiers had made a deep impression upon the minds of their compatriots stationed elsewhere in New Jersey. "Our pleasure in Elizabethtown is over," complained the chaplain of the Third Waldeck Regiment. "One can no longer lie down to sleep without thinking: this is your last night of freedom. Elsewhere people are accustomed to undress themselves when going to sleep; here, however, it is otherwise. We go to bed

[39] Great Britain, Historical Manuscripts Commission, *Report on the Manuscripts of Mrs. Stopford-Sackville, of Drayton House, Northamptonshire*, Vol. II (Hereford, 1910), pp. 55-6.
[40] Glyn, *Journal*, pp. 39-40.

fully clothed and ready to travel. . . . We have everything for our necessity and pleasure, save only quiet."[41]

Frequent attacks upon outposts and patrols during the first few days of the new year did nothing to allay the anxiety at Elizabeth-Town, and on January 7 the town was abandoned by the British.[42] Other exposed garrisons were brought in at the same time; and by January 10 the King's men had been crowded into their new quarters. Some fourteen thousand British, Hessian, and Ansbach troops were now distributed along the river and the shore from Raritan Landing, just above New Brunswick, to the Old and New Blazing Star ferries opposite Staten Island, with the chief concentrations in the towns of New Brunswick and Perth Amboy, and small outlying detachments stationed at Powles Hook and the Sandy Hook lighthouse.[43]

Such a striking change in the military situation profoundly affected the spirit of the people in New Jersey. For weeks they had been chafing under the arrogance of the army of occupation. Now that Washington had outgeneralled Cornwallis, placed himself in a strong position from which he dominated the whole country from the Hudson to the Delaware, and forced the enemy to huddle together in a few towns, the inhabitants of New Jersey eagerly joined in harrying the insolent invaders. Although the American army had been weakened by the desertion of many of the Pennsylvania militia who, not grasping the significance of the Princeton maneuver, had fled in small parties to the Delaware during the march northward,[44] their loss was compensated by assistance from the New Jersey militia. The upsurge of resentment against the British, which had encouraged such widespread guerrilla activities during the month of December,

[41] Waldeck, *op. cit.*, p. 25.

[42] *ibid.*, pp. 25-6; *N.J.A.*, 2nd S., Vol. I, pp. 257, 258; Washington, *Writings*, Vol. VI, p. 487; Kemble, *op. cit.*, pp. 105-6; Münchhausen, Journal, Jan. 31, 1777.

[43] Kemble, *op. cit.*, p. 107; Glyn, *Journal*, p. 39.

[44] *Pennsylvania Archives*, 1st S., Vol. V, p. 180.

grew in intensity as news of the discomfiture of Cornwallis spread through the countryside.[45] Farmers who had taken the oath of allegiance to the King, had received "protections," and had been stripped of their belongings in contemptuous violation of the amnesty, now seized their muskets, joined in small parties with their neighbors, and assisted in driving in the regulars from all exposed and outlying posts. Many a neighbor must have envied the man living near Princeton who, it was said, discovered two Hessian fugitives in his stable and made them prisoners with the help of his dog and his pitchfork. The impression of one British officer that "the revolt all at once became universal" was somewhat exaggerated; but it was apparent that there was no safety for small parties of the King's troops outside their restricted lines.[46]

Not only the soldiers of the royal army but the Loyalists as well suffered in the general resurgence of Revolutionary sentiment. The country south of Raritan Bay, where Loyalism had flourished while British prestige was high, became once more unsafe for active supporters of the Crown,[47] and throughout the state those who had shown particular zeal in welcoming and assisting the British army were seized, thrown into jail, and heavily fined. Their property was taken from them by Whigs who, having been plundered by the British and Hessians, saw no reason why they should not indemnify themselves at the expense of the King's adherents. Regular legal proceedings to sequestrate the estates of persons hostile to the new government did not become common for some time after this; but known or suspected Tories could find no protection, and were subjected to lawless plundering. In order to give his troops an extra incentive to activity, Washington had ordered on December 31 that

[45] Washington, *Writings*, Vol. VI, p. 470; *Am. Arch.*, 5th S., Vol. III, p. 1449.
[46] Hall, *op. cit.*, pp. 268-9; Collins, *op. cit.*, pp. 30-1; Whitehead, *Perth Amboy*, pp. 339-40; Gordon, *Am. Rev.*, Vol. II, p. 416.
[47] *N.J.A.*, 2nd S., Vol. I, pp. 276-7.

all property taken from the enemy by his soldiers should be divided among the captors in proportion to their pay. He had expressly exempted civilian property from this regulation, in order to prevent indiscriminate looting; but the New Jersey militia, who had more personal grudges against individual inhabitants of the state than did the Continental soldiers, and who were near enough home to dispose of plunder, were guilty of much wanton pillaging as they moved about the countryside.

The position of New Jersey as the cockpit of the war was beginning to have its inevitably disastrous effect upon the morale of the people. So divided in sentiment that it was impossible for one faction ever completely to root out the other, and living, in great part, in places which were exposed throughout the contest to sudden raids from either army, the inhabitants grew more bitter and more brutal as the tides and backwashes of war swept over them again and again. When Howe's forces spread over the state in the winter of 1776, the Whigs had paid—and, as is always the case, paid with interest—for their harshness to the Tories during the preceding months. Now that the British troops had in turn been driven away, many of the Revolutionists avenged themselves upon their political opponents for what they had suffered at the hands of the military. Retribution was cruel and undiscriminating, and many of the more reasonable Whigs shuddered as they saw the excesses which were adding to the intensity of partisan hatred. Early in February, Governor Livingston, shocked by the lawless depredations of militiamen and other persons and stung by a sharp protest from Washington, issued a proclamation aimed at stopping the abuses; but the state government was weak, and irregularities persisted.[48] The frenzy of war was

[48] Fraser, op. cit., Vol. I, pp. 544, 561, 649-50, Vol. II, pp. 871, 908; Washington, Writings, Vol. VI, pp. 459-60, Vol. VII, pp. 56-7; Collins, op. cit., pp. 40-1; N.J.A., 2nd S., Vol. I, pp. 272, 283-4; Thomas Lowrey to Joseph Reed, Jan. 8, 1777, in Washington Papers, Vol. 39.

upon the land, and there was little will to peace or reconciliation among the leaders of either contending party.

So New Jersey passed an uneasy winter, the Whigs dominant and intolerant, the Tories nursing their growing resentment and waiting for the moment of revenge. Meanwhile, the eyes of all were fixed with anxious expectancy upon the two camps: one protected by the hills about Morristown, where Washington was engaged in his never ending struggle to turn his ragged and shifting force into an efficient army; the other in the villages along the Raritan, where the British and Hessian troops, squeezed uncomfortably into close confinement, cursed their luck and their tedious surroundings, and thought longingly of better times past and to come.

CHAPTER VII ☼ *A SEASON OF ATTRITION*

FOUR months and more of dreary garrison life dragged on heavily for the royal forces cooped up in the Raritan villages. While General Howe was enjoying in New York as gay a social season as the pleasure-loving officers and the complaisant upper-class Tories could devise,[1] the winter had become for his subordinates in New Jersey something quite different from the period of relaxation to which they had looked confidently forward. They had settled down in a district already ravaged by months of war. Perth Amboy, in particular, was no longer recognizable as the well kept, aristocratic little community it had been a year or two earlier. During the months of occupation by the American forces in the previous summer and autumn, most of the inhabitants either had fled the town voluntarily or had been expelled by the authorities for fear they might communicate with the enemy on Staten Island. In their absence, buildings had gone to rack and ruin under the rough usage of the military, and furnishings and personal property had been destroyed, stolen, or damaged beyond repair. The occupation of the town by the British brought back few of the original inhabitants: some of them were prevented by the Whigs from returning, and, in view of the evil reputation which the royal forces had made for themselves that winter, there was scant inducement to settle again in a town where every available corner was used to house a foreign soldier.[2]

Into this devastated community troops and yet more troops were driven as the activity of the Americans at the turn of the year rendered outlying positions untenable. To

---

[1] George Otto Trevelyan, *The American Revolution*, 4 vols. (New York, 1909-1912), Vol. III, pp. 141-2; Creswell, *op. cit.*, pp. 243-5; Oscar T. Barck, *New York City during the War for Independence* (New York, 1931), pp. 74, 82, 170.

[2] Whitehead, *Perth Amboy*, p. 231.

find accommodations for these newcomers was an almost insoluble problem. An entire company received only two rooms in which to sleep, and frequently it lacked mattresses, straw, or any other covering to soften the hard floor. A whole regiment was quartered in a church. Stables were made into bunk-rooms by the addition of shelves nailed along the walls, and open sheds were hastily transformed into barracks by the boarding-up of the exposed sides and the introduction of some of the primitive eighteenth century stoves to combat the winter cold that crept in at all the cracks. Still the soldiers came; and at last the possibility of squeezing them in was exhausted. For a time, many lay in the open; and the latest arrivals were kept aboard ships anchored close to shore.[3]

Beyond Perth Amboy, a post was established at the hamlet of Bonhamton, which, though considered too insignificant to be one of the winter cantonments in December, now overflowed with a good-sized garrison stationed there to maintain the communication between the two principal British strongholds in New Jersey. Farther along, at New Brunswick, were the headquarters of Lord Cornwallis, with a sizable force posted in the town and at various defensive outworks which had been constructed nearby.[4] As the more fortunate British officers and the leading Tory ladies in New York imitated the social life of London, so the officers stationed in New Brunswick and some of the residents of the town gave forth a pale reflection of the gayety of New York. There were formal calls, dances, and other diversions; and some young ladies, though professedly Whig in sentiment, were so dazzled by the unwonted brilliance of life that they let their political principles fall into temporary abeyance while

[3] Waldeck, *op. cit.*, pp. 27-8; Col. Joseph Reed to Gen. Sullivan, Jan. 10, 1777, in Otis G. Hammond, ed., *Letters and Papers of Major-General John Sullivan, Continental Army* (Concord, N.H., 1930) (hereafter referred to as *Sullivan Papers*), Vol. I, p. 310.

[4] Glyn, *Journal*, p. 39; Map No. 3, "Sketch of Brunswick," in the Hills Atlas of manuscript maps, Map Division, Library of Congress.

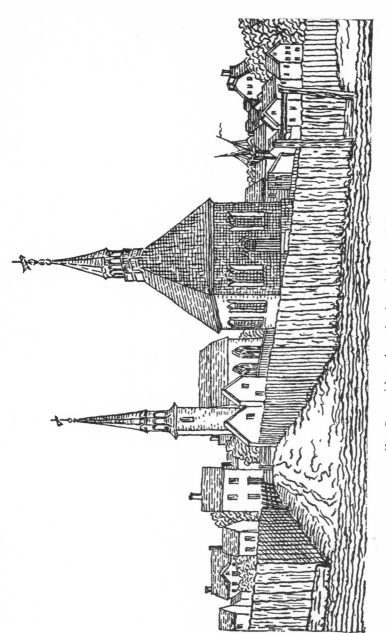

New Brunswick at about the time of the Revolution

(From a contemporary sketch by Archibald Robertson, adapted by Gustaf Lundin)

they accepted the attentions of the fascinating military gentlemen from overseas.[5] Yet to the officers, imbued with the sophisticated tastes of their class and period and familiar with the colorful London throngs who paraded in the Rotunda at Ranelagh or danced at the Pantheon in Oxford Street, life in the bleak little town of New Brunswick, with its handful of fluttering provincial ladies, must have seemed dull enough.

What made the situation worst, however, was neither overcrowding nor tedium, but lack of food. No sooner had the British shut themselves up in New Brunswick and Perth Amboy than Washington threw up an invisible but almost impenetrable wall about the garrisons. Though the principal American camp was beyond the hills at Morristown, patrols of Continentals and militia were constantly roaming over the countryside to capture any of the British who might wander away from their quarters. The farmers of the surrounding district were by this time mostly hostile to the invaders; and the sharp watch kept by the American soldiers effectually prevented any considerable traffic in provisions between town and country by such of the inhabitants as might otherwise have been inclined to overlook past injuries for the sake of some hard money. To make certain that Cornwallis should not supply the wants of his army from nearby farms, Washington dispatched parties of soldiers who systematically collected and moved to a distance all stores of provisions, livestock, and forage upon which they could lay hands and which seemed in danger of falling into the possession of the British.[6]

[5] Graydon, *op. cit.*, pp. 265-6; Letter of Margaret Livingston to Susan Livingston, June 9, 1777, in Livingston Papers, Massachusetts Historical Society, Vol. II.

[6] Glyn, *Journal*, p. 41; "A Campaign Journal, from Nov. 29, 1776, to May 6, 1777," in *Princeton Standard*, New Series, Vol. III, No. 19 (May 8, 1863); Washington, *Writings*, Vol. VII, pp. 15, 96-7, 119-20; *N.J.A.*, 2nd S., Vol. I, pp. 331, 334; Israel Putnam to George Washington, Feb. 8, 1777, in Washington Papers, Library of Congress, Vol. 40.

Hardly a foraging party could leave New Brunswick or Perth Amboy without being set upon by the Americans; and nearly every morsel of food which the men of the besieged garrisons brought in from the neighboring districts for themselves or their horses had been paid for in nervous irritation, in lead, and in blood. Washington's men had an exasperating and almost uncanny knowledge of when and where such excursions were to take place: wherever the British foragers went, complained one of their officers, their opponents appeared in force, "notwithstanding the Orders were given, but a few hours before the Troops moved." The newspapers, letters, and diaries of those early months of the year 1777 are filled with accounts of clashes between detachments of the two armies, and Cornwallis was forced to protect his expeditions with forces as great as two thousand men.[7] In course of time, the British came to look upon these harassments as a normal phenomenon of life. "Nothing very particular," runs an entry in one officer's diary for what he evidently considered a dull week in March; "our Foraging Parties meet with the Rebels as usual, and a Man or two Killed now and then." When a detachment from Perth Amboy made a successful excursion without being molested, the *New York Gazette* regarded the occurrence as sufficiently unusual to be reported to its readers.[8]

It was not only in the collection of provisions and forage from the surrounding countryside that the British were hampered. The bulk of supplies for the garrisons, brought in from New York by water, reached Perth Amboy without serious difficulty, but from that point to New Brunswick had to run the gauntlet of American sharpshooters. On the overland route, the country offered

[7] Glyn, *Journal*, pp. 42, 43; Kemble, *Journal*, pp. 108-12; Waldeck, *op. cit.*, p. 29; *N.J.A.*, 2nd S., Vol. I, pp. 294-5, 296-7, 305-6, 307-8, 310; Trevelyan, *op. cit.*, Vol. III, pp. 141-2; Whitehead, *Perth Amboy*, p. 341; Washington, *Writings*, Vol. VII, pp. 95, 118.

[8] Kemble, *op. cit.*, p. 111; *N.J.A.*, 2nd S., Vol. I, p. 309.

many places where the provision convoys could be attacked and disorganized. By water up the Raritan, transportation was hindered part of the time by ice, and, when the river was open, by detachments of Americans who posted themselves on the south bank and opened fire upon the boats slowly ascending the stream.[9]

Although the British were not driven from New Jersey by such annoyances, they did suffer severely from them. The garrison at New Brunswick was badly straitened for provisions: the soldiers were put upon salt rations, and the tables of the officers lacked those delicacies to which the gentlemen were accustomed. Wanting fresh food, the troops grew sickly. In March, the Loyalists enrolled in Cortlandt Skinner's brigade, the New Jersey Volunteers, had to be sent off to Long Island to regain their health. By the end of May, the soldiers, particularly the Hessians, were succumbing rapidly to the scurvy: as many as fifteen were sometimes buried in a day. Even more than the men, the horses sickened and died. Hay was a bulky article to be transported any distance; and the Americans had stripped the surrounding districts so completely of all kinds of forage that, in the words of one officer, "it was with the utmost difficulty our light cavalry and carriage horses could subsist." Such horses as did not die were badly weakened by their scanty diet; and Washington, happy to lessen the mobility of the British artillery, baggage trains, and forage wagons, took care to

[9] A favorite place for such an ambush was a spot known as the "Roundabouts," where the Raritan, flowing in a narrow channel, curved past a wooded point just below the mouth of South River. From this spot, the American riflemen did good execution upon the helpless crews and guards of the vessels; and on February 26, according to one account, several boats were sunk by shots from a battery of fieldpieces which had been temporarily erected either at the Roundabouts or at some point not far away. Glyn, *Journal*, pp. 40-1; Creswell, *op. cit.*, pp. 238-9; Hall, *op. cit.*, p. 270; Waldeck, *op. cit.*, p. 28; Whitehead, *Perth Amboy*, p. 341; William McAlevy *et al.* to Gen. Putnam, Feb. 7, 1777, in Washington Papers, Vol. 40; Putnam to Washington, Feb. 8, *ibid.*; Map No. 246 in the British Headquarters Maps, Clinton Collection, William L. Clements Library, Ann Arbor, Mich.

226 Cockpit of the Revolution

have removed from the neighborhood of the hostile garrisons not only provisions and cattle but wagons and such horses as might be appropriated for draft purposes to replace those lost during the winter.[10]

These troubles by no means constituted the sum of the inconveniences suffered by the unhappy royal army as the winter wore on. Fuel became scarce, and such fences as had hitherto escaped burning were brought in and used to warm the soldiers shivering in their improvised quarters. Several houses in Perth Amboy burned down—a serious loss in a town where every square foot of floor space was so precious. Smallpox made its appearance, along with the disorders which poor living induced. Finally, the Americans, in an unending series of minor annoyances, kept the nerves of the garrisons almost as thoroughly on edge as those of Rall's brigade had been in December. Never more than a few days passed without some new alarm: either a foraging party would be fired upon, or outposts would be driven in or captured, or someone would report seeing a strong party of rebels hovering about near by, or a garrison would be kept on the alert an entire night to meet an expected assault which never came. In the vicinity of New Brunswick, a considerable number of redoubts and flèches were thrown up to render the defenders of the town more secure; still, so an American spy reported, there was grave apprehension among the troops lest the rebels should deliver another surprise attack. The memory of Trenton had not grown dim.[11]

[10] Trevelyan, *op. cit.*, Vol. III, pp. 141-2; Glyn, *Journal*, p. 41; Hall, *op. cit.*, p. 270; Washington, *Writings*, Vol. VII, pp. 97, 118, 119; Dickinson to Washington, March 13, 1777, in Washington Papers, Vol. 43; Putnam to Washington, Feb. 18, *ibid.*, Vol. 41; *Sullivan Papers*, Vol. I, pp. 310-11, 361.

[11] *Sullivan Papers*, Vol. I, pp. 310-11; Jones, *op. cit.*, p. 43; Waldeck, *op. cit.*, pp. 27-30; Von Jungkenn MSS., 1:35; Putnam to Washington, Feb. 8 and 18, 1777, in Washington Papers, Vols. 40 and 41; Dickinson to Washington, Feb. 13, *ibid.*, Vol. 41; Münchhausen, Journal, Feb. 14, 1777; Glyn, *Journal*, pp. 42-3.

Privations, discomfort, and discontent were by no means confined to the invaders. The Americans at Morristown were scarcely happier or more comfortable than their adversaries in New Brunswick, and Washington had to struggle with difficulties which Cornwallis was spared. Chief among his worries was the old problem of keeping an army together. In all reasonableness, he might well have expected his troubles in this respect to be over. From every part of the country came news of a revival of Revolutionary ardor in consequence of the victory at Trenton. "It was a most happy stroke," wrote General Arnold from Rhode Island, "and has greatly raised the sinking Spirits of the Country."[12] In Loudoun County, Virginia, a young Englishman confined within the state through no wish of his own ground his teeth in private over the change in the situation of affairs.

"The minds of the people are much altered," he fumed in his journal on January 7. "A few days ago they had given up the cause for lost. Their late successes have turned the scale and now they are all liberty mad again. Their Recruiting parties could not get a man (except he bought him from his master) no longer since than last week, and now the men are coming in by companies. Confound the turncoat scoundrels and the cowardly Hessians together. . . . Volunteer Companies are collecting in every County on the Continent, and in a few months the rascals will be stronger than ever. Even the parsons, some of them, have turned out as Volunteers and Pulpit Drums or Thunder, which you please to call it, summoning all to arms in this cursed babble. D—— them all."[13]

For all this patriotic bustle, however, it was months before any considerable number of recruits arrived in Morristown. Washington became uneasy as his victorious army gradually melted away. The Philadelphia Associators were

[12] Arnold to Washington, Jan. 13, 1777, in Washington Papers, Vol. 39.
[13] Creswell, *op. cit.*, pp. 179-80.

disinclined to participate in a long winter campaign, particularly since they had sent their blankets with the baggage to Burlington when Washington left Trenton for Princeton. "They have undergone more fatigue and hardship," declared the general, "than I expected Militia (especially Citizens) would have done at this Inclement Season,"[14] and they lingered on at Morristown day after day from a reluctance to leave the commander-in-chief in too weakened a situation; but towards the end of January they departed for home. Although Mifflin's brigade of county militia from Pennsylvania remained in camp past the time when its enlistment was expired, its ranks were greatly thinned by desertions. The arrival of some seven hundred of the Massachusetts militia in the middle of January to act as a stopgap was soon counterbalanced by the departure of a somewhat greater number of New England Continentals whose terms of service had expired.

"The fluctuating state of an Army, composed Chiefly of Militia," observed Washington on January 19, "bids fair to reduce us to the Situation in which we were some little time ago, that is, of scarce having any Army at all."[15] Early in April, he complained: "Except for a few hundred from Jersey, Pennsylvania, and Virginia, I have not yet received a Man of the new Continental Levies";[16] and towards the end of the same month, he declared: "It is shameful, and at the same time a most Melancholy consideration, that at this late day, after a much longer indulgence than we could reasonably, or had any right to expect, we should be in such a condition, as not to justify a hope of a successful Opposition to the movements of the Enemy."[17] Soon after this, however, regiments began to arrive. By May 20, there were slightly over eight thousand Continental troops in New Jersey; and, as the new recruits were enlisted for three

[14] Washington, *Writings*, Vol. VI, p. 470.   [16] *ibid.*, p. 350.
[15] *ibid.*, Vol. VII, p. 29.   [17] *ibid.*, p. 454.

years or the duration of the war, the commander-in-chief had for the first time since the opening of hostilities a force possessing some degree of permanence.[18]

Particularly alarming in these doubtful months was the number of desertions. Bad living conditions doubtless contributed to the exodus from the army; the lure of freely offered British gold helped likewise; and Washington himself laid the chief blame upon the irregularity with which his troops were paid. Another very powerful incentive was the temptation to desert from one corps and, by joining a different one, to receive the bounty with which an attempt was made to render enlistment in the army more attractive. The practice of deserting and reenlisting for profit became, as Washington said, "a kind of business," which the officers found great difficulty in checking.[19]

Deserters revealed a complete indifference as to the plight in which their action might leave their former comrades. Thus, on the night of February 9, every man of the artillery company stationed at Princeton ran off, leaving the rest of Putnam's force without anyone to work the cannon in case of an attack. In explaining the matter, Putnam informed Washington:

"We were some Days without Rum, when a fresh Supply came they expected to receive all their back Rations at once, this however I would not comply with, for beside the bad Precedent, there would be not a Man of them fit for Duty."[20]

[18] Fitzpatrick, *George Washington Himself*, p. 291; MS. in Washington's handwriting, "Arrangement, & present Strength of the Army in Jersey 20th May 1777," in Washington Papers, Vol. 47.

[19] Washington, *Writings*, Vol. VII, pp. 199, 480; Sullivan to Washington, May 23, 1777, in Sparks MSS., 49, Vol. II, p. 224; Washington to Col. Baylor, June 19, 1777, in Armstrong Collection, photostat in Princeton University Library MSS., AM 10047.

[20] Putnam to the Hon. Thomas Wharton, Feb. 10, 1777, MS. in possession of the Hon. H. E. Pickersgill of Perth Amboy.

Angered by this refusal, the artillerymen went off to slake their thirst in more congenial surroundings.

Removal of some of the soldiers' legitimate grievances, coupled with such severe repressive measures as the threat of capital punishment, together with subtler forms of pressure, checked the desertions. In early June, Washington was able to inform Sullivan with some degree of satisfaction:

"By paying off the Troops and keeping them well supplied with provisions &c^a desertions have become much less frequent. A Story has got into our Camp which has a happy effect. It is that the East India Comp^y purchase all deserters of the Crown and send them out. It is believed by the Soldiers here and I wish you could circulate it in your Quarter. This should be done seemingly with indifference, drop it at table before the Servants."[21]

The matter of keeping the army well supplied with provisions, which Washington mentioned so casually in this letter, had been no simple task. Few military commanders in modern times have had to grapple with the results of such inefficient and disorganized auxiliary services as handicapped Washington throughout most of the war. Time and again, when already beset with strictly military problems calling for all his intelligence and energy, he was forced to take upon his shoulders the responsibility for keeping his followers from starving. In this first winter at Morristown, there was no such acute crisis as those through which the army was destined to pass repeatedly in subsequent winters. Yet even now the men who were supposed to keep the soldiers fed were proving unequal to the task, and the commander-in-chief was obliged to intervene.

Joseph Trumbull, the commissary general, remained away from camp, despite repeated pleas from Washington that he join the army and attempt "to prevent every thing from

[21] Washington, *Writings*, Vol. VII, pp. 82-3, 111-12, 480-1; *Sullivan Papers*, Vol. I, p. 375.

runing into a State of distraction."[22] A number of deputy commissaries scattered about the countryside worked at cross purposes, bidding against one another for provisions until they had raised prices to "a most extravagant rate." The supplies of food that reached the camp through their efforts were scant; but the volume of complaints, rumors, charges, and countercharges which poured in upon the commander-in-chief was generous. There were frequent hints of corruption among the purchasers; and, in such a disorganized and ill-supervised branch of the public service, it would have been remarkable indeed if no irregularities had occurred. Meanwhile, the troops were going hungry. On February 22, far from being able to enjoy a happy celebration of his birthday, Washington was writing angrily to Matthew Irwin, Deputy Commissary of Issues:

"The Cry of want of Provisions comes to me from every Quarter. Genl. Maxwell writes word that his People are starving; Genl. Johnston, of Maryland, yesterday inform'd me, that his People could draw none; this difficulty I understand prevails also at Chatham! What Sir is the meaning of this? and why were you so desirous of excluding others from this business when you are unable to accomplish it yourself? Consider, I beseech you, the consequences of this neglect, and exert yourself to remove the Evil."[23]

The commander-in-chief had neither time nor authority to investigate the abuses of the commissaries and to reform the chaotic system of provisioning. What could be done by independent action, he did. On December 27, the Continental Congress had vested him for six months with sweeping powers, including the right "to take wherever he may be, whatever he may want for the use of the Army, if the inhabitants will not sell it, allowing a reasonable price for the same." On the strength of this resolution, Washington,

[22] Washington, *Writings*, Vol. VI, pp. 457, 477-8; Vol. VII, pp. 160-1, 325-6.
[23] *ibid.*, Vol. VII, pp. 160-1, 183, 189.

on January 11, authorized a subordinate, Captain Francis Wade, "to collect all the Beef, Pork, Flour, Spirituous Liquors &c. &c. not necessary for the Subsistence of the Inhabitants, in all the parts of East Jersey, lying below the Road leading from Brunswick to Trenton." As fast as the farmers, either voluntarily or under duress, brought these supplies in, Wade was to transport the goods to Newtown in Bucks County, Pennsylvania; for Washington, who did not like his situation at Morristown and expected the British to advance again upon Philadelphia at any time, seems to have been unwilling to have large magazines laid up east of the Delaware. In order to move the stores to Pennsylvania, Wade was empowered to impress such wagons as might be necessary.[24]

At the end of the month, however, the special commissary sent to his commander from Allentown a letter full of mournful complaints. He was without either men or money: the few Philadelphia militia who for a time had been helping him collect stores had gone home, and he could get no funds from the officer who was supposed to provide them. He had no salt to use in preserving whatever fresh meat he could procure. Worst of all, he reported that various stores of provisions and cattle belonging to the army, particularly some which had been brought together at Princeton, had been unceremoniously appropriated by members of the New Jersey militia and other persons with no legal right to them. So far, his efforts to recover the property had met with little success. Finally, there were no storehouses at Newtown capacious enough to hold any large supply.[25]

Such were the difficulties which beset every attempt to supply the army with what it needed to eat. As late as the end of May, General Greene was reporting to Washington that the regiments stationed under him at Bound Brook were

[24] Washington, *Writings*, Vol. VI, pp. 496-7.
[25] Francis Wade to Washington, Jan. 29, 1777, in Washington Papers, Vol. 40.

insufficiently provided even with the restricted and unwhole-some diet to which they were then accustomed.[26] On the whole, however, for most of the winter and spring, the American troops seem to have been better fed than in the first weeks at Morristown. The presence of the British in New Brunswick and Perth Amboy gave Washington a reason and an excuse for stripping the country more ruthlessly than he would have cared to ordinarily, and the temporary grant of extraordinary powers from Congress furnished him with the authority. Somehow, then, the army managed to live on what the farmers of New Jersey had raised. It was not during this winter that the world was to behold the spectacle of the American troops starving amidst the prosperity of the people in whose name they were fighting.

Other privations beset the soldiers who settled down amidst the New Jersey hills at the beginning of January. Immediately after his arrival there, Washington informed Congress that many of his men were "quite bearfoot and ill clad in other respects"; and one New Jersey observer speaks of seeing "the roads full of naked, half dead soldiers." Occasional testimony from other sources indicates that clothing and equipment for the troops remained inadequate for some time; but in this respect, as in that of food, there is no parallel at Morristown in 1777 for the horrible conditions at Valley Forge a year later.[27]

More serious than lack of food or insufficiency of clothing was sickness in camp—an evil for which the other distresses paved the way. An ill-balanced diet, the lowered resistance of the soldiers due to exposure, and presumably also the imperfect sanitary conditions of the hastily established camp, led to the appearance of fevers and dysentery. Venereal

[26] Greene to Washington, May 23 and May 27, 1777, in Washington Papers, Vol. 47.

[27] Washington, *Writings*, Vol. VI, p. 470; Collin, *Journal*, p. 237; Zebulon Butler to Washington, May 29, 1777, photostat in Washington Papers, Vol. 47; Washington to Charles Young, June 10, 1777, photostat in Princeton Library MSS., AM 10046.

disease, too, was not unknown. Most alarming of all was the outbreak of smallpox. The spread of this plague among the soldiers worried the commander-in-chief, for, as he wrote to Dr. Shippen, "Should the disorder infect the Army, in the natural way, and rage with its usual virulence, we should have more to dread from it, than from the Sword of the Enemy."[28]

Under the circumstances, Washington made up his mind early in February to have the soldiers in camp inoculated with the disease, and he instructed Dr. Shippen to take the same action at Philadelphia with all the new recruits on their way to Morristown. This decision meant that the inhabitants of the whole countryside near the camp must undergo the same experience, since the soldiers passing through the mild form of the smallpox induced by the treatment could communicate it in its full virulence to any of the rest of the population who were not inoculated. Consequently, it was decided to quarter the troops in small companies in the houses of the people in Morristown and the nearby villages and countryside, and have soldiers and civilians alike inoculated and cared for by the army physicians.[29]

When this project became known, it created considerable dismay among the population. Twenty-three householders of the village of Hanover sent a petition to Washington, pleading for an abandonment of the plan. They offered several reasons for their request, the chief ones being that the district had been stripped of provisions suitable for feeding invalids, and that the hardships of war and the exigencies of militia service had left many households both

[28] Washington, *Writings*, Vol. VI, p. 473, Vol. VII, pp. 75-6; Margaret Morris, MS. Journal, pp. 26, 28-9; Nathanael Greene to Washington, May 23, 1777, in Washington Papers, Vol. 47; "Copy of a Court of Inquiry ordered by Gen¹. Sullivan July 6, 1777," *ibid.*, Vol. 50; Collin, *Journal*, p. 237.

[29] Washington, *Writings*, Vol. VI, pp. 473-4, Vol. VI, p. 105; Ashbel Green, *The Life of Ashbel Green* (New York, 1849), p. 88.

impoverished and shorthanded, and hence unable to bear the burden of accommodating soldiers. Several of the most prominent men of the same township, under the leadership of the minister, waited upon the commander-in-chief personally to ask whether it would not be possible to isolate the army from the population during the immunization period. Washington replied that there would be far less danger for the inhabitants if they were regularly inoculated and cared for by trained army physicians than if they were exposed to infection by the inevitable contacts with the inoculated troops. Accordingly, the original program was carried out without seriously incapacitating the people; and, as Washington was able to write at the beginning of March, the scheme was "attended with amazing Success." By his firm and intelligent action both the army and the civil population were saved from what was, before the nineteenth century, one of the worst and most common accompaniments of war—the irresistible sweep of pestilence.[30]

Much more difficult to conquer than the ills which attacked the bodies of the soldiers was the gradual disintegration of their morale during the long, dull months in Morristown. The temptation to illegal personal enrichment, which brought the New Jersey militia into such bad repute at this time, was not unknown to the Continental troops. During the winter, efforts were made to prevent their plundering the inhabitants on the pretext that the property seized belonged to Tories; but in June the people of the state were still complaining of the same abuses. Any opportunity for gain afforded by a special type of duty was eagerly seized upon. Governor Livingston complained in February that the military detachments which had been placed in

[30] Washington, *Writings*, Vol. VII, p. 230; Green, *op. cit.*, pp. 88-94; petition from inhabitants of Hanover, N.J., Feb. 12, 1777, in Washington Papers, Vol. 41.

charge of some of the Delaware ferries were demanding exorbitant fares from the passengers.[31]

Demoralization among the troops also took other forms, of greater or lesser degrees of seriousness. The inhabitants of Morris County, among whom the Puritan tradition of the early settlers was still strong, were shocked by the casual profanity of the soldiers, especially the officers, and even more by the cheap and unprofitable manner in which the men of the army passed their leisure time. Gambling became an all-absorbing preoccupation. One person in whose home a number of officers were quartered for the winter later reported that he could not recall ever having seen any of the officers diverting themselves otherwise than by playing cards—"their standing amusement, or rather their employment, both by day and by night"—except that now and then they engaged in a little rifle practice. The widespread American characteristic of preferring amusements for which a minimum of intellectual activity or of individual self-expression is required—a phenomenon for which the mass-civilization of the machine age is often blamed—seems to be as old as our national independence.[32]

Fearing that the prevalence of gambling would undermine the morale of the efficient military organization which he was trying to create, Washington issued early in May a drastic order forbidding "all officers and soldiers playing at cards, dice or at any game except those of exercise for diversion, it being impossible if the practice be allowed at all, to discriminate between innocent play for amusement and criminal gaming for pecuniary and sordid purposes."

In promulgating this ruling, the general expressed the hope that "officers, attentive to their duty, will find abun-

[31] Washington, *Writings*, Vol. VII, pp. 16-17, Vol. VIII, p. 213; Col. Samuel Thatcher to Capt. Butterfield, March 5, 1777, in Ford House MSS., Morristown National Historical Park; Livingston to Washington, Feb. 22, 1777, in Washington Papers, Vol. 41.

[32] Green, *op. cit.*, pp. 92-3.

dant employment in training and disciplining their men, providing for them, and seeing that they appear neat, clean and soldier like. Nor will anything redound more to their honor, afford them more solid amusement, or better answer the end of their appointment, than to devote the vacant moments they may have to the study of military authors."[33]

Alas for such vain hopes! There was probably no other time during the whole war when the officers of the American army were so little interested in the welfare of the service as during the first seven or eight months of the year 1777. They quarrelled with one another and were consumed with jealousy whenever one of their number received a promotion. Accustomed as we are at the present day to regard an army— at least in theory—as an impersonal organization in which the interests of the individual are completely subordinated to the efficiency of the service, we are startled, if we read Washington's correspondence, to realize how completely foreign this conception seems to have been to the minds of many of his officers.

Their mentality was a curious blend of the individualism which was already so strongly developed in the American character and of an aristocratic self-consciousness inherited or imitated from the European social structure. Washington himself wished to have a sharp social as well as military distinction between the officers and the common soldiers, and declared that in the selection of officers "the true Criterion to judge by (when past Services do not enter into the Competition) is, to consider whether the Candidate for Office has a just pretention to the Character of a Gentleman, a proper sense of Honor and some reputation to loose."[34] Many of the officers, confident of their social superiority and their merits, combined inordinate personal ambition with that childish glorification of selfishness then euphemis-

---

[33] *N.J.A.*, 2nd S., Vol. I, pp. 372-4.
[34] Fitzpatrick, *George Washington Himself*, p. 258. Used by special permission of the publishers, The Bobbs-Merrill Company.

tically known as a "sense of honor." All too often they lacked a corresponding sense of responsibility, and the results were unfortunate for discipline. When the Continental Congress made some promotions in the army early in the year 1777, a number of officers felt themselves slighted, and immediately sent in their resignations to Washington, quite ignoring the harm which their withdrawal might do to the service. The harassed commander-in-chief, already burdened with more than enough problems for one man, was called upon to exercise all his tact in persuading his sulky subordinates to remain with the army.

His difficulties with the officers did not stop here. In an attempt to hasten the forwarding of new men for the dwindling army, and to bring back to camp soldiers who had long been absent on the plea of sickness, Washington had sent out as recruiting officers such subordinates as he could spare. The results of their activity, however, appeared to be negligible, and the general became convinced that they were wasting their time in idleness and dissipation. Wherever he turned, he met irresponsibility and selfishness, and there must have been times when he felt that he was carrying the burden of the war almost alone. On April 12, he wrote to the president of Congress, lamenting the slow progress of recruiting, and continuing with a frank expression of his discouragement:

"If the Men that are raised, few as they are, could be got into the Field, it would be a matter of some Consolation, but every method that I have been able to devise, has proved ineffectual. If I send an Officer to collect the Sick or Scattered of his Regiment, it is ten to one but he neglects his duty, goes home on pleasure or Business and the next I hear of him, is, that he has resigned. Furloughs are no more attended to than if there was no limitation of time, and in short Sir, there is such a total depression of that Military Ardor, which I hoped would have inspired every Officer, when he found his pay genteely augmented, and the Army put upon a respectable footing, that it seems to me, as if all public Spirit was sunk into the means of making money by the Service, or quarrelling upon the most trivial points of Rank."[35]

Even while wrestling with these problems and discouragements occasioned by the state of the Continental army, Washington was also having difficulties with that inexhaustible source of trouble, the New Jersey militia. Hardly had he reentered the state when, on December 31, he had issued a proclamation addressed "To the Friends of America in the State of New Jersey," calling upon the militia to help drive the enemy from the state. The response was less gratifying than first indications promised. Large numbers of farmers preferred paying a fine to entering into military service, and it soon became evident that many of those who did turn out were less interested in serious fighting than in looting their neighbors. Disgusted by this selfishness in the people upon whom he had counted to help him, Washington wrote to Governor Livingston on January 24:

"Their Officers are generally of the lowest Class of People; and, instead of setting a good Example to their Men, are leading them into every Kind of Mischief, one Species of which is, Plundering the Inhabitants, under pretence of their being Tories. A Law should, in my Opinion, be passed, to put a Stop to this kind of lawless Rapine; for, unless there is something done to prevent it, the People will throw themselves, of Choice, into the Hands of the British Troops. But your first object should be a well regulated Militia Law; the People, put under good Officers, would behave in quite another Manner; and not only render real Service as Soldiers, but would protect, instead of distressing,

[35] Washington, *Writings*, Vol. VII, pp. 398 *et passim*; *Sullivan Papers*, Vol. I, p. 370; Washington to Col. John Patton, April 14, 1777, photostat in Princeton University Library MSS., AM 10040; Washington to David Greer, photostat, *ibid.*, AM 10043.

the Inhabitants. What I would wish to have particularly insisted upon, in the New Law, should be, that every Man, capable of bearing Arms, should be obliged to turn out, and not buy off his Service by a trifling fine. We want Men, and not Money."[36]

Livingston agreed with Washington in attributing the failings of the militia to the weaknesses of the existing regulations. For weeks he struggled with the state legislature to obtain the passage of a law which would render the service more efficient and which, above all, would no longer permit the payment of a fine to serve as a loophole for escape from military obligations. The pronounced antipathy of the Quakers, however, towards laws establishing compulsory military service and the indifference or concealed Loyalist sentiments of a large section of the population prevented the passage of any legislation answering Washington's requirements. Livingston wrote him on March 3:

"Our long expected Militia Bill in its present form, and as it will undoubtedly pass . . . admits of a Composition for actual Service for £3 to £20. . . . I cannot make our Assembly sensible of the Importance of an effectual Militia Law; or if they be, they are so unduly influenced by the Fear of disobliging their Constituents, that they dare not exert themselves with the requisite Spirit for the Exigencies of War."[37]

The governor was indeed in a difficult situation. Far from being hostile to the Quakers, he respected their conscientious scruples, and was disinclined to force them into arms. Others, however, were less considerate. Early in February General Putnam, who disliked the Quakers, sent a lieutenant to Salem County, where the sect was strongest, and authorized him to collect fines from the persons refusing to march with the militia. Livingston, as soon as he heard

[36] Washington, *Writings*, Vol. VI, p. 460, Vol. VII, p. 57.
[37] *ibid.*, Vol. VII, p. 263; Livingston to Washington, Feb. 10, 1777, in Washington Papers, Vol. 41; same to same, March 3, *ibid.*, Vol. 42.

of this step, issued orders countermanding it, and was promptly supported by Washington. The imposition of fines, declared the governor, immediately introduced "the invidious Distinction between Rich & Poor, which is always attended with disagreeable Circumstances." Furthermore, the law provided that all such fines, as soon as collected, should become the property of the militia company to which the delinquent belonged. "This being the Case," Livingston informed Putnam, "it is really the Interest of every Man willing to go, to discourage every other from going; as the money he receives is in Proportion to the Number of Delinquents. . . . Moreover, this Practice will greatly retard the Inlistment in the continental Service. Because the poorer Sort, who will chiefly compose the new Service, will, by these Means, receive so much in Fines, as to have little Inducement to enter for the sake of the Bounty."

In calling out the militia, the governor continued, he had acted "without founding my orders upon any particular Law of this State. I Did it by virtue of the fundamental Principles of the Constitution, by which the Commander in Chief must, in case of an actual Invasion, have authority to compel every person capable of bearing Arms to assist in repelling it. In this View of the Matter, as I was not regulated by any particular Law; so I intended to admit of no Compositions; and our People begin now to be so convinced that they must either turn out freely, or will be compelled to do it, as long as the Enemy's Troops remain in this State; that I fear the Method you propose will re-introduce that Reluctance & Backwardness of which they began to be happily cured."[38]

By this somewhat irregular substitution of broad general powers for specific legislation, Livingston stopped for the time being the levying of fines; but his optimistic belief that

[38] Putnam to Livingston, Feb. 10, 1777, in Washington Papers, Vol. 41; Livingston to Putnam, Feb. 13, 1777, *ibid.*; Washington, *Writings*, Vol. VII, pp. 186-7, 189.

the militia would finally be induced to turn out more whole-heartedly was scarcely justified by the course of events. The new law was so ineffective as to evoke disparaging comment from Washington, and the militia remained undependable. As in the past, service was rendered only by the willing; and the men of this minority, as is usually the case with people who assume burdens, were overworked to atone for the deficiencies of their lethargic fellow citizens.[39] The most generally faithful of the militia, from the time the British entered New Jersey, were the men of Morris County. Their neighbors in the nearby districts showed far less ardor. In Bergen County, the chief stronghold of Loyalism in the state, only the feeblest response answered any summons to arms. The Sussex militia were bluntly characterized by General Dickinson as "extremely unfriendly to the cause in general." In Monmouth, according to General Putnam, there was good reason to believe that many persons "engaged in our Service with a View to assist the Enemy by betraying it," and that some of them carried on a regular correspon-dence with refugees. As for the inhabitants of Essex, Gen-eral Maxwell recommended "a strict hand" in dealing with them, "because so many of them is protection Men and they will think that we are in Jest with them if we do not insist on their coming out." He urged that guards be "sent round to bring out those that did not come out agreeable to orders & to serve that part a month without pay, for there is a great number of Villains here that laugh's at all orders."[40]

Washington approved of Maxwell's suggestion, and re-quested the assistance of Brigadier General Dickinson in calling out all the men that could be procured. It was im-

[39] Washington, *Writings*, Vol. VII, pp. 286, 344; Livingston to Washington, April 4, 1777, in Washington Papers, Vol. 44.
[40] *N.J.A.*, 2nd S., Vol. I, p. 271; Dickinson to Washington, Feb. 13, 1777, in Washington Papers, Vol. 41; Maxwell to Washington, Feb. 17, 1777, *ibid.*, Vol. 41; Putnam to Washington, Feb. 26, 1777, *ibid.*, Vol. 42.

possible, however, to pump martial spirit into the farmers by force, and throughout the spring the cooperation of the militia remained irregular. The men of Salem and Cumberland Counties were praised by Livingston for turning out "with great Spirit"; the inhabitants of Burlington, on the other hand, the governor characterized as "exceedingly dilatory in their motions." Cape May was too distant, too thinly populated, and too exposed to render any assistance; and the farmers of Middlesex were too much worried by the presence of the British in their very midst to wish to move far from their own doorsteps. Gradually, Washington was learning that not in every state could he count upon such wholehearted zeal as that with which the militia of New England, for all their cantankerousness, had turned out and helped to keep the British shut up in Boston in 1775 and 1776. New Jersey was not Massachusetts; and there was as much divergence in the feelings and opinions of its inhabitants as there was variety in their origins, economic status, religion, and social traditions.[41]

All classes of people, however, irrespective of their sentiments, felt the effects of the war if they were within the range of operations of either army. The inhabitants who suffered the most were probably those living in the British garrison towns. Like the troops quartered there, they had to endure the overcrowding and the shortage of provisions; and, in addition, they felt the detrimental effects, upon property and spirit, of continual contact with the soldiery. To be sure, the English, German, and Loyalist regiments lent a certain new and spectacular brilliance to the aspect of the little Raritan towns as they thronged the streets in their uniforms of varying colors and designs. But even the sight of Highlanders wearing bonnet, tartan, and kilt—a uniform which soon proved to be impractical in the face of the cold

[41] Livingston to Washington, April 4, 1777, *ibid.*, Vol. 44; same to same, May 2, 1777, *ibid.*, Vol. 46; Washington, *Writings*, Vol. VII, pp. 158, 159.

blasts of a New Jersey winter and the mosquitoes of a New Jersey summer—could not compensate the citizens long for the trouble inflicted by the army.

The royal troops were brutalized by the harshest kind of discipline, and many of them were so lacking in *esprit de corps* that they did not hesitate on occasion to rob even one another. From such hardened men, the citizens could expect little consideration; and, even if the worst excesses of December were not repeated later in the winter in Perth Amboy and New Brunswick, where the general officers could exercise a stricter supervision, yet the influence of the rough, licentious soldiers upon manners and morals was inevitably harmful. Added to all these evils was the insistent and ever present evidence of the cruel waste of war, as wagonloads of the dead and wounded rolled back into town again and again from foraging expeditions.[42]

In the British outposts, where discipline was laxer than under the eye of the higher officers in town, the soldiers seem to have behaved themselves as badly throughout the winter as they had done in the rest of New Jersey upon their first arrival. Raritan Landing, wrote one of its inhabitants, suffered greatly at the hands of its garrison:

"I could not have thought there was such a lot of blackguards in the world. I have said, and have no reason to recall it, 'That if the Devil had a permission to send the worst crew from Tophet, these people, if they may be allowed the title, would outdo them in swearing, lying, stealing and blackguarding. . . . They have stole the chief of my loose estate, all my meat and flour, hay, horses, a hundred and more bushels of wheat, two hogshead of lampblack, beds & bedding. . . . I am not alone; all my neighborhood, that had any thing to lose, fared the same fate. You would hardly know the landing. Not a pannel of fence left stand-

---

[42] Dunlap, *op. cit.*, Vol. I, pp. 293-4; Whitehead, *Perth Amboy*, p. 347; Collins, *Brief Narrative*, pp. 37-8.

ing in a mile, all the wheat fields open, some houses burnt down, some pulled down and burnt. . . . We have nothing comfortable to eat or drink, everything dear. . . . If such people are to rule and reign on earth, then the Devil must be stiled the God of this world; I wish I lived in a cave on bread and water, rather than live as I do."[43]

If conditions within the British lines were thus almost intolerable, the vicinity of the American camp at Morristown was by no means a paradise. To be sure, there was less to fear from the soldiers; but here, as on the Raritan, there was neither adequate housing nor sufficient food for everyone who had flocked into town. The high cost of living and the other hardships endured in common do not seem to have produced complete harmony among the American refugees who had taken up residence in Morristown. Washington, already harassed by the bickerings and jealousies of his officers, found himself obliged to intervene to compose a dispute between Lord Stirling and old Mrs. Livingston, a social leader from New York. The patient but rather weary tone of the general's admonitory note to Stirling gives a hint of the nerve-racking life he was leading:

"The present situation of public affairs affords abundant causes of distress, we should be very careful how we aggravate or multiply them, by private bickerings. . . . All little differences and animosities, calculated to increase the unavoidable evils of the times, should be forgotten, or, at least postponed."[44]

Outside the encampments and garrisons of the two armies, the people were not subjected to the same constant pressure as within the lines; but throughout the central portion of the state no one was allowed to forget for long that a war

---

[43] *N.J.A.*, 2nd S., Vol. I, pp. 391-2.

[44] Washington, *Writings*, Vol. VIII, pp. 21-2; Stirling to Washington, May 6, 1777, in Washington Papers, Vol. 46; Peter van Brugh Livingston to Gerard Bancker, March 3, 1777, in Rutgers University Library (letter loaned by the Misses Baldwin and Mr. George V. N. Baldwin).

was in progress. The lower Raritan valley and the adjoining regions were swept almost clean of cattle and provisions by parties from the hostile forces, which followed one another in rapid succession. Hardly a wagon was left in the possession of the farmers near New Brunswick. The Americans made their extensive collections even in districts which were out of the immediate range of the enemy, but which might be invaded from New York or might, through the Tory partisanship of the inhabitants, supply the garrisons by means of a clandestine trade.[45]

Such official confiscations, accompanied by payment or by promises to pay, caused trouble enough for the people of the state. Much worse were the irregular depredations by Continentals and militiamen, which even repeated admonitions from Washington and Livingston failed to stop. The usual pretext given was that the property appropriated belonged to Tories; and certainly there must have been a great temptation to rifle the houses of noted Loyalists who had fled to the British or were confined within the American lines. In January, New England troops on their way home from camp plundered Captain Archibald Kennedy's mansion on the Passaic. At about the same time, the well stocked store belonging to Robert Drummond, the principal merchant of Acquackanonck, who had forsaken his former Whig principles and joined the British, was looted. In March, the home of Stephen Skinner just outside Perth Amboy was visited and robbed, to the great terror of Mrs. Skinner, who was still living there.[46]

Naturally enough, British propagandists made the most of all these depredations. On February 3, the *New York Gazette and Weekly Mercury* declared:

[45] Washington, *Writings,* Vol. VII, pp. 96-7, 119; "A Campaign Journal," in *Princeton Standard,* New Series, Vol. III, No. 19 (May 8, 1863); *N.J.A.,* 2nd S., Vol. I, pp. 277, 331, 334; Putnam to Washington, Feb. 8, 1777, in Washington Papers, Vol. 40.
[46] *N.J.A.,* 2nd S., Vol. I, pp. 251 n., 263-4, 271-2, 309-10.

"The Ravages of the Rebel Army in and about the Jersies are shocking to Humanity. Several Persons upon the bare Suspicion of being well-affected to legal Government, have had their Property seized, and their Houses and Furniture entirely demolished. They have so harassed the poor Farmers in general, that all Agriculture is stopt, and every Prospect is opened to an approaching Famine. The Rebels have also forced away almost all their Cattle, and left many Scores of Families in the most melancholy Situation of Poverty and Distress."[47]

In the same vein, the *Gazette* reported on April 14:

"On Friday last a Party of 50 Men came into Town from West Jersey. . . . The Whole Country is so oppressed with the Villainy and tyrannical Proceedings of the Rebels, that the Inhabitants are almost every where ready to rise, when the King's Troops shall take the Field."[48]

Less than a week before, on the other hand, the *Pennsylvania Gazette*, a Whig newspaper, had printed an item of completely contradictory import:

"A Gentleman, late from Head-Quarters in the Jersies . . . remarks, that he could not have believed it was in the power of any events to have made so great an alteration in the sentiments and spirits of a people in so short a time, as the enemy's rout and ravages made among the Jerseymen. The specimens of British Government exhibited on their momentary triumphs have fully gratified any hankering the inhabitants might have to see it established. The repeated failure of their military operations has cast such reproach on their arms, that those who were frightened with Gen. Howe's success and begged his pardon, have almost to a man returned to the cause, and are now fighting for the defence of their country; being resolved at all hazards to prevent any future ravages."[49]

[47] *N.J.A.*, 2nd S., Vol. I, pp. 278-9.
[48] *ibid.*, p. 338.
[49] *ibid.*, pp. 336-7.

How much truth there is in any of these partisan accounts is difficult to determine. Certainly the New York journal erred in picturing the people as waiting for an opportunity "to rise, when the King's Troops shall take the Field." When Howe finally marched into the interior of the state in June 1777, the farmers rose indeed, and flew to arms, but against him. On the other hand, as we have already seen, dislike of the British did not necessarily mean willingness even to serve in the militia; and the American gentleman's description of the Jerseymen as "almost to a man . . . fighting for the defence of their country" must have brought sarcastic smiles to the faces of Generals Putnam, Maxwell, and Dickinson if they read the item in the Philadelphia newspaper.

In general, the division of public opinion seems to have altered very little after the beginning of the year 1777, and the only change in the following years was the progressive intensification of partisan hatred. In certain parts of the state there had grown up so widespread and deep-rooted an antipathy to the revolution that during the rest of the war no threats, violence, or cajolery could bring the inhabitants to look favorably upon it. Bergen County was generally regarded as irretrievably Loyalist, and the activities of the American authorities in that district were directed towards keeping the Tories as harmless as possible. Of the English Neighborhood, today called Englewood, it was said that not a person was to be depended upon by the Whigs, almost every man being a spy.[50] Although there were a number of ardent and energetic Whigs in Hackensack, the fertile lands about that town and in the neighborhood of Paramus and the falls of the Passaic were the source of large supplies of provisions and forage which passed to the British troops in New York by way of Powles Hook. Washington did

[50] Letter of Capt. Isaac Beal, April 20, 1777, in Washington Papers, Vol. 45.

what he could to halt the traffic; but the combination of
loyal zeal and thirst for profit was too much for the vigilance
of the Whigs, particularly since detachments of royal troops
were sent out from time to time as far as the English Neighborhood to guard the wagons bearing provisions towards the
Hudson.[51]

Similar conditions prevailed in a considerable part of
Monmouth County, where the long, unsettled shoreline
made it particularly difficult to detect illicit trade with the
British. A party of some three hundred militia under Lieutenant Colonel David Forman was stationed on the shore
to check the trade; but the detachment had a seacoast of
one hundred miles to guard, and Forman despaired of performing his task efficiently. He was acquainted with the
two routes to Sandy Hook over which horses were taken
to the British post at the lighthouse; but he did not dare to
station permanent guards to block the roads, for fear the
men might be surprised; and he had no artillery with which
to defend such works as he might erect at strategic spots.[52]

Elsewhere in the state, the Tories were unable to render
much effective assistance to the British troops, either because,
as in Sussex County, where they were numerous, they were
remote from the royal garrisons, or because, as in Essex
County, where they were near the shore, they were kept
under surveillance by a Whig majority.

Late in January, Washington made an attempt to solve
the Tory question in drastic fashion. On the strength of the
resolution by which Congress on December 27 had vested
him with the right "to arrest and confine persons . . . disaffected to the American cause,"[53] the commander-in-chief
issued a proclamation on January 25, ordering that all who
had taken protections from Howe and sworn allegiance to

[51] Washington, *Writings*, Vol. VII, pp. 165, 179; Alexander McDougall to
Washington, Feb. 11, 1777, in Washington Papers, Vol. 41.
[52] David Forman to Richard Peters, May 27, 1777, *ibid.*, Vol. 47.
[53] *Am. Arch.*, 5th S., Vol. III, p. 1613.

the King should either deliver up their protections to the nearest officer of the militia or the Continental army or withdraw with their families into the British lines. Anyone failing to comply with this order within thirty days would be deemed an adherent of the King of Great Britain, and treated as a common enemy of the American States. By later orders, Washington expanded the regulation so that persons who chose to join the British were unable to take with them anything but their clothing and such household furniture as they could transport without the use of wagons or carts, which he was unwilling to have fall into the hands of the enemy.[54]

Such a decree could not be effective in a region where the Tories were so numerous and the agencies of law enforcement so weak as in New Jersey.[55] The state continued to abound with Loyalists, and almost the only result of the proclamation was that Washington was subjected to sharp censure by people who feared a military dictatorship. Abraham Clark, a delegate from New Jersey to the Continental Congress, wrote to a friend on March 7:

"It must render any man Unpopular to speak in favour of those who joined the Enemy & took Protections, but I think the Gen[rls] Proclamation a Violation of our Civil Rights. . . . It is Notorious the Gen[rl] directly counter Acted a Resolve of Congress of the 9th of March last, Strictly forbidding Any Officer to impose or require Any Oath of the Inhabitants, and he requires an Oath of allegiance to the *United States* when such an Oath is Absurd before our Confederation takes place. . . . In many other instances the Procla[a] is exceptionable, and very improper, and I believe was the Production or at least set on foot by some too much in the Gen[rls] Good Graces, he is too much

[54] Washington, *Writings*, Vol. VII, pp. 61-2, 142-3, 188, 189-90.
[55] *N.J. Exec. Corr.*, p. 46.

incumberd to attend to every thing, & tho' I believe him honest, I think him fallible."[56]

Clark introduced into Congress a motion to call the proclamation into question;[57] but the committee to whom the motion was referred reported in favor of Washington's action and the matter was soon dropped.

Amidst all the heated discussion over the treatment of Loyalists, and the growing bitterness between the political parties, there were some individuals who succeeded in keeping on a reasonably good footing with both sides. Characteristic of these were the five Van Horne sisters—"all handsome and well bred"—who professed to be Whigs, but who nevertheless stayed with their mother in New Brunswick most of the winter and remained on the best of terms with the British officers, thereby scandalizing old friends like the Livingstons, who held stricter views.[58]

At Bound Brook lived a family, also named Van Horne, who performed prodigies in the difficult art of being all things to all men. The head of the family, a retired colonel of the militia and before the war a prosperous merchant in New York, had withdrawn upon the outbreak of hostilities to his country seat just outside Bound Brook. Here he received all comers, British and American alike, with a most generous welcome. "His hospitality ought certainly to have been recompensed by an unlimited credit on the public stores," writes one American officer who passed through in the summer of 1777. "His house, used as a hotel, seemed constantly full. It was at this time occupied by Colonel Bland, of the Virginia cavalry, and the officers of his corps. . . . Notwithstanding the number of guests that were to

[56] Abraham Clark to Elias Dayton, March 7, 1777, in Sparks MSS., 49, Vol. II, p. 215.

[57] *N.J. Exec. Corr.*, p. 26; Fitzpatrick, *op. cit.*, pp. 284-6.

[58] Graydon, *op. cit.*, pp. 265-6; Margaret Livingston to Susan F. Livingston, June 9, 1777, in Livingston Papers, Massachusetts Historical Society, Vol. II.

be provided for, there appeared no deficiency in accommodation; and we supped and lodged well."[59]

This hospitality was offered with equal cordiality to adherents of the King, and Mr. Van Horne maintained friendly connections with persons living behind the British lines in New Brunswick. "Nothing can prove more strongly the integrity of his conduct," writes one innocent contemporary, "than the esteem in which he is held by both parties." According to one account, Cornwallis, on the morning in April 1777 on which he delivered a surprise attack at daybreak upon the American detachment stationed under General Lincoln at Bound Brook, had breakfast with the Van Hornes, and General Lincoln, who had slipped off to the woods when the British came, returned after the enemy left, and ate dinner with the same family.[60]

There seem to have been no American troops at the Van Horne establishment, however, on the autumn day in 1779 when the Baron and Baroness von Riedesel, prisoners since Burgoyne's surrender in the fall of 1777, and now travelling from captivity in Virginia to New York to be exchanged, stopped to spend the night at Bound Brook. They were very kindly received by the Van Hornes, who "gave themselves out for royalists," and, on the departure of the guests the next morning, begged to be recommended to Cornwallis. At Elizabeth-Town, however, the baron and his wife found that Congress had refused to ratify the exchange of prisoners, and that they must turn back. On the return trip, they stopped overnight once more with the gracious Loyalist family who had recently been so hospitable to them. Great was their astonishment to discover that "three days had wrought . . . a wonderful change in the sentiments" of the Van Hornes. A number of American officers were now staying at the house, and the prim baroness was shocked in

[59] Graydon, *op. cit.*, pp. 263, 278-80.
[60] *ibid.*, pp. 263, 265; Chastellux, *op. cit.*, Vol. I, pp. 143, 150-1.

more ways than one to find "the daughters of these pretended royalists on the most familiar footing with the anti-
royalists, and allowing them all kinds of liberties." Forced
to choose between maintaining their reputation as good
Loyalists with a royal officer going back to captivity, and
remaining on a good footing with the young soldiers now
on the spot, the Van Hornes did not hesitate. The gay party
went on, and "during the whole night," reports the horrified
baroness, probably with some exaggeration, the revellers
could be heard singing: "God save great Washington! God
damn the King!" "Upon our departure the next morning,"
she adds, "I could scarcely conceal my indignation."[61]

The Van Horne girls, indeed, had a way with them when
it came to getting along with military men. Before long the
eldest of them was married to Stephen Moylan, colonel of
Dragoons; and a French traveller who stopped at the house
in 1780 found the next oldest "on terms of great familiar-
ity" with another young officer.[62] Possibly their principal
charm was their freedom from embarrassment in trying sit-
uations. A month after making their former visit, the von
Riedesels went through Bound Brook again on their way to
New York. They had not intended to stop this time with
their double-dealing former hosts; but, by a strange coincidence, the carriage broke down before the very door
through which they had last departed with such suppressed
wrath. So, while the vehicle was being repaired, the baroness
had to accept the deceptive hospitality which she now
scorned. Apparently not in the least perturbed, however, by
the upsetting circumstances under which their guests had
last seen them, the Van Hornes requested once more, as the
involuntary callers were departing, that they be remembered
to their old friends like Cornwallis in New York, and gave
renewed assurances of their devotion to the King. This time
they seem to have dwelt upon Mr. Van Horne's former

[61] Riedesel, *op. cit.*, pp. 164-5.   [62] Chastellux, *op. cit.*, pp. 151-4.

service in the militia, giving the impression that he was now looking back with fond pride to a career as colonel in the royal army. The baroness, however, was not impressed. "I answered coldly," she says, "that I believed he did not need our recommendations; which reply he was welcome to take as he pleased."[63]

During the first five months of 1777, however, neither the Van Hornes nor any of the other political weathervanes living between the encampments could engage in such carefree social life as they later enjoyed after the British had left the state. The grim antagonism of the two armies lying so close together cast a gloom over New Jersey; and it must sometimes have been a strain for people like the Bound Brook opportunists to greet all comers with a smile when life was so very uncertain. Although from January until June no military engagements of any considerable importance took place on New Jersey soil, there was scarcely an intermission in the series of skirmishes between minor detachments. From the latter part of January, Washington maintained a considerable number of troops at Princeton under General Putnam; for most of the winter a force of varying strength was stationed at Bound Brook; and advanced bodies of militia or Continentals occasionally made their headquarters at other points. The recurrent clashes between detachments from these posts and stationary or roving parties of the British occasionally involved as many as one or two thousand men; but such an engagement rarely lasted long enough to be decisive.

On January 20, a party of some four hundred New Jersey militia under General Dickinson, with the assistance of about fifty Pennsylvania riflemen, attacked and routed a British foraging expedition of approximately equal strength not far from Somerset Court House on the Millstone River. The incident aroused among the Americans a delight out

63 Riedesel, *op. cit.*, p. 167.

of all proportion to its magnitude; for the raw militia, equipped with only one fieldpiece as against three for their adversaries, had faced the British regulars firmly and compelled them to retreat. Among the British, on the other hand, the clash apparently caused some embarrassment. The *New York Gazette and Weekly Mercury*, which never failed to record with an impressive and sometimes imaginative wealth of detail any defeat of the Americans, confined itself, in its issue published a week after the affair, to one brief and coldly uninterested sentence:

"A Skirmish has happened in the Jersies between a foraging Party of the King's Troops, and a large Body of the Rebels, in which it is reported, we have lost several waggons, but no authentic Particulars are come to hand."[64]

On April 13, the British sought balm for their injured pride in attempting to surprise a small American detachment stationed under General Lincoln at Bound Brook. Two columns under Cornwallis which had marched up opposite sides of the Raritan converged on the village and nearly trapped the Americans; but Lincoln was able to escape with most of his men up the slopes of Newark Mountain with not a moment to spare. Cornwallis took back with him a few score prisoners, three captured pieces of artillery, some baggage and stores, and all of Lincoln's papers, from which the British were interested to learn what an exact knowledge of their position at New Brunswick the Americans possessed. If the jaunt had been planned as a British version of the surprise at Trenton, it had failed notably.[65]

More successful was a series of raids directed against small parties of soldiers or against prominent Whig civilians

[64] "A Campaign Journal," in *Princeton Standard*, New Series, Vol. III, No. 18 (May 1, 1863); *N.J.A.*, 2nd S., Vol. I, pp. 272, 275-6; Washington, *Writings*, Vol. VII, p. 48.

[65] Washington, *Writings*, Vol. VII, p. 427; *N.J.A.*, 2nd S., Vol. I, pp. 342-4; Glyn, *Journal*, pp. 44-5; "A Campaign Journal," in *Princeton Standard*, New Series, Vol. III, No. 19 (May 8, 1863).

living in outlying districts beyond the protection of the main American force. Bergen County, in the lower part of which ten or twelve hundred Loyalist troops were stationed, became the chief center of this new form of violence: the kidnaping of political opponents not actually engaged in military service. In vain did the Revolutionary party rage: there was little that could be done except to retaliate in kind. Many of the Loyalist raiders were natives of Bergen County, thoroughly at home on the ground on which they were operating; the widespread sympathy for them among the other inhabitants of the district rendered their activities easy and handicapped any force which came to oppose them.[66] The country was full of spies eager to warn Tory soldiers of impending attacks, and to betray into their hands any weak parties of rebel troops. Some measure of vengeance could now be exacted for the excesses with which the Whigs, on returning to power after the battles of Trenton and Princeton, had punished the Tories for the sins of the British troops. With a sweep more violent than ever, the pendulum of fratricidal hatred was swinging back again. The civil war in New Jersey had advanced another step.

[66] *N.J.A.*, 2nd S., Vol. I, pp. 54-5 n., 287, 288, 295, 310, 342, 354, 378-9, 384; Washington, *Writings*, Vol. VII, pp. 168-9; Kemble, *op. cit.*, p. 114; Letter of Carl Leopold von Baurmeister, Feb. 16, 1777, in Von Jungkenn MSS., 1 :27; Putnam to Washington, Feb. 18, 1777, in Washington Papers, Vol. 41; Adam Stephen to Washington, May 15, 1777, *ibid.*, Vol. 47; Nathaniel Heard to Washington, May 14, *ibid.*; Isaac Beal to Stephen, April 20, *ibid.*, Vol. 45.

CHAPTER VIII ✹ *STATESMANSHIP AND POLITICS*

IN comparison with the stirring military operations and the social turmoil in New Jersey during the years 1776-1783, political activities were barren of excitement and color. No such radical changes in governmental structure took place as might have been expected in a state where so many poor and discontented inhabitants were to be found, and where the tradition of flouting constituted authority was so well established. That the classes lowest in the economic scale exercised almost no voice in modelling the new government must be explained by their dispersion, their frequent remoteness from centers of political importance, their ignorance, their lack of organization and of competent leadership, and their position as a fairly small minority in a province of normally prosperous farmers.

From the beginning, the Revolutionary movement in its political phases tended to be led by men of substance and political experience; the majority of farmers were content to follow such leadership along paths which did not diverge too far from well trodden ways. Even those inhabitants of East Jersey who had engaged for so many years in rioting against the Proprietors or against lawyers were by no means all poverty-stricken social malcontents. Many were owners of sizable and flourishing farms, who resented encroachment upon their hard-won prosperity by Proprietors, creditors, or the law. Irritable though they might be, especially at times of economic depression, men of this kind were not disposed to regard their troubles as permanent. Once the Board of Proprietors had been paralyzed by the war, and some of the specific grievances of past years had been removed, they were not inclined towards sweeping changes. In the woes of their less successful fellow citizens they felt no undue interest, and the idea of revising political institutions in favor of the poor backwoodsman would scarcely have occurred to them.

We need not be surprised, then, that the Constitution of 1776 made no drastic alteration in the franchise. Before the change of government the right of voting for members of the legislature had been open to any freeholder who owned one hundred acres of land, or was worth £50, current money of the province, in real and personal estate.[1] Under the new constitution, the requirement of land-holding was dropped, but in order to enjoy the franchise an inhabitant must be worth £50 in "clear Estate," and have resided for a year preceding the election in the county in which he claimed a vote.[2] Some geographical favoritism was abolished. Under the colonial government, the cities of Perth Amboy and Burlington had each been entitled to elect two members to the Assembly, a representation equal in each case to that of a county. In the overturn of 1776, the special privileges of the two towns ceased. At the same time, the number of deputies to be chosen annually from each county was raised from two to three, but no attempt was made to apportion representation according to the number of inhabitants; the sparsely settled county of Cape May had as many delegates as Essex with its much greater population.[3]

Like the franchise, the qualifications for serving in the Assembly were but slightly changed by the new dispensation. Formerly, a member had been required to own a thousand acres of land, or be worth £500 in real and personal estate; now the provision in regard to the thousand acres was dropped, but a candidate must still be "worth Five Hundred

[1] *Acts of the General Assembly of the Province of New Jersey* . . . (Burlington, 1776), Chap. X, Sec. 1.

[2] New Jersey Constitution of 1776 (in Peter Wilson, compiler, *Acts of the Council and General Assembly of the State of New Jersey* . . . [Trenton, 1784]), Chap. IV.

[3] *ibid.*, Chap. III; Acts of the (Provincial) General Assembly, Chaps. X, CXXV, CCCCLXXIV.

Pounds, Proclamation Money, in Real and Personal Estate"
in the county which he was to represent.

Along with the Assembly, the Council of the earlier period
was retained by the state constitution. For this body, new
qualifications must now be established, for the members had
formerly been appointed individually by the Crown upon
the recommendation of the governor. By the new frame of
government, representation on the Council became geographical, each county electing one delegate annually. In
an evident attempt to ensure that the board should have
much the same social complexion as in colonial days, eligi-
bility was made dependent upon the possession of real and
personal property worth a thousand pounds.[4]

At first sight, it may appear strange that the new state
should be eager to perpetuate any of the characteristics of
a governmental organ which in the past had been so unpopular. Throughout the eighteenth century, there had almost
constantly been bad blood between the Council and the
Assembly, and, as we have already seen, a majority of the
upper house aligned themselves openly or secretly on the
side of British authority when the Revolution came—a fact
which can scarcely have been unsuspected by the framers
of the constitution. Why, then, should this ancient source
of friction be retained? The answer is, of course, that the
men of 1776 aimed not less at preserving the advantages
than at avoiding the evils of the past. In their opinion, the
undesirability of the Council in its old form lay not in its
social composition, but in the appointment of its membership by irresponsible authority. In making it elective, and
forbidding it to prepare or alter money bills, they believed
they were sufficiently restricting its independence, and were
safe in placing it in all other respects on an equal footing
with the Assembly. To them, the drawing of its membership

[4] N.J. Constitution, Chaps. II, III.

from the wealthy class was not an evil, but an advantage, though perhaps a dangerous one.

Social ideals were in a curious stage of transition in America during the late eighteenth century, and nowhere was the confused blending of old values and new more striking than in New Jersey. The democratic sentiment which had been growing up out of American conditions over a long period of time, and which in the course of the next sixty years was to triumph throughout most of the country, was already perceptible, and gaining vigor. It was definitely tempered, however, by the accepted class distinctions which had been imported from Europe with the founding of the colonies and had but gradually lost their force. Probably it would have been unsafe in the New Jersey of 1776 to express the opinion voiced by Governor Winthrop of Massachusetts almost a century and a half earlier, that "a Democratie is, amongst most civil nations, accounted the meanest and worst of all forms of government." On the other hand, it would have aroused less opposition to declare with the same gentleman that among the population "the best part is always the least, and of that best part the wiser part is always the lesser."[5] To most people, the term "the wealthier class" was still synonomous if not with "the better class," then at least with "the wiser class." The Jerseyman of 1776 believed he had a democracy, and he gloried in it; but this conviction did not shake his adherence to traditions of social differentiation. The wealthy and well born, he thought, had advantages of education and experience which fitted them for political leadership and which should be used; but, he added—and here was a new idea—these people, once put into office, must be watched sharply to make sure they did not betray the interests of the people for their own benefit.

[5] Samuel Eliot Morison, *Builders of the Bay Colony* (Boston, 1930), pp. 92, 95. By permission of the publishers, Houghton Mifflin Company.

An illuminating exposition of this point of view is found in the columns of *The New Jersey Gazette* for May 12, 1779. The writer, after the fashion of the times, failed to sign his name, but sent in his contributions over the modest pseudonym, "A True Patriot." His anonymity has been preserved to this day, but from his many letters, published over a considerable period of time, and dealing with various matters in the public eye, we gather that he was a reasonably well informed person, interested in the affairs of the times, and characterized by a pronounced agrarian bias. Hence his meditations upon the New Jersey constitution, probably being representative of widely held views, are worth attention. "Wisdom and virtue," he declares, "the two necessary qualifications of good civil rulers, are no hereditary endowments of human nature. The very titles of honour and wealth expose such to the danger of oppressing others for their support." On the other hand "the many imperfections incident to human nature, will ever prevent the majority of every nation to be fitly qualified to manage civil government. Comparatively few are fit to direct the great machine of state." From these premises it follows that, under the best governmental system, "the people at large have the sole power of annually electing such officers of state as are to be entrusted with the most invaluable rights, liberties and properties of the people."

Judged by this standard, the Constitution of New Jersey was a happily conceived scheme. "Our Legislature is annually to be appointed on a fixed day, only by the free voices of the people. And in order to give the community an opportunity of improving by the wisdom and learning (which are generally on the side of the rich and wealthy), without exposing them to danger, this Legislature is divided into two branches; the most learned and rich being thus generally chosen in the Council, will not have that opportunity by subtility and sophistry, to mislead the more unlearned, though honest, in the Assembly, to betray the common interest to their private emolument, they would have, were they mixed with them in one body. All money matters and impeachments for mal-administration, are for that reason committed to the Assembly."[6]

Here is an interesting point of view indeed. Of dutiful subordination to a superior social class, in the seventeenth century manner, there is no trace; but respect for the ability and experience of the wealthy persists. To put those qualities to work for the good of the community, under proper safeguards, is considered legitimate and desirable. Yet there was no doubt in the mind of "A True Patriot" that the rich—meaning particularly the mercantile class—constituted a latent menace to the state, and that too great an encouragement of them would result in subverting the constitution. He was also fearful of what this class might accomplish in the Continental Congress, through delegates from less carefully governed states. "The spirit of the different constitutions on this continent," he explained, "will point out to you what you have particularly to guard against. That of ours, with some others, is truly democratical; That of some borders upon Aristocracy. Hence you will find the latter always favour plans calculated for the advantage of the rich . . . the former such as have a tendency to benefit the commonalty. In perusing the New York constitution it appears evident to me that the powers of government are thrown into the hands of the rich and wealthy in the two cities. The manifest conduct of the merchants and traders among us, have fully showed throughout the course of this contest, what kind of patriots and governors the body of them are, worthy individuals excepted. . . . It appears highly probable to me, that men who have thus carried their point against the commonalty in their own state, being delegated to the august Council of the empire, will endeavour

[6] *N.J.A.*, 2nd S., Vol. III, pp. 350-7.

to favour every scheme which may have the same tendency in the other states."[7]

Whatever concessions were made to wealth, then, in the new constitution from considerations of expediency, the people of New Jersey were inclined to look upon it as a democratic instrument and to fancy themselves as pleasantly radical. Subtle and less subtle indications of this new spirit, and of the efforts to flatter it, are to be found in the contemporary press. Contributors to the voluminous political discussion carried on in the columns of *The New Jersey Gazette* were fond of passing themselves off as plain farmers, though the style or the content of their communications is frequently such as to cast suspicion upon these claims. "Though I am a poor writer, and not quite perfect in spelling," are the opening words of one well written letter, which concludes with a specious assumption of rustic modesty: "And ye who are able penmen and well wishers to your country, I expect will take the matter in hand, and represent it in a clearer light than I can."[8]

Governor Livingston, a keen observer and expert manipulator of public opinion, was not averse to encouraging democratic predilections through the sprightly contributions which, under the pen name "Hortentius," he was accustomed to send to the *Gazette*. In September 1778 he published a short essay which satirically particularized "some eminent advantages peculiar to the old government, of which we are most lamentably deprived by our independency and republicanism." In the course of this discussion, he remarked:

"That the vulgar should be flattered by our muggletonian, tatterdemalion governments, is not to be wondered at, considering into what importance those whimsical ragamuffin constitutions have elevated the heretofore dispicable and insignificant mobility. But I am astonished that men of fashion and spirit should prefer our hotchpotch, oliverian,

[7] *ibid.*   [8] *ibid.*, pp. 31-2.

oligarchical anarchies, to the beautiful, the constitutional, the jure divino, and the heaven-descended monarchy of Britain. For pray how are the better sort amidst our universal levelism, to get into offices? How is a gentleman of family, who is always entitled to a fortune, to be promoted to a post of profit, or station of eminence in these times of insubordination and fifth monarchynism? Why, he must deport himself like a man of virtue and honor, (which abridges him of a thousand innocent liberties) and would in almost any other employment yield him ten times the amount of his emoluments. . . . Besides, it is not only the smallness of our salaries, and the necessity of having an adequate degree of merit to get into office, (a condition never exacted by the generosity of monarchs) but the comparative scarcity of offices themselves, that must make every man of laudable ambition eternally regret our revolt. . . . For the present governments being manufactured by the populace, who have worked themselves into a persuasion of I know not what, of public weal and public virtue, and the interest of one's country, it has been ridiculously imagined that there ought to be no more offices in a state than are absolutely requisite for what these deluded creatures call the benefit of the commonwealth. Under the old constitution, on the contrary, whenever the crown was graciously disposed to oblige a gentleman, (and the royal coffers at the happy juncture of princely munificence happened to shew rather too much of their bottoms) an office was instantly invented for the purpose. . . . Thus every humble suitor who had a proper introduction was always sure of being genteely provided for, without either consulting a mob, or losing any time about the wild chimera of public utility."

Having paid this oblique tribute to republican civic virtue and frugality, Livingston touched upon the appealing theme of democratic simplicity of manners as against the degenerate sophistication of Europe:

"We have irretrievably lost, by our fatal revolt, another important advantage, I mean the late useful and uninterrupted influx of the British gallantry, and all the politeness of the Court of London. While we received our governors and other principal officers immediately from the fountain-head of high life and polish'd manners, it was impossible for us to degenerate into our primitive clownishness and rusticity. But these being now unfortunately excluded, we shall gradually reimmerse into plain hospitality, and downright honest sincerity; than which nothing can be more insipid to a man of breeding and *politesse*."[9]

Such democratic sentiments were implicit rather than explicit in the new political order, and can hardly be called conclusive evidence of a genuine revolution. It was in the complete break with the British type of administrative system that the new government made its most sweeping innovation. With vivid memories of the long struggles between colonial assemblies and royal governors, the framers of the new system determined that no strong executive should be raised up again to pit his will against that of the chosen representatives of the people. The governor was to be elected annually by a joint session of the Council and the Assembly at their first meeting. No qualifications were established for the office, other than that it be filled by "some fit Person within the Colony"; evidently it was felt that the legislators were more to be trusted with recognizing suitability than were their constituents. The governor was to preside over the Council and have a casting vote in that body. He was to constitute a court of last appeal in all causes of law, with power to grant pardons to criminals after condemnation. He was to be captain-general and commander-in-chief of all the militia and other military forces of the state, chancellor, ordinary, and surrogate-general; he was empowered to employ any three or more of the Council to act as a Privy Council in case

[9] *N.J.A.*, 2nd S., Vol. III, pp. 416-20.

of need; and he was to give commissions to the civil officers of the state. In general, he was to "have the supreme executive power," but his influence on legislation was to be negligible: no mention is made of even a suspensory veto.[10] Other important officials, the treasurer, secretary, and attorney general of the state, were to be chosen for the same term and in the same manner as the governor.

As the executive arm of the government was made completely subordinate to the legislative, so was the judicial. The theory of "checks and balances," which was to rise into nationwide prominence on the wave of political conservatism a few years later, found no support among the New Jersey republicans of 1776, proud of establishing what they regarded as a popular government. Judges and clerks of the various courts and justices of the peace were to be appointed by the Council and Assembly, the judges of the Supreme Court for a term of seven years, the others for a year at a time. All might be reappointed; and all were liable to dismissal by the Council on impeachment by the Assembly. "A True Patriot" has a word of explanation upon this subject:

"Though prejudices, derived from our former very different constitution, may urge reasons in favour of judges being independent, both as to their offices and salaries, yet their conclusions will by no means hold good in our present constitutions. I acknowledge they ought to be independent of the individuals whose cases they are to judge; but hence does not follow that they ought to be independent of the community at large, whose interest they are bound to promote, by an impartial distribution of justice."

On the other hand, it would be unwise to elect them directly:

"Because the duty of civil officers is to execute the laws upon subjects, and mostly upon neighbors and acquaintances, it is evident what tendency it would have to relax

[10] Constitution, Chaps. VII, VIII, IX, XII.

the most wholesome and necessary laws, in case those magistrates were to be elected by these their neighbours: Therefore their appointment is committed to the joint body of the people's Representatives."[11]

In order to prevent any abuse of this arrangement, and preserve the legislature "from all Suspicion of Corruption," it was provided that no judge of any court, sheriff, "or any other Person or Persons possessed of any Post of Profit under the Government, other than Justices of the Peace," should be entitled to a seat in Assembly; on being elected and entering upon his legislative duties, every such person was to be considered as having vacated his other office.[12]

Except for various county or local posts, such as those of sheriffs, coroners, and constables, no further governmental machinery was set up by the constitution. The functions and nature of the various courts were not established, and the creating and filling of all branches of administration was left by implication in the hands of the legislature. Every effort was made to minimize shock and disturbance to the people at large in the transition from the old to the new order. A recent compilation of the law of the province was declared valid, except in such points as it should conflict with the new charter; and the common law of England, together with as much of statute law as had previously been practised in the colony, was retained with the same reservation.[13]

As an insurance against dangerous innovations, the new instrument of government included several articles of the nature of a bill of rights. "The inestimable Right of Trial by Jury" was guaranteed, "as a Part of the Law of this Colony, without Repeal for-ever." Criminals were assured equal privileges of witnesses and counsel with their prosecutors. Freedom of religion and the equal right of all Prot-

---

[11] *N.J.A.*, 2nd S., Vol. III, pp. 351-2.   [13] *ibid.*, Chaps. XIII, XIV, XXI, XXII.
[12] Constitution, Chap. XX.

estants to hold office were promised, and it was provided that there should be no officially established sect, and that no person should ever be obliged to pay taxes or tithes towards the support of any church.[14]

The constitution was not submitted to the voters of New Jersey for ratification. Evidently it was believed that the charter might at any time be altered, as it had been drawn up, without direct reference to the people, for it prescribes no procedure for amendment, and requires that every member of the legislature bind himself by oath not to repeal the sections providing for annual elections, trial by jury, and religious freedom.[15]

It is not entirely surprising that the new frame of government was thus casually put into operation, and was regarded as susceptible of change without a solemn referendum. Those who drafted the instrument in 1776 were frankly uncertain as to the outcome of the war. In their preamble, they said nothing to indicate that they felt themselves to be establishing a constitution that was to last for ages. On the contrary, they pointed out that the hostile acts of the King of Great Britain had dissolved his authority, cited the advice of the Continental Congress to substitute another form of government, and declared that the document had been drawn up "not only for the Preservation of good Order, but also the more effectually to unite the People, and enable them to exert their whole Force in their own necessary Defence." The general tone of the charter is that of a provisional arrangement: New Jersey is referred to throughout not as a "state" but as a "colony"; and the instrument closes with an interesting though superfluous paragraph:

"Provided always, and it is the true Intent and Meaning of this Congress, That if a Reconciliation between Great Britain and the Colonies should take Place, and the latter be again taken under the Protection and Government of the

[14] Constitution, Chaps. XVI, XVIII, XIX, XXII.   [15] *ibid.*, Chap. XXIII.

Crown of Great Britain, this Charter shall be null and void, otherwise to remain firm and inviolable."

The Constitution thus diffidently launched proved to be workable enough in time of peace, but inadequate to the wartime needs of a state torn by internal dissensions and ravaged by contending armies. In particular, the executive arm of the government, which had deliberately been made the weakest, was found to need strengthening to meet the emergencies which arose when the legislature was not in session, or which by their nature could not well be handled by so large and cumbersome a body. To provide a temporary remedy for this failing, a law was passed in March 1777 creating a Council of Safety to be composed of twelve men under the presidency of the governor. This body was authorized temporarily to fill military offices which might fall vacant during recesses of the legislature, "to cause the Laws of this state to be faithfully executed," to call out such of the militia as might be necessary for enforcing its orders, and to draw on the state treasurer for any sum up to £1,000 in the exercise of its powers. Most important of all, the Council of Safety was granted power to apprehend anyone "disaffected to, or acting against the Government," or even suspected of such offenses, and, after examination of witnesses, to commit such person to jail. In order to facilitate these various operations, each member of the board was vested with the powers of a justice of the peace in respect to criminal matters.[16]

This measure was frankly an experimental one, and was enacted for only a few months; but it proved so useful that in September 1777, upon its expiration, it was revived and extended. Members were now vested with all the powers of justices of the peace, with the discretionary right to exercise them in civil matters. The council was permitted

[16] *Acts of the General Assembly of the State of New Jersey* (published irregularly from 1777 on at Burlington), Chap. XXII (March 15, 1777).

to convert any building into a legal jail in case of need; to examine persons incurring the death penalty by being apprehended on their way to join the enemy; to grant pardons to such offenders on their declaring their willingness to enlist on a United States war vessel; to issue passports for travel through any parts of the state, and to delegate this power; to send into the British lines at discretion the wives and children of residents of the state who had gone over to the enemy; to remove at will persons accused of certain grave offenses against the state, from counties where the Toryism of the inhabitants would render a fair trial difficult to any other county for trial; to detain in jail for punishment by due process of law or to deport to the enemy's lines any persons believed dangerously disloyal who refused to take the oaths of abjuration and allegiance; to imprison disaffected persons as hostages for the release of citizens kidnaped by the British; and to take from dangerous Tories all arms and ammunition they might possess, giving compensation according to the judgment of two or more appraisers.

These were extraordinary powers, susceptible of abuse if they fell into the wrong hands, and justifiable only by the military emergency. As long as the state was imperilled by hostile armies, however, some such drastic provisions were necessary, and the law was renewed for brief periods, with slight alterations, in December 1777 and April and June 1778. After the British had left Philadelphia, and conditions in New Jersey became more stabilized, such precautions were no longer necessary, and the Council of Safety was allowed to lapse in October 1778, when the law of June 20 expired.[17]

In addition to the legal organs of government, there continued to function throughout the state, during most of the war, certain semiofficial bodies which were a heritage from the days when British authority was being supplanted. From

[17] *Acts of the General Assembly*, Dec. 8, 1777, April 4, 1778, June 20, 1778.

time to time the citizens of towns or counties met formally, passed resolutions on matters of public interest, and elected committees of correspondence to exchange views with other committees within or without the state. There seems to have been no legal authorization of such activities, but they were frequently led by citizens of prominence and did not partake of the subversive nature which had characterized the work of similar committees from 1765 to 1776, so we find no record of any opposition to them on the part of the government.[18] Doubtless they were a useful means of familiarizing the legislators with the sentiments of their constituents, and as such were welcomed. Extra-legal organizations of a much more sinister sort, the retaliatory associations which flourished in Monmouth County, despite official disapproval, and avenged themselves upon the property and persons of Tories or alleged Tories for the activities of Loyalist raiders, will be more pertinently discussed later in this chapter.

No time was lost in putting the new government into full swing. The first legislature reestablished the system of courts formerly existing in the colony, ordered that proceedings pending in any court at the time of the Declaration of Independence were to be continued as if there had been no interruption, and authorized the prosecution of any crimes or offenses committed and of any indictments preferred before July 1776.[19] It imposed upon all officers, civil and military, oaths or affirmations abjuring allegiance to the King of Great Britain and promising fidelity to the government established under the authority of the people.[20] Concerned for the dignity and the safety of the state, the legislature, before another year had passed, made the punishment of high treason identical with that for murder, with the addition of

[18] *N.J.A.*, 2nd S., Vol. III, pp. 429-32, 503-4, 519, 583-5.

[19] Wilson, *Acts of New Jersey*, Chap. IV (Oct. 2, 1776), Chap. XLI (Sept. 20, 1776).

[20] *ibid.*, Chap. II (Sept. 19, 1776).

forfeiture of the offender's estate. Thereby New Jersey rejected the cruel and inhuman British penalty of drawing the victim to the gallows, hanging him, cutting him down alive, burning his entrails, cutting off his head, and quartering him—a practice, remarked Livingston, which "none but a Savage, or a British Subject, can think of without Horror."[21]

In an attempt to secure the perfect operation of democratic electoral machinery, a law of June 4, 1777, established rules for the nomination of candidates, imposed penalties for corrupt practices, and prescribed the use of ballots in all counties except Morris, Essex, Middlesex, Monmouth, Cumberland, and Cape May.[22] Unhappily, time was to show once more that stern realities conflicted sadly with ideal principles. Just as it had proved necessary to entrust the executive temporarily with far-reaching powers, in violation of the theory of legislative supremacy, so it was found that the free use of the secret ballot brought serious danger. New Jersey came to a conclusion at which every revolutionary community seems to arrive sooner or later, however unwillingly, but which is never shared by outsiders who cry out at suppression of liberty: that until the new government is firmly established it cannot afford to be too punctilious in dealing with inhabitants working secretly, by every available means, to restore the old order. How deeply rooted this belief had become in New Jersey is shown by a law passed, surprisingly enough, in September 1782, when

[21] Wilson, *Acts of New Jersey*. Chap. XLI; *Votes and Proceedings of the General Assembly of the State of New Jersey* (published irregularly; hereafter referred to as *Votes of Assembly*), Sept. 8, 1777.

[22] *Acts of Assembly*, Chap. XXX (June 4, 1777). These exceptions are puzzling. Of the counties in which use of the ballot was compulsory, Bergen and Sussex swarmed with Tories, Burlington and Gloucester were regarded with suspicion by the Whigs, and Salem was none too zealous in support of the Revolution; so it may have been thought safer for the Whigs to vote secretly there. On the other hand, Hunterdon and Somerset were at least as Whiggish as Middlesex, and more so than Monmouth, so this explanation seems to fall to the ground.

the British menace was actually much less imminent than in 1777, but when the long years of strife and violence had stamped the thinking of the inhabitants with indelible bitterness and suspicion. This decree pointed out at considerable length the peril of penetration by pro-British elements "into the Legislature, and into Posts of Trust, Profit and Influence"; emphasized the need for "the preserving of our Legislature pure and altogether uncontaminated with the least Blemish of Toryism or Anti-Republican Principles, the eternal Pest of all free Governments"; and ordered that in all elections during the rest of the war voting should be *viva voce* and not by ballot.[23]

This measure was by no means the only or the most serious respect in which political activities in New Jersey fell short of ideal standards during the years following 1776. Far from presenting a picture of vigorous, disinterested, and harmonious action by statesmen and constituents alike, as the emergency demanded, the political history of the period shows us an endless round of factional quarrels, personal rivalries, legislative inefficiency, corruption, and charges of corruption. The historian who attempts to disentangle the web of jealousies, intrigues, and personal grudges half-revealed in the correspondence of the time finds himself baffled. In all this confusion, however, a few clear facts can be discerned.

Political animosities among the firm Revolutionists seem to have centered in two leading figures of the time: William Livingston, who was governor of the state throughout the war; and Abraham Clark, who served in Congress during most of the same period, with an interval on the Legislative Council in 1778-1779. These two men, both able politicians and untiring supporters of the war, and both members of the same Presbyterian congregation at Elizabeth-Town,[24] were

[23] Wilson, *Acts of New Jersey*, Sept. 27, 1782.
[24] *N.J.H.S.P.*, Vol. III, p. 80.

at loggerheads almost constantly. How far back their animosity extends it is difficult to say. As early as June 1776, their political paths crossed, when Clark was elected a delegate to the Continental Congress in place of Livingston, who had served since 1774. In compensation, the displaced representative was appointed commander of the militia, but having had no military experience, he was reluctant to accept such a post. "Mʳ Livingston hath declined," wrote Clark on June 26, "and seems much Chagarened at his being left out of Congress, and there is not wanting some who endeavour to persuade him that it was through my means to Supplant him, which was far from true, I used my Endeavours to get him continued in, and it is much against my Will that I am Appointed."[25]

Before long the disappointed candidate swallowed his "Chagarene," and undertook to do what he could with the militia. With characteristic humorous modesty, he wrote to a friend from his "markee tent" in the encampment at Elizabeth-Town Point on August 29: "You would be astonished to see how grand I look, while at the same time I can assure you I was never more sensible (to use a New-England phrase) of my own nothingness in military affairs."[26] He threw himself unstintingly into the more than Herculean task of building a disciplined military organization out of the disorganized mob of militia, a labor under which, as he soon wrote, "my ancient corporeal fabrick is almost tottering." Fortunately for the state, Livingston was soon spared the necessity of wasting his abilities on such an impossible undertaking: on August 27 he was elected governor of New Jersey, a post in which his unusual gifts were to find full scope.

[25] Lucius Q. C. Elmer, *The Constitution and Government of the Province and State of New Jersey* . . . (Newark, 1872), pp. 60-1 ; Clark to Elias Dayton, June 26, 1776, in Sparks MSS., 49, Vol. II.

[26] *Am. Arch.*, 5th S., Vol. I, p. 1210.

In his new capacity, Livingston came into contact with many of the same problems with which Clark was concerned; but the differences in the positions of the two men, as well as their temperamental dissimilarities, caused them to regard matters from sharply contrasting points of view. As an executive who discovered all too soon how difficult it was to run the faulty machinery of the new state with any approach to the efficiency demanded by constant emergencies, and as the chief civil functionary in a district which was a center of military operations, the governor soon came to appreciate both the problems raised by endemic civil war and the perplexities which faced the commander-in-chief of the Continental army. Clark, on the other hand, spent most of his time at Philadelphia, where the atmosphere tended to be somewhat more theoretical than it was nearer the battlefields, and where the fascinating game of Continental politics sometimes overshadowed other matters.

Thus we find that Livingston became a warm friend and admirer of Washington, whereas Clark could never bring himself to regard any soldier, other than his personal friends, without suspicion. Although the understanding between the governor and the commander-in-chief was not perfect during the retreat across New Jersey in 1776, the two men soon developed a deep mutual respect. Whoever reads their correspondence during the years of the war cannot fail to be struck by the confidence which each evidently felt in the integrity and ability of the other, and there can be no question as to the valuable services which Livingston rendered the army at such critical times as the hungry winter of 1779-1780.[27] If proof were needed of the admiration which the governor came to feel for the leader

[27] See Washington Papers, *passim*. On March 2, 1778, Livingston informed Washington: "As for the personal friendship of your humble Servant, if it is worth having at all, you have it upon the solid principles of a full Conviction of your disinterested Patriotism; and will continue to have it, while that Conviction continues to exist, all the Devils in hell, and all the envious intrigues upon Earth, notwithstanding."—Washington Papers, Vol. 68.

of the army, it is to be found in an ode "To His Excellency General Washington," which appeared in the *New Jersey Gazette* in April 1778, over the well known signature of "Hortentius," and which, after extolling the merits and accomplishments of its hero, wound up by giving him a throne in Heaven beside those of Hampden, Sidney, Brutus, and other "patriot demi-gods."[28]

To Clark, on the contrary, there was nothing of the demigod in Washington, or in anyone else he knew. "Tho' I believe him honest, I think him fallible," was about as fulsome a remark as the grumpy descendant of the Puritans would make about the Virginia gentleman.[29] The difference in the attitudes of the two New Jersey statesmen was strikingly illustrated after Washington issued a proclamation on January 25, 1777, commanding all who had taken protections from Howe either to surrender the papers and swear allegiance to the United States, or to depart to the British lines. Clark, as we have seen,[30] took steps in Congress to have the commander-in-chief censured for such an exercise of power; and he seems to have been supported in this attempt by at least one other New Jersey delegate, Jonathan Dickinson Sergeant.[31] Livingston, on the other hand, wrote to Washington after Clark had stirred up the controversy, and expressed warm approval of the grant of extraordinary powers from Congress by virtue of which the general had issued the proclamation. "I heartily congratulate my Country," declared the governor, "that they have seen the Necessity of the Measure. I could only wish that it had been done a twelvemonth ago."[32]

There were other points on which the two antagonists found occasion to differ. Clark was a native of the district

[28] *N.J.A.*, 2nd S., Vol. II, pp. 135-7.
[29] Clark to Dayton, March 7, 1777, in Sparks MSS., 49, Vol. II.
[30] Above, Chap. VII. [31] Fitzpatrick, *op. cit.*, p. 285.
[32] Livingston to Washington, Feb. 15, 1777, in Washington Papers, Vol. 41.

which had been settled by New Englanders, and which
had maintained its traditions and its cultural connection
with the older colonies. While in Congress, and apparently
with the occasional support of the other outstanding New
Jersey delegate, John Witherspoon, he cooperated closely
with the New England representatives, who formed probably the most astute bloc in the assemblage and were very
influential in directing Continental policy. In marked contrast was the position taken in such matters by Livingston,
who had moved to New Jersey from New York but a few
years earlier. He had no ties to bind him to the Yankee
outlook on life; indeed, his background of Dutch tradition inclined him to look with suspicion on the views and
activities of persons coming from east of the Hudson. During
the early stages of the war, the New Englanders, together
with Clark and Witherspoon, worked energetically to have
independence declared, and regarded with some misgivings
a policy of close cooperation with the French. Livingston,
on the other hand, was strongly inclined to question the
expediency of severing all ties with the Empire before a
clear agreement with France had been secured.[33] After independence had been irrevocably decided upon, and the
French alliance had become a fact, these points were no
longer a source of disagreement; but the governor of New
Jersey still cherished his suspicions of the delegates from the
states to the eastward. In December 1778, he offered some
advice to John Fell, who had recently been elected a
representative in Congress:

"Unless Congress is altered much for the better since I
had the honour of representing this state in that respectable
Assembly, you will discover more or less of a party spirit.
As I know you despise all intrigue & cabal I mention this
to make you vigilant in discovering where it lies & with

[33] John Durand, translator and editor, *New Materials for the History of
the American Revolution Translated from Documents in the French Archives
and Edited* . . . (New York, 1889), pp. 165, 238; Elmer, *op. cit.*, p. 61.

proper vigilance you doubtless will discover it. The interest of New Jersey is intimately connected with that of the Middle Colonies as they used to be called & I could therefore never see the policy or propriety of our Delegates throwing themselves into the arms of those of New England & Virginia as has generally been the case instead of cultivating a kind of fraternity with those of New York Pennsylvania & Maryland which I think ought to be the case."[34]

As the years wore on, Livingston's distrust of Yankee politicians grew more pronounced. In 1780, the French minister reported to his superiors at home that the governor had worked out a plan for a confederation of the states which would exclude New England.[35] The same year, Clark was writing of "the Genius & Political Ideas of the New England states & New Jersey" as if they were identical.[36] Maintaining their sharp opposition on such an important point, the old antagonists could scarcely be expected to bury their differences on others.

To be sure, when the two men were faced by the same problems under the same circumstances, they tended to work together more harmoniously. For a brief period in the years 1778 and 1779, Clark was a member of the New Jersey Council from Essex, and his activity in this position won Livingston's admiration. The latter informed a friend in December 1778: "We have . . . passed many valuable & spirited Laws, & dispatched more business than usual, which is principally to be ascribed to M^r. Clarke who has indeed great talents for Legislation & is a man of indefatigable industry."[37] Unhappily, the reconciliation which this handsome tribute seemed to foreshadow was not thorough: in

[34] Livingston to Fell, Dec. 14, 1778, copy in Box 2, Livingston Papers, Massachusetts Historical Society.
[35] Durand, *op. cit.*, pp. 238-9.
[36] Clark to Josiah Hornblower, Oct. 31, 1780, in Room 118, State Library, Trenton.
[37] Livingston to Nathaniel Scudder, Dec. 14, 1778, Livingston Papers, Box 2.

February 1780, we find the two men quarrelling again in the acrimonious tone of deep-rooted dislike.[38]

Clark's "indefatigable industry" was of great service to New Jersey. He was tireless in his attendance at Congress while a delegate,[39] and he did not hesitate bluntly to demand action from the state legislature when, over his opposition, measures were approved at Philadelphia which seemed to him to speak for themselves "in a Language which in New Jersey will be better understood than Relished."[40] Undoubtedly, he was a political force to be reckoned with, though it is difficult to estimate the strength of his following, or to trace the ways in which he manipulated it. When he tried to obtain an appointment from Congress for his pastor and good friend, the Rev. James Caldwell, he found that "the wheels drag heavy, a Presbyterian Clergyman is not with some a Popular Name." We may suppose he applied some oil to the wheels, for in time Caldwell became assistant commissary-general.[41] Clark was less successful in caring for another of his intimates, Elias Dayton, colonel in the Continental army. Promotions in the service were made by Congress, and competition was keen: Clark's best efforts failed to obtain advancement for his friend, and Dayton's correspondence for years is filled with complaints over his misfortunes and with threats to resign.[42] The colonel's young son, Jonathan, however, through someone's good offices, was commissioned paymaster in the army as early as 1776—an appointment which occasioned considerable acid and embarrassing com-

[38] Livingston to Clark, Feb. 1, 1780, *ibid.*   [39] *N.J. Exec. Corr.*, pp. 279-80.
[40] Clark to Hornblower, Oct. 31, 1780, in State Library, Trenton. This communication was called forth by what Clark considered the very dangerous measure of voting half-pay for life to officers of the army.
[41] Clark to Elias Dayton, March 7, 1777, in Sparks MSS., 49, Vol. II; *N.J.A.*, 2nd S., Vol. I, p. 147 n.
[42] *N.J.A.*, 2nd S., Vol. I, p. 518; Clark to Dayton, March 7, 1777, Sparks MSS., 49, Vol. II; Dayton to Clark, Dec. 21, 1780, *ibid.*; Washington, *Writings*, Vol. XI, p. 50.

ment in New Jersey by political enemies of the Clark-Cald-well-Dayton faction.[43]

If Clark was not invariably successful as a political manipulator, his chief opponent also had to cope with mounting difficulties as the years of war rolled by. Livingston's first election to the governorship was not accomplished without some slight unpleasantness. On the first ballot he was tied with Richard Stockton; the latter then withdrew his candidacy, under some involved circumstances which shortly led to a controversy between Stockton and John Stevens. This dispute finally reached such a point that both parties memorialized the legislature on the subject.[44] Nothing came of the confused and petty disagreement; but to Livingston, already smarting under his failure to be reelected to Congress, it must have been disagreeable to enter upon his new office to the accompaniment of such an undignified squabble.

During his first difficult term, in the course of which the state almost ceased to function, the new governor conducted himself with such vigor and efficiency that in November 1777 he was unanimously reelected.[45] Such a pleasant state of affairs could not last. No man of Livingston's dynamic personality, strong convictions, and sharp tongue could hold high office for long in those troubled days without running afoul of many people. His increasing bitterness towards the British and their adherents won him the implacable enmity not only of the avowed Tories within the British lines, but also of the large number of people in the state who, while outwardly conforming to the new order, secretly wished for the success of the Crown, or deplored the struggle and all its violence. Although his contributions to the *New Jersey Gazette* appeared over the signature "Hortentius," it was generally known from whose pen they proceeded—indeed,

[43] Caldwell to Dayton, Sept. 10, 1776, Sparks MSS., 49, Vol. II.
[44] See Stockton's memorial, and Stevens' reply, in the Stevens Papers, Stevens Institute, Hoboken.
[45] *Votes of Assembly*, Nov. 1, 1777.

there was no other pen in New Jersey capable of their type
of biting satire, or, occasionally, of simple rollicking humor.
These essays, though inevitably of very uneven quality, must
have been most effective as propaganda; but there were conservative souls to whom it seemed undignified for the
governor to engage publicly in such gibes, thrusts, and
bludgeonings—particularly since on rare occasions he used a
coarseness of expression distasteful to the modern reader
but common enough in the political controversies of the day.

All the disgruntled elements seem to have combined to
embarrass Livingston in the closing days of the legislative
session in the summer of 1778, and at the joint meeting of
the new Council and Assembly held in October to elect a
governor. He wrote to a friend about it some months later:

"You was witness to the attempts made at the close of the
last session for raising a storm against me to be improved at
the then approaching election. My Persecutors however made
a very contemptible figure in joint meeting. Had the opposition been any way respectable, I should have thought it
my duty to have resigned tho' elected by a considerable
majority. . . . But the minority being so very trifling, such
a step could have served no other purpose than that of gratifying their personal malice, to which I confess I was by no
means disposed. In revenge for their disappointment, they
began the present year with treating me with such insult as
no consideration whatever save that of sacrificing my private
rights to the public could have induced me to bear. . . .
They cannot I think injure me, & what is of more consequence their motives are now too well understood for them
to injure the public. They endeavor indeed as usual to per-
plex & to obstruct every spirited measure, but they are as
constantly outvoted; & will soon become so generally
suspected as to be utterly despised."[46]

[46] Livingston to Theophilus Elmer, Dec. 9, 1778, in Livingston Papers,
Box 2.

Although the storm of opposition blew over for the time being, it had one regrettable effect. Among the complaints against Livingston made at the joint meeting had been one about his improper conduct in publishing the "Hortentius" articles.[47] Like the other accusations, these objections seem to have carried little weight with the legislature; but the governor evidently decided that it would be prudent for him to desist from literary activity. After the month of October 1778, the columns of ponderous political controversy in the *New Jersey Gazette* are enlivened by no more of the sprightly observations of Hortentius—a sad change for the reader of today who wades through the endless treatises by "Eumenes," "A True Patriot," "Honestus," and others.

Livingston's adversaries were by no means silenced: the next year at voting time they renewed their attack. It can scarcely have been a coincidence that at the end of September 1779, about two weeks before election day, the attention of the Assembly was called, ostensibly by a routine incident, to a charter of incorporation which the governor had granted to the First-Day Baptist Society of Hopewell, Cumberland County, a year and a half earlier. Jealous of its privileges, once the matter was raised, the house unanimously resolved that the charter was void, and that the power of granting patents and charters was vested solely in the legislature. The Council was requested to concur in these resolutions, but demurred. Pointing out that the session was nearing its close and that numerous members had already departed, so that a representative expression of opinion could not be secured, and doubtless suspecting that the raising of such a question at that time was intended to furnish campaign ammunition, the upper house suggested that consideration of the matter be left to the next legislature. To this proposal the Assembly refused to assent, reiterating

[47] Livingston to Isaac Collins, Feb. 22, 1779, in Livingston Papers, Box 2.

in spirited resolves its firm conviction of its rights in the matter.[48] The incident had no particular importance; but it had put upon official record, for such use as might be made of it, the unanimous opinion of the chief legislative body that the governor had exceeded his powers.

All this had been done under the guise of regular legislative routine; but a more open attack was soon to attract wide attention. In the *New Jersey Gazette* for October 27, 1779, appeared an essay by one "Cincinnatus," entitled "Hints humbly offered to the consideration of the Legislature of New-Jersey, in their future choice of a Governor." Although the article did not mention Livingston by name, it obviously was a sarcastic denunciation of him. In thinly veiled allusions it scorned him as "a foreigner," with "little or no landed interest within the State" to make him cautious in expending tax money; aspersed his legal attainments; intimated that he was too prone to issue proclamations on his own initiative; ridiculed his speaking ability; condemned the "Hortentius" letters; designated him "a thorough and complete coward"; painted him as an implacable enemy of the Quakers; represented his travels about the state (actually necessitated by the dangerous situation of his home at Elizabeth-Town) as motivated by a dislike for his family; sneered at his well known lack of elegance in dress; and denounced him as a turncoat because, having formerly been opposed to independence, he was now so zealous in persecuting those who still were.[49]

It was a clever attack, with enough truth in its allegations to support its appeal to a varied array of prejudices and emotions. Livingston's reputation, however, was too secure to be seriously affected by any such scurrility, and he was triumphantly reelected, as indeed he was to be for years, long after the war was over. The Council was incensed at

[48] *Votes of Assembly*, April 11, 1778, Sept. 29, 1779, Oct. 6, 1779.
[49] *N.J.A.*, 2nd S., Vol. III, pp. 711-13.

the anonymous publication, particularly since "Cincinnatus" had taken occasion, in passing, to cast a gratuitous aspersion upon the College at Princeton. In the opinion of the house, the letter constituted "not only a Slur upon the Seminary of Learning in this State, and the President and Tutors thereof, but also a tacit Charge against the Legislature of this State as being greatly deficient in Point of Integrity, or Ability, and Judgment in the Choice of a Governor, and an express Declamation against our excellent Constitution; and also an unjust, false and cruel Defamation and Aspersion of His Excellency the Governor; all which evidently tends to disturb the Peace of the Inhabitants, and promote Discord and Confusion in the State, and to encourage those who are disaffected to the present Government." Hence, though professing a belief that "the Freedom of the Press ought to be tolerated as far as is consistent with the Good of the People, and the Security of the Government established under their Authority," the Council felt that some steps should be taken to punish the offender. It resolved that Isaac Collins, printer of the *Gazette*, should be required to inform the Legislature who the author of the libelous article was, and at whose request it had been published.

The Assembly refused, by a vote of 17 to 11, to concur in this action, and thereby set an admirable precedent for freedom of the press in New Jersey.[50] Unhappily, one cannot be sure that the action of all those who took this stand was motivated by abstract considerations of liberty. Prominent on the side of the majority in this case are several men who seem by their records to have constituted a clique of malcontents in the Assembly, and whose votes, year after year, were recorded against most of the measures proposed.

Of such members "A True Patriot" warned the voters in 1778 when he counselled them to scrutinize carefully the legislative records of candidates for reelection. "Take notice

[50] *Votes of Assembly*, Oct. 28, 1779.

of their *yeas* and *nays*," he admonishes. "A few you will find
in every proposed case, on the *nay* side. You have great reason to suspect this proceeds from a *temporizing* principle.
Only consider, it will afford as good a plea to compromise
matters with the enemy, to have it in their power to shew by
their records that they have opposed all business, as any
whatever."[51]

Such suspicion of chronic dissenters—the fear of "boring
from within" which haunts every revolutionary government—appears to have been widespread. In December 1778,
Governor Livingston complained with characteristic vehe-
mence to a friend about the conduct of John Cooper, member
of the Council for Gloucester County:

"Cooper according to custom has used all his little arts
to retard every necessary measure, & enjoys the satisfaction
(if his crooked soul could take delight in any thing) of
having his *nays* on record as monumental of his zeal in the
cause of Toryism, & old England. What the creature can
mean unless it be to support an interest in a disaffected
County is perfectly inscrutable. He not only knows himself
to be suspected of infidelity to America by the very broad-
est hints from many of the Council but has by one of them
been called a Tory to his face at a full board; & still persists
in his opposition to every measure *ne respublica detrimentum
capiat* with [the] shamelessness of a Cataline. I wish he
would also imitate that arch-Traitor to his Country in withdrawing himself from its Senate & openly avowing his
treachery."[52]

Worse things than concealed and probably ineffectual
Toryism and rancorous personal animosities characterized
the politics of New Jersey during the war years. Not content
with the unusual opportunities for men of political talents
to rise into prominence in the excitement of the times, or

[51] *N.J.A.*, 2nd S., Vol. II, pp. 450-1.
[52] Livingston to Nathaniel Scudder, Dec. 14, 1778, in Livingston Papers,
Box 2.

with the various forms of war profiteering which were within the law, numerous individuals resorted to corrupt practices to hasten their advancement in public life, or utilized official positions to make illegitimate profits.

Early in November 1777, two petitions were brought into the Assembly, complaining of illegal proceedings in the recent election of representatives in Monmouth County. After examining witnesses, the house voted, 13 to 12, to set aside the election, and ordered a new one. Of the three men thus rejected, one, James Mott, Jr., was voted in again, and continued active in the Assembly for several sessions, distinguishing himself by the consistency with which he voted against proposed legislation. A second, Kenneth Anderson, had the satisfaction of returning triumphantly to resign his seat in favor of "an Office under the Government"—presumably the Continental government—to which he had been appointed. The third, Kenneth Hankinson, failed of reelection, and was replaced by Peter Schenck;[53] but it was not long before he was implicated in another scandal.

As hatred for the Loyalists grew implacable, legislation was passed for confiscating their estates, and commissioners were appointed in each county to sell the property at public vendue. By May 1779, inhabitants of Monmouth were complaining to the legislature that the commissioners for their county were engaging in practices which made fair sales impossible. A committee appointed by the Assembly to look into the matter found enough justification for the charges to require a thorough investigation; and a joint committee for that purpose, from both branches of the legislature, was delegated, with powers to summon and question witnesses, call for papers, and have affidavits taken.

The hearings extended over several months, and enough of the testimony has been preserved to show us that some

[53] *Votes of Assembly*, Nov. 4, 5, 11, 12, and 26, 1777; Feb. 11 and 18, March 11, 1778.

of the simple Jerseymen of the eighteenth century had a natural gift for corruption. The practices to which the commissioners resorted in order to enable favored individuals to buy the properties for sale were varied and interesting. Sometimes they neglected to advertise the auctions according to law. Sometimes they failed to publish detailed inventories of the forfeited estates, so that no buyers except insiders knew the value of what was offered for sale. On one occasion at least, presumably for the benefit of persons living in the immediate vicinity, they "Sold at Middletown fourteen Plantations or Tracts of Land Not only on a Very Stormy Day, when But few People Could be Expected to Attend, But by an Early hour in the afternoon, and Some of them Greatly under their Saleable Value, though they might Agreeable to their own advertisements, have Continued the Sales from Day to Day, and thereby Perhaps have Greatly Promoted the Interest of the State." Their favorite device, however, was to limit the bidding to a specified number of minutes: at the end of that time, no matter how fast the offers were coming in, they would close the sale after a bid by their favorite.

It was impossible to controvert these disturbing findings of the investigating committee. On September 30, 1779, the day the report was presented, the Assembly resolved, by a vote of 21 to 4, "That Samuel Forman, Kenneth Hankenson and Joseph Lawrence, Commissioners appointed for taking Charge of and selling the forfeited Estates of certain Fugitives and Offenders, having abused the Trust reposed in them, to the great Injury of the State, ought to be discharged from their Appointment." For some reason, no effective steps were taken to make this vote of censure operative. In December, the Council passed a resolution authorizing the attorney general to bring suit against the commissioners for £100,000; but, after being ordered a second reading in the lower house, the measure was allowed to fall into

oblivion. In February and March another bill from the
Council and one prepared by members of the Assembly were
read, both providing for the dismissal from office of the
offending agents; after some deliberation, the Council bill
was rejected, and consideration of the Assembly measure
was postponed to the next sitting. Meanwhile, three members were delegated to examine the commissioners' accounts.
This committee failed to report, and the bill for dismissal
was never again brought up for discussion. By May 1781, it
had even ceased to appear on the list of unfinished business
compiled at the beginning of each sitting. The faithless
stewards got off scot-free, and the enterprising Mr. Hankinson evidently suffered no loss in prestige by having been
thus publicly discredited on two separate occasions: in 1781
he was serving as tax collector for Monmouth.[54]

    This remarkable failure to take action upon a flagrant
case of corruption was by no means unique. In the spring
of 1778, complaints were made against the conduct of several magistrates of Hunterdon County; after investigation,
the Assembly voted by 25 to 4 to impeach one of them, William Cleayton. A committee was appointed to draw up articles of impeachment; but it, too, never reported and no effort
seems to have been made to bring either it or Cleayton to
account.[55] At almost the same time that the Monmouth
commissioners were being arraigned, a petition from a number of inhabitants of Sussex County was presented to the
Assembly, charging the agents for forfeited estates in their
district with similar objectionable practices. The three
members from Sussex were instructed by the house to look

    [54] *Votes of Assembly*, May 17, June 10, Sept. 21, Sept. 22, Sept. 30, Dec. 16,
Dec. 22, and Dec. 24, 1779, Feb. 25, March 9, and March 15, 1780; following
MSS. in Public Record Office, Trenton: Representation to Assembly by eleven
residents of Monmouth County, May 8, 1779; report of committee, Sept. 30,
1779 (incorrectly endorsed "May 1779"); depositions by David Rhea, William
Schanck, and others, dated June 2, 1779.
    [55] *Votes of Assembly*, April 16, June 9, June 12, June 13, June 17, June 18,
and Sept. 25, 1778.

into the charges; and that was the last that was heard of the matter.[56]

One prominent individual of the day flits through many of these scandals with airy persistence, but is never caught, and still tantalizes the mind of the historian. David Forman, of Monmouth County, brigadier general in the militia, had many enemies—all Tories or other undesirables, he said; good, honest people, they insisted. In the affair of the fraudulent Monmouth election of 1777, Forman was charged with aiding in the "undue practices." He was summoned for interrogation by the Assembly, and, when the house refused his request to have the examination postponed in view of his pressing military obligations, he resigned his commission in a huff.[57] A year and a half later, his name was brought into the investigation of the Monmouth commissioners for forfeited estates when it came to light that on one occasion he had been a beneficiary of their irregular methods of sale.[58]

In the interval between these two scandals in which he was but a subsidiary, he was involved in one entirely of his own. On January 1, 1778, he sent Washington a memorial setting forth that with his partners he was erecting extensive salt works on Barnegat Bay, which would be of great value in supplying the army with the much prized necessity, and which would be made larger if he could be assured of a military guard to secure them against raids from the sea.[59] The commander-in-chief, who had been favorably impressed by Forman's energy and ability in the militia, transmitted the memorial to Congress, without specific recommendation,

[56] *ibid.*, May 3, 1779. In this connection it is interesting to note that Shaffer, a member of the committee, had been one of the minority to vote against unseating the improperly elected Monmouth delegates in 1777. Can he have had a lurking tenderness for evil-doers?

[57] *Votes of Assembly*, Nov. 5, 1777; Forman to Washington, Nov. 7, 1777, in Washington Papers, Vol. 60.

[58] Deposition by David Forman (not the general), June 2, 1779, in Public Record Office, Trenton.

[59] Forman to Washington, Jan. 1, 1777 (memorial and accompanying letter), in Washington Papers, Vol. 64.

but with implied approval. Meanwhile, he permitted Forman, though no longer a military officer, to retain at the salt
works, as a guard, a party of Continental troops who happened to be in the vicinity.[60]

It was not long before the neighbors began to complain.
One Trevor Newland, who was involved in a dispute with
Forman over the ownership of the lands on which the works
were going up, carried to the New Jersey Council a protest
over the use of the troops. After listening to testimony by
the complainant, by Forman, and by the captain of the
soldiers in question, the legislators announced that they
could not see "that the Troops so stationed have been of any
use to the Publick; but that they have been employed in
collecting Materials, and erecting Buildings to promote the
private Interest of Individuals." The works were not yet
producing salt, they pointed out, and would probably not,
"at least for some Months to come, furnish a Quantity
equal to the Production of divers other Works in this State,
which are therefore better entitled to the Protection of the
Publick." For this reason, the Council held that the stationing of the troops thus, "aiding the Purposes of private
Interest," was improper and burdensome to the public; and
it requested the governor to transmit its views to the commander-in-chief.[61]

Forman wrote to Washington at once, explaining that
Newland was "an avowed Enemy to the American Cause
and would do every thing in his power to prevent the manufacturing of that necessary & very much wanted Article
Salt." He intimated, in addition, that Livingston disap-
proved of the Council's action, and would be happy to explain the situation if consulted in an unofficial capacity.[62]
The governor, however, refused "to fault the Resolutions

[60] Washington, *Writings*, Vol. X, p. 412, Vol. XI, p. 149.
[61] Resolution of Council, March 11, 1778; copy in Washington Papers,
Vol. 69.
[62] Forman to Washington, March 13, 1778, in Washington Papers, Vol. 69.

of the Council; I only intended," he declared, "to have given you my Sentiments had I been requested to do it, on the rise & Origin of the Prosecution, & not on any thing that appeared before the Board on the hearing, or the Resolutions of the Council in consequence thereof. . . . Many of the Inhabitants of the County of Monmouth, are unhappily actuated by a Party Spirit, this Spirit has probably had its share in exciting the Clamour against Coll: Forman & . . . I have reason to think from Depositions in my Possession, that M.ʳ Newland is not friendly to our Cause."[63]

Such a very tepid corroboration of part of Forman's excuse was not enough to override the conclusion of the Council that he had been enjoying a supply of free labor at public expense. On March 25, Washington wrote Forman: "To avoid the imputation of partiality and remove all cause for censure, both with respect to you and myself, I am induced to direct [that the troops now at the works] . . . may for the present join and act with Colo. Shreve's Regiment, in the purposes of common defence."[64] Thereafter, the canny Monmouth salt maker had to hire his own help.

A few years later, in 1782, the irrepressible David was again in trouble as a result of his peculiar flair for combining profit with patriotism. By now, he was a judge, but his high office had by no means imbued him with a spirit of judicial detachment. He had become head of the Association for Retaliation, a band of violent Whigs, among whom there appeared for perhaps the first time in the life of America as an independent nation the spirit later to be embodied in the Ku Klux Klan, the vigilantes, the Black Legion, and kindred organizations. During the years of increasingly cruel civil war, Monmouth County, with its long, exposed coastline and its stretches of swamp and wilderness where outlaws could safely lurk, had suffered from innumerable

---

[63] Livingston to Washington, March 14, 1778, in Washington Papers, Vol. 69.
[64] Washington, *Writings*, Vol. XI, pp. 148-9.

raids by regular British forces, by exiled Loyalists, and by violent men of no principle who seized upon the disorders of the times as an excuse for leading a life of brigandage. Ostensibly as a means of combating these outrages, the Association had been formed to wreak vengeance upon the persons and property of helpless Tories living in the country. Victims were plundered or imprisoned at will by this irresponsible brotherhood, and there can be little doubt that the innocent suffered with the guilty. Under the cover of patriotic service, many a fine robbery was committed, and the Assembly, though helpless to enforce its disapproval, condemned the Association in uncompromising terms.[65]

In this illegal organization Forman was a leading spirit, and as such he issued orders for plundering and imprisonment which were scarcely compatible with his judicial function.[66] The matter came to a head when petitions from victims precipitated a legislative investigation in October 1782. By a vote of 18 to 15, the Assembly found Forman guilty of some of the abuses charged; but he had, as usual, kept his tracks well covered: by a vote of 21 to 12, the house agreed that the charges were not sufficiently supported to ground an impeachment.[67]

The career of David Forman is an example of the practices on the borderline of ethics in which a man of ability could engage in those days without serious interference or loss of public standing. That he escaped trouble is comparatively easy to understand. More difficult to explain is the laxity with which the Assembly treated such notorious examples of corruption as Hankinson, whose misdeeds were a matter of public record. The examples which have been cited of failure by the legislators to proceed against office-

[65] *Votes of Assembly*, Sept. 23, 25 and 29, Oct. 2, 1780.
[66] This was not a new departure for him. As early as 1777, one opponent had declared: "He has chose to act against all Christian laws, and follow the Dictates of some African Tyrant."—Petition of Robert Lawrence to Assembly, Oct. 7, 1777, in Room 118, State Library, Trenton.
[67] *Votes of Assembly*, Oct. 29 and Nov. 21, 1782.

holders whose delinquencies were proven or strongly indicated are not the only ones to be found in the journals of the house. Such remissness on the part of the Assembly, one is tempted to conclude, may have arisen from the pressure of work which prevented its members from attending properly to all the duties that devolved upon them. This impression is strengthened by the lists of unfinished matters of business prepared at the beginning of each sitting which, despite the frequent arbitrary omission of important items by the committees in charge of the compiling, continued to lengthen as year followed year. Yet even a casual reading of the journals of the house reveals that, like occasional legislators of any age, the delegates sometimes gave much attention to comparatively trivial affairs, while neglecting matters of serious importance. At that time the Council and Assembly still exercised some of the functions which are delegated to executive or judicial authorities today; and the Assembly passed a good many hours—not too uninterestingly, perhaps—in listening to testimony brought by persons petitioning for divorce. It also found time, while urgent matters waited, to pass an act, elaborated in great detail, "to prevent idle and disorderly Persons misspending their Time at Publick-Houses, and for the Suppression of other Immoralities."[68]

If the home politics of New Jersey during the years of the war were all too frequently marked by trivial preoccupations and corruption, the record of participation by the state in Continental politics is a much more creditable one. Just as among the members of the League of Nations in recent years the sincere advocates of enlightened international cooperation have been for the most part the smaller and weaker countries, whereas the larger powers with few exceptions have tended to follow selfish and archaic policies, so, among the states casually cooperating through the Conti-

[68] *Acts of Assembly*, May 28, 1779.

nental Congress, New Jersey with its notable deficiencies in
territory, population, and wealth, sometimes championed
measures for the general good which ran counter to the
greedy ambitions of its larger neighbors.

Next to the matter of winning the war, the problem which
loomed largest in the minds of American statesmen during
the years after 1776 was that of confederation. The Congress at Philadelphia, with the cumbersome administrative
machine which had grown up under it, was an organization
lacking legal authority or executive force. Its decrees took
the form of "recommendations" to the states; its attempts
to administer a war were the despair of Americans and the
amazement of foreign observers.[69] By the end of 1777, after
over a year of discussion and wrangling,[70] a set of Articles
of Confederation had been drawn up, which aimed to provide a workable federal government and were submitted to
the states for ratification.

In New Jersey, where the need for a general American
union was felt with particular sharpness, the Articles were
looked upon with misgiving, for it was held that they did
not place sufficient restrictions upon powerful individual
states. Instead of accepting the proposed confederation at
once, the legislature sent to Congress, in June 1778, a number of objections to the scheme as it stood. The absence of
any oath, test, or declaration to be imposed on delegates to
Congress was held to be dangerous, as it might permit the
representatives of a number of powerful states to carry matters with a high hand, in violation of the covenant, and to
the detriment of the country as a whole. To a state like New
Jersey, engaging in a negligible amount of foreign commerce, and lying at the mercy of its neighbors for imports
and exports, it seemed a regrettable omission to entrust the

[69] Durand, *op. cit.*, pp. 174-6.
[70] See, for example, letter of Abraham Clark, Aug. 1, 1776, in Sparks MSS.,
49, Vol. II.

regulation of trade to the separate states. In the opinion of the legislature, such power should rest exclusively with Congress, and the proceeds of duties levied "ought to be appropriated to the Building, Equipping and Manning of a Navy for the Protection of the Trade and Defence of the Coasts, and to such other publick & general Purposes as to the Congress shall seem proper and for the common Benefit of the States."

The perpetual bone of contention—whether slaves should be counted as part of the population of a state in laying obligations upon it or giving it power—was to plague the framers of the federal Constitution a decade later, and it cropped up now. At Philadelphia, the Southern forces had won a partial victory: Article 9 provided that Congress might fix quotas of armed land forces from each state in proportion to the number of its white inhabitants. This provision met with a cold reception in New Jersey. Antislavery sentiment had been growing rapidly in the state during the past few years; moreover, the results of a drain of manpower for military purposes were already being sharply felt, and self-interest demanded that no future advantage in this respect should be conceded to the Southern states without a struggle. Not unwilling to indulge in a little didacticism, the legislature, in attacking the objectionable provision in Article 9, quoted the embarrassing passage from the Declaration of Independence concerning the equality of men, life, liberty, and the pursuit of happiness. After this preliminary flourish, it went on to point out the injustice of the apportionment plan, even "should it be improper, for special local Reasons, to admit . . . [Negroes] in Arms for the Defence of the Nation." In every state, it was pointed out, whatever the composition of its population, some of the inhabitants must remain at home in time of war "to till the Ground and labour in mechanick Arts and otherwise." Where the population was entirely white, these workers were included in calculations of the ability of the state to furnish troops; why should the same principle not hold true in states where the people employed in necessary occupations were blacks?

All these objections, as well as others included in the representation sent to Congress, were subsidiary to the chief source of uneasiness for New Jersey: the future of the unsettled lands west of the Appalachians, to which several states asserted they had good title, but to which New Jersey could lay no claim. The legislature suggested that the boundaries and limits of each state should be finally determined as soon as possible or that at least the principles upon which this was to be done should be established. In its sixth comment, however, the representation came to the heart of the matter:

"The ninth Article provides, that no State shall be deprived of Territory for the Benefit of the United States. Whether we are to understand that by Territory is intended any Lands, the Property of which was heretofore vested in the Crown of Great-Britain, or that no Mention of such Lands is made in the Confederation, we are constrained to observe, that the present War, as we always apprehended, was undertaken for the general Defence and Interest of the confederating Colonies, now the United States. It was ever the confident Expectation of this State, that the Benefits derived from a successful Contest were to be general and proportionate, and that the Property of the common Enemy, falling in Consequence of a prosperous Issue of the War, would belong to the United States, and be appropriated to their Use. We are therefore greatly disappointed in finding no Provision made in the Confederation for empowering the Congress to dispose of such Property, but especially the vacant and unpatented Lands, commonly called the Crown Lands, for defraying the Expences of the War, and for other such publick and general Purposes. The Jurisdiction ought, in every Instance, to belong to the respective States, within the Charter or determined Limits of which such Lands may be seated; but Reason and Justice must decide, that the Property which existed in the Crown of Great-Britain, previous to the present Revolution, ought now to belong to the Congress in Trust for the Use and Benefit of the United States. They have fought and bled for it in Proportion to their respective Abilities, and therefore the Reward ought not to be predilectionally distributed. Shall such States as are shut out by Situation from availing themselves of the least Advantage from this Quarter, be left to sink under an enormous Debt, whilst others are enabled, in a short Period, to replace all their Expenditures from the hard Earnings of the whole Confederacy!"[71]

Although the question of western territory was of such deep concern to New Jersey, its suggestions, when read in Congress, were heard with small favor by members from most other parts of the Continent. States like Virginia and Massachusetts, which cherished claims to land extending as far west as the Pacific, were by no means disposed to relinquish their advantages. Pressure must have been brought to bear upon the New Jersey members, for one of them, Nathaniel Scudder, wrote to the Assembly on July 13, 1778, to urge the unconditional ratification of the Articles.

Confederation was a matter of the utmost exigency, he pointed out. The states had entered upon a treaty with France as a confederated people; what would be the reaction of the French ambassador, whose arrival was imminent, should he discover "that we are ipso facto unconfederated, and consequently what our enemies have called us, 'a rope of sand'!" Unanimous ratification was necessary; only New Jersey, Maryland, and Georgia stood out; Georgia was about to join the rest, and Maryland would probably accede if New Jersey should set the example. After Con-

[71] *Votes of Assembly*, June 15 and 16, 1778.

gress had entered the recent objections upon its minutes, it had voted not to "admit any emendations in the plan of confederation." In Scudder's view, every state was subjected to some disadvantages by the covenant. "Indeed," he asserted, "upon the whole I am fully of opinion that no plan can or will ever be adopted more equal or less generally injurious to the confederated states than the present. I also declare it as my opinon that, if the general business of emendation were to be fairly taken up by Congress tomorrow, several alterations would be made exceedingly disadvantageous to the smaller circumscribed states, and which perhaps might more than counterbalance the obtaining what we apply for."

Such being the case, the delegate was in favor of confederation, even under disadvantages, in preference to endangering the union. He was inclined to minimize the importance of the western question: as the other states grew in population and wealth, he thought, their shares of the public debt would become greater, and New Jersey's smaller. In settling its accounts with its soldiers at the end of the war, Scudder conceded, states without western lands would be at a disadvantage; but, "as the larger states will doubtless rejoice to have their frontiers immediately enlarged, and will vie with each other in courting so great an accession of inhabitants, there will probably be no greater expense than barely that of locating the lands, our quota of which cannot be any very considerable sum."[72]

At about the same time, the president of Congress wrote to Livingston, expressing the hope that the "patriotism and good sense" of New Jersey would lead it to ratify the Articles, "trusting to future deliberations to make such alterations and amendments, as experience may shew to be expedient and just." Livingston was not impressed, and made no secret of his belief that some of the patriotism and

72 *N.J. Exec. Corr.*, pp. 119-22.

good sense should be shown by Congress, who had it in their power to make at once the alterations for which they were referring New Jersey to a vague future.[73]

The legislature, too, was inclined to persist in its refusal, but finally, on November 20, 1778, it authorized its delegates to ratify the Articles. In so doing, it expressly adhered to its former objections, but made them subordinate to its "full Conviction . . . that every separate State-Interest ought to be postponed to the general Good of the Union." With an optimism perhaps more apparent than genuine it put on record its "firm Reliance that the Candour and Justice of the several States will, in due Time, remove, as far as possible, the Inequality which now subsists."[74]

This was handsomely done, but New Jersey had small thanks for its action. In the course of the following year, ignoring the appeal to subordinate state interest to the good of the nation, Virginia opened an office for the sale of lands in the western territory. At once the most doleful forebodings were aroused among the people of New Jersey. If the states with possessions beyond the mountains should begin in earnest to pay off their war debts by the sale of wilderness lands, the comparative position of states which must resort to taxation would be a deplorable one, and might lead to a widespread emigration from them. The legislature was petitioned to send a remonstrance to Congress "setting forth, in the warmest Terms, the Injustice of permitting any State to assume a Right of disposing of vacant and unappropriated Lands, commonly called Crown Lands, for its own private Emolument; and urging the Propriety of opening an Office for the Sale of such Lands for the general Benefit of the United States."[75]

[73] *Votes of Assembly*, Sept. 14, 1778.
[74] *ibid.*, Sept. 25, Nov. 14; Wilson, *Acts of New Jersey*, Chap. CIX (Nov. 20, 1778).
[75] *Votes of Assembly*, Nov. 3 and Dec. 22, 1779.

A committee appointed by the Assembly to consider the problem brought in, at the end of the year 1780, a very able report. It fixed its attention particularly upon Virginia's claims to the western territory, and demolished them neatly. Among other evidences, the committee adduced an impressive number of quotations from prominent Virginia officials of the years preceding the war as proof that the colony had recognized that its title to the territory in question, if it ever existed, had passed to the Crown.[76]

Doubtless from considerations of tact, the Assembly refrained from officially communicating this barbed report to Congress, though it entered it upon its public journals for all the world to see. Before the end of the year, the two houses of the legislature did send a "Representation and Remonstrance" to Philadelphia, drawing attention to their previous utterance on the subject of the western territory and expressing their amazement at the action of Virginia in assuming to dispose of the lands "when on the plainest Principles of the Law of Nations, of Reason, Truth and Justice, they are become, by the Revolution, vested in Congress, for the Use of the foederal Republick they represent." Flatly they declared "that they acknowledge no Tribunal but that of Congress competent to be the Redress of such a Grievance." Nevertheless the remonstrance carefully avoided any tone of acrimony, and invoked "the conciliat-

---

[76] *Votes of Assembly*, Dec. 20, 1780. Of interest is the committee's comment on the famous phraseology in the charter of 1609, on which Virginia's claim was based: that the territory of the colony should embrace "all that Space or Circuit of Land lying from the Sea Coast of the Precinct aforesaid, up into the Land throughout, from Sea to Sea, West and Northwest." If the lines, remarked the report, "are run agreeably to the Construction put on them by Virginia, that is a northwest line from the northernmost Extent of their Grant on the Sea Coast of the Atlantic, the said Line will wind in a spiral Manner round the Globe, and at last terminate in the North Pole, without ever touching the South Sea." A glance at the globe or map will show that this is true, unless the Arctic Ocean be considered part of the Pacific.

ing Influence of Equity, Moderation and liberal Affections"
upon the treatment of all disputes between the states.[77]

These were admirable sentiments; but throughout history
appeals to sweet reasonableness have proven notoriously
ineffective in dealing with collective bodies of human beings.
New Jersey had no way of backing up its demands, and it
is not likely that in the normal course of events they would
have been more seriously regarded than the protest of two
years earlier. What saved the situation was the circumstance
that the "foederal Republick" to which the legislature had
appealed did not in fact exist. The state of Maryland, circumscribed, like New Jersey, by definite boundaries, but less
trusting, had firmly refused to ratify the Confederation
until the western lands should be ceded to the Union, and
it held out until the larger states capitulated in 1781.

Even this agreement did not completely solve the problem. Virginia had agreed to make the cession, but execution
of the promise was deferred for several years. In October
1781, seven months after Maryland had made the Confederation operative by ratifying the Articles, several citizens
of New Jersey were complaining to the Assembly that the
Virginia government had dispossessed them of a tract of
land called "Indiana," to which they claimed title. The legislature at once informed its representatives in Congress that
it was "unsatisfied with the partial Concessions made by the
State of Virginia," and instructed them to cooperate with
the delegates of other interested states to make "a warm and
spirited Address to the United States in Congress assembled,
for the Redress of Grievances."[78]

In the course of the next few years, interstate wrangles
of this particular type disappeared, as the cession of trans-
Appalachian territory became complete. New Jersey could
not lay claim to having worked very effectively for the
creation of the national domain, having thrown away its

[77] *Votes of Assembly*, Dec. 29, 1780.   [78] *ibid.*, Oct. 3, 4, 5, 1781.

chief weapon, abstention from the Confederation, early in the struggle; but at least it had consistently pleaded for an enlightened policy. In the turmoil of Continental politics its record was one of cooperation and reasonableness contrasting strikingly with the selfishness of some of its sister states.

The disposal of the "Crown lands" was not the only question of Continental interest, arising in the course of the war, upon which New Jersey took a firm stand. In 1779, the legislature voiced its unqualified opposition to the proposed grant of half-pay for life to all army officers, informing Congress that it considered this step "contrary to the very Spirit of a Republican Government, as introductive of the Practice of Pensioning, which has always been held in the utmost Detestation by a free People, as creating a Distinction in the Community, invidious in its Nature, dangerous in its Tendency, and productive of Inconvenience and Injury to the Officers themselves, as well as to the Community at Large."[79] It is not impossible that parsimony as well as principle entered into the issuance of this statement, for New Jersey was none too generous with its troops. Nevertheless, anyone acquainted with the pernicious effects which seem to follow inevitably whenever veterans of a war are made a privileged caste, irrespective of their needs, must rejoice that, through the insistence of New Jersey and other states, no official step was taken at the close of the Revolution which would have set off one section of the community as the recipient of special favors for life.

Aside from the privilege of fighting for the enlightened principles which New Jersey usually supported in matters of Continental interest, the delegates representing the state in Congress led no enviable life. First among their troubles was unending financial embarrassment. Wherever Congress met, whether at Philadelphia, Baltimore or York, Pennsylvania, prices seemed to be unconscionably high, and at few

[79] *Votes of Assembly*, Dec. 7 and 14, 1779.

periods, if any, during the war was the pay of the New Jersey representatives adequate to their needs. Through their correspondence runs a mournful refrain which seems to vary little from delegate to delegate: my private fortune is being ruined while I serve the state here for a miserable pittance. One of them, Nathaniel Scudder, set forth at some length, in a letter of October 1779, the reason why he could not accept reelection: during his term of service he had suffered all sorts of embarrassments for want of funds, and another year's attendance would ruin him. He concluded:

"I say not these things as the least Reflection on my Constituents, or under an Expectation of any further Compensation than my legal Wages for my past Service, but sincerely for the Benefit of the State, least *that same* Necessity, which now compels my Declination, may soon occasion other faithfull Servants to retire from it's Service; when possibly their Places may be filled by ambitious designing Men, or by others, who being Persons of like contracted Fortunes with myself, may not perhaps so fully withstand those powerfull lucrative Temptations, which *here* surround us, as I firmly boast *I have* done."[80]

In the opinion of some observers, indeed, such stern virtue as that to which Scudder confessed had departed from the delegates by the end of the war. While the Continental Congress was sitting at Princeton in August 1783, under the presidency of Elias Boudinot of Elizabeth-Town, and Silas Condict was another member for New Jersey, the secretary of the body wrote to his wife:

"The President of Congress has not provided a house for himself, nor is it likely he will find one here to suit him. I find Elizabethtown has been talked of at his table as a proper place for the residence of Congress. He has a house there which he says has twenty rooms, and which he will let

[80] Scudder to John Stevens, Oct. 26, 1779, in Stevens Papers, Stevens Institute. See also *N.J. Exec. Corr.*, pp. 25, 27, 109-11, 142, 156.

for the use of the President. It is true the place is infested with mosquitoes in summer and lying low, and near marshes may be liable to intermittents in the Spring and Fall, but these are trifling when it is considered that by fixing the residence of Congress there the value of his estate will be increased and he will have an opportunity of letting his house at a good rent. But yet I am inclined to believe this will be opposed by his colleagues; for Mr. Condit has found a lodging in this town at $3 a week, which enables him to lay up money. And there is reason to fear that at Elizabethtown, which is so near New York, it will cost him at least four. This would be a clear loss of $52 a year which is no trifling consideration, and which I daresay will have due weight with some others. There are other weighty consideration which might be mentioned."[81]

Other worries than financial ones pressed upon the delegates. There was constant anxiety and uncertainty over affairs of the nation as the ill-managed war dragged on and on. There was the exasperation attendant upon trying to accomplish anything through the cumbersome process of Congressional recommendation and state execution. Finally there was, for the conscientious, the enormous burden of administrative duties which devolved upon everyone in proportion to his willingness, and kept a man like John Fell busy day and night.[82]

All these sources of nervous strain did not make the tempers of the delegates any too sweet. Not infrequently they were quarrelsome, suspicious of one another, and ready to pass on their grievances to the people at home. Clark intimated strongly in 1781 that he was the only completely conscientious representative from his state.[83] John Fell complained openly in 1779 that Witherspoon and Frelinghuysen treated him "with the greatest unpoliteness, they take

[81] Charles Thompson to his wife, Aug. 21, 1783, reproduced in *N.J.H.S.P.*, N.S., Vol. VI, p. 235.
[82] *N.J. Exec. Corr.*, pp. 142, 280.　　　　　[83] *ibid.*, pp. 279-80.

upon them to leave Congress when they Please & without leave, by which the State in course is not Represented."[84]

Such outbursts clearly indicate that the dissensions and animosities afflicting the internal politics of New Jersey followed its delegates even into Congress. Quarrelling and recrimination seemed to be the order of the day in all phases of political activity. To many a mild-mannered citizen of the state, unable to appreciate the value of the experience in self-government that was being gained and the importance of the new pride in democratic institutions which was growing up, it must have seemed that the Revolution had brought New Jersey nothing but factionalism and bickering. Such observers might well have been pardoned had they dismissed all the politicians of the time with the words which one confirmed contributor to the *New Jersey Gazette* angrily flung at another: "You seem to throw the gantelope to all around you."[85]

[84] John Fell to Livingston, March 25, 1779, in Room 118, State Library (reproduced, with regularization of spelling, punctuation, and, occasionally, grammar, in *N.J. Exec. Corr.*, pp. 141-2). Frelinghuysen's comment is printed in *N.J. Exec. Corr.*, pp. 155-6.

[85] *N.J.A.*, 2nd S., Vol. IV, p. 111.

CHAPTER IX ✿ *THE CAMPAIGN OF 1777 OPENS*

"MUCH depends upon our taking the Field early with a powerfull force," wrote Washington on January 24, 1777. While the British army was still shaken by the blows it had received in the recent campaign, and before it should have had time to obtain reinforcements from home, he wished to inflict upon it another crushing stroke. Given a strong enough force at this time, he thought, the Americans could not fail to be victorious; the enemy might well be driven from New Jersey; and a vigorous policy would establish the revolutionary cause so firmly that for the future it would have "but little to dread" from the soldiers of the King.[1]

To carry out such a course of action, however, many new recruits for the army were indispensably necessary; and of such reinforcements there was no sign. Week after week, month after month dragged by; the puny force at Morristown dwindled and then at last began to increase only with painful slowness. Winter was over, and spring came; the prowling American detachments continued to keep the British in a state of discomfort, nervous irritation, and ill-health; and still Washington's army was too feeble to take advantage of the situation. In the hope that others might see opportunities where he could find none, the commander-in-chief called a council of war at the beginning of May. He asked his officers to advise him whether a general attack upon the British garrisons would be justified. Their answer was regretful but unanimous; the American soldiers were both too

[1] Washington to Brig. Gen. George Clinton, Jan. 24, 1777, in Armstrong collection, photostat in Princeton University Library MSS., AM 10035.

few and as yet too ill-disciplined to give the undertaking any reasonable prospect of success.[2]

It was a trying ordeal to have to sit passive while a favorable opportunity for striking the enemy grew more and more remote; still more trying was the uncertainty as to how the British might take advantage of their opponents' weakness. As early as January 20, Washington harbored uneasy suspicions that Howe and Cornwallis were gathering their forces in preparation for an advance either upon Morristown or upon Philadelphia, "as I cannot suppose them," he remarked, "so much uninformed of our strength as to believe they are acting upon a Defensive Plan at this hour."[3]

In the middle of February, Howe sent six battalions of British troops from Rhode Island to Perth Amboy, though that town was already so overcrowded that the newcomers had to be kept aboard the ships. In the course of a few days, the commander of the royal forces followed in person, and proceeded to New Brunswick. Washington was now convinced that a new advance across New Jersey towards Philadelphia was imminent. So uncomfortable were the troops on the Raritan that it was incredible Howe would concentrate more of them in the garrisons without good reason. The King's soldiers, according to Washington's information, which was probably an underestimate, amounted to at least ten thousand, "well disciplined, well officered, and well appointed"; the Americans could muster barely four thousand "raw Militia, badly Officered, and under no Government." If the British should move out in force across the New Jersey lowlands, their great superiority in numbers would keep them safe from successful attack, and would enable them to sweep up from the country enough horses

[2] Washington, *Writings*, Vol. VII, p. 395; minutes of a Council of General Officers, May 2, 1777, in Washington Papers, Vol. 45; Washington to Col. Joseph Ward, April 21, in Ford House MSS., Morristown National Historical Park.

[3] Washington, *Writings*, Vol. VII, p. 38.

and forage to solve the transportation problems which had grown serious as their own horses in New Brunswick sickened and died. Should Howe neglect this opportunity to assume the offensive, Washington declared to his brother, "there can be no Impropriety, I conceive, [in] pronouncing him a Man of no enterprize, as circumstances never will, I hope, favour him so much as at present."[4]

Without much confidence, the leader of the forlorn band at Morristown made plans for harassing the British force on its march, arranged that in case of an alarm all boats along the Delaware from Easton to Bristol should be collected immediately on the west side of the stream, and sent a warning to Philadelphia that the stores there might have to be moved at a moment's notice.

Once more, however, General Howe declined to take advantage of what seemed to be a very favorable opportunity. After staying a few days in New Brunswick, he returned to New York, and the expectations of the Americans and some of his subordinates that a military operation of consequence was in prospect were not borne out. His visit to the garrisons may have confirmed him in the belief that for the present it was as well not to expose his army unnecessarily to the attentions of the ever alert rebels; for while in New Jersey he had had a taste of the guerrilla warfare to which his troops were by now accustomed. When he was on his way back from New Brunswick to Perth Amboy, his escort was attacked by a party of nearly a thousand Americans, and there was sharp fighting for a few minutes before the assailants were repulsed. Such an incident was scarcely a temptation for the general to leave the city where he was having such a pleasant sojourn and to begin another cam-

[4] Washington, *Writings*, Vol. VII, pp. 168, 198, 222-3; Washington to Robert Morris, Feb. 22, 1777, in Armstrong collection, photostat in Princeton University Library MSS., AM 10037; Münchhausen, Journal, Feb. 14, 1777; Alexander Hamilton to Gen. McDougall, March 10, 1777, in Washington Papers, Vol. 42.

paign before the winter was over. The bleak March landscape was not inviting, and Howe had already had some
experience of New Jersey mud. It is reasonable to suppose
that he wished for good dry roads before he exposed the
wagons of his army to attack from the swift-moving enemy
lurking in the hills.[5]

Eventually, the British commander decided not to attempt
again to march across New Jersey to the Delaware. Although
his goal was still Philadelphia, it seemed more advisable
to approach it by sea. On April 2 he wrote to Lord George
Germain announcing his change of plans. There would be
much difficulty and delay on the overland route, he explained; so it would probably be necessary to abandon New
Jersey altogether in favor of an advance upon the city by
water.[6] The Colonial Secretary replied on May 18, giving
his approval to this plan. He expressed the hope, however,
that the enterprise should be finished in time to permit
Howe to cooperate with the army which was scheduled to
advance during the summer from Canada up the Richelieu
River and Lake Champlain and down the Hudson. "If we
may credit the accounts which arrive from all quarters,"
wrote Germain cheerfully, "relative to the good inclinations
of the inhabitants, there is every reason to expect that your
success in Pennsylvania will enable you to raise from among
them such a force as may be sufficient for the interior defence
of the province and leave the army at liberty to proceed to
offensive operations."[7]

Long before this letter was written in London, however,
Howe had made up his mind not to assist the northern army.
On April 5, he had warned Sir Guy Carleton, the general com-

[5] Washington, *Writings*, Vol. VII, pp. 164, 177, 187-8; Kemble, *op. cit.*,
pp. 110-11; Waldeck, *op. cit.*, p. 29; Greene to Washington, Feb. 20, 1777, in
Washington Papers, Vol. 41; James Irvine to Washington, March 3, *ibid.*,
Vol. 42.

[6] Historical Manuscripts Commission, *Report on Stopford-Sackville Manuscripts*, Vol. II, pp. 63-4.

[7] *ibid.*, p. 67.

manding in Canada, that the only assistance the latter could probably expect from New York would be the opening of the lower Hudson to shipping, at the moment blocked by American forts.[8] The decision to move towards Delaware Bay instead of Lake Champlain seems to have been made in pursuit of that ever tempting will-o'-the-wisp, a Tory majority in the population which would rise up to welcome and assist the delivering army of the King. "I flatter myself," Howe informed Carleton, "and have reason to expect the friends of Government in that part of the country will be found so numerous and so ready to give every aid and assistance in their power, that it will prove no difficult task to reduce the more rebellious parts of the province."[9]

The same storm of controversy which has raged about other aspects of Howe's American career has enveloped the campaign of 1777. It would not be pertinent to our story to investigate here the possible importance of other factors in shaping Howe's plan of campaign—such factors, for instance, as his desire (revealed or invented by him in later years) to draw the American army into a general engagement under conditions favorable to the British.[10] Whatever the truth as to his purposes may be, it is certain that he had chosen his course of action by the beginning of April, and that he kept his own counsel remarkably well. Few even of his own officers knew anything of his plans: as one of the Hessians wrote back home, "His Excellency General Howe is very secretive about his undertakings."[11] Up until the last minute, neither the American nor the royal army had any idea what form the campaign was to take.

American spies were permitted to ferret out such secrets as that the British were about to attack Morristown, or that, while the main army was advancing by land towards Phila-

[8] *ibid.*, pp. 65-6.
[9] *ibid.*, p. 66.
[10] Howe, *Narrative*, pp. 19-21.
[11] Johann Friedrich von Cochenhausen to Baron von Jungkenn, March 17, in Von Jungkenn MSS., 1:29.

delphia, a force of Loyalists under Cortlandt Skinner was to march from Bergen into Sussex County, to aid a rising of the Tories there. So seriously did Washington take this latter rumor that he rearranged the stations of the militia to intercept any such march by Skinner's corps. Meanwhile, other spies brought the news that carpenters in New York were working on pontoons for the artillery and on a floating bridge to be flung across the Delaware three miles above Trenton; and there was every indication that New Jersey was to be the scene of a lively campaign.[12]

On the nineteenth day of May the soldiers in New Brunswick were moved out of town to camp along the hills on the west bank of the Raritan, and two days later the garrison at Perth Amboy also left its cramped winter quarters for an encampment in the open. After the long season of discomfort and close confinement, it was a welcome relief for the soldiers to be out amidst the fresh green of woods and fields and the acres of blossoming orchards. Only a sensitive poet," exulted the chaplain of a German regiment, "would be able to describe all the charms of the spring which a gracious Providence, after a disturbed and hateful winter, has let us experience. He may apply all his power of imagination, inspired by the Muses, to the task of describing spring in Jersey, but to him who has seen and blissfully lived through this young and laughing month of May here, all such descriptions will be mere dead pictures. Its beauty can only be experienced, not described."[13]

The Americans agreed that the British had greatly bettered their situation by extending their lines beyond the towns. "The Enemy," remarked one of Washington's sub-

---

[12] Washington, *Writings*, Vol. VII, pp. 177, 443-4, 460-1; Philemon Dickinson to Washington, March 13, 1777, in Washington Papers, Vol. 43; deposition of John Haynes, April 15, *ibid.*, Vol. 45.

[13] Waldeck, *op. cit.*, pp. 30, 31; letter of Carl Leopold von Baurmeister, June 2, 1777, in Von Jungkenn MSS., 1:36.

ordinates, "are in possession of a fine Country, well Supplyed w^t green Lamb, Veal, Beef, Mutton & pretty girls."[14]

More important to Washington and his officers, however, than the question of how the King's troops were enjoying their new surroundings was the problem of Howe's intentions in making the change. Was this move merely a sort of grand picnic designed to restore the health and spirits of the army before it evacuated the state to participate in some other enterprise, or was it the preliminary to a campaign in New Jersey? There were strong indications pointing to both conclusions, and the Americans were thoroughly perplexed.

By the first week in May, there was a great bustle of activity in the two British garrison towns. Boat after boat, filled with soldiers and women, slipped down the Raritan to Perth Amboy, where a number of transport ships were waiting. Probably the soldiers seen by the American observers on these trips down the river were the numerous sick and wounded of the garrison; but the watchers had no way of knowing that. Upon the transports lying at anchor in the mouth of the river were loaded as fast as possible the light baggage of the army and all camp equipment except canteens, hatchets, kettles, and haversacks; aboard the vessels went also a chosen few of the woman camp followers, in the ratio of four women to every fifty men to be transported, while all other women and children and the sick of the army, together with the heavy baggage, were sent to New York.[15]

All this seemed to point to an abandonment of New Jersey and an expedition by sea. This impression was strengthened by the fact that Howe's troops were being drawn from Kingsbridge on the Hudson and moved to Staten Island, where they could be easily embarked upon the vessels which had been prepared for their reception. Several regiments, it was known, had received orders to hold themselves in readiness

[14] *Sullivan Papers*, Vol. I, p. 353.
[15] Israel Putnam to Washington, May 10, 1777, in Washington Papers, Vol. 46; Glyn, *Journal*, pp. 49, 51-2.

to go aboard. Furthermore, twenty transports, each capable
of holding twenty horses, were being fitted up. Such elaborate preparations for an embarkation must have some purpose. On the other hand, by the beginning of June it was
reported that the British had mounted a number of flat-
bottomed boats on wheels in New York and on the Raritan,
were demolishing the fortifications at Perth Amboy, and were
drawing together in New Brunswick all their troops already
in New Jersey and some reinforcements from New York
as well. Considerable numbers of wagons, together with
some of the boats on wheels, were brought over from New
York to New Jersey, and everything seemed to be in preparation for a speedy push overland towards the Delaware.[16]

Various were the speculations about Howe's intentions;
but until he chose to reveal his plans there was little that the
Americans could do but watch and wait. At the end of May,
Washington had moved his army from Morristown to the
Middlebrook valley, behind the First Watchung Mountain
a short distance north of Bound Brook. Not only was this
position a natural stronghold from which the Americans
might defy attack: it was within eight miles of New Brunswick and threatened any overland expedition which the
British were likely to make.

In order to render his force more compact and effective,
Washington drew in his outlying posts on the southeast,
though Sullivan's detachment, now increased to over 1,600
men, remained at Princeton. The removal of the guards and
patrols of Continentals which heretofore had afforded some
protection to the northeastern part of the state led the
inhabitants of that section to offer themselves more readily
for militia duty; and by the first of June seven hundred
militiamen were gathered at Newark, Elizabeth-Town, and

16 *Sullivan Papers*, Vol. I, pp. 350, 360-5, 375-6; Washington, *Writings*,
Vol. VIII, pp. 150, 234.

Rahway, ready to assist Washington in hampering any move of the enemy.[17]

The American commander was wary, and did not let himself be misled by any preconceptions. All appearances, he asserted, pointed to an advance upon Philadelphia by the British; "but appearances are deceiving, false colours are often thrown out to mislead or bewilder, this may be the case now." By remaining at Middlebrook, he was not only in a position to embarrass any excursion in the direction of the Delaware, but able as well to move quickly to the defense of the Hudson fortresses if Howe should make a swift advance in that direction to assist the invasion from Canada. Sullivan was warned to keep a vigilant watch upon the enemy, in case they should move towards Princeton. All but a few of the boats and scows on the Delaware were sent up the river to a place on the Pennsylvania shore a few miles above Coryell's Ferry, and arrangements were made to seize the other craft, if necessary, at a moment's notice. General Arnold, at Coryell's Ferry, prepared to contest any attempt of the British to cross the Delaware; four galleys and ten armed boats patrolled the stream; several pieces of heavy artillery were set up on the west bank; and great numbers of the Pennsylvania militia and state troops hastened to defend the river against a crossing.[18]

During the second week of June, it became apparent that the long awaited move was imminent. On the ninth, nearly two thousand soldiers crossed from Staten Island to reinforce the garrison at Perth Amboy; two days later, Howe proceeded to New Brunswick with nearly his entire force, leaving only four regiments to guard the town at the mouth of the Raritan.[19] A corresponding activity began immediately

[17] *Sullivan Papers*, Vol. I, p. 354; Washington, *Writings*, Vol. VIII, pp. 118-19, 163-4; *N.J.A.*, 2nd S., Vol. I, p. 389.

[18] Washington, *Writings*, Vol. VIII, pp. 150-1, 157; *Sullivan Papers*, Vol. I, pp. 347, 348; Benedict Arnold to Washington, June 16, 1777, in Washington Papers, Vol. 49.

[19] Münchhausen, Journal, June 9 and 11, 1777.

to animate the American headquarters. Now that it was fairly certain that the British effort was actually to take place in New Jersey, and that the bustle on the banks of the Raritan was not merely a deception calculated to distract attention while a blow was struck elsewhere, Washington's staff considered it safe to bring in reinforcements from the Highlands of the Hudson; accordingly an urgent message was sent to Peekskill ordering Putnam, the officer in command there, to dispatch to Middlebrook all the Continental troops at his post except a garrison of one thousand. At the same time, Sullivan was ordered to call out immediately all the militia in his vicinity, and to move his force from Princeton to Rocky Hill, where he could not be cut off from the rest of the army by a surprise movement of the British, but whence he could quickly retreat to the rough uplands of Sourland Mountain. Sullivan's men and the militia were to harass the enemy constantly in their movements, but under all circumstances to avoid a general engagement.[20]

At New Brunswick and Piscataway, meanwhile, strong fortifications were being thrown up with great speed, to make easier the defense of those posts by the small guard which it was purposed to leave when the main British army pushed forward. The change of living conditions since the advent of spring, the prospect of action after months of torpor, the arrival of strong reinforcements from outside New Jersey, and the presence of the popular commander-in-chief had worked a great improvement in the spirit of Howe's troops. One young Hessian officer asserted:

"Everyone in our army wishes that the rebels would do us the favor of giving us a real battle: they would certainly be beaten. I believe that no more select corps can exist than the one General Howe has here. I am too young and have

[20] Washington, *Writings*, Vol. VIII, pp. 234-5; *Sullivan Papers*, Vol. I, pp. 380-1, 383-5; letter of John van Emburgh, June 12, 1777, in Washington Papers, Vol. 49; minutes of a Council of General Officers, June 12, in Washington Papers, Vol. 49.

seen too little to expect my judgment on this matter to find acceptance; but all the Hessian and veteran English officers say that they have never seen such a corps—meaning in quality, of course. Of the Englishmen, the grenadiers, light infantry, and light dragoons, and of the Hessians, the grenadiers and Jägers are the *élite* of the corps. Every fellow serves with joy, and everyone would rather cut loose today than tomorrow."[21]

How many men there were in this force it is impossible to say; General Howe himself later gave the number as eleven thousand, but other estimates are larger, and no reliance can be placed upon any assertion which Sir William made when defending his conduct. In any case, the British seem to have been as outstandingly superior to the Americans in numbers as they were in discipline. Howe's purpose apparently was twofold: to make a night march and cut off Sullivan's detachment from the main army; and, by feigning an advance upon Philadelphia, to draw Washington down from his strong position in the hills and lure him into a general engagement. Owing, however, partially to bad luck and chiefly to poor management, the British commander failed in both these purposes.[22]

At eleven o'clock on the night of June 13, the entire army, except for six regiments left behind as a garrison for New Brunswick, was scheduled to be in motion in two divisions; but various misunderstandings and accidents to the wagons delayed the departure until almost daybreak, so that Sullivan received ample warning of the movement and slipped off with his men to Flemington. The British column, after marching some three miles on the highway to Princeton, turned off on a road to the right, and proceeded to Somerset Court House, where a party of two hundred Americans dis-

[21] Münchhausen, Journal, June 11-13, 1777.
[22] Howe, *Narrative*, p. 16; Kemble, *op. cit.*, p. 121; *N.J.A.*, 2nd S., Vol. I, pp. 398, 476; Chastellux, *op. cit.*, Vol. I, p. 157; Münchhausen, Journal, June 8, 1777.

puted passage over the Millstone and inflicted a number of casualties before retiring in good order into the woods.[23]

The division under Cornwallis encamped near Somerset Court House, with the advance guard posted three or four miles from the village on the road leading to Coryell's Ferry. The second division, under General von Heister, took up a position at Middlebush, six miles from New Brunswick and two miles from the Court House. That the British should halt in a spot so near the American camp, instead of attempting a swift and secret push to the Delaware, aroused Washington's suspicions; and these were confirmed when it was reported to him that Howe had left behind in New Brunswick his baggage and provision wagons, and all or most of his bridges and boats. Finally, when the royal army began throwing up some redoubts on June 16, with the evident intention of staying where it was for a time, it became unmistakably clear that Howe's purpose was merely to tempt the American army away from its strong position into a battle in the lowlands.[24]

Washington declined the invitation. He was very secure in his stronghold behind the Raritan and Watchung Mountain, and he had sent to Peekskill for reinforcements. His right flank, which was the weakest in point of natural defensibility, he strengthened by erecting some redoubts and a long breastwork and by drawing in a detachment from Sullivan's corps. With these precautions taken, the position of his army was almost impregnable, and he saw so reason why he should not leave to Howe the initiative in further operations. For the British commander, on the other hand, the situation was becoming somewhat embarrassing. Even if he could bring on from New Brunswick his boats and his

[23] Münchhausen, Journal, June 14; Washington, *Writings*, Vol. VIII, pp. 243-4; John André, *Major André's Journal* . . . (Tarrytown, N.Y., 1930), p. 26; *Sullivan Papers*, Vol. I, pp. 390-1.

[24] Münchhausen, Journal, June 19; *Sullivan Papers*, Vol. I, pp. 393-4; Washington, *Writings*, Vol. VIII, pp. 261, 266-7.

318 Cockpit of the Revolution

pontoon bridge, it would be most unwise to hazard a crossing of the Delaware, with an increasing force waiting on the opposite shore to dispute his passage, and upon his flanks and rear Washington's army and a rising militia eager to inflict all possible damage and destroy his communications.[25]

According to one account, Colonel Mawhood, who since his engagement at Princeton had defeated a party of Americans on at least one occasion, and whose ferocious contempt for the rebels' bravery had not lessened, volunteered to head an attack up one of the passes leading to Washington's camp, in the hope that the resulting skirmish would bring on a general engagement.[26] Howe refused his consent. In order to reach the only vulnerable American position, the right flank, the attackers would have needed to make a long circuit around the end of the First Watchung Mountain to somewhere in the vicinity of Pluckemin, thereby exposing themselves to the danger of being cut off. If it had already proved impossible to maintain a long chain of posts in the level country between New Brunswick and Trenton, the perils were far greater in the rolling terrain of the Millstone and upper Raritan valleys. General Howe had learned his lesson: "No man in the world," wrote one of his aides, "can be more cautious than he is—which is unavoidably necessary in this cursed cut-up land."[27]

What made the situation even more difficult for him was the alacrity with which the militia were turning out to harry the invaders. Old scores were not yet settled, and respect for the military prowess of the King's troops had sunk very low during the winter and spring. The spirit of the farmers at this time, declared one contemporary, would "do them honor

---

[25] *Sullivan Papers*, Vol. I, p. 393; Washington, *Writings*, Vol. VIII, pp. 243-4, 259-61; Galloway, *Letters to a Nobleman*, pp. 61-2, 66-7; George S. Mott, "The First Century of Hunterdon County," in *N.J.H.S.P.*, 2nd S., Vol. V, pp. 102-3; Chastellux, *op. cit.*, Vol. I, p. 147; Gordon, *American Revolution*, Vol. II, pp. 470-1; Hall, *op. cit.*, pp. 291-2; Howe, *Narrative*, pp. 15-16.
[26] Hall, *op. cit.*, p. 291.
[27] Münchhausen, Journal, June 16; Howe, *Narrative*, pp. 15-16.

to the latest ages.—Never," he continued, "did the Jerseys appear more universally unanimous to oppose the enemy; they turned out old and young, great and small, rich and poor. Scarcely a man that could carry a musket was left at home."[28] Washington frankly attributed in large part to the activity of the militia Howe's eventual decision to return to New Brunswick without undertaking any serious offensive operation.

These eager militiamen, together with a small number of Continentals, annoyed the enemy unremittingly. During the long winter, the Americans had become expert in guerrilla tactics, and now their skill was exercised under the most favorable circumstances. British sentinels were killed by shots proceeding from out of the darkness; patrols making their rounds in broad daylight were greeted with deadly fire from thickets or barns; and if an officer ventured beyond the lines to reconnoiter the American position, he was likely to find himself surrounded in an instant by a swarm of horsemen who made him gallop back in hot haste.[29] Even the gentle promptings of love were not sacred to the ubiquitous rebels. One night two young lieutenants of the grenadiers slipped out to visit a pair of sisters who lived about fifty paces beyond the British outposts, and with whom they had formed a tender friendship during the previous period of occupation in December. A third sister, excluded from the happy reunion, slunk wrathfully away from the house, and before long the lovers were brusquely interrupted by a party of militia, who carried off the gallants amidst the lamentations of the bereft ladies.[30]

Four days and five nights Howe lingered near the Millstone, vainly waiting for Washington to come out and attack

[28] "A Campaign Journal," in *Princeton Standard*, New Series, Vol. III, No. 20 (May 15, 1863).

[29] Washington, *Writings*, Vol. VIII, pp. 270-1, 287; André, *op. cit.*, p. 28; Münchhausen, Journal, June 14-18.

[30] Münchhausen, Journal, June 19; Kemble, *op. cit.*, p. 121.

him; four days and five nights his men were made the helpless targets of continual sniping. The road to New Brunswick, along which his provisions had to be brought, was infested with ambushes. At length the British commander grew weary of this unprofitable excursion, and early in the morning of June 19 the crack troops of the royal army, who had come out of New Brunswick with such confidence and eagerness, were marched back in humiliation to their old quarters. The start was made so early and was such a surprise to the Americans that Washington had little opportunity to embarrass the retiring force. A few shots, mostly ineffective, were fired upon the British as they passed through the countryside; and the King's soldiers, in return, set fire to some buildings on their way. The great expedition into the interior of New Jersey, which had engaged the anxious attention of the Americans for so long, had taken place with no result but the burning of a few houses.[31]

If it was not possible to draw Washington out by making a demonstration below his camp, the same purpose might be accomplished by other means. Howe's bag of tricks was not yet quite exhausted. For the moment, he seemed to be resigned to the failure of his excursion. On June 19, the army arrived in New Brunswick. During the two following days, several regiments left the town for Perth Amboy; and before daybreak on the morning of June 22 the rest of the army began to march off.

So large was the force to be moved that, long before the evacuation was complete, parties of Americans were hovering in the vicinity to see what mischief they could do. Had it not been for the weather, which had suddenly become rainy, the British would have met with rougher treatment than they actually received. Sullivan had worked out a detailed plan for an attack upon New Brunswick, and Wash-

---

[31] Münchhausen, Journal, June 19; Washington, *Writings*, Vol. VIII, pp. 266-7; *N.J.A.*, 2nd S., Vol. I, p. 405.

ington had arranged to move the army down from Middle-brook to support his advanced detachments. The downpour, however, which was bad alike for men, arms, and ammunition, led him to keep most of his troops under cover, since he could see no decisive advantage to be gained by pursuing the enemy at this juncture. In this decision he may have erred: one of Howe's adjutants later expressed the positive opinion that if the Americans had attacked the retreating column in force at several points simultaneously, they must inevitably have inflicted severe damage, since it was too unwieldly and too cramped for space in the narrow road to avoid being thrown into confusion.[32]

As it was, the British and Hessians were by no means undisturbed in their retirement: swift American detachments hovered about, a constant threat, and attacked when occasion offered.[33] Without suffering any great harm, but in a hasty and undignified retreat which contrasted strikingly with their first triumphant entry into New Jersey, the British marched down the Raritan; and New Brunswick, the headquarters of the army of occupation for over six months, was again in the hands of the Americans. The retiring troops, sullen and humiliated over the inglorious outcome of the campaign, wreaked their vengeance upon the countryside through which they passed, and no officer prevented them. House after house on the road to Perth Amboy went up in flames: as far as one could see, reports one English civilian who travelled with the army, there were blazing homes. People who had gathered on the neighboring heights to watch the departure of the hated invaders found their view obscured by a pall of smoke hanging in the wet, heavy air over the entire road from New Brunswick to Perth Amboy.

[32] Münchhausen, Journal, June 20, 21, 22; Sullivan Papers, Vol. I, pp. 395-400; André, op. cit., p. 29.

[33] Münchhausen, Journal, June 22; N.J.A., 2nd S., Vol. I, p. 477; Creswell, op. cit., pp. 240-2; Washington, Writings, Vol. VIII, pp. 281-3, 298-9; André, op. cit., pp. 30-1.

Thus the royal army, which had so long outstayed its welcome in the Raritan valley, bade farewell to its involuntary hosts.[34] Like an awkward guest, however, who cannot depart without making several false starts, it was to rush back briefly and embarrassingly before it disappeared for good.

Howe's withdrawal caused jubilation among the Americans. Washington, who had not escaped criticism for his failure to attack Howe when the latter was encamped on the Millstone, decided, in accordance with the general desire, to follow the British. Already they were crossing from Perth Amboy to Staten Island, and were preparing to board the waiting transports; and the Americans were eager to fall with tooth and nail upon the last of the retreating army. On June 24, as soon as the rain stopped, Washington moved down from the hills to the vicinity of Quibbletown. He sent forward Lord Stirling, with a strong detachment, to the Short Hills in the vicinity of Metuchen Meeting House, and stationed light parties close to the British lines. Despite the eagerness of his officers, he was uneasy. On the day before he moved into the lowlands, he wrote to Joseph Reed:

"If General Howe has not maneuvred much deeper than most People seem disposed to think him capable of, his Army is absolutely gone off panic struck; but as I cannot persuade myself into a belief of the latter, notwithstanding it is the prevailing opinion of my Officers, I cannot say that the move I am about to make towards Amboy accords altogether with my opinion, not that I am under any other apprehension than that of being obliged to loose Ground again, which would indeed be no small misfortune as the Spirits of our Troops, and the Country, is greatly reviv'd (and I presume) the Enemys not a little depress'd, by their late retrograde motions."[35]

[34] Washington, *Writings*, Vol. VIII, p. 281 ; Creswell, *op. cit.*, p. 242 ; *N.J.A.*, 2nd S., Vol. I, pp. 406, 407, 415, 477.
[35] Washington, *Writings*, Vol. VIII, pp. 295, 298-9.

These forebodings were well justified. The news that the American army had forsaken its strong position was precisely what Howe had been waiting for. Preparations for embarking the troops went ostentatiously forward, and a brigade of Hessians was actually sent aboard transports; but, late in the afternoon of June 25, secret orders were sent out for the vessels to move at once to Perth Amboy and debark their men, equipped with three days' rations. Similar orders were sent to the commanders of the regiments on Staten Island, who were to have their men on the shore opposite the town, in readiness to cross, at eight in the evening. Greatly to Howe's annoyance, however, strong contrary winds delayed the movement of the troops across the water, so that it was midnight before the last of the Hessians from the transports had been set ashore at Perth Amboy.[36]

At about one in the morning of June 26, the first British column, under Cornwallis, set off on the road to Wood-bridge; two hours later the second division, marching under the immediate command of General Vaughan and accompanied by Howe, departed on the road to Bonhamton. After proceeding a few miles, both columns turned into roads leading towards Scotch Plains, and continued northward upon somewhat parallel routes, flanking on either side the low chain of the Short Hills in which the American advanced detachment under Stirling and Maxwell was posted. The late start and the vigilance of the American pickets prevented a complete surprise: after a few of Stirling's outlying parties had accidentally collided with the British columns, the alarm was given and the rest of the advance was made under continual fire from thickets, in the effective American style. In the neighborhood of Ash Swamp, not far from Scotch Plains, the main body of men under Maxwell and Stirling twice made a vigorous stand, apparently in order

[36] Münchhausen, Journal, June 24 and 25; André, *op. cit.*, p. 31; Hall, *op. cit.*, p. 295.

to protect some wagons which were being hastily removed to the hills. Superiority of numbers soon told, and the American force, with the loss of three small but good French cannon and some seventy or eighty prisoners, withdrew hastily to the mountain to avoid being surrounded.

Alarmed by the swift approach of the enemy, and fearful lest Howe should get between him and the safety of Middlebrook, Washington moved his army from Quibbletown to the passes in Watchung Mountain, where he could offer an effective resistance even to an overwhelming force. The British pressed briskly on, apparently in an attempt either to gain one of the passes ahead of the Americans, or to cut off more of the outlying rebels. Somewhere between Metuchen Meeting House and Scotch Plains, the two columns united—whether before or after the brush with Stirling's force is not clear[37]—and from that point they advanced as far as Westfield. The galling fire from concealed snipers continued all the way, and the weather was insufferably hot, particularly for the Hessians, who had to make the unusual exertion while burdened with elaborate and heavy uniforms. Many dropped dead along the way from heat and exhaustion; and one of Howe's subordinates admitted that in the course of the day the army suffered more than seventy casualties from the shots of the enemy and the burning rays of the sun. American estimates of Howe's losses ran much higher, and the British in turn made the usual extravagant and unverifiable assertions about the numbers of rebels killed and wounded, which do not agree at all with Washington's optimistic but vague report on the subject.[38]

[37] It cannot be determined which British column was involved in this action, or whether both were. The journals of officers in both divisions claim the victory for their own columns. Although the varying accounts are not to be reconciled, the weight of the evidence seems to point to the right column as having borne the brunt of the action after it had been joined near Metuchen Meeting House by the other division.

[38] Münchhausen, Journal, June 26 and 27; Hall, *op. cit.*, pp. 295-6; André, *op. cit.*, pp. 31-3; *N.J.A.*, 2nd S., Vol. I, pp. 415-16, 428-9, 477-8; Kemble, *op. cit.*, p. 123, Washington, *Writings*, Vol. VIII, pp. 307-8; Obrist-Lieutenant

The aggressive sortie from Perth Amboy was effective in checking the eagerness of Washington's followers to pursue the royal troops, but failed in what was probably its chief purpose: to catch the American army at a disadvantage and force a battle. On June 27, the British returned at a leisurely pace as far as Rahway, without being disturbed. Many dwellings of those unfortunate enough to live along the route of the march were plundered and burned, and all cattle discovered were appropriated and driven along. The King's soldiers were leaving a part of the country which had proved notably unresponsive to their efforts to win back its love for their gracious sovereign, and they were taking full advantage of the opportunity to pay their final respects to such undutiful stubbornness.[39]

Having failed again to draw Washington into a pitched battle or to dislodge him from his mountain fastness, Howe saw no reason for lingering in New Jersey. On June 28, the very day on which the army arrived back in Perth Amboy, evacuation of the town began. For two days it continued, and on June 30 the last of the remaining troops were embarked under the guns of the *Vigilant*, a powerful battery-ship anchored at the mouth of the Raritan. For a quarter of an hour after the last boatload had left, Howe remained with a few of his officers on an elevation near the shore, to see if any American troops were approaching. Washington's men, however, had learned a lesson of caution from the recent maneuvers, and, although parties of them had come fairly close to the lines during the past two days, not an American soldier was as yet ready to enter the deserted town. Satisfied with the results of their inspection, the British officers went down to the shore and got into a waiting

von Dincklage, diary (MS. transcript), in German Papers, New York Public Library, June 26, 1777; Maxwell to Stirling, July 2, in Washington Papers, Vol. 50.

[39] André, *op. cit.*, p. 33; Dincklage, Journal, June 26 *ff.*; Washington, *Writings*, Vol. VIII, pp. 311-13; *N.J.A.*, 2nd S., Vol. I, p. 415.

boat. General Howe was the last man to step aboard. Whether he knew it or not, in his survey from the hilltop he had taken final leave of an ungrateful province. Never again was he to set foot in New Jersey, where his most hopeful schemes had more than once met unexpected ruin.[40]

By this undisputed embarkation, some of the sting of leaving the state was removed; but there was not a little discontent in the British army over the ineffectiveness of the recent campaign. Howe was personally popular in the army because of "his good nature, and gracious behaviour to all ranks in the service, as well as a pretty equal distribution of justice in the line of his profession"; but even loyalty to the commander could not check the angry tongues of some of the officers. While the Americans were rejoicing over the turn of events, and the militia of New Jersey were taking credit to themselves for stopping an invasion of Pennsylvania and driving the invaders out of their state, Howe's followers were nursing a feeling of injured corporate pride, which grew more galling with each passing month. "Never," declared one well informed observer over a year later, "was an Army more chagrined than by this Retreat. The first as well as the inferior Officers complained loudly, and perhaps, in so doing, indiscreetly. The Infection of Discontent from this Period has spread among us. I can scarce hear a Man speak on that Subject but in Passion or Despair."[41]

As yet, however, the army had but little to criticize in comparison with what was to follow. Even as he had thrown away the fruits of the campaign of 1776 by an unwise step in December, the general was now entering upon an expedition that would ruin British military plans for the year 1777. Once more the hopes of the King and his ministers were to be drowned in the waters of the Delaware.

[40] Münchhausen, Journal, June 29-30, 1777; Dincklage, Journal, June 30; André, op. cit., pp. 33-4; Washington, Writings, Vol. VIII, pp. 309-10, 315, 322, 324.
[41] Hall, op. cit., p. 297; Kemble, op. cit., p. 124; Ambrose Serle to Lord Dartmouth, Aug. 30, 1778, in Stevens, Facsimiles, Vol. XXIV, No. 2066.

CHAPTER X ☼ *A SUMMER INTERLUDE*

AFTER the inglorious beginning of their campaign and the evacuation of New Jersey, General Howe's troops remained for several weeks on Staten Island. Gradually, while the Americans watched with interest, they were embarked on the fleet of transports lying in Raritan Bay. Between the ships and the city of New York a swarm of small boats was constantly plying to and fro, carrying baggage and stores to the vessels and transporting the busy officers who were supervising the operations. Evidently some sort of expedition was in preparation; but what its goal was to be the Americans had no way of knowing.

While waiting to see what was going to happen, Washington concluded that it was safe to dispense with the services of the militia, who, except for the inhabitants of lethargic Burlington County,[1] had turned out with unexpected alacrity to interfere with the recent British operations. By July 1 the embattled Jerseymen had been discharged, with thanks, except for a few guards. The general's words of warm appreciation for their "late Spirited Behaviour"[2] had gone far to wipe out memories of the days when cooperation between militia and Continentals had left much to be desired. As a concrete sign of this reconciliation between New Jersey and the army, Washington sent several wagonloads of meat and flour to be distributed among the inhabitants in the vicinity of Westfield and Ash Swamp whose homes had been robbed and devastated by the British army in its last foray.[3]

Except for a small garrison at Powles Hook, the royal occupation of the state was now but an unpleasant memory; yet the American army lingered on. Washington was reluctant to quit his commanding position in the Watchung

---

[1] *N.J. Exec. Corr.*, pp. 68, 70-1, 91.
[2] Washington, *Writings*, Vol. VIII, pp. 287, 325-6.
[3] *ibid.*, Vol. VIII, p. 341 ; *N.J.A.*, 2nd S., Vol. I, p. 422.

Mountains until the direction of Howe's next move should become apparent. Logically, Sir William might be expected to sail up the Hudson as far as he could go and then proceed overland to cooperate with General Burgoyne, who was approaching Ticonderoga from Canada. Past experience had shown, however, that the logical thing was precisely what the British commander might not be expected to do. Furthermore, David Forman of Freehold in Monmouth County, who had organized a fairly efficient system of collecting information about activities on Staten Island, reported that a number of brigs, schooners, and sloops had been prepared for taking horses aboard, and that the stalls on these vessels had been lined with sheepskins with the wool on, to keep the animals from chafing.[4] Since precautions of this nature would be totally unnecessary for an expedition up the Hudson or over the landlocked waters of Long Island Sound, Washington concluded that some more ambitious enterprise, either to eastern New England or to Philadelphia or the Southern states, might be in prospect.

Until this uncertainty should be resolved, the situation of the commander-in-chief was, to use his own words, "truly delicate and embarrassing." Should the army move away from Middlebrook towards the Hudson fortresses to help guard against the probable British advance up the river, Howe would be able to land his troops at South Amboy and march without hindrance across New Jersey to Philadelphia. If, on the other hand, the American force should stay where it was, the enemy, in a swift offensive, might be able to overpower the North River forts before Washington had time to go to their rescue. "Thus let us examine matters as we will," he declared, "difficulties stare us in the face."[5]

As news of the northern campaign became progressively more alarming and a minor British expedition up Long

4 David Forman to Washington, July 6, 1777, Washington Papers, Vol. 50.
5 Washington, *Writings*, Vol. VIII, pp. 326-7, 329-31, 363-4, 366.

Island Sound to Fairfield harbor suggested the possibility that Howe was about to attack the Highland forts from the rear, Washington was forced to make a decision, and moved gradually northward with his army. He had advanced some distance into the state of New York when unexpected messages from New Jersey sent him hastening southward again.[6]

On Sunday, July 20, one hundred and sixty vessels of the royal fleet fell down from Staten Island to Sandy Hook Bay, where they were joined the next morning by fifteen more transports and men-of-war, and later by thirty small brigs, schooners, and sloops. For another day the great fleet lay quiet; and then, early in the morning of July 23, the vessels one by one hoisted sail and weighed anchor. For hours, while observers on the New Jersey shore watched intently, the countless white sails tacked back and forth across the bay until finally the last of them had cleared the Hook and the long procession stood out to sea, where until sundown it could be seen steering a southeast course before a favoring wind.[7]

The report of the sailing reached Washington at the same time that another incident convinced him that Philadelphia was the object of British designs. In an attempt to keep the main American army out of the way until a swift attack on Philadelphia by way of the Delaware could be delivered, Howe sent an emissary with a false message to General Burgoyne sewed in his coat and instructions to let himself and the message be captured by the Americans. This letter informed Burgoyne that Howe's sailing to the southward was but a ruse intended to decoy Washington in that direction, and that he really intended to go to Boston, from which place he would cooperate with the invasion from Canada.[8]

[6] *ibid.*, pp. 341, 342, 344, 353, 371-3, 377-9, 386, 390, 406, 409, 471-2; *Sullivan Papers*, Vol. I, pp. 411-12, 414-15.

[7] André, *op. cit.*, p. 34; Forman to Washington, July 23, in Washington Papers, Vol. 52; Col. Stephen Moylan to Washington, July 23, *ibid.*

[8] *Report on the Stopford-Sackville MSS.*, Vol. II, pp. 72-3; *Sullivan Papers*, Vol. I, pp. 418-19.

Once more Sir William underestimated his adversary's intelligence. The ruse was clumsily executed, and Washington was not deceived for a moment. "To me," he informed Putnam, "a stronger proof could not be given that . . . [General Howe] is not going to the Eastward, than this Letter adduces. It was evidently intended to fall into our hands, the complexion of it, the circumstances attending it &ca., evinces this beyond a doubt in my Mind."[9] He acted swiftly, and once more New Jersey swarmed with American soldiers, as the Continental army, in several divisions following different routes, hastened across the state to the Delaware. On July 26, the British fleet was seen a short distance off Little Egg Harbor, beating towards Cape May against a south wind; a few days later the armada was at the Delaware Capes. Most of the American army now crossed over into Pennsylvania to resist the threatened invasion; but all further motion was abruptly halted at the beginning of August, when it was learned that the British had left the mouth of the Delaware and sailed out of the range of vision of watchers on Cape May, on a course bearing east-northeast before a fresh, favoring wind.[10]

Howe had abandoned the plan of going up the Delaware. The natural and artificial obstructions in the channel and the number of American small armed vessels which had been collected in the river would prevent his fleet from getting very far upstream; and the marshy, cut-up nature of the territory where he would probably have to land his men would greatly assist the opposing forces.[11] So the British fleet sailed away to carry out the original plan of coming up Chesapeake Bay; but the wide circuit to the eastward with which it began the journey perplexed and alarmed the Americans. That Howe

[9] Washington, *Writings*, Vol. VIII, pp. 468, 484-5.
[10] *ibid.*, Vol. VIII, pp. 487-8, 492-3, 496, 497, 500-5, Vol. IX, p. 1; John McGinnis to Col. Bradford, July 26, Washington Papers, Vol. 52; Thomas Mifflin to Washington, July 27, *ibid.*; letter of John Hunn, July 31, *ibid.*
[11] Howe, *Narrative*, p. 23.

might be going to attack New England and cooperate with Burgoyne now seemed as likely as that he might be aiming for the Chesapeake. Worried and uncertain, but unwilling to march his troops unnecessarily in the excessive heat, the commander-in-chief moved slowly northward with his main army, and General Sullivan, who was still in New Jersey, was posted with his division at Hanover in Morris County to await further developments.[12]

For almost two weeks thereafter, nothing definite was heard about the British vessels. Stationed at Hanover with nothing to do, Sullivan decided to employ his spare time to advantage by striking a blow at the depleted garrison of Staten Island—a project which had suggested itself to Washington a couple of weeks earlier. The expedition, which took place on August 22, was a failure, like all other attacks on the island. Some eighty of the Loyalist New Jersey Volunteers were captured by Colonel Matthias Ogden's two New Jersey regiments of Continentals, with the help of some militiamen—here was civil war with a vengeance! —but the British made up for this loss by the number of American stragglers and members of the rear guard whom they took prisoner.[13]

On the same day on which this fiasco occurred, Washington, having had news of the British from the Chesapeake, bade Sullivan join him at once, and New Jersey was soon left with nothing but its own militia for defense against any incursion which Sir Henry Clinton, Howe's *locum tenens* in New York, might see fit to launch.[14] The dreaded blow soon fell. Clinton believed the time was ripe for "a small diversion" to forestall the unlikely possibility that the New Jersey militia might move to help resist either Howe's

[12] *Sullivan Papers*, Vol. I, pp. 429-30; Washington, *Writings*, Vol. IX, pp. 1, 4, 6, 9-10, 21, 43.
[13] *Sullivan Papers*, Vol. I, pp. 437-42, 445, 459-60, 485-532; *N.J.A.*, 2nd S., Vol. I, pp. 452-3, 457-60, 463, Vol. II, pp. 45-6; Kemble, *op. cit.*, pp. 41-2; Washington, *Writings*, Vol. IX, pp. 115-17.
[14] *N.J. Exec. Corr.*, pp. 94-5.

march from Chesapeake Bay towards Philadelphia or Burgoyne's slow advance from Canada. At the same time that he was thus keeping Jerseymen worried, he would be able to replenish his supply of livestock and horses. From September 11 to September 15 large parties of his troops scoured most of Bergen County and part of Essex. The inhabitants were able to offer but little resistance, and panic spread swiftly. Rumor declared that six thousand of the enemy were about to ravage a wide expanse of countryside and capture Morristown. Before hastily summoned reinforcements from Morris and the western counties could hasten up, the invaders had withdrawn, but they had thrown a severe fright into the people of New Jersey.[15]

Clinton's raid came at the worst possible time for Washington's plans. On September 11, the Americans had failed at Brandywine Creek to stop Howe's northward advance from Chesapeake Bay, and on September 26 the British entered Philadelphia. Before the occupation of the city, Washington was anxious to enlarge his army in order to throw what obstacles he could in the way of Howe's progress; and, after the capital had fallen, he was equally in need of a large force capable of annoying the enemy and cutting off their communications. As yet, the British fleet was not able to pass the obstructions in the Delaware; and, if supplies were to be carried from the ships to the city, they would have a long and difficult overland journey. Could the Delaware be kept shut against the fleet, and the American army be sufficiently reinforced to play havoc with Howe's land communications, Washington was not without hope, as he informed John Hancock on September 23, that Sir William's

[15] *N.J.A.*, 2nd S., Vol. II, pp. 42-4; Kemble, *op. cit.*, p. 132; Washington, *Writings*, Vol. IX, pp. 218-19; Hall, *op. cit.*, p. 325; Dickinson to Washington, Sept. 13, 16, and 17, Washington Papers, Vol. 56; Col. W. Malcom to Washington, Sept. 13 and 14, *ibid.*; Dickinson to Cadwalader, Sept. 14, *ibid.*; Putnam to Washington, Sept. 14, *ibid.*; Col. A. Burr to Malcom, Sept. 14, *ibid.*; Gen. Alexander McDougall to Washington, Sept. 17, *ibid.*; Dickinson to Hancock, Sept. 18, *ibid.*

acquisition of Philadelphia might "instead of his good fortune, prove his Ruin."[16]

For this reason, the commander-in-chief was doing his utmost during those feverish autumn days to obtain, among other reinforcements, a strong body of New Jersey militia to serve with him for a few weeks. Governor Livingston had approved the application, and General Dickinson had been assembling in the western part of the state as large a number of men as he could collect. The irruption from New York and Staten Island sent Dickinson hastening with most of his force to help repel the invaders; and after they had returned to their own territory he informed Washington that the recent excitement had changed the mood of the people. They were now fearful, he declared, that the incursion might be repeated, and were loath to leave their own state; so that whereas, had it not been for the alarm, he thought he might have been able to march to the assistance of the army with four thousand men, he doubted that now he could prevail upon more than half that number to enter Pennsylvania.[17]

Dickinson himself was detained in New Jersey to arrange for militia guards in the exposed area in the northeast, and it was General David Forman of Freehold who finally joined the army on September 29 with about eight hundred men.[18] For the next month, Livingston, Dickinson, and Forman had their hands full in attempting to meet the pressing demands upon the militia for various purposes. They had to struggle against a marked public apathy, for the people were growing war-weary and had little inclination to shoulder arms until the necessity was thrust upon them.[19] Matters had grown worse, if anything, since one traveller

[16] Washington, *Writings*, Vol. IX, p. 259.
[17] Dickinson to Washington, Sept. 20, Washington Papers, Vol. 56.
[18] Washington, *Writings*, Vol. IX, pp. 268, 269, 270, 271, 277-8, 284.
[19] Dickinson to Washington, Sept. 16, in Washington Papers, Vol. 56.

passing through the state in July had found a discouraging state of affairs:

"General Washington, with the little remnant of his army at Morristown, seemed left to scuffle for liberty, like another Cato at Utica. Here and there, we saw a militia man with his contrasted coloured cape and facings; and we found besides, that Captains, Majors and Colonels had become 'good cheap' in the land. But unfortunately, these war-functionaries were not found at the head of their men: They, more generally, figured as barkeepers, condescendingly serving out small measures of liquor, to their less dignified customers. Still they were brimfull of patriotism, the prevailing feature of which was, to be no less ardent in their pursuit, than fervent in their hatred of Tories."[20]

Such militiamen as had been induced to join Washington went with heavy hearts, committed themselves only for very short terms, and soon revealed such anxiety to be at home again that on October 6 the commander-in-chief instructed Forman to take them back to New Jersey, discharge them, and make every effort to replace them.[21] Three days later Governor Livingston, with the consent of the legislature, authorized Forman to raise two thousand militia from Burlington, Sussex, Monmouth, and southern Middlesex Counties, to serve under his command with the Continental army; but from the beginning the unhappy officer ran into difficulties. The men had not yet all been divided into classes for alternation in service, so that he had trouble in calling out the number he was authorized to summon. The two classes from Hunterdon which had been assigned to his brigade had been drawn off to help Dickinson guard the district near New York. The Monmouth militia, though willing to turn out, had become so alarmed by recent minor pillaging raids into their territory that they had persuaded the legislature to forbid their being called away from their own county. He

---

[20] Graydon, *op. cit.*, pp. 282-3.   [21] *N.J. Exec. Corr.*, pp. 104-5.

received no answer at all to his appeal to Sussex County. In disgust, he informed Washington on October 15: "I do not belive I shall Collect three Hundred men." Finally he was informed by the commander-in-chief that if he had any men to spare he should send them not to Pennsylvania but to the fort being constructed at Red Bank on the New Jersey shore of the Delaware a few miles below Philadelphia.[22]

While the officers had been struggling with such poor results to rouse the militia, the period for sending men out of the state had passed. By this time, the campaign had entered a new phase, and chief interest had shifted from land operations to the struggle of the British fleet to ascend the Delaware. No longer was the war something which, except for such unpleasant but minor matters as occasional raids, had been removed away from New Jersey to another area. Once more the theater of major operations had returned to the borders of the state, and a decisive contest was about to be fought out upon the waters and along both banks of the Delaware. The summer interlude was over; New Jersey was on the point of witnessing on its own threshold the most spectacular struggle of the entire Revolution.

[22] Livingston to Washington, Oct. 10, Washington Papers, Vol. 58; Forman to Washington, Oct. 11, *ibid.;* Washington, *Writings,* Vol. IX, p. 402. Meanwhile, another emergency drew off a force of militia in a different direction. At the beginning of October, Clinton sent a force up the Hudson, which burned the towns of Kingston and Esopus and seemed about to attack the river forts in an effort to aid Burgoyne. In answer to an urgent appeal from Washington, Livingston sent a force of a thousand militia temporarily into the state of New York to support General Putnam, and Dickinson's guard in the Elizabeth-Town-Passaic area was thereby reduced to a skeleton.— Washington, *Writings,* Vol. IX, pp. 339-40, 356; Livingston to Washington, Oct. 10 and 12, in Washington Papers, Vol. 58; Dickinson to Washington, Oct. 24, *ibid.,* Vol. 59.

CHAPTER XI ☼ *THE DEFENSE OF THE DELAWARE*

WHEN Admiral Lord Howe's ships appeared in Delaware Bay in the autumn of 1777 and began to thread their way cautiously among the sandbanks and up the tortuous channel, they were but realizing a possibility which the Americans had long dreaded and prepared to resist. Months before, there had been sunk at a narrow place in the channel a few miles below Philadelphia a triple row of the strange instruments known as chevaux-de-frise. These devices were heavy frames of timber, sunk to the bottom of the river with stones. Massive iron prongs, rising at an angle almost to the surface of the water at low tide and pointing downstream, offered a deadly obstacle to any wooden vessel incautious enough to run against them. A row of these spaced close together presented an impenetrable barrier to ships of any considerable size, and they were so heavy that two vessels would require several hours to move a single one of them away.[1]

For the defense of this barrier, a comprehensive scheme had been devised. A fleet of small armed vessels was stationed above it to repulse such British ships as might ascend the narrow principal channel of the Delaware, two or three at a time, in order to reach and lift the obstructions. The lighter of these defending craft would enjoy much greater freedom of action than the enemy vessels, in being able to maneuver over shallows and to slip around the chevaux-de-frise by way of the unobstructed secondary channel between the Pennsylvania mainland and the islands—a passage too shallow for the hostile men-of-war. Both the river fleet and the impediments in the main channel were protected by an

[1] Lamb, *op. cit.*, p. 232; Green's view on defense of the Delaware, Washington Papers, Vol. 53.

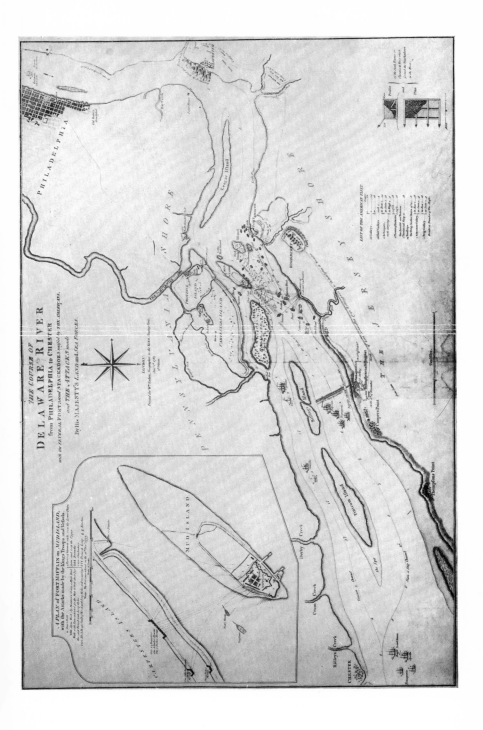

THE COURSE OF
DELAWARE RIVER
from PHILADELPHIA to CHESTER
with the SEVERAL FORTS and STACKADOES raised by THE AMERICANS
and THE ATTACKS made
By His MAJESTY'S LAND and SEA FORCES.

LONDON
Printed for Wm Faden, Geographer to the KING, Charing Cross,
June 1st 1778.

A PLAN of FORT MIFFLIN on MUD ISLAND,
with the Attacks made by the King's Troops and Vessels.

LIST OF THE AMERICAN FLEET.

PHILADELPHIA

PENNSYLVANIA SHORE

PENNSYLVANIA

THE JERSEY SHORE

Timber Island

MUD ISLAND

CARPENTERS ISLAND

CHESTER

extensive fortification in midstream, begun in the days of British rule, left unfinished for some years, and carried nearer to completion, under the name of Fort Mifflin, after a false alarm of invasion by sea in April 1777 had produced a burst of frenzied activity among the defenders of the river. Fort Mifflin was situated on Mud Island, a low bank of sand and mud close to the main channel and just above the chevaux-de-frise. In order to be entirely effective in controlling the upper river, it would have required a supporting work on Red Bank, an eminence on the New Jersey shore about a mile and a half away and slightly upstream; but construction on this second project, begun in the spring of 1777, was soon halted.[2] Fort Mifflin was generally regarded as well-nigh impregnable, and fortification work in New Jersey was concentrated on a supplementary defensive position at Billingsport, a commanding elevation some five miles farther down the river, where another line of chevaux-de-frise was sunk.[3]

It soon became clear, however, that in defending the Delaware the Americans must choose either Billingsport or Fort Mifflin as the center for effective resistance, since the Continental army had neither men nor artillery enough to hold both points strongly.[4] Early in August, when General Howe seemed to be threatening Philadelphia by water, Washington urged upon Congress the advisability of making Mud Island their chief reliance. Billingsport, he pointed out, was too remote to be effectively supported by the American army, and, if besieged in force, could not possibly hold out for more than fifteen or twenty days. Whether it would be better to abandon the post in advance, or whether the delay imposed on the British by a temporary opposition would be

[2] General Philip Schuyler to Washington, April 16 and 22, 1777, in Washington Papers, Vol. 45; Owen Biddle to Washington, April 19, ibid.
[3] Washington, Writings, Vol. VII, p. 411; Chastellux, op. cit., Vol. I, pp. 252-3; Pennsylvania Archives, 1st S., Vol. IV, p. 784; N.J. Exec. Corr., p. 63.
[4] See the opinions of Greene, Knox, Reed, and Wayne scattered through Volumes 50, 53, 54, and 55 of the Washington Papers.

worth the "disagreeable impressions" made upon the public mind by an unsuccessful resistance, he left it to Congress to decide. Of one point he felt certain: Fort Mifflin was far more easily defensible, because the New Jersey shore was too distant to be within effective cannonading range, and because the Pennsylvania shore, though nearer, could be made unsuitable for the erection of hostile batteries by opening embankments and flooding the low-lying islands into which it was cut up by creeks. So long as the upper river was controlled by American shipping, he believed, the garrison of Fort Mifflin could be provisioned and reinforced; and from below the British would be held off by the chevaux-de-frise.[5]

Even before the general's recommendations had reached Congress, Howe had appeared in Chesapeake Bay, and it had become evident that the advance upon Philadelphia would be by land. Nevertheless, the Delaware must still be kept closed to British shipping. Sir William might take Philadelphia; he might scour the surrounding countryside; but in the long run a large part of his provisions and all his military supplies must come to him by water. The overland route by which he marched was far too long to be maintained as his chief line of communication with the outer world while Washington's detachments were moving about the countryside. After Philadelphia fell, the British fleet under Admiral Howe moved around from Chesapeake to Delaware Bay. Could it be kept away from the city, the army of occupation must eventually find its position there intolerable, for land transportation along the marshy western shore of the river was both difficult and exposed to interference by the Americans.

For this reason, preparations for keeping the river shut went on vigorously; and, in general, Washington's suggestions were followed. Fort Mifflin, which had been com-

[5] Washington, *Writings*, Vol. IX, pp. 46-52.

menced upon too ambitious a plan to be completed in time, and which had been designed, according to one engineer, "without any Judgment," was made as respectable as time and resources would permit. At the end of September, it received a garrison of two hundred Continental soldiers under Lieutenant Colonel Samuel Smith, who remained in command until the arrival, in the middle of the next month, of an experienced foreign officer, the Baron d'Arendt. More chevaux-de-frise were sunk in the river and a boom was stretched across part of the channel to complete the barrier. At the same time, Congress resolved to offer some resistance at Billingsport, and a force of about two hundred fifty militia was stationed there. Cooperating with these garrisons was the American fleet, consisting almost entirely of the Pennsylvania state navy under the command of Commodore John Hazelwood, and composed of thirteen galleys, two floating batteries, two xebecs, one ship, one brig, numerous smaller craft, fourteen fireships, and a number of fire-rafts.[6]

By the beginning of October, the defenses were complete upon the success of which depended the permanence of Howe's occupation of Philadelphia. They were pitiful enough. Behind the ramparts at Billingsport, the handful of militia, far too few to hold the extensive fortification, nervously awaited the advance of the enemy. Though the officers passed brave resolutions not to abandon the post

[6] Lamb, *op. cit.*, p. 231; Washington, *Writings*, Vol. IX, pp. 260-1; Col. Samuel Smith to Washington, Oct. 2, 1777, in Washington Papers, Vol. 57; Washington, *Writings*, Vol. IX, p. 321. Besides these vessels, there were, further up the river, two frigates, the *Delaware* and the *Montgomery*, in active use, and two unfinished ones, the *Washington* and the *Effingham*—all in the Continental service. The two latter were manned only with skeleton crews, and were not used during the campaign; and the *Delaware* was captured by the British when she grounded during an attack upon Philadelphia on the day after Howe entered the city. The *Montgomery* joined the Pennsylvania fleet and the few smaller Continental vessels at Fort Mifflin.—Washington, *Writings*, Vol. IX, p. 299; Comm. Hazelwood to Washington, Oct. 12, 1777, in Washington Papers, Vol. 58; Continental Navy Board to Washington, Oct. 26, *ibid.*, Vol. 59; Capt. John Montresor, *Journal*, in *New York Historical Society Collections*, 1881, p. 459.

"till the last extremity," their words were hollow, and they were in a mood to decamp as soon as any considerable landing party should approach.[7]

At Mud Island, the garrison was in a more determined temper, but its surroundings and prospects were gloomy enough. Baron d'Arendt, when he arrived, some time later, was to describe the fort with feeling as "the worst that I have ever seen," and he had good reason for this judgment. Like Billingsport, Fort Mifflin had been laid out on far too grandiose a plan for the men available; eight hundred soldiers would have been required to man it adequately, even without an allowance for a necessary reserve. Washington, who, as usual, was suffering from a shortage of troops, and did not dare, by weakening his army north of Philadelphia, to expose to a British raid the stores at Easton, Bethlehem and Allentown and the various hospitals of the army, had not felt able to spare more than the two hundred men whom Smith had brought with him. Last-minute alterations had not been able to remedy some of the deficiencies of the fortification. On the south and east there was a high, thick redoubt of stone, fitted with loopholes, and solidly built upon piles, which had been started under the colonial government in the year 1772. It was described by one New England soldier as "some of the grandest wall of hewn stone that I ever saw," and, since it was built with large embrasures, it was the chief shelter for the soldiers during the siege. The work also contained some "magnificent barracks"; but aside from these advantages there was little to be claimed for it. On the north and the west there were no ramparts: such defenses as existed there were chiefly the wooden barracks, four wooden blockhouses, and a wall of palisades.

The fort was almost level with the water, and was cold and damp; so soft was the mud on which it was built that all

[7] Col. Samuel Smith to Washington, Oct. 2, 1777, in Washington Papers, Vol. 57.

material for the construction of earthworks had to be brought from the mainland. Indeed, the one advantage of the soil was that it nullified the efforts of the British batteries, later constructed on the Pennsylvania shore, to set fire to the wooden structures with inflammatory shells, for, as the engineer in charge of the British operations noted with chagrin, the instant such projectiles fell on the island, they were immersed in the mire.[8]

Colonel Smith, placed in such a cheerless situation, and feeling no confidence in either the Pennsylvania navy or the garrison at Billingsport, cast an apprehensive eye upon Red Bank, which the American leaders had neglected to continue fortifying, or to garrison. He fully expected the British to seize that point and establish a battery there, which not only would drive away the vessels supposed to supply Fort Mifflin with ammunition and provisions, but would also be able, he felt sure, to break down by constant cannonading the flimsy wooden walls of the fort and lay it open, on all sides except that of the stone redoubt, to an assault by soldiers in boats.

As for the navy, stationed for the most part between Fort Mifflin and Billingsport, it was almost paralyzed by fear. Commodore Hazelwood, though a well meaning man, lacked both the extraordinary ability and the qualities of inspiring leadership which the crisis demanded. Throughout the Delaware campaign, discipline was lax in the navy and morale was poor; at the beginning of the struggle the spirit of the crews was at its very lowest ebb. Even in the shallow waters of the Delaware, with which they were thoroughly familiar, it was no pleasant prospect for these men, most of them inexperienced in fighting, to defy with their handful

[8] Montresor, *op. cit.*, pp. 414-17; letter of Ebenezer David, Nov. 5, 1777, in John Carter Brown Library, Brown University; letter of Baron d'Arendt, Oct. 24, 1777, copied in Major Fleury's Journal, Oct. 29, Washington Papers, Vol. 58; William Faden, map and diagram, *The Course of the Delaware River. . .* (London, 1785).

of little boats the navy which for nearly two centuries had been the most formidable in the world.

"So general a discontent and Panic runs through . . . the fleet," lamented Smith on October 2, "that neither Officers nor men can be confided in, they conceive the River is lost if the enemy gets Possession of Billingsport nothing can convince them of the contrary, & I am persuaded as soon as that fort is taken that almost all the fleet will desert, indeed from their disposition I am induc'd to believe they will openly avow themselves and desert their Officers with their Crew (which has been the case with two) perhaps with their Gallies. The Officers and Mens Wives have been permited to remain in the City who have sent down to the fleet, to whom they have given prodigious accounts of the enemies force & sweet pretty promises aded to them have I am of Opinion caused this very general Desertion disaffection and Panic. . . . Your Excellency will find there is little dependence to be put in the fleet, and with four hundred Men the enemy will take the River without endangering one of thier Ships, for after they have weighed the obstructions at Billingsport which will soon be done, they will then fortify Red Bank and drive all the shiping from between us and it."[9]

These gloomy forebodings seemed in a fair way of fulfilment. On the very day that Smith confided his fears to Washington, a detachment from Howe's army, of a strength estimated at fifteen hundred men, crossed the Delaware to the New Jersey shore several miles below Billingsport. The garrison promptly evacuated the fort, after removing the stores and spiking the cannon. The next morning, a detachment of two or three hundred militia under General Silas Newcomb advanced to meet the enemy, and exchanged a few shots; but, finding itself outnumbered and in danger of being surrounded, it fell back, without suffering any

[9] Col. Samuel Smith to Washington, Oct. 2, 1777, in Washington Papers, Vol. 57.

serious casualties, to Haddonfield, while the British took possession of the abandoned stronghold.[10]

What both Washington and Smith had dreaded from the surrender of Billingsport now happened in full measure. The fleet was panic-stricken, and wild rumors as to the activities of the British were current. On the night after the fall of the fort, five officers and eighteen men deserted from the American vessels, and a great part of the rest, asserted Smith grimly, were only awaiting a good opportunity to follow their example.[11] His greatest fear, however —that the British would now move on to Red Bank and establish themselves in the unfinished fort there—was not realized. To be sure, Colonel Sterling, the British officer commanding the party which had taken possession of Billingsport, seems to have requested permission to occupy Red Bank; but his suggestion was ignored by headquarters. Howe's subsequent excuse for failing to seize this strategic spot was that the fortification was far from being complete at this time, that before a corps could have been securely established there, it would have needed to be "supplied with stores and provisions, with great difficulty, while exposed to the annoyance of the armed galleys and floating batteries; and [that] before the army was drawn nearer to Philadelphia the support of a post, so detached, would have been very precarious."[12] For similar reasons, presumably, he made no attempt at this time to hold Billingsport permanently: on October 10, Sterling evacuated it, after burning the gun-carriages and platforms and destroying the works.[13]

[10] Smith to Washington, Oct. 3, 1777, Washington Papers, Vol. 57; Gen. Silas Newcomb to Livingston, Oct. 4, in Livingston Papers (Mass. Hist. Soc.), Vol. II.

[11] Smith to Washington, Oct. 3, Washington Papers, Vol. 57.

[12] *ibid*. and same to same, same date; Galloway, *Letters to a Nobleman*, pp. 79-81; Hall, *op. cit.*, pp. 317-18; Howe, *Narrative*, p. 29.

[13] Washington, *Writings*, Vol. IX, p. 350; Smith to Washington, Oct. 6, Washington Papers, Vol. 57.

While the British force was somewhat weakened by the absence of the detachment sent to occupy Billingsport, Washington delivered a surprise attack against Howe's army at Germantown on October 4. Although the assault was unsuccessful, the audacity with which it was delivered and the losses which it inflicted upon the enemy did much to restore confidence in the American cause, and dispelled the exaggerated rumors which were current in the fleet concerning the completeness of Howe's triumph. By October 6, the panic had been dispelled, so Smith reported. Desertions had stopped, and a few runaways had actually returned to duty. Infused with this renewed confidence, the men of the galleys on October 6 drove away some ships which were making an effort to raise one of the chevaux-de-frise, and in the course of the evening, Hazelwood cleared the whole river of British shipping as far down as Chester.[14]

This evidence of power brought further self-assurance to the crews. Their minds were relieved of worry still more when, on October 7, upon the urgent representation of Colonel Smith and a representative of the Pennsylvania Navy Board, Washington ordered the First and Second Rhode Island Regiments of Continental troops under Colonel Christopher Greene and Colonel Israel Angell to occupy and strengthen the fort at Red Bank. His changed attitude towards this position was shown in the solemn tone of his instructions to Colonel Greene, the commander:

"The post with which you are now intrusted is of the utmost importance to America, and demands every exertion you are capable of, for its security and defence. The whole defence of the Delaware absolutely depends upon it, and consequently all of the Enemy's hopes of keeping Philadelphia and finally succeeding in the object of the campaign."[15]

[14] Smith to Washington, Oct. 6 and 7, 1777, Washington Papers, Vol. 57; Washington, *Writings*, Vol. IX, pp. 308-9, 321.
[15] Washington, *Writings*, Vol. IX, pp. 326-7, 328-9, 333-5.

With Greene went a skilled French engineer, the Chevalier de Mauduit du Plessis, who was to have charge of the artillery and of any new construction. His skilled eye perceived at once that Fort Mercer, as the work was now called, was, like the other fortifications on the river, much too large for a small garrison, and by no means perfect in design. Under his direction, one end of the structure was selected for use, and was put into a condition in which it could easily be defended by the five or six hundred men. By this judicious reconstruction, Fort Mercer became much more formidable than either of its sister strongholds on the Delaware.[16]

While these steps were being taken to secure the upper line of chevaux-de-frise, the British vessels were making continual efforts to move away part of the lower barrier. Whenever they seemed to be making progress, Hazelwood's fleet would swarm around them, and, having more guns on board the light-draft galleys than could be brought into action by the few larger British ships which could get near the obstruction, the Americans almost invariably were able to chase away the hostile vessels. As soon as the galleys retired, however, the British would return to their posts, and the process would have to begin again. Such a campaign used quantities of ammunition; and once more the poverty of the Americans hampered their efficiency. Not enough military stores were available to carry on the naval warfare as vigorously as it should have been prosecuted if the determined British fleet was to be kept off. "For God Sake," pleaded Commodore Hazelwood in one letter to Washington, "give us ammunition & all is Safe."[17]

Such an outburst on the part of the commodore was rare. In general he maintained a good humor which circumstances

[16] Chastellux, *op. cit.*, Vol. I, pp. 260-1; Ebenezer David, letter of Nov. 5, 1777, in John Carter Brown Library.

[17] Hazelwood to Washington, Oct. 10 and 15, 1777, Washington Papers, Vol. 58; Smith to Washington, Oct. 14, *ibid.*

frequently failed to warrant. By nature he seems to have been a simple and optimistic soul, and there was no thought of sarcasm in his mind, we may be sure, when he cheerfully informed Washington on October 10: "We fear nothing but want of Ammunition, Provisions & desertion of our Men, otherwise should be quite easy."[18] Two days later, however, he was obliged to apologize for not having stormed a battery the British were erecting on the Pennsylvania shore:

"Our Fleet is so reduc'd by desertion that four of the Galleys have not Men enough to Man One, and if I should land a number of those on board the other Galleys I can have no dependence on their return. . . . If your Excellency could furnish me with One hundred and fifty Men acquainted with the water, it would enable me to support the pass effectifly."[19]

Moved by this appeal, Washington attempted to fill the commodore's requirements. Colonel Greene was ordered to draft for service aboard the vessels such of his Rhode Islanders as were at home on the water, and efforts were made to obtain seamen elsewhere, but the navy at no time during the campaign became a dependable weapon.[20]

Affairs began to wear a serious aspect not only for the navy but for Fort Mifflin as well. The men of the garrison, exhausted by overwork in the damp, unhealthful fort, began to sicken rapidly. Smith became alarmed, and begged Washington for reinforcements. "Your Excellency will see the Necessity of sending me more Men," he wrote, "at least one hundred indeed one hundred fifty will not be too much, for every day our Men fall Sick. I have within four days thirty-four men Sick in Garrison the remaining will soon be worn out with fatigue as I am obliged to keep them on

[18] Hazelwood to Washington, Oct. 10, 1777, Washington Papers, Vol. 58.
[19] Hazelwood to Washington, Oct. 12, 1777, *ibid.*
[20] Washington, *Writings*, Vol. IX, pp. 369, 370; Continental Navy Board to Washington, Oct. 26, 1777, in Washington Papers, Vol. 59.

constant duty. . . . I conceive one chief reason of my Men being so very sickly is their want of Cloathing & Blankets. Your Excellencys Order to the Cloathier has never . . . been comply'd with. I have at least 60 of this small number without Breeches many of whom have scarce Ozn^a. enough to cover their Nakedness, never were Poor wretches in such a Situation as they are, had it not been for some Cloathing Capt Blewer lent me, they must all have perished before this."[21]

Added to these physical discomforts for the garrison of Fort Mifflin was a growing uneasiness of mind as the British offensive preparations on the Pennsylvania shore gradually assumed more menacing proportions. The confidence with which Washington and his officers had assumed that the enemy could not erect batteries near enough the fort to be effective was now proved to have been unjustified. Across the shallow secondary channel of the Delaware from Mud Island was a marshy region divided from the mainland and intersected by creeks. The principal sections of this area were known as Carpenter's Island and Province Island; but these two divisions were frequently referred to collectively under the name of the latter. Over this low-lying ground, the British gradually began to extend approaches to Fort Mifflin, utilizing for the purpose whatever higher points they could find. By a strange coincidence, the engineer in charge of throwing up the works intended to demolish the fort was Captain John Montresor, the same man who had drawn for the Pennsylvania colonial government the plans for fortifying Mud Island; so his labors were made easier not merely by intelligence and skill, but also by a thorough knowledge of the ground.

Slowly but formidably the British approached. During the night of October 8, a battery of two twelve-pounders was raised at the mouth of the Schuylkill River, on the

[21] Smith to Washington, Oct. 14, Washington Papers, Vol. 58.

north bank, and several attacks from American vessels failed to destroy it.[22] Although the battery was too far from Fort Mifflin to do serious damage, it protected the mouth of the Schuylkill from the American fleet, and permitted the British to move artillery and implements of construction across to Province and Carpenter's Islands without hindrance. Two nights after this initial move, a second battery was raised on Carpenter's Island, on a dike in a flooded meadow. The new work was only five hundred yards west of Fort Mifflin, and with its howitzer and mortar menaced the ill-protected north side of the fort. A warm cannonade from three American galleys and a floating battery the next day induced two officers and fifty-six privates stationed at the fortification to surrender; but the Americans could not destroy it, and it was soon repossessed. The next day, after a heavy preliminary cannonade, a party crossed the water from Fort Mifflin in an attempt to storm the work; but they were obliged to return without glory or success.[23]

Two more batteries were completed during the night of October 14, one equipped with two eighteen-pounders and constructed in front of the pest-house on a slight elevation on Province Island a considerable distance from the fort; the other threatening Mud Island with a small howitzer and a mortar from a distance of only six hundred yards. With these preparations completed, Montresor's men had done all they could to invest Fort Mifflin, and as the fog lifted from the river on the morning of October 15, all four batteries opened fire. Much to the disappointment of the British, the effects of the attack were negligible. Their artillery was too light to be effective in making breaches; and the explosive shells and red-hot shot from the mortars

[22] Montresor, *op. cit.*, pp. 463-4; Smith to Washington, Oct. 9, Washington Papers, Vol. 58.

[23] Montresor, *op. cit.*, pp. 464-5; Wm. Bradford and John Hazelwood to Washington, Oct. 11, Washington Papers, Vol. 58; Hazelwood to Washington, Oct. 12, *ibid.*

and howitzers, which had been expected to drop behind the walls and set fire to the wooden structures, buried themselves harmlessly in the mud.[24]

Obviously, the first plan to reduce Fort Mifflin had failed. Three weeks had gone by, Howe reminded his engineers reproachfully, since his arrival in Philadelphia, and the rebel stronghold was as formidable an obstacle as ever. He could spare no more artillery to increase the effectiveness of the siege; and his supply of ammunition was running so low that he could not afford to waste it in showering Mud Island with ineffective shots.[25] Provisions were becoming dangerously scarce. Something drastic must be done, or the position of the British army in Philadelphia would become untenable.

Something was done. Plans were laid to send over a picked force to take possession of Red Bank. Once established on that commanding eminence, the British would have another and more effective base from which to bombard Mud Island; and, what was more important, they would be able to drive away the American fleet and starve Fort Mifflin out.

On October 21, a strong detachment of Hessians under Colonel von Donop, consisting of all the Jägers, three battalions of grenadiers, and a regiment of foot—perhaps twelve hundred men in all—crossed the Delaware from Philadelphia to Cooper's Ferry and proceeded southward. Meeting with no effectual opposition from the militia, von Donop's force passed the night at Haddonfield, and reached the vicinity of Red Bank at about one o'clock the following afternoon. In the neighborhood of the fort they captured one Captain Clark, who had been sent out to reconnoiter, and who now did his best to help out his comrades by giving the Hessians an exaggerated estimate of their numbers. Nevertheless, the attacking party confidently

[24] Montresor, *op. cit.*, pp. 465-9; Wm. Bradford to Washington, Oct. 15, Washington Papers, Vol. 58.
[25] Montresor, *op. cit.*, p. 467.

set up eight fieldpieces and two howitzers, then summoned the fort to surrender in the King's name, threatening that there might be no quarter should battle be risked.[26] Colonel Greene's deputy, if local tradition is correct, answered promptly and pointedly: "We'll see King George damned first," he said, "we want no quarter!"[27]

It was now about half-past four in the afternoon, and von Donop wasted no more time. The cannon and howitzers opened fire and the battalions advanced upon the fort from two directions. Approaching from the northeast, the larger column soon made its way across the ditch and the wall of the old fortification; and, thinking they had captured the work, the men raised a cry of victory. Between them and the main citadel, however, was an abattis, or thicket of cut-down trees with the ends of branches sharpened and pointing outward—a device serving the same purpose as barbed-wire entanglements today. While attempting to break through this obstruction, the Hessians were suddenly exposed to a withering fire from the fort proper and from a projection which partially flanked the abattis. At the same time, the ships and row-galleys stationed in the river below swept the ranks of the attackers from the flank and the rear with a deadly rain of projectiles. Flesh and blood could not long withstand this ordeal. Officers and men were mowed down; von Donop fell, mortally wounded; and the survivors soon fled to the protection of the woods.

[26] Von Jungkenn MSS., 7:5.
[27] Mickle, *Reminiscences of Old Gloucester*, p. 68. This account of the exchange of remarks may be apocryphal; for, unfortunately, historic conversations frequently prove on investigation actually to have been less sprightly than tradition makes them. However, the colloquy between Col. Olney, Greene's representative, and the two officers sent by von Donop, as reported in a letter of a member of the garrison, follows somewhat similar though less epigrammatic lines. According to this source, Olney closed by saying for Greene "that he would defend the Fort as long as he had a man, & as to Mercy it was neither sought nor expected at their hands." Letter of Ebenezer David, Nov. 5, 1777, in John Carter Brown Library.

Meanwhile the smaller column, attacking from the southeast, succeeded in forcing its way through the abattis and crossing the moat, but was unable to climb all the way up the parapet. Some of the men, isolated on a ledge, were captured in a sally made by part of the garrison; the rest retired to safety with their comrades of the other column. The action had lasted a scant forty minutes, but it had been bloody and decisive: the shattered regiments were in no mood for further fighting, and, leaving behind them their dead and many wounded, they made their way back to Philadelphia.[28]

While the Hessians, demoralized by their crushing failure, were hastily retreating, encumbered with baggage, cannon, and considerable numbers of wounded men, an admirable opportunity was offered to the militia of the vicinity to harry them and perhaps to inflict further serious harm. On the very day of the battle, Washington was writing to General Silas Newcomb, the commander of the militia in southwestern New Jersey, to fall upon the rear of the enemy in case they should invest the fort.[29] Newcomb did not, to be sure, receive this letter in time; but the situation was one of which any person with the slightest degree of military sense or energy would have taken advantage. A member of the garrison, who happened to be absent when von Donop's force landed, and just failed to reach the fort before the assault began, pleaded with Newcomb to attack the Hessians from the rear; but his urgings fell upon deaf ears. "Such stupidity, such infamous Conduct I never saw," he raged; "if the Salvation of the Brave Men in the Fort if the Salvation of America had ought depended upon them all had been lost."[30] So the defeated and panic-stricken Hessians

---

[28] Von Jungkenn MSS., 7:5; Chastellux, *op. cit.*, Vol. I, pp. 261-5; letter of Ebenezer David, Nov. 5, 1777, in John Carter Brown Library.

[29] Washington, *Writings*, Vol. IX, p. 413.

[30] Letter of Ebenezer David, Nov. 5, 1777, in John Carter Brown Library.

retired undisturbed to Cooper's Ferry and were transported quickly across the river.

The losses of the Americans in this engagement were very small, but those of the attacking force were heavy, and a large proportion of those hit were killed. Estimates of the Hessian casualties range from one hundred fifty to five hundred; and the inhabitants of the vicinity who flocked in the next day to view the scene of carnage beheld a gory spectacle. "About two hundred were lying on straw in two large rooms," writes Pastor Collin of Swedesboro, "some without arms or legs, and others again with their limbs crushed like mush by langrel, some floated in blood, and they told me that some had died for lack of something to bandage their wounds with. . . . Outside of the house lay two piles of arms and legs."[31]

Among the casualties was Colonel von Donop, one of the most humane of the German officers. He had made a favorable impression upon the inhabitants of New Jersey during the preceding December by his forbearance, and his correspondence shows that he did not regard the Whigs with the same contemptuous lack of understanding as did most of his fellow officers. For several days after the battle, he lingered on in agony, and in those final unhappy hours he had time to reflect upon the reasons why he was dying before his time in a foreign land. When Mauduit du Plessis, in accordance with his request, came to inform him that his end was near, von Donop, if tradition be true, uttered the only intelligent remark that has been recorded as falling from a Hessian officer's lips during the war.

"It is finishing a noble career early," he said, "but I die the victim of my ambition, and of the avarice of my sovereign."[32]

[31] Ebenezer David, letter of Nov. 5; Mickle, *op. cit.*, p. 70; Hall, *op. cit.*, p. 417; Collin, *Journal*, pp. 240-1.
[32] Chastellux, *op. cit.*, Vol. I, p. 266.

As soon as Washington heard that the enemy had dispatched a body of troops to New Jersey, probably to storm Red Bank, he had written at once for a large force of New Jersey militia to relieve the post; and, even after the assault had proved unsuccessful, he was anxious to have a reinforcement of militiamen for the weak garrisons of Forts Mercer and Mifflin in case of a renewed threat. On October 22 and 23 he requested assistance from Governor Livingston, from General Dickinson, commanding at Elizabeth-Town, from General Forman, commanding in Monmouth County, and from General Newcomb, in charge in the southwestern counties nearest to Red Bank. The response was disappointing. Although Livingston was completely sympathetic with the request, and saw the urgency of the situation, his term of office had just expired; and, as the state legislature had not yet met to reelect him, he considered himself powerless to issue any orders. Dickinson was eager to help, and as senior general in New Jersey ordered Forman and Newcomb to march at once, with all the men they could collect, to Red Bank. In the district where he himself was stationed, however, the inhabitants were too fearful of another descent from New York to go willingly towards the Delaware. "The Reports of our intended march to Red-Bank," he informed Washington on November 1, "has lessen'd the numbers at this Post, the Troops being Eastern men, not chuseing to abandon (as they term it) this Part of the State— . . . thus it is with the militia, they will undertake to judge for themselves."[33]

Even before receiving Washington's request, Forman had prepared to march for Red Bank with one hundred men, all that could be spared from the duty of guarding the saltworks on the Monmouth shore. Going on ahead of this detachment, he tried to rouse the farmers in Burlington

[33] Washington, *Writings*, Vol. IX, pp. 411-12, 413, 419-20, 431; Philemon Dickinson to Washington, Oct. 26, and Nov. 1, 1777, Washington Papers, Vol. 59; Livingston to Dickinson, Oct. 26, *ibid.*

County; but, as usual with persons on his errand in that quietistic region, he met with an apathetic reception. "Neither our Late sucksesses," he reported, "or the Danger in haveing their Country ravaged gives y^t spring to their spirits y^t is Necessary to bring them out—I have however in the Most Express manner ordered the Colo^{ls} to Exert themselves and am in hopes y^t a few Days will produce two or three hundred men." The heavy rains which fell in the days following the attack on Red Bank delayed the advance of the Burlington and Monmouth militia; but by October 30 the first of them had begun to arrive.[34]

As for the lower counties, General Newcomb's province, their response was so feeble as to arouse considerable indignation. The blame for this lethargy lay chiefly upon Silas Newcomb himself, who, though pious and well meaning, was lacking in all the qualities normally expected in a military leader. During the previous winter, he had been removed by Washington from his rank as colonel of the first New Jersey brigade of the Continental army. At that time, the commander-in-chief wrote to Livingston:

"Notwithstanding I believe that Colonel Newcomb is a Gentleman of great goodness and integrity, and cannot entertain the Slightest doubts of his bravery; yet I am too well persuaded that he is not equal to such a Command.— Many qualities, independent of personal Courage, are requisite to form the good officer.—Among these, Activity claims a first rank; indeed it is indispensably necessary. Of this I fear he does not possess a Sufficient share."[35]

As a brigadier general of the militia, Newcomb now revealed the same traits which had made him unacceptable both to his superiors and to his subordinate officers when he was in the Continental service. "General Newcombs Conduct," remarked Livingston tartly to Washington, "is such

---

[34] Forman to Washington, Oct. 26 and 29; Washington Papers, Vol. 59.
[35] Washington, *Writings*, Vol. VII, p. 134.

The Defense of the Delaware

as might naturally be expected from a Gentleman who was made a General, because your Excellency did not think him fit for a Collonel."[36]

After Forman arrived with his recruits from Monmouth, he wrote to Washington on October 26:

"The lower Militia under Gen¹ Newcomb have not as yet produced a Single Man—as being elder in Command then Newcomb I have taken the Liberty this Day to Issue orders for their Immediate Assembling, and Will from time to time do every thing in my power to Assemble them."[37]

To such attempts to stir up activity in his district Newcomb opposed a passive resistance. Feeling his honor affronted by Forman's intervention in his sphere, he flatly refused to render him any account of the state of his brigade. "I think I could be able to Collect a respectable body of Militia," complained the energetic officer from Monmouth, "was I able to overcome the Obstinacy of or to displace Gen¹ Newcomb."[38]

Washington passed on this complaint to Livingston, who brusquely admonished the offender to give Forman "every Aid by your influence & encouragement as a Man of your reputed Zeal for your Country's Service ought to do."[39] Spurred by this rebuke, the slothful commander at last began to act; by November 9, he had about five hundred of his brigade assembled in the vicinity of Red Bank—a much better showing than that made by Forman's men, only sixty of whom had arrived. Newcomb's lethargy, however, had so exasperated his critical colleague from Monmouth that by this time he had gone to Princeton to complain to the legislature. There Forman became involved in one of his quarrels with the Assembly over his political activities, and

---

36 Livingston to Washington, Nov. 5, Washington Papers, Vol. 60.
37 Forman to Washington, Oct. 26, *ibid.*, Vol. 59.
38 Same to same, Oct. 29, *ibid.*
39 Washington, *Writings*, Vol. IX, pp. 469, 473, 485; Livingston to Newcomb, Nov. 5, Washington Papers, Vol. 60.

356 Cockpit of the Revolution

resigned his commission. Despairing of receiving any adequate reinforcement from a state so handicapped by dissensions, Washington at last ordered a detachment from the Continental army under Brigadier General Varnum to take post at Woodbury and assist either or both of the forts as needed. The new addition raised to sixteen hundred the number of men sent to the garrisons from the Continental army.[40]

Despite the disappointment over the New Jersey militia, the general aspect of affairs on the Delaware at the end of October was not unfavorable. One more small redoubt, sheltering a thirteen-inch mortar, had been erected by Montresor on Carpenter's Island on the night of October 20, nearer to Fort Mifflin than any of the other British works; but, like the earlier batteries, it failed to do as much damage as had been hoped. Equally fruitless was another threat which the British made with their most formidable weapons, when they finally succeeded in breaking through the lower chevaux-de-frise, and the way was open for their ships of war to move upstream to a point within cannon shot of Mud Island.

The first of the obstructions at Billingsport was removed on October 11; but it was not until the day of the engagement at Red Bank that a second one was lifted away and six vessels were able to pass through. They sailed up the river, apparently with the intention of assisting the attack on Fort Mercer by creating a diversion at the upper chevaux-de-frise. The Americans, however, gave them no opportunity to take the initiative. While a few of the galleys were doing such good execution upon von Donop's corps as it assailed the fort, the rest, in cooperation with the floating batteries, opened a vigorous fire upon the approaching ships; and, when the land engagement was over, the cannon-

[40] Brig. Gen. James Mitchell Varnum to Washington, Nov. 6 and 9, Washington Papers, Vol. 60; Forman to Washington, Nov. 7, *ibid.*; Livingston to Washington, Nov. 9, *ibid.*; Washington, *Writings*, Vol. IX, pp. 476-7.

ade became so warm that the British vessels were obliged to fall back downstream. During this retreat, the largest of the ships, the *Augusta*, of sixty-four guns, ran aground near the New Jersey shore.

It was then too late in the day for the Americans to inflict much further damage, but the stranded vessel failed to free itself during the night, and the next morning the attack was renewed in force. Before long the helpless ship caught fire. It was impossible for the other British vessels to rescue the crew, for the Americans kept up a rain of shot upon their victims, and any near approach to the *Augusta* was rendered even more perilous as her own guns were discharged at random by the spreading heat of the flames. Many of those aboard saved themselves by jumping into the river and swimming to their friends; but over a hundred men are said to have perished as the blaze finally reached the powder magazine and the *Augusta* exploded with a report that shook the entire surrounding countryside. Nor was this the sum of Admiral Howe's misfortunes on that day. An eighteen-gun sloop, the *Merlin*, also ran aground, and was set afire by her crew as they abandoned her. While these disasters were taking place, Lord Howe's vessels had gradually been falling downstream; now they moved out of range of the Americans, and the first attack by water upon Fort Mifflin was over.[41]

The damage, however, had not all been suffered by the British. Their vessels and their land batteries together had kept up a heavy fire upon Fort Mifflin until noon, and in this, the first really violent bombardment to which Mud Island had been exposed, the fort suffered considerable

[41] Hall, *op. cit.*, pp. 417-18; Washington, *Writings*, Vol. IX, pp. 380, 392-4, 428-9 (Washington confused the chronological relationship of the naval engagement and the attack on Red Bank in this letter), 477; Wm. Bradford and John Hazelwood to Washington, Oct. 11, Washington Papers, Vol. 58; Hazelwood to Washington, Oct. 26, *ibid.*, Vol. 59; Von Jungkenn MSS., 7:5; *N.J.A.*, 2nd S., Vol. I, pp. 480, 492-3; Montresor, *op. cit.*, pp. 468-9; *N.J.H.S.P.*, Vol. L, pp. 228-9.

damage. A shell destroyed one of the blockhouses, blew up some ammunition, and upset several cannon. Another started a blaze in the barracks, and even the palisades caught fire. Strangely enough, however, during all this turmoil, the only casualty suffered by the garrison was one captain wounded; for the men, lying in the shelter of Montresor's great wall, were safe from the shells of Montresor's batteries.[42]

Certainly, the brothers Howe had made but scant progress in their weeks of labor, and the prospect of getting the fleet up to Philadelphia before the army should be starved out was none too bright. To make matters worse, there began on October 25 a period of wet weather which two days later turned into a furious tempest. The repairs which General Howe's troops had been making to the dikes on Province and Carpenter's Islands, previously broken down by the Americans, were overflowed by the swollen currents of the Delaware and the Schuylkill. Sweeping over the low islands for three days, the flood waters carried away a bridge, a wharf, and some boats, and rendered useless the newly constructed batteries. Under the accumulation of all these misfortunes, it is small wonder that Captain Montresor wrote gloomily in his notebook on November 1:

"We are just now an army without provisions or Rum, artillery for Beseiging, scarce any ammunition, no clothing, nor any money. Somewhat dejected by Burgoyne's capitulation, and not elated with our late manoeuvres as Dunop's repulse and the Augustas and Merlin being burnt and to compleat all, Blockaded."[43]

[42] Letter of Baron d'Arendt, Oct. 24, copied in Fleury's Journal, Oct. 29, in Washington Papers, Vol. 58.

[43] Montresor, *op. cit.*, p. 472 n.; Ambrose Serle, Lord Dartmouth's representative with the fleet, was likewise pessimistic. Having made the unpleasant voyage with the army around the Capes and up Chesapeake Bay in the stifling heat of midsummer, and then back again to the lower Delaware, he was doubtless growing thoroughly bored by the monotony of life aboard the inactive vessels. "I own, My Lord," he wrote from Newcastle on October 28, "I am not charmed with the present Appearance of our Affairs. We have had Victories, it is true: I shall rejoice more than I can at present, when I perceive them to

While the hopes of the British sank, and those of the Americans rose, so that a pious and observant Rhode Islander in the Red Bank garrison was finding nothing more immediate than "the growing extortion in the land, [and] the increasing infidelity & profanity in the Army" to make him "rejoice with trembling,"[44] an unforeseen weakness was bringing nearer the sudden collapse of the river defense.

In making plans for blocking the Delaware, the American leaders had paid but little attention to the subordinate or Tinicum channel which runs between the Pennsylvania shore and the long-extended archipelago composed of League, Mud, Hog, Low, and Tinicum Islands. This passage, it was asserted, was far too shallow to permit the entrance of any of the British ships; and at the same time it gave to the light-draft vessels of the Pennsylvania navy a convenient route for passing around the chevaux-de-frise and operating wherever their presence would be most effective.

It was true that royal men-of-war could not ascend the Tinicum channel; but where small American boats could go, small British boats could also go, and did. On the night of October 19, twelve flat-bottomed boats and a whaleboat from Admiral Howe's fleet crept stealthily upstream between the islands and the Pennsylvania shore, and, ironically enough, escaped discovery or interference until they had left Mud Island far behind and were passing the British battery at the mouth of the Schuylkill. Not having been forewarned

be real Advantages. I wish it may never be found, that cunctando perdidimus rem.—But this is so delicate a Subject, that I am persuaded Your Lordship will fully pardon me in saying nothing further upon it." (Stevens, *Facsimiles*, Vol. XXIV, No. 2068.)

Such delicacy did not trouble the Americans. As the spirits of the British went down, theirs went up. An adjutant of General Howe, who visited Red Bank on October 30 to inquire about the Hessian prisoners, was so annoyed by the impudent good spirits of the Americans that he refused an invitation to dine with the American officers, "because Green, though he was very courteous, nevertheless showed a great pride, partly on account of the repulse of our attack upon his fort, and also on account of the news they had that Burgoyne was captured with his entire force." (Münchhausen, Journal, Oct. 30.)

[44] Letter of Ebenezer David, Nov. 7, in John Carter Brown Library.

of this venture, and supposing that the craft which they heard passing were American, the force on shore opened fire and killed one seaman. At four in the morning, however, the flotilla arrived at Philadelphia, and the first trip by water from Admiral Howe's fleet to General Howe's city was complete.[45]

This was only a beginning. Three nights later, eight flat-bottomed boats made the trip to the Schuylkill without having a shot fired at them by the Americans. It is an interesting commentary on eighteenth century ideas of necessities that these vessels bringing supplies to an army in need of so many things were loaded with hogsheads of rum. Twenty-four more boats filled with provisions reached the army before daybreak on October 26, and more followed every two or three nights. On November 11, two brigs and two sloops laden with food started to make the run, and all but one sloop passed through the heavy American fire, bringing enough salt, provisions, and ship's bread to supply the army for three weeks.[46]

Hazelwood's fleet was powerless to stop these operations. The batteries on Province and Carpenter's Islands, though they could do little damage to Fort Mifflin, made the western channel virtually impassable to the American galleys and boats during the day; and at night the weather was so stormy during much of late October and early November that the commodore considered it unsafe to station his vessels away from the shelter of land. As a result of these conditions and of the depleted state of the crews, the water patrols about Mud Island were highly irregular and of varying effectiveness.

By the defenders of Fort Mifflin, this inactivity on the river was regarded as a base defection, and was bitterly resented. They were less concerned about the traffic of the

---

[45] Montresor, *op. cit.*, p. 468.

[46] *ibid.*, pp. 469, 471, 473, 474, 475; Münchhausen, Journal, Nov. 11; Brig. Gen. J. Potter to Washington, Nov. 12, Washington Papers, Vol. 60.

British provisioning vessels than about the possibility of hostile troop movements over the water; for they lived in dread of a sudden nocturnal descent upon Mud Island by boatloads of soldiers ready to land and storm the fort. To them, it seemed inexcusable for Hazelwood not to keep a large and active water guard on duty every night. Smith, d'Arendt, and Major Fleury, the able French engineer in charge of strengthening the fort and repairing damages to it, complained sharply to the commander-in-chief about the commodore's neglect of their safety; and no plea for harmony that Washington, Greene, or Varnum could make lessened the increasing dislike felt for Hazelwood by the men whose nerves were being strained beyond endurance by the constant danger, discomfort, and fatigue of life on Mud Island.[47]

The commodore himself was almost distracted by the disparity between the capabilities of his fleet and the demands upon it. Of the thirteen galleys at his disposal, he had seamen enough to man only five; and of the numerous armed boats only the same small number were supplied with crews. "The Fleet is now so poorly Mann'd," he lamented to Washington on October 26, "& the constant cry from Fort Mifflin is to guard that Post, that I know not how to act without more assistance. Col¹ Green & Angel can spare no men [as] they are afraid of being attacked and as to the Vessels at Borden-town[48] I am informed they have not Twenty private Men on board, so that I expect no assistance from there."[49]

---

[47] Washington, *Writings*, Vol. IX, pp. 409-11, 459; letters of Baron d'Arendt, Oct. 24 and 26, copied in Fleury's Journal, Oct. 29, Washington Papers, Vol. 58; letter of Fleury, Oct. 26, *ibid.*; Smith to Washington, Oct. 26, *ibid.*, Vol. 59; letter of Fleury, Oct. 28, *ibid.*; Hazelwood to d'Arendt and Smith, Oct 26, *ibid.*; Varnum to Washington, Nov. 3, *ibid.*; same to same, Nov. 6, *ibid.*, Vol. 60; letter of Ebenezer David, Nov. 7, 1777, in John Carter Brown Library.

[48] The unfinished frigates of the Continental navy.

[49] Hazelwood to d'Arendt and Smith, Oct. 26, Washington Papers, Vol. 59; Hazelwood to Washington, Oct. 26, *ibid.*

Much more serious than the provisioning of Howe's army from the fleet, and in final effect more dangerous to the Americans than the threat of a storming of Mud Island by boat, was the use of the Tinicum channel by the British to bring up several pieces of heavy artillery with which the strength of the batteries opposite Fort Mifflin was increased. By November 3, six twenty-four-pounders had been carried up to Province Island; and, after a couple of false starts, the works to hold these cannon were built as an extension of the first battery erected on Carpenter's Island, directly opposite the fort.[50]

Meanwhile, Admiral Howe's fleet began to push forward again from Billingsport towards the upper chevaux-de-frise. General Varnum did what he could to harass the British ships by erecting upon a small eminence on the New Jersey shore between Billingsport and Red Bank a battery of two good-sized cannon with which he drove several of the vessels from their stations.[51] It was evident, nevertheless, that the crisis of the struggle for the Delaware was approaching. On November 8, Washington informed Varnum that the British were about to make a formidable attack upon Fort Mifflin, and requested him to warn the commodore of the prospective operation; at the same time he importuned Livingston to send to the river strongholds "as respectable a force . . . as the Circumstances of the state will permit."[52]

The defenders of the river were ill-prepared to meet the emergency. There were some four hundred fifty men stationed within Fort Mifflin, and slightly more than five hundred in Fort Mercer. On Mud Island the men were more miserable than ever. As early as October 22, there had been a sharp frost; and, after the water which flooded the island during the storms at the end of the month had subsided, the

50 Montresor, *op. cit.*, pp. 472, 473, 474; Faden, map, *The Course of the Delaware River.*
51 Varnum to Washington, Nov. 6, Washington Papers, Vol. 60.
52 Washington, *Writings*, Vol. X, pp. 21, 25.

cold set in bitterly. On November 11, there was a northwest wind as frigid as in the depth of winter, and in some places there was ice half an inch thick. So urgent had the need of clothing become that Varnum was obliged to send out officers among the Tory Quakers of Salem, "directing them to proceed with Humanity and Tenderness; But at all Events, to procure the Articles necessary for the Garrisons."[53] The soldiers in Fort Mifflin continued to succumb at an alarming rate to the hardships of their existence. Of the two hundred men, completely officered, whom Smith had taken with him to the island early in October, all but sixty-five privates and four officers had been sent away to the hospitals by November 9. The Sixth Virginia Regiment, which had come in later as a reinforcement with one hundred twenty men, had only forty-six left fit for duty; and the First Virginia Regiment, a later arrival, was proportionately weakened. Smith cast much of the blame for his sickness upon "a want of Rum"; but he also offered a more convincing explanation: "For some time past there has not been one night without one two or three Alarms, one half of the garrison are constantly on fatigue & guard." The Baron d'Arendt had been obliged to go away because of ill-health, and Smith himself was so worn out that he asked to be relieved.[54]

Within the fort itself, there were dissensions among the officers. Major Fleury wrote to a friend: "While Baron d'Arendt was present, he understands the Military Art, and my Opinions in point of fortification were his—but he is absent and you know there are persons who know a great deal without having ever learnt—and whose obstinacy is equal to their Insufficiency." Altogether, the spirit on Mud Island, though determined, was far from happy. Experi-

[53] Montresor, op. cit., pp. 469, 471, 474-5; Washington, Writings, Vol. IX, p. 462; Col. Christopher Greene, return of men at Fort Mercer, Oct, 27, in Washington Papers, Vol. 59; Fleury's Journal, Oct. 29, ibid., Vol. 58, and Nov. 14, ibid., Vol. 60; Varnum to Washington, Nov. 6, ibid., Vol. 60.
[54] Smith to Washington, Nov. 9, Washington Papers, Vol. 60.

enced men like Fleury, who watched the new battery going up on Province Island and then looked at the pitiful palisades in the line of fire, wondered how long the puny structure would stand up and whether the fort would ever receive the fascines, or bundles of sticks, long since ordered from the mainland for supporting the walls in place of the earth which could not be procured.[55]

The time for speculation was not long. On November 9, Smith had estimated that by the twentieth of the month, if it was not attacked sooner, Fort Mifflin ought to have been brought into "a good posture of defence"; but on the very day after he made this prediction, General Howe opened his grand offensive. The new battery with its powerful artillery joined the ones which had already been used; and for the entire day a furious cannonade continued. The Americans replied vigorously, but they suffered far more damage than they inflicted. Cutting down the palisades four or five at a time, the projectiles from Carpenter's Island soon laid open a great part of the side of the fort nearest to them, nearly destroyed the barracks in that quarter, seriously damaged the blockhouses, dismounted three of the blockhouse guns, and put out of commission one cannon in a battery. Amidst all this devastation, the officers and men of the garrison, sheltered behind Montresor's massive wall, remained unhurt; but, as Smith wrote to Washington, they were "already half Jaded to death with constant fatigue," and could not hold out much longer. He suggested the advisability of destroying the works on Mud Island and transporting the cannon to the New Jersey shore, whence the chevaux-de-frise could be protected as effectively as from the low-lying island.[56]

[55] Fleury to Hamilton, Nov. 1777, Washington Papers, Vol. 59; Fleury, Journal, Nov. 4-6, *ibid.* Fleury's strictures were not directed against Smith, whose intelligence he praised.

[56] Smith to Washington, Nov. 10, Washington Papers, Vol. 60.

That night the Americans had no time to repair their works, for Howe's batteries now continued their bombardment even after dark.[57] On November 11, the second day of the cannonade, Varnum reported that every defense of Fort Mifflin was almost destroyed, and that Smith, wounded and brought over to New Jersey, still wished to evacuate the fort. Nevertheless, since the loss of men had as yet been small, Varnum determined to maintain the resistance.[58]

It was indeed an open question whether, if the Americans held out, Howe would be able to stay in Philadelphia until his guns had battered Fort Mifflin to pieces. There were rumors that the British were discouraged, and about to evacuate the city. Such supplies as could be brought up by the small boats did no more than cover the bare necessities of the army, and beef had become so scarce and so expensive in Philadelphia that the soldiers were put on reduced rations.[59]

During the six-day bombardment of Mud Island, the Americans administered one minor setback to the attackers. On November 14, two floating batteries which the British had built in the Schuylkill ventured forth to the Delaware to attack Fort Mifflin; but one was driven back into the tributary river and the other was so warmly cannonaded from the Island that its crew jumped overboard and the artillery was later removed.[60]

Aside from this one small incident, conditions grew progressively worse for the Americans as one day of ceaseless cannonading followed another. Major Fleury, who, though slightly wounded, remained in the fort after all the rest of the garrison had been relieved from Red Bank, was almost

[57] Münchhausen, Journal, Nov. 10, 11.
[58] Varnum to Washington, Nov. 11, Washington Papers, Vol. 60.
[59] Nathanael Greene to Washington, Nov. 14, Washington Papers, Vol. 60; Benjamin Randolph to Washington, Nov. 15, ibid.; John Clark, Jr., to Washington, ibid.
[60] Montresor, op. cit., p. 476; André, Journal, p. 63; Münchhausen, Journal, Nov. 12-14.

beside himself with anxiety to procure materials for repairing the damages wrought by the hostile fire. "As long as my Workmen would remain with me," he wrote in his journal on November 13, "I employed them in covering the two western Blockhouses, with Joist within and without and filling the interstices with rammed earth—General Varnum has sent me neither Ax, Fascine, Gabion nor Palisade, altho he promised me all these Articles, I suppose it has not been in his power it is impossible however with watery mud alone to make works capable of resisting the Enemys 32 Pounders."[61]

At daybreak on November 15, the British batteries which, as Varnum informed Washington, had "kept up a constant Cannonade and Bombardment all the night, so as to prevent, in a great Measure, the necessary Repairs to the Breeches," began to fire with even greater vigor. Simultaneously, three men-of-war, two frigates, and a galley from Admiral Howe's fleet set sail to come up the river with the tide. At eight o'clock they were within range of Mud Island, and began to add their fire to that of the land batteries. This was the most violent cannonade that Fort Mifflin had yet had to endure; but worse was yet to come. Up the Tinicum channel crept two fair-sized vessels, which at high tide had crossed the shallowest bar: one, the *Vigilant*, an old ship cut down so as to draw little water, but carrying fourteen twenty-four-pounders, and the other a sloop with six eighteen-pounders. These two new adversaries anchored right off the fort, between it and Carpenter's Island, and poured their shot into the defenses.

Participants on both sides agreed that the roar of cannon which lasted for the rest of the day was overwhelming in its intensity. It was like "a constant thunderstorm," remarked one Hessian officer; and a man aboard one of the American vessels declared: "Such a cannonade I believe, was

[61] Fleury, Journal, Nov. 13, in Washington Papers, Vol. 60.

never seen in America." Peaceful Quakers of the vicinity, who by this time had become hardened to the noise of battle, shuddered anew at the unprecedented din. Realizing that this was the supreme test, the defenders of the barricade fought desperately. Hazelwood's galleys, floating batteries, and boats and the Continental sailing vessels poured shot and shell into the royal fleet: the *Isis* alone received thirty-four shots which passed quite through her. What made the struggle hopeless for the Americans, however, was the unexpected presence of the *Vigilant* so near Fort Mifflin. Not only did the heavy guns of this vessel, in combination with artillery on Carpenter's Island, destroy the right battery of the Americans; snipers posted in the tops of the masts fired with muskets directly down into the fort and shot any persons who appeared on the cannon platform. Captain Lee, the commander of the artillery, and Major Fleury, who was in charge of the infantry engaged in shooting at the tops of the *Vigilant*, remained at their posts until all their men were either killed or wounded and the cannon were broken to pieces. Major Simeon Thayer of the Second Rhode Island Regiment, who was in charge of the defense, moved about everywhere, encouraging his men; but everywhere, though the garrison fought bravely, he found all too evident the shattering effect of the assault.

Unless the *Vigilant* could be removed, there was no hope of saving the fort. Commodore Hazelwood ordered six of his galleys to attack the vessel and take it; but, after the little American craft had warped around to the west side of the island and the crews looked down the narrow channel, swept by the fire of the land batteries, to the formidable ship which seemed well able to take care of itself, they returned with the report that the enterprise was impossible.

By early afternoon, all the cannon in the fort except two were disabled, the ammunition was nearly exhausted, the great wall was at last half-demolished, the palisades had been levelled, and the remnants of the blockhouses were being splintered away bit by bit. A piece of flying timber knocked Fleury senseless and killed Captain Lee, the courageous artillery officer. Still the defenders would not surrender, and throughout the rest of the day the two remaining guns continued at intervals to bark defiance of the King. On the Pennsylvania shore, a force of English troops stood in readiness to embark in small boats to storm the fort as soon as General Howe should give the signal. The signal, however, never came. The British commander always avoided what he considered unnecessary effusion of blood; and he knew that the stronghold, which had been reduced to little more than a heap of rubbish, could not resist for another day.

He was right. After darkness had come, Major Thayer sent over to Red Bank most of the men remaining in the garrison, while he stayed with a small rear guard until the greater part of the stores had been removed, the guns had been spiked, and what remained of the buildings had been set ablaze. Then, at two o'clock on Sunday morning, November 16, the last survivors of Fort Mifflin rowed over to the shelter of Red Bank.

When a bleak dawn came a few hours later, the American flag was still visible through snow flurries, floating over the wreckage on Mud Island. At half-past seven, a boatload of British sailors rowed across the water and pulled down the banner; they found the cannon dismounted and splashed with blood, the works lying in ruins, and the dead scattered about either unburied or thrust into shallow trenches. About an hour later, a detachment of redcoats crossed over and began cleaning up the débris and throwing up a battery. Mud Island had reverted to the King. The fight for the Delaware was almost over.[62]

[62] Fleury, Journal, "October" [November] 15, 1777, in Washington Papers, Vol. 58; Hazelwood to Washington, Nov. 15, ibid., Vol. 60; C. Greene to Gen. Potter, Nov. 15, ibid.; Varnum to Washington, Nov. 14 and 15, ibid.; Varnum to Washington, Nov. 16 and 17, ibid., Vol. 61; Münchhausen, Journal, Nov.

After the fall of Fort Mifflin, the American fleet had no choice but to retire from the neighborhood of the British batteries and vessels. Fort Mercer, deprived of support from the river, was in a precarious position: a bombproof magazine was almost completed, but otherwise there was no security against shells, and in case of a siege the post, it seemed, must inevitably succumb to a long-continued bombardment.[63] Anxious to retain and strengthen this foothold in New Jersey, Washington dispatched sizable reinforcements under General Nathanael Greene;[64] but events outstripped their arrival.

Late in October, the British had reoccupied and strengthened Billingsport; and on November 18, a strong corps under Lord Cornwallis crossed the Delaware to that post from Chester. They were joined by several regiments of Germans which had been sent from New York, so that a formidable expeditionary force was now collected in New Jersey. On the following day, after hearing a report that Cornwallis was advancing towards Red Bank, Varnum and Colonel Greene moved out most of the garrison, and had a considerable quantity of powder strewn about the fort in preparation for blowing it up. Until the enemy should appear, a number of the men were employed in carrying off the stores and some of the artillery. Finally, on the evening of November 20, it seemed unwise to remain any longer, for it was rumored that the British were in the immediate vicinity. The last of the garrison marched out, the powder was ignited, and, with a thunderous detonation, Fort Mercer passed into history.[65]

15 and 16; Dincklage, Journal, Nov. 15; André, *Journal*, p. 64; Hall, *op. cit.*, pp. 420-1; *N.J.A.*, 2nd S., Vol. I, pp. 493-6; *N.J.H.S.P.*, Vol. L, p. 229.

[63] Christopher Greene to Washington, Nov. 17, Washington Papers, Vol. 61.

[64] Washington, *Writings*, Vol. X, pp. 77-80, 83-6, 100-1.

[65] Adam Comstock to Washington, Oct. 27, in Washington Papers, Vol. 59; Jos. Reed to Washington, Nov. 18, *ibid.*, Vol. 61; John Clark to Washington, Nov. 19, *ibid.*; Capt. Charles Craig to Washington, Nov. 19, *ibid.*; Varnum to Washington, Nov. 19 and 20, *ibid.*; Ebenezer David to Nicholas Brown, Nov. 23, in John Carter Brown Library; André, *op. cit.*, p. 64; *N.J.A.*, 2nd S., Vol. I, p. 504.

Billingsport had fallen; Fort Mifflin had fallen; Red Bank had fallen. The last of the defenses of the Delaware, the combined Continental and Pennsylvania navies, no longer could hope for any support from the land below Philadelphia. Their problem was to slip by the batteries of the city without damage. On the night of November 19, thirteen galleys rowed quietly up the river, and, by hugging the New Jersey shore, crept safely past the enemy without being detected. At three o'clock in the morning of November 21, a brig, a schooner, and several smaller sailing vessels attempted to follow the example of the galleys; but in the bright moonlight they were discovered and subjected to a hot fire from the hostile batteries. The schooner and one of the smaller vessels ran aground on the New Jersey shore and were set on fire by their departing crews; the others succeeded in making their escape. It now seemed useless to hope that the brig, xebecs, sloops, floating batteries, and fireships which had not yet attempted the trip could be carried safely past the city; so they were abandoned near Gloucester and given to the flames.

From the Pennsylvania shore the soldiers of Howe's army and the Tory inhabitants gazed upon a spectacle of which they fully appreciated both the magnificence and the meaning. The darkness at the river's edge was stabbed by the flashes from the city batteries playing upon the vessels, whose white sails gleamed in the moonlight as they made their way upstream along the opposite shore. Farther down the Delaware, the blazing ships, set in motion by the tide, drifted slowly upstream, their flaming hulls and superstructures mirrored in the water. When the heat of the conflagration grew more intense, the loaded cannon aboard the vessels discharged themselves with a roar that mingled with the crash of the British guns. One by one, as the fire reached the powder magazines, the doomed ships exploded into the air with tremendous reports; and when quiet settled over the river at last, the American fleet had disappeared from the lower Delaware.[66]

This was Howe's moment of greatest triumph. He was now securely confirmed in his occupation of the capital of the confederacy, the place where the Declaration of Independence had been signed and whence the Continental Congress had, in a makeshift way, directed the activities of the Americans since the spring of 1775. The triumph, however, was a hollow one. Already his false strategy had caused the capture of Burgoyne's army in the north; and Washington's force, defeated but not destroyed, and encamped only a few miles from Philadelphia, was playing its old game of waiting for a favorable opportunity to strike. The struggle for the Delaware, though it had ended in victory for the brothers Howe, had by no means been a disgrace for the Americans. The courage and tenacity with which the defenders of the barricades had maintained themselves for weeks against overpowering numbers and superior equipment, thereby protracting the campaign until it was too late for Howe to think of further offensive operations that season, was in striking contrast to the almost complete collapse of American resistance just a year before. The opposition to British rule and to the British army was growing firmer and better organized. Although the states of the Union, and New Jersey in particular, had much to suffer in the coming years from the depredations of the royal army, and still more from the desperate conflicts between the contending parties among the inhabitants themselves, yet the most critical stage of the struggle was past. Whether they knew it or not, Howe and his successors, after the conclusion of the campaign of 1777, were fighting a rear-guard action.

[66] Münchhausen, Journal, Nov. 21; Dincklage, Journal, pp. 146-7; N.J.A., 2nd S., Vol. I, p. 496; N. Greene to Washington, Nov. 21, Washington Papers, Vol. 61; [Joseph Stansbury,] poem "Mud Island" in MS. volume of Loyalist Rhapsodies, 1775-1783, Library of Congress; Montresor, op. cit., p. 478.

CHAPTER XII ☼ *HOWE'S TRIUMPH CRUMBLES*

THE bitter struggle for domination of the lower Delaware was followed during the closing weeks of the year 1777 by a slackening of military activity. Both armies needed a breathing-spell: the victorious British to consolidate their position for the winter, and the Americans to work out a new plan of action suited to the changed circumstances. Before the end of November, most of the six thousand men under Cornwallis had recrossed the river from Gloucester Point, taking with them such livestock as they had been able to collect in the vicinity. Although the Americans were itching, as one impatient colonel wrote, "to give em a floging before they Leave the Gerseys"[1] the retiring enemy were so well protected by the guns of their fleet lying in the river, and by the swampy nature of the ground, that they were able to make a leisurely withdrawal, and lost only a few prisoners to a small American party under the Marquis de Lafayette.[2]

At the same time, Greene's corps was hurriedly summoned to join the main army by Washington, who saw in the return of Cornwallis and his command a threat that Howe might launch a strong offensive in Pennsylvania while the American forces were divided.[3] Only a detachment of horse was left at Haddonfield under Captain Lee to patrol the countryside and protect it as well as might be from the depredations of the small royal garrison still remaining at Billingsport.[4] New Jersey, it seemed, was about to enjoy a

[1] Col. Adam Comstock to Greene, Nov. 25, 1777, in Washington Papers, Vol. 61.

[2] Brig. Gen. J. M. Varnum to Washington, Nov. 19 and 21, 1777, in Washington Papers, Vol. 61; Greene to Washington, Nov. 21, 22, 24, 25, 26 and 28, *ibid.*, Vols. 61 and 62; *N.J.A.*, 2nd S., Vol. I, pp. 488, 496-7.

[3] Washington, *Writings*, Vol. X, pp. 104-5, 107-8.

[4] Lee to Washington, Dec. 3, 1777, in Washington Papers, Vol. 62.

respite from warfare. All eyes were now turned upon the hostile armies encamped no great distance from each other in Pennsylvania.

In assuming that Howe was about to resume offensive operations, Washington had once more overestimated his adversary's enterprise. The British commander, after a strenuous season of campaigning, was no more disposed to maintain the initiative during the winter months than he had been a year earlier. This time, moreover, he felt much less cheerful over his accomplishments. Once more his rosy hopes of a mass rising of Tories to aid his triumphant arms were being revealed as overoptimistic; and now the disappointment was doubly serious, for on no other ground than the liberation of a strong body of suppressed Loyalists throughout the middle colonies could his abandonment of Burgoyne be justified. Indeed, in the depth of the gloom into which Howe had now fallen, he began to regard his position almost as that of the defender of a beleaguered city. Far from planning further advances, he was beginning to worry about the prospects for the next summer's campaign; and on the last day of November he wrote to Lord George Germain what can only be regarded as the letter of a disillusioned and discouraged man. No longer could he look upon himself as a bringer of peace who would be welcomed by a substantial part of the population; now he must openly admit that "the people at large" were in opposition to his measures, and that he was in the position of a foreign invader whose conquest of the country must be a long and disagreeable labor.[5]

Not all the prominent occupants of the city of Philadelphia shared this pessimistic view. Ambrose Serle might admit to Lord Dartmouth at the beginning of December: "Since [the opening of this campaign] . . . I own my Ideas are

[5] Historical MSS. Commission, *Report on Stopford-Sackville MSS.*, Vol. II, p. 81.

lowered upon the management of the War";[6] but his friend
Joseph Galloway wrote to the same dignitary on the same
day in an altogether different tone: "I will venture to give
it as my opinion that the Rebellion in the middle Colonies
is in its last languishing Stage, and in another year must be
ended provided vigorous and proper Measures are pursued."[7]

So far as southwestern New Jersey was concerned, there
seemed to be at least as much justification for Galloway's
optimism as for Howe's gloom. The advent of the royal
army, bringing weapons and support for the suppressed
Tories, precipitated an upsurge of Loyalist sentiment similar
in nature to that which had swept the eastern part of the
state a year earlier, but even more violent in its manifestations. West Jersey offered a fair field of activity for aggressive
adherents of the King. In the long established, prosperous
communities near the river, to be sure, the dominant Quakers
tended to maintain an attitude of aloofness from the struggle, though many of them leaned towards Toryism and few
were reluctant to make an honest penny by selling provisions
to Royalist Philadelphia. Among the more volatile population of the back settlements, on the other hand, partisanship
in political matters had become as passionate as it had long
been in religious disputes, and carnal weapons now supplanted spiritual.

The activities of the Tories began mildly enough as
friendly commercial relations with the conquering army.
After the Howe brothers had established control over Philadelphia and the entire stretch of the river below it, sympathizers in West Jersey lost no time in opening a brisk
trade with the city. For some months they had been suffering
from a growing scarcity of imported goods and hard money;
now with comparative ease they could satisfy their need for
sugar, tea, molasses, strong liquors, and coin, by furnishing
the hungry British army with native products. Adequate

[6] Serle to Dartmouth, Dec. 3, 1777, in Stevens, *Facsimiles*, Vol. XXIV.
[7] Galloway to Dartmouth, Dec. 3, *ibid*.

policing of the innumerable small steams tributary to the river was impossible for the few American soldiers whom Washington could spare from Pennsylvania or for the feeble Revolutionary government; so the clandestine trade went on with no serious interruption throughout the winter and spring.[8]

In December, the Continental Congress authorized Washington to subject to trial by court martial anyone engaged in the act of supplying intelligence or provisions to the enemy who might be caught within thirty miles of any British post in New Jersey, Pennsylvania or Delaware, but this measure could not act as a deterrent where there were no troops to enforce it.[9] The sporadic arrests which were made by the Revolutionary authorities and the savage reprisals occasionally visited on offenders by irregular groups of Whigs[10] served not to overawe but merely to infuriate the Tories. Those who found their neighborhoods too warm for them went over to the British lines, and during the winter a considerable number of them were organized in Philadelphia as the West Jersey Volunteers, a unit of Howe's army, under the command of Daniel Cozens, a tavern-keeper of Gloucester. In January 1778, they established themselves at Billingsport, where the abandoned American fortifications had been reduced to defensible compass and converted into a strong base for raids into the unprotected countryside. This force of refugees now became an object of intense hatred to its victims, and launched upon a career of violence which permanently precluded any reconciliation with the Whigs. At

[8] As early as July 1777, inhabitants of Cumberland County had been going aboard British vessels lying in Delaware Bay and receiving detailed instructions for cooperation with landing parties; but these plans were discovered in time by the Revolutionary authorities and came to nothing.—"Account of Cumberland Tories," July 30, 1777, in Public Record Office, Trenton.

[9] *N.J.A.*, 2nd S., Vol. I, pp. 505-6; Livingston to Washington, Jan. 15, 1778, in Washington Papers, Vol. 65; Collin, *Journal*, pp. 244-5.

[10] On Easter Sunday, 1778, for example, one participant in the forbidden trade was seized in Swedesboro, tied to a tree near the church, and flogged so severely that he died of the effects.—Collin, *Journal*, p. 246.

the moment, few of its members could have seen that this was but the opening chapter of their military careers, and that circumstances would force them to continue fighting for their King for long, weary years.[11]

As the winter wore on and spring came, the demoralization in the southwestern counties grew progressively worse. Parties of American militia, British regulars and Loyalists prowled about the countryside, rarely engaging in pitched battles, but swooping down upon families in the dead of night, kidnapping prominent adversaries, burning, plundering, and wantonly destroying whatever enemy property they could lay hands on. As the district was of almost negligible military importance, little attention was paid to it by the staff of either army, so that breaches of discipline which might have been punished elsewhere passed here without reproach. No one was safe from violence or capture, and normal social relationships were completely disrupted. "Everywhere distrust, fear, hatred and abominable selfishness were met with," writes Pastor Collin of Swedesboro. "Parents and children, brothers and sisters, wife and husband, were enemies to one another."[12]

Nor was the southwestern section of the state the sole part to feel the bitterness of that cheerless winter. Not only from Philadelphia, but from that other center of foreign occupation, New York, the poison of sporadic warfare spread into the adjoining districts, effectually preventing any healing of the social lesions created during the preceding year. Bergen County, which Livingston had referred to in July as "almost totally revolted,"[13] defied repeated attempts

---

[11] Collin, *op. cit.*, p. 245; Jones, *op. cit.*, pp. 51, 54-5; Israel Shreve to Washington, April 7, 1778, in Washington Papers, Vol. 71.

[12] Collin, *Journal*, pp. 243-9; Israel Shreve to Washington, March 28, 1778, Washington Papers, Vol. 70; same to same, April 7, *ibid.*, Vol. 71; *N.J.A.*, 2nd S., Vol. II, p. 218. Shreve writes to Washington on March 28: "This Country is in a miserable Situation the inhabitants afraid of every person they see." (Washington Papers, Vol. 70.)

[13] Livingston to Washington, July 11, 1777, Washington Papers, Vol. 51.

to restore it to republican order. For the most part, the southern section of the county was dominated by the British strongholds of Powles Hook, Staten Island, and New York; but from time to time swift-moving detachments of militia-men swept down from the safer regions in the north and west, harassed the flourishing trade between inhabitants and royal garrisons, and made off with horses, livestock, and provisions. Kidnappings, ambushes, and sundry thrilling escapades kept life from growing dull for such of the popula-tion as attempted to carry on the business of life in the no-man's land between royal and rebel spheres of control.[14] Occasional parties of the British and Loyalists carried destruction and terror farther afield by embarking on small vessels and making surprise descents along the coast. In November 1777, they burned the saltworks at Shrewsbury; the following April they did the same at Squan Inlet; and in May they fell upon Middletown Point, destroyed the grain storehouse of John Burrowes, the "Corn King," and hustled off the wealthy owner to captivity.[15]

However unhappy an effect the proximity of hostile forces may have had upon the life of the common citizens in the northeastern counties, there were not a few individuals for whom the abnormal conditions opened the way to prosperity. It was not only in Bergen that shrewd traders succeeded in eluding the vigilance of the American authorities and smuggling supplies into the welcoming arms of the British. According to common report, quantities of provisions found their way to the enemy from Shrewsbury, Middletown Point, and Perth Amboy. It was an open secret that Elizabeth-Town, the home of such intransigent rebels as Abraham Clark and William Livingston, was also the center of flour-

[14] *N.J.A.*, 2nd S., Vol. I, pp. 427, 429, 481, 486, 505; Vol. II, pp. 32, 47-8, 218; letter of W. Malcolm, "Rampough," Sept. 13, 1777, in Washington Papers, Vol. 56.

[15] *N.J.A.*, 2nd S., Vol. I, p. 485, Vol. II, pp. 160, 170-1; Shreve to Washing-ton, April 7, 1778, in Washington Papers, Vol. 71; Andrew Brown to Col. Anthony White, May 28, 1778, *ibid.*, Vol. 75.

ishing commerce with Staten Island, by which, according to the governor, "the enemy as I am informed is plentifully supplied with fresh Provisions, & such a Quantity of British Manufactures brought back in Exchange as to enable the Persons concerned to set up Shops to retail them."[16]

Had this clandestine traffic been confined to articles of normal trade, it would have been annoying enough to the American authorities; what made its existence intolerable was the mounting evidence that less tangible but more dangerous items were being exchanged across the lower Hudson and the Sound: military intelligence, propaganda and schemes for undermining the independence of the state. This communication was carried on in part furtively, in part quite openly under the protection of flags of truce granted all too readily by many military officers to inhabitants of the area who alleged reasons of business for their presence on Staten Island. Under this pretext, complained the Whigs, a thriving trade was pursued, the little specie in the state was drained out to pay for foreign luxuries, secrets of the army were betrayed, and a flood of counterfeit bills, printed in New York, was let loose on the state to depreciate the currency.[17] Stirred by repeated allegations of this nature, the New Jersey legislature as early as June 1777 had made it a capital offense for any of its citizens to attempt to enter the enemy lines without a written pass from the commander-in-chief of the Continental army, the governor of the state, or commander-in-chief of the militia.[18] The prohibition was ineffective: two months later Livingston was obliged to publish a proclamation forbidding the issuance of passes by militia officers,

---

[16] *N.J. Exec. Corr.*, pp. 91-2; *N.J.A.*, 2nd S., Vol. I, pp. 514-15; Livingston to Washington, Nov. 22, 1777, in Washington Papers, Vol. 61, and Jan. 12, 1778, *ibid.*, Vol. 65.

[17] *Sullivan Papers*, Vol. I, pp. 433-4. If this last charge was true, it indicated a work of supererogation on the part of the British, for the paper money issued by the Revolutionary authorities was already, by 1777, proving itself capable of an alarming depreciation without outside assistance.

[18] *N.J.A.*, 2nd S., Vol. I, p. 465.

and to request Washington's assistance in checking the "constant Communication" with the enemy.[19]

No legislation or proclamation, however drastic, sufficed to stop the intercourse, which continued throughout the war. Sympathizers with the royal cause who lived near the shore could always be conveniently "captured" by detachments of the British and held for a suitable period of time; and it was usually found, in the opinion of General Maxwell, that people who had been on the island came back "with the addition of seven devils more than they were possessed of before, by the connections they have formed on the other side, and no doubt but some of them is sent over to us by the Enemy."[20] General Campbell, in command of the royal forces on the island, particularly infuriated the Americans by sending over his flags of truce—ostensibly on legitimate errands—in charge of refugee Tories, who, as Livingston complained, "being intimately acquainted at Elizabeth Town, & frequently not sufficiently watched by our Militia Officers at that Port, generally make it an Opportunity of sowing the seeds of disaffection among their old Cronies."[21]

Besides these native supporters whom they thus openly flaunted in the faces of the New Jersey authorities, the British had secret agents scattered throughout the state, who disseminated propaganda and collected information. In the spring and summer of 1777, two men were discovered to have been enlisting for the royal army, one from among the inhabitants of Morris County, the other, boldly enough, from among the Continental troops![22] How many other agents engaged in similar enterprises may have escaped

[19] Proclamation of Aug. 14, 1777, in Washington Papers, Vol. 53; Livingston to Washington, Aug. 15, *ibid.*, Vol. 54.

[20] Maxwell to Governor and Legislature of New Jersey, April 26, 1779, in Room 118, State Library, Trenton.

[21] Livingston to Washington, April 15, 1778, in Washington Papers, Vol. 72.

[22] Examination of Peter Young and Henry Mowerson, May 6, 1777, in Public Record Office, Trenton; record of court martial held by order of Brig. Gen. Deborre, July 31, 1777, in Washington Papers, Vol. 52.

detection one can only surmise, but there can be no doubt that a smoothly functioning espionage service kept the British informed of every important military development among the Americans. When General Philemon Dickinson launched a surprise attack upon Staten Island at the end of November 1777, he kept his plans secret from his own field officers until eight o'clock in the evening of the enterprise; by three in the morning, General Skinner of the New Jersey Volunteers had learned of the project, and the expedition failed in consequence.[23]

One constant center of intrigue and spying which the Americans were slow in eliminating was formed by the group of prominent Loyalists of the state who were granted freedom, not unlike that of distinguished prisoners of war, after giving their paroles to conduct themselves properly. Of these people, probably the most troublesome was Captain Archibald Kennedy, the unpopular landowner of Horsimus, who was confined on parole to his wife's farm near Newark. By January 1778, Governor Livingston and his Council had enough evidence of Kennedy's activities as an informer of the British and as a distributor of secret letters from New York to initiate an investigation. Once more, however, the strange laxity which allowed so much corruption and disaffection to go unpunished throughout the years of the war seems to have intervened. Nothing came of the inquiry, and in April 1779 General Maxwell was still complaining to the legislature of the notorious fact of the captain's correspondence with the enemy, and demanding action against such "Licensed Spies."[24]

[23] Whitehead, *Perth Amboy*, pp. 107-8; Dickinson to Washington, Nov. 28, 1777, in Washington Papers, Vol. 62.

[24] Copies of depositions by Robert Niel, Robert Nicholls, and Nathaniel Camp, Jr., Jan. 12, 1778, and letter from Livingston to Washington, Jan. 13, in Washington Papers, Vol. 65; Maxwell to Governor and Legislature of New Jersey, April 26, 1779, in Room 118, State Library, Trenton. In their dealings with subversive and destructive elements, the Revolutionary leaders of New Jersey, like many men of other times and places, could testify to the peculiar deadliness of the female of the species. In July 1777, Joseph Hedden, a mag-

Not all the secret communication between the lines, of course, was carried on in the interest of the British. By mid-summer of 1777, the commandant in New York was so suspicious of the "evil practices" apparently followed "by persons passing and repassing to and from this city and the Jersey shore in small craft" that he restricted such intercourse to persons with suitable authorization, and completely prohibited it after sunset, on pain of military execution.[25] Such instances of alarm on the part of the royal authorities, however, seem to have been infrequent, and it is clear enough that the chief sufferers from the clandestine activity were the Americans.

The difficulties raised by busy Tories, open and concealed, were not the only troubles besetting Jersey officials during the winter of 1777-1778. Even among Whigs a general deterioration of public morale complicated the problems facing the hard-pressed Livingston and his assistants. For the war-weary population of the state, constantly reminded that war was wasteful and brutal, there remained little of the patriotic glamor which had enveloped the early phases of the struggle. To be sure, the military situation was much less discouraging than it had been a twelvemonth earlier. Except for the districts within easy striking distance of

istrate of Newark, complained distractedly of the conduct of certain Tory women of the town, whose husbands had gone off to join the enemy and who showed great ingenuity in keeping their property out of the hands of the rebel authorities. (Hedden to Livingston, July 9, in P.R.O., Trenton.) "Cherchez la femme" was a principle strongly endorsed also by General Maxwell, who, in the same letter in which he complained of Captain Kennedy's activities, offered even more pointed remarks about one Mrs. Chandler of Elizabeth-Town, presumably the wife of a prominent Loyalist Anglican clergyman. "In the way of giving intiligence to the Enemy," he declared, "I think her the first in the place. Thare is not a Tory that passes in or out of New York or any other way, that is of consequence but what waits on Mrs. Chandler, and mostly all the British Officers going in and out on Parole, or Exchange, waits on her—in short she Governs the whole of the Torys and many of the Whigs. I think she would be much better in New York, and to take her Baggage with her that she might have nothing to come back for." (Letter of Maxwell to Governor and Legislature, April 26, 1779, in Room 118, State Library, Trenton.)

[25] *N.J.A.*, 2nd S., Vol. I, p. 443.

New York or Philadelphia, the menace of British arms was comparatively remote. Until the very end of the winter, no military operations of any importance took place in the state, barring a couple of fruitless raids on Staten Island made by the militia in October and November.[26] Yet the very removal of the greatest danger permitted the appearance of a spirit of dissension among the Whigs which had not existed during the emergency of 1776-1777. Mismanagement, corruption, and selfishness, all too evident in both military and civil administration, offered occasion for widespread grumbling, and the occasion was not neglected. "People here," wrote Washington's aide-de-camp, Colonel Tilghman, from Trenton in February, "begin to think freely and speak freely of Men and Measures. The designs of the factions are seen thro' and the authors reprobated, as I am told by all Ranks of People."[27]

Much of this widespread criticism was well founded. In much of it, on the other hand, as it appeared in the press, honest denunciations of corruption or inefficiency were mingled with disingenuous diatribes proceeding from self-interest, personal enmity, or distrust of the growing democratization of government.[28] Whatever their origin, the complaints coincided with an increasing public apathy towards the war—a state of mind reflected in the intensification of the old problems of the militia. Insubordination and undependability on the part of the citizen-soldiers became more marked, if possible, than ever.

On November 21, Brigadier General Varnum announces grimly to Washington that he is having no success in drawing

[26] *N.J.A.*, 2nd S., Vol. I, pp. 485, 487; Washington, *Writings*, Vol. X, p. 134; Dickinson to Washington, Oct. 4 and Nov. 28, 1777, in Washington Papers, Vols. 57 and 62; letter of John Neilson, Nov. 28, in James Neilson Papers, Rutgers University Library.

[27] Tilghman to Washington, Feb. 19, 1778, in Washington Papers, Vol. 67.

[28] See, for example, the "Thoughts on the present state of the Army," printed in the *New Jersey Gazette*, Dec. 24, 1777 (*N.J.A.*, 2nd S., Vol. I, pp. 522-5).

a body of three hundred militiamen from Haddonfield to
Mount Holly: "I have ordered them here, but am just told
'they dont like the manouvre.' "[29]

The same day General Greene reports from Burlington
that "from the temper of the People there appears no great
prospect" of any turnout for service; and shortly thereafter he bemoans the poor state of the commissary's department and the unwillingness of the inhabitants to furnish
supplies for such militiamen as may report for duty.[30] In
January, Colonel Joseph Ellis, successor of the slothful
Newcomb, makes a complaint similar to Greene's; a few
weeks later he asserts that the fluctuating numbers under
his command seldom or never exceed five hundred; and in
March he offers a series of gloomy details:

"I have repeatedly call'd on the Coll.[s] at Burlington but
without Effect; not a single man of them appears, nor do I
hear there is any motion of the kind among them—We can
get but very few from Salem or Cumberland as they plead
the Necessity of guarding their own Coast which I think
not unreasonable—Gloucester of late is little better, they
being discouraged at the Weakness of the Post in part, &
partly for want of their Pay, which with some Company's is
several months in Arrear—Coll Otto's Battalion have chiefly
revolted to the Enemy & have made Prisoners of a Number
of their Officers, those who have escaped dare not stay at
their Homes: Coll. Somers's Battalion upon the last call
for two Classes have not sent twenty men—The market to
Philadelphia is now open nor is it in my Power to stop it
with about fifty men which is all I have at present. . . .
Without some standing force we have little to expect from
the Militia who being alone not sufficient to prevent the

[29] Varnum to Washington, Nov. 21, 1777, Washington Papers, Vol. 61.
[30] Greene to Washington, Nov. 21 and 22, *ibid.*

incursions of the Enemy, each one naturally consults his own Safety by not being found in Arms."[31]

So widespread was the disinclination to military service that in March the manager of the Hibernia Furnace in Morris County attributed his good fortune in enjoying a constant labor supply to the law which exempted ironworkers from militia duty, and to the choice of foundry labor by local farmers as the lesser of two evils.[32]

It would not be fair to blame the people of New Jersey too severely for this slackening of patriotic enthusiasm. They could point to all too many examples of misbehavior and faithless stewardship on the part of other Americans entrusted with important functions in the management of the war, and might well ask why more should be demanded from them than from others. In February 1778, while Governor Livingston was struggling with the militia problem and other perplexing matters, he was suddenly called upon to shoulder an additional burden of which he might reasonably have expected to be free. The shivering Continental army at Valley Forge was on the verge of starvation; and Washington, in his extremity, called upon the dependable chief executive of New Jersey for assistance, especially in the matter of impressing wagons to transport supplies. Livingston complied with the request, but added:

"These Sir, are very temporary Expedients. It is impossible for this State to cure the blunders of those whose Business it is to provide the Army; and considering what New Jersey has suffered by the war, I am justly certain it cannot hold out another year if the rest will not furnish their proportionable share of Provisions. And for my own part, tho' I would rather spend the remainder of my days in a wigwam at lake Erie than be the most splendid Vassal of any arbitrary Prince on Earth, I am so discouraged by

[31] Col. Joseph Ellis to Washington, Jan. 15, 1778, in Washington Papers, Vol. 65; Feb. 8, *ibid.*, Vol. 67; March 23, *ibid.*, Vol. 70.
[32] *N.J.H.S.P.*, N.S., Vol. VIII.

our public mismanagement, & the additional load of Business thrown upon me by the Villainy of those who pursue nothing but accumulating Fortunes to the ruin of their Country, that I almost sink under it."[33]

The governor had ample reason for anger. One of Washington's aides-de-camp, coming to New Jersey at this juncture to obtain supplies for the army, reported to his chief:

"Gentlemen from every part of the province . . . all agree that the failure in the Commissary's department has been intirely owing to neglect. Ten thousand Barrels of pork might have been as easily collected as one thousand which has been the extent of all the purchases and one half of that trifling quantity has been consumed at the small posts here, by the sailors at Bordentown, and the Commissaries and Quarter Masters themselves, who like Locusts oppress the people and consume what they gather up. In short Sir the complaints against the underlings in these two departments are universal. There is not a Cross Road, or a Village of three houses but a deputy Commissary and Quarter Master is fixed there,—to do nothing."[34]

Even more painful to observe than these evidences of mismanagement in the commissariat were the results of inefficiency on the part of another auxiliary army service with important centers in New Jersey. Appalling conditions in the several military hospitals in the state forced the governor in December 1777 to bring matters to the attention of Congress. The mortality rate among the patients was so high, he pointed out, that unless a reformation of conditions should be carried out, "General Washington will be able before next Spring, with the same melancholy Propriety that he did last winter, to call himself a General without an Army."

Dr. Benjamin Rush of the Princeton hospital reinforced Livingston's denunciation with a depressing picture of overcrowding, unsuitable food, and the total inadequacy of such

[33] Livingston to Washington, Feb. 16, 1778, in Washington Papers, Vol. 67.
[34] Tilghman to Washington, Feb. 1778, *ibid.*

necessary supplies as sheets, blankets, and shirts. Of hospital discipline there was none: "The men by going out where they please catch colds—they sell their arms—blankets—& clothes to buy rum, or provisions that are unsuitable for them—they plunder & insult the inhabitants, while within doors they quarrel and fight with each other—disobey their Surgeons—matrons & nurses, and thus defeat the most salutary plans that can be devised for their recovery."[35]

If the sight of such melancholy conditions persistently reminded Jerseymen in general that the war was still in progress, the people of Trenton had special reason not to forget the state of the country. Their little town was crowded to the bursting point with sailors quartered there when the Delaware fleet was decommissioned in the closing weeks of 1777, and with a considerable body of cavalry. It had originally been Washington's intention to winter all his light horse in Trenton, but when General Pulaski arrived with them at the beginning of January he found the village unable to contain his entire force. The community had never fully repaired the damages suffered during the period of Hessian occupation; building materials and workmen were still scarce; and the provisions and fodder available in the vicinity had been almost exhausted by the needs of the heavy traffic in army supplies passing through the town in recent months. Pulaski found himself obliged to scatter his men and horses over a territory extending as far away as Chatham; but enough of them remained in Trenton to brawl with the sailors, offer the inhabitants exhibitions of poor discipline, and consume the provisions grudgingly furnished by tradesmen who displayed no optimism as to the value of the certificates they were given in payment.[36]

[35] Livingston to Henry Laurens, Dec. 25, 1777, Washington Papers, Vol. 63; Rush to (Washington ?) Dec. 26, *ibid.*; Livingston to Washington, March 2, 1778, *ibid*, Vol. 68.

[36] Washington, *Writings*, Vol. X, pp. 232-3, 234-5, 304, 352; Magistrates of Trenton to Washington, Jan. 2, 1778, in Washington Papers, Vol. 64; Pulaski

Such, in rough outline, is the picture of life in New Jersey during its second dreary winter of the war: guerrilla activity and the constant menace of British raids in the northeast and the southwest; the discomforts and disorders of an over-crowded garrison town in Trenton, which was nevertheless rapidly becoming the most important community in New Jersey; defeatist propaganda, low morale, corruption and maladministration throughout the state; and the open scandal of illicit trade with the enemy wherever a weak government was unable to make its restrictions felt.

For a period of about four months this condition of affairs was enlivened by no military operations of any consequence; but as winter merged into spring the sporadic activities of the opposing forces increased in scope until they culminated in the campaign of June 1778.

In the latter part of February and the beginning of March, rival foraging expeditions of considerable strength, the American under General Wayne, supported by Captain Barry of the Continental navy, and the British divided between Lieutenant Colonel Abercrombie and Colonel Sterling, were active in the territory between Salem and Mount Holly. Neither sortie was entirely successful. Wayne complained that the inhabitants "being (if possible) more toriestically Inclined [than] those in the State of Penn[a].," had concealed their cattle in the swamps until the Americans had gone and the royal troops appeared.[37] The British, on the other hand, although they took away a much needed supply of tar and a good stock of cattle and fodder, were obliged to abandon some of their acquisitions upon the approach of the rebels, and return with some precipitation and little dignity to Pennsylvania. Wayne reported with glee that Colonel Aber-

to Washington, Jan. 9, 12, and 20, *ibid.*, Vol. 65; Major Benjamin Tallmadge to Washington, Feb. 9, *ibid.*, Vol. 67.

[37] Wayne to Ellis, Feb. 20, 1778, in Washington Papers, Vol. 67; Wayne to Barry, Feb. 23, 1778, *ibid.*, Vol. 68; Wayne to Washington, Feb. 25, *ibid.*; Barry to Washington, Feb. 26, *ibid.*; Wayne to Washington, Feb. 26, *ibid.*

crombie, who had gone to Salem, "hearing that the Militia were Collecting in Great Numbers—and that we were Advancing from Mount Holly— . . . took the *Horrors* and passing by Water got safe to Phil.ª the same Evening— leaving his whole Collection of Cattle &cª behind for the owners to take again."[38]

A few weeks later the British recouped their prestige and replenished their larder by a more successful expedition. Colonel Mawhood, whose low opinion of American valor had not improved since the battle of Princeton, landed near Salem on March 17 with a sizable force of regulars and New Jersey Loyalists, and gathered up from the fat countryside between Alloways and Salem Creeks a supply of cattle, horses and provisions. Though he met no effective opposition, he was threatened by several small detachments of Americans which were guarding the bridges over Alloways Creek, and which might embarrass the rear of his force when it reembarked. Instead of wasting time and strength by a frontal attack on these opponents, Mawhood eliminated them by stratagems with which the simple-minded and inexperienced countrymen were unable to cope. The detachment at Quintin's Bridge was lured into an ambush by a sham retreat, and suffered heavy losses. The post at Hancock's Bridge, nearest to the Delaware, was surprised on the night of March 20 by a party which landed near the mouth of the creek, stole through the woods, surrounded the sleeping Americans and put them to the bayonet, to the last man, before any resistance could be organized.[39]

The cold-blooded ruthlessness of this coup aroused great indignation. As if still not satisfied with what he had done, the colonel, before he left New Jersey, took one more action which is one of the most illuminating examples that can be

[38] Wayne to Washington, March 5, *ibid.*, Pulaski to Washington, March 3, *ibid.*; Lieut. J. G. Simcoe, *Military Journal* (New York, 1844), pp. 38-45.

[39] Simcoe, *op. cit.*, pp. 46-53; Elijah Hand to Livingston, March 21, 1778, in Washington Papers, Vol. 70.

found of the workings of the eighteenth-century British military mind. Despite the blow which the militia at Quintin's Bridge had suffered, there was still a small force posted there. To this handful of embattled farmers Mawhood now sent an ultimatum threatening, in case they should not lay down their arms and return home, to arm the Tories, "attack all such of the militia as remain in arms, burn and destroy their houses and other property, and reduce them, their unfortunate wives and children to beggary and distress."[40] From the point of view of the British officers, this was a perfectly justifiable proceeding, for, as we have seen, they regarded war as a professional activity in which laymen, especially of the lower classes, should not presume to meddle. Interference by the militia was characterized by one of Mawhood's subordinates as "contrary to common prudence and the rules of war."[41] There could be no valid ground of objection, then, to repressing such irregularity by drastic measures. This attitude, however, was not shared by the New Jersey farmers, and Mawhood's fulminations made no greater an impression upon them now than had General Howe's more than a year earlier. Colonel Elijah Hand, in charge of the militia, returned a spirited refusal and remonstrance against Mawhood's ruthless policy, couched, however, in much more courteous terms than his adversary had deigned to use. In the exchange of notes, indeed, Hand bore away all the honors. He appealed to Mawhood as "a Gentleman, brave, generous and polished with a genteel European education," and the blustering of the Briton appeared to particular disadvantage beside the ironically deferential concluding sentence of the American farmer's reply: "My prayer is, Sir, that this answer may reach you in health & great happiness."[42]

Whether or not Mawhood had the grace to be shamed by this dignified protest, he departed without doing further harm. The brave, polished and genteel gentleman had accom-

[40] *N.J.A.*, 2nd S., Vol. II, p. 168.   [42] *N.J.A.*, 2nd S., Vol. II, pp. 168-70.
[41] Simcoe, *op. cit.*, p. 41.

plished the object of his expedition: he had gathered a good supply of forage and he had revived the honor of British arms by a couple of cheap victories over a handful of armed rustics. Colonel Abercrombie need no longer suffer from "the Horrors."

Before two months had passed, another sharp blow was struck from Philadelphia—this time up the river. Since the end of the autumn campaign, the remnants of the American navy on the Delaware had been laid up at Bordentown. For fear that the most valuable vessels, the unfinished frigates, *Washington* and *Effingham*, might fall into the enemy's hands, they had been scuttled at the beginning of November on Washington's orders; but before another month had passed, the commander-in-chief was obliged to consent unwillingly to their being raised again to provide quarters for the officers and crews whose vessels had been abandoned below Philadelphia.[43] Early in the spring of 1778 the row-galleys, the most mobile units of river defense, appear to have been dismantled and sunk, and their cannon moved overland to places of safety; from that time on there was no force of armed American watercraft capable of offering resistance to a British excursion upstream.

Taking advantage of this situation, and having diverted the attention of the armed forces in New Jersey by landing a foraging expedition near Cooper's Ferry, Howe sent out, on the night of May 7, a small armada, consisting of several row-galleys, a brig and a schooner, which proceeded without molestation up the river to Bordentown. There they burned the frigates, which the surprised Americans had not had time to sink according to their plan for such an emergency. A number of smaller vessels lying in nearby creeks, a quantity of naval stores, with their storehouses, and the

[43] Washington, *Writings*, Vol. IX, pp. 445-8; Francis Hopkinson and John Wharton to Washington, Nov. 28, 1777, in Washington Papers, Vol. 62; George Everett Hastings, *The Life and Works of Francis Hopkinson* (Chicago, 1926), pp. 222-5.

home of Joseph Borden, one of the most prominent Whigs in town, were also given over to the flames, and a few militiamen who attempted a resistance were killed. Thereupon the raiders reembarked and crossed to the Pennsylvania shore, where they performed similar exploits before returning to Philadelphia. The blow had been an unpleasant one for the Americans, and, as Washington pointed out, an avoidable one.[44] The loss, however, was hardly serious, since the value of the frigates was questionable so long as the Howe brothers had the lower river bottled up. The chief result of the raid, as of all such activities by the King's troops throughout the war, was the further exasperation of the inhabitants. At the very time this expedition took place, Lord North's conciliatory proposals were being discussed, and his commissioners were hopefully on their way across the Atlantic to negotiate a settlement. As the *New Jersey Gazette* bitingly commented:

"Thus do these people seek peace; and thus would they conciliate the affections of the Americans!—At the very time that terms are pretended to be offered, and proposals of accommodation, as they say, on the point of being made, fire and sword are carried to our habitations, and these Instruments of violence are committing every species of rapine, plunder and cruelty! This is the application of Lord North's Sermon on the 19th of February last!"[45]

The military authorities at Philadelphia, indeed, were already planning much more extensive operations in New Jersey, and were not troubling themselves overmuch about the peace mission. Sir William Howe's resignation from his command, rendered inevitable by his mismanagement of two campaigns, had been accepted without many tears at White-

[44] Washington, *Writings*, Vol. XI, pp. 7-8, 12-13, 378-9; Col. Wm. Bradford to Washington, March 5, 1778, in Washington Papers, Vol. 68; same to same, March 14, *ibid.*, Vol. 69; Anthony Wayne to Washington, March 14, *ibid.*; Shreve to Washington, May 4, *ibid.*, Vol. 73; Moylan to Washington, May 8, *ibid.*; *N.J.A.*, 2nd S., Vol. II, pp. 207-8, 217-18.

[45] *N.J.A.*, 2nd S., Vol. II, p. 208.

hall, and Sir Henry Clinton, his designated successor, had
already arrived at Philadelphia from New York. The new
commander was not inclined by temperament to conciliate
his enemies, and the instructions he had received from Lord
George Germain indicated that one at least of Lord North's
colleagues felt little faith in a policy of soft words.

Nothing could reveal more sharply the bankruptcy of
British policy in 1778 and the lack of resource in governmental circles than this letter in which Germain outlines
for Clinton a plan of campaign for the coming season. The
chief operation recommended by the Colonial Secretary is
the systematic ravaging of the American coastline from New
York to Nova Scotia, by the burning of all shipping found
in the creeks and harbors, all wharves, and all stores and
materials for shipbuilding. So important does the King consider this scheme, declares Germain, that, in order to release
enough troops to carry it out, Clinton is authorized even to
evacuate Philadelphia if necessary. After the program of
destruction in New England is carried out, the instruction
continues, "it is the King's intention that an attack should
be made upon the southern Colonies, with a view to the
conquest & possession of Georgia & South Carolina"; and
in the meantime every possible "diversion" permitted by the
forces available is to be made in Virginia and Maryland.
"Should the success we may reasonably hope for," the letter
winds up, "attend these enterprizes, it might not be too much
to expect that all America to the south of the Susquehannah
would return to their allegiance, and in the case of so happy
an event, the northern provinces might be left to their own
feelings and distress to bring them back to their duty, &
the operations against them confined to the cutting off all
their supplies & blocking up their ports."[46]

For the execution of this policy of mean-spirited harassments, which British officers themselves wryly referred to as

[46] Historical MSS. Commission, *Report on Stopford-Sackville MSS.*, Vol. II,
pp. 96-9.

"a buccaneering war,"[47] no fitter commander could have been found than Sir Henry Clinton. A man of cold heart and limited vision, he was unpopular even with many of his own officers, who questioned his ability and resented his brusque manners.[48] In contrast to Howe, who, for all his faults, seems never to have been happy in warring upon a civilian population, the new commander-in-chief appears to have taken a positive pleasure in carrying out Germain's program of ruthless attrition. Under Clinton, indeed, the policy was extended beyond its original scope, and New Jersey in particular was drawn into its range. In the coming years, the state was to suffer keenly from a series of deliberate persecutions which reached their climax in the senseless destruction of Springfield in 1780.

Some foreboding of these things crept into the mind of the observant Governor Livingston in the spring of 1778. In a message to the Assembly on May 29, even while rejoicing in the new French alliance, and foretelling the downfall of "haughty Britain," probably after only one more campaign, the chief executive struck a note of prophetic warning: "But how speedily soever she may be doomed to final Perdition, it is our Duty to guard against the vindictive Effects of her expiring Struggles. When all the Horrors of Desperation seize her, and utterly hopeless of Conquest, she determines to rise above herself, by some signal stupendous Act of Barbarity, (having like the Devil in the Apocalypse, great Wrath because she knoweth that she hath but a short Time) she may attempt to desolate what she finds it impossible to subdue."[49]

In the spring of 1778, however, Clinton's chief and immediate menace to New Jersey lay in his decision to evacuate Philadelphia and the Delaware valley completely, and

[47] See marginal note on letter of Stirling to Washington, Oct. 14, 1778, in Washington Papers, Vol. 87.
[48] Kemble, *Journal*, pp. 139, 150, 156, 166.
[49] N.J. Assembly, *Votes & Proceedings*, May 29, 1778.

march most of his troops overland to New York. This step in the execution of the Germain-Clinton plan was kept secret even from some British officials who had every right to be informed of it;[50] but by the latter part of May the preparations for removal were so far advanced that everyone in both armies was aware of them.

Washington faced a characteristic dilemma. If his antagonist actually were planning to abandon the Delaware without striking another blow, and to cross New Jersey, an admirable opportunity might present itself to the Americans to harry the retiring force. On the other hand, by moving prematurely to intercept the probable line of march before the British got all their forces across the river, Washington would expose his camp at Valley Forge, with its stores and its three thousand sick, to a possible sudden attack from Philadelphia. Hence all that he could do was to hold his army in readiness for a quick departure, reinforce Colonel Shreve's two regiments of Continentals in New Jersey with two more under General Maxwell, and urge General Dickinson to raise the militia speedily in case the British should actually pass the Delaware.[51]

By June 18, the last of the Philadelphia garrison had crossed to New Jersey, and Clinton's army took up its slow, straggling march across the state. Since the nature of the Pine Barrens forbade a direct push to the coast, the main body followed a circuitous path through Evesham, Morristown, Mount Holly, Crosswicks, Allentown, Freehold and Middletown to Sandy Hook, with another column under General Knyphausen diverging for part of the way over a

[50] It is characteristic of the obscurity of British policy at this period that the conciliation commissioners who sailed for America in the spring of 1778, expecting to urge Lord North's proposals from the vantage point of a magnanimous victor, knew nothing of the impending move until they arrived in the Delaware and were confronted with what one of them called "the extraordinary change of measures which makes the river at this moment as busy & as mortifying a spectacle as any Englishman ever saw."—Historical MSS. Commission, *Report on Stopford-Sackville MSS.*, Vol. II, p. 115.

[51] Washington, *Writings*, Vol. XI, pp. 437, 445-8, 451-2, 468-70.

shorter route through Imlaystown. At no time during the war can His Majesty's troops be said to have moved with lightning speed, and this march was no exception. The distance by road between Cooper's Ferry and Freehold can scarcely have exceeded sixty miles; yet, except for Knyphausen's division, the army did not arrive at the latter point until June 27, nine days after it had finished crossing the Delaware.[52]

Part of this delay was due to the activities of the New Jersey militia, which began sniping at the British as early as June 19, and continued to impede their progress by tearing up bridges in the line of march. Skirmishes at Evesham and Crosswicks and on the road between Allentown and Freehold served to annoy and to delay, but not seriously to inconvenience Clinton's force, and there was little earnest attempt to put into effect the threat of being "Burgoyned" which the British found scrawled conspicuously at various places along their line of march.[53] One is struck, indeed, by the contrast between the comparative inactivity of the inhabitants of this vicinity and the vigor with which the farmers of more northerly counties harried Howe's men during his spring promenade in 1777 and resisted Knyphausen's expedition to Springfield in 1780. The failure to hamper Clinton effectively is particularly striking in view of the fact that, as reported by militia officers in the vicinity, his line of wagons was more than two miles long, the flanks of his columns were very extensive, and many of his camp followers straggled about unarmed.[54]

Nature did her best to make up for the Jerseymen's deficiencies. The first two or three days saw a heavy rainfall which did nothing to improve poor roads; and the wet spell was followed by a heat wave of uncommon intensity and unprecedented duration. To the soldiers, still wearing their

[52] André, *op. cit.*, pp. 74-8.   [53] *ibid.*, pp. 75-7; Simcoe, *op. cit.*, pp. 63-8.
[54] Dickinson to Washington, June 20, 1778, in Washington Papers, Vol. 77; Richard Howell to Maxwell, June 20, *ibid.*

heavy European uniforms and plodding along sandy lanes under the load of their knapsacks and accumulating plunder, the march under the blazing sun became a nightmare, made worse, as they moved on toward Freehold, by a water scarcity to which the militia contributed by stopping up wells along the way.[55] Hundreds of the men, Hessians particularly, collapsed under the strain, and hundreds more deserted along the line of march.[56]

In order to minimize demoralization in the ranks, Clinton issued stern orders against plundering and destruction, even going so far as to threaten any offender with instant execution, and offering a reward of twenty-five guineas for information which would convict any incendiary.[57] Despite these injunctions the King's army once more left destruction and destitution in its wake even in this region of generally sparse settlement: houses were burned, personal goods were stolen, and horses and cattle were driven along with the invaders. So outrageous was the conduct of his soldiers that Clinton felt obliged to comment in his general orders of July 5: "The irregularity of the Army during the March reflected much disgrace on that discipline which ought to be the first object of an Officer's attention."[58]

As soon as it became evident that the British move to the left bank of the Delaware was not a ruse, the American army was set into motion, and by June 22 it had crossed to New

[55] André, *op. cit.*, p. 78; Dincklage, Journal, pp. 164-5; Charles W. Parker, "Shipley: The County Seat of a Jersey Loyalist," in *N.J.H.S.P.*, N.S., Vol. XVI, p. 130.

[56] Dickinson to Washington, June 21, in Washington Papers, Vol. 77; Washington to Gates, June 27, *ibid.*, Vol. 78; Washington to Patrick Henry, July 4, *ibid.*, Vol. 79.

[57] "Sir Henry Clinton's Orderly Book," in *Collections of the New York Historical Society*, 1883, pp. 595, 598.

[58] *ibid.*, pp. 598, 602-3; Diary of John Hunt, in *N.J.H.S.P.*, Vol. L, p. 232; MS. notes of Rev. E. G. Foote in Sharpe Collection, Rutgers University Library; Maxwell to Washington, July 1, Washington Papers, Vol. 78; William Willcocks to Stirling, June 26, *ibid.*; Steuben to Washington, June 27, *ibid.*

Jersey at Coryell's Ferry.[59] What should be done from this point on was a puzzle to Washington. He was not convinced that General Dickinson was right in the unqualified conclusion to which he had come after directing the obstructive resistance of the New Jersey militia to the British advance for several days: that Clinton's aim was to draw the American army into a general engagement.[60] On the other hand, there was no doubt that the slow pace of the enemy could scarcely be attributed to the obstacles thrown into their way.[61] To this day it is difficult to explain Clinton's delay on any other basis than the customary sluggishness of the royal high command. No less perplexing than the question of the adversary's motives was the problem of correct procedure for the Americans. To expose the still none-too-efficient American army to possible destruction in the lowlands of central New Jersey, where no friendly mountains offered a refuge in case of defeat, was a course for which the commander-in-chief could not lightly decide. On the other hand, to permit so disorderly an enemy to make his journey across the state unchallenged and unscathed might lower dangerously such prestige as Washington's motley fighters still enjoyed.

A council of war to which he referred the matter on June 24 decided against risking a general engagement, but recommended sending fifteen hundred men to harry the left flank and the rear of the enemy, in conjunction with other Continental troops and militia already on the spot, while the main body should hold a position enabling it "to act as circumstances may require."[62] In separate supplementary opinions, several of the officers, including the competent

[59] Washington to Livingston and to Dickinson, June 21, 1778, Washington Papers, Vol. 77; Joseph Clark, Diary, in *N.J.H.S.P.*, Vol. VII, p. 106.

[60] Dickinson to Washington, June 23, Washington Papers, Vol. 78; Washington to Dickinson, June 24, *ibid*.

[61] Minutes of Council of War, and attached documents, June 24, in Washington Papers, Vol. 78.

[62] *ibid*.

Greene, the impetuous Wayne, and the three foreigners, Lafayette, du Portail, and Steuben, urged conditionally that more vigorous action be taken, and that no reasonable opportunity be lost to strike an effective blow. As Greene put it: "People expect something from us & our strength demands it. I am by no means for rash measures but we must preserve our reputation."[63]

Washington had already sent out detachments to cooperate with the militia in annoying the enemy: now on June 25, he reinforced these troops and put Lafayette in general command of all advanced parties, with instructions to give the enemy "every degree of annoyance," even attacking with his entire force should a suitable opportunity present itself.[64]

Scarcely had this assignment of duty been made when General Lee, though confessing "I do not think that this detachment ought to march at all," demanded to be put in charge of it, on the grounds that as second in command of the army he would be slighted if he were passed over.[65] Considerably embarrassed by this sudden request, but anxious, as usual, to avoid offending any of his staff, the commander-in-chief solved the problem by sending out a further reinforcement under Lee, who was given command over the entire advanced corps, with the sole proviso that he should not interfere with any plan already formed by Lafayette for attacking the enemy.[66]

When, therefore, two days later the Americans had drawn close enough to Clinton's retiring army to attack it in force, the man in charge of the important operation was, by a malign twist of fate, not the energetic Lafayette but the unstable Charles Lee, who had already been in treacherous communication with Howe while a captive and who made

[63] ibid.
[64] Washington, Writings, Vol. XII, pp. 113, 114, 115, 117.
[65] ibid., p. 119 n.
[66] ibid., p. 119.

no secret of his disapproval of the very enterprise he was now undertaking.

The last opportunity to strike at the British presented itself as they withdrew from Freehold, or Monmouth Court House, on Sunday, June 28; once they should gain the rolling country about Middletown, a few miles away, they would be comparatively safe from molestation. Accordingly, despite the fact that Clinton's force was now arranged in much more formidable order than at any other time in the course of the long march, with the baggage protected by a strong rear guard,[67] Washington ordered Lee, early in the morning of July 28, to attack, "acquainting him at the same time, that I was marching to support him."[68]

After several unnecessary delays, Lee, who "appeared irresolute & confused,"[69] finally brought up his men into contact with the enemy at about eight in the morning. Before there was any chance, however, for battle to be fairly joined, he began falling back with part of his force, to the amazement of his subordinates in charge of other detachments, who had no choice but to abandon excellent positions and retire along with their general. The British, seizing the opportunity, pressed on and threw the bewildered American troops into confusion as no word came from Lee to make a stand. Such was the situation which Washington found when he approached Freehold at the head of the main American army and was met by his demoralized advanced corps. Taking personal charge of affairs, as he had at Princeton, but this time not without uttering what Lee later called "very singular expressions," the commander-in-chief was able to rally and re-form his men, check the advance of the enemy, and force them back before dark to approximately the positions held at the outset of the battle. During the course of the

[67] Lamb, *op. cit.*, p. 241; Hamilton to Washington, June 28, in Washington Papers, Vol. 78.

[68] Washington, *Writings*, Vol. 142.

[69] Copy of opinion by David Forman in Washington Papers, Vol. 50.

night, the British withdrew quietly from the field, and by
daybreak were too far away to be pursued over the sandy
roads through the intense heat.[70]

By his prompt and cool action, Washington had undoubtedly retrieved a dangerous situation, and prevented a totally
unnecessary and disgraceful rout. Once the initiative was lost
to the Americans, however, by Lee's strange conduct, it was
too late to inflict any severe damage upon the British before
they left New Jersey. Although the Americans claimed a
victory because their enemy quit the field, the triumph was
a hollow one, and Clinton, safely at Sandy Hook, was able
to congratulate his men upon the success of their march and
upon "the noble Ardour shown by that part of the Army
who repulsed so superior a number of the Enemy on the 28th.
of June."[71]

One happy result did emerge from the annoying battle.
General Charles Lee, who had been a source of dissension
and trouble ever since he joined the Americans, was now
permanently disgraced. While awaiting trial by court martial, he wrote some characteristically impudent letters to
Washington, in the course of which he referred contemptuously to the latter's "tinsel dignity."[72] His effrontery failed,
however, to save him before the court, which found him
guilty of "disobedience of orders, in not attacking the enemy
. . . agreeable to repeated instructions," and of "misbeha-
viour before the enemy . . . by making an unnecessary and
in some few instances a disorderly retreat." He was accordingly sentenced to be suspended for twelve months from

[70] ibid.; account by Wayne and Scott, June 30, ibid., Vol. 78; Washington,
Writings, Vol. XII, pp. 139-46; André, op. cit., pp. 78-81; Clark, op. cit., p. 106.
A very full and careful study of the Monmouth campaign is to be found in
William Stryker's The Battle of Monmouth (Princeton, 1927). Its value is
lessened by the absence of good maps or plans.
[71] "Sir Henry Clinton's Orderly Book" in Collections of the New York Historical Society, 1883, p. 602.
[72] Lee to Washington, June "28", June 30, and July 1, 1778, in Washington
Papers, Vol. 78.

any command in the armies of the United States[73]—a mild enough punishment, but one that ruined his career. The removal of such a dangerous intriguer from the army might well have been worth an even more serious military disappointment than the fiasco at Freehold.

Washington profited not only by the disgrace of Lee, but also by an increase in prestige which brought about the eclipse of General Gates. The latter's adherents in Congress had been pressing his case, as a rival of the Virginian, until a dangerous split was developing. "The evacuation of Philadelphia and the battle of Monmouth decided the question," the French minister wrote home in November 1778, "and the partisans of General Gates are reduced to silence."[74]

After the excitement attendant upon Clinton's march and the engagement at Freehold, New Jersey soon relapsed into quiet. The British already had a number of vessels waiting at Sandy Hook;[75] and, after lingering a few days in the Highlands, the troops were ferried over to Manhattan, Long and Staten Islands.[76] Even before the enemy had quit the state, the assembled militia, anxious to return to their farm work and to avoid the strain of soldiering in the heat, dispersed in spite of all the efforts of their commanders to hold

---

[73] Judgment of the Court Martial, in Washington Papers, Vol. 81. The whole case of Charles Lee is interestingly discussed in John Fiske's *Essays Historical and Literary* (New York, 1902), and George H. Moore's *The Treason of Charles Lee* (New York, 1860).

[74] Durand, *op. cit.*, pp. 167-8.

[75] South Amboy. Jun 28th 1778 Sunday afternun
    Sir
    Thes Comes to inform you that thar is three or four Ships now at the Huck I think Very ner the shouer with upords of forty sale of Slups and Squeners agrat maney flatbotom bots on the Est side of Stat Island this morning I had aman in middeltown he informed me thar was no Enmey thar yet on the South Side of the Island thare is But one armed Squener and Two Small Bots The Wessels from The Hook Ceeps Passing and Repassin Very Much—Sir i am your most Humbl Sarvent—James Morgan Capt
    To
    His Exelency Genriel Washenton—Washington Papers, Vol. 78.

[76] Simcoe, *op. cit.*, p. 73; Maxwell to Washington, July 5, Washington Papers, Vol. 79; Washington to Arnold, July 11, *ibid.*

them.[77] Washington, meanwhile, suspicious of possible British designs on the Hudson, moved slowly northward through New Brunswick and Newark to Paramus. There, in the middle of July, he heard of the arrival off the coast of a French fleet under Count d'Estaing, and crossed the Hudson at once with his army to Westchester County, where he planned to give the British in New York "every jealousy" in his power, and, if possible, strike an effective blow.[78] The story of how the remaining weeks of the summer were frittered away while Washington vainly hoped for a joint naval and land offensive against New York does not fall within the scope of this work. So far as New Jersey was concerned, the campaign of 1778 was over. A small detachment of Continentals under Maxwell was left at Elizabeth-Town, and observers were stationed in Monmouth County to watch British shipping.[79] Aside from this handful of soldiers, there were few signs of military activity to be seen in the state, and New Jersey, after two years of alarums and excursions, settled down into a period of comparative tranquillity.

[77] Dickinson to Washington, June 29 and June 30, *ibid.*, Vol. 78.
[78] Washington, *Writings*, Vol. XII, pp. 178-80.
[79] *ibid.*, pp. 281, 295, 296-7, 298.

CHAPTER XIII ☼ *THE CLOSING YEARS*

THE two years between the Battle of Monmouth and the skirmish at Springfield saw no military engagements of importance in New Jersey. The state settled into an uneasy repose, marked by incessant petty raids, outbursts of lawlessness, recurrent problems of hunger for the inhabitants and the transient armies, and the rapid growth of war profiteering and kindred manifestations of a declining public morale.[1]

Some few communities enjoyed an unwonted degree of prosperity. What had been one of the least developed regions of New Jersey—the long, sparsely settled coast—had leaped into new prominence as a result of wartime conditions. From Raritan Bay to Cape May, enterprising individuals bestirred themselves to share in the golden harvest of profits. Tiny hamlets like Toms River and Tuckerton now found their harbors crowded with more and larger vessels than they had ever seen before, and their lanes and houses bustling with teamsters, militiamen, laborers, adventurers, and business-men. At the Forks of the Mullica River, a small boom town grew up to enjoy a brief flush of prosperity before disappearing entirely within a few years after the restoration of peace.[2] This wave of business activity was based on three factors: foreign commerce, salt manufacturing, and privateering—and the greatest of these was privateering. The harbors lying behind the shallow and difficult passages through the barrier beaches offered a safe refuge from King

[1] "Our political stupor & security, owing to our last years successful campaign, & a thirst for the Mammon of unrighteousness, is truly lamentable." —Livingston to Washington, May 8, 1779, in Washington Papers, Vol. 106.
"A most mortifying consideration is our declension of public spirit; and as the Depreciation of Patriotism has kept full pace with the depreciation of the Currency, I really dread the Continuance of the war as a Member of the Confederacy at large & the total loss of all the honour acquired by this State, as connected with it in particular."—Same to same, Oct. 8, 1779, *ibid.*, Vol. 118.
[2] Alfred M. Heston, *Absegami* (Camden, N.J., 1904), Vol. I, pp. 151-3.

George's warships, and were at the same time conveniently close to the trade routes leading to New York from Europe and the West Indies. Even before Manhattan Island fell to the British, privateers operating from Little Egg Harbor had taken several rich prizes.[3] With the enemy headquarters established so near by, after the autumn of 1776, and a constant flow of supply vessels offering tempting opportunities, legalized piracy from the lonesome inlets of New Jersey became a flourishing business. By 1778 and 1779, no vessel bound for New York was safe from attack unless escorted by a ship of war or itself heavily armed. The Jersey seahawks were no respecters of persons. An oyster boat from Long Island, a brig from Ireland laden with butter and linen, a brigantine of His Majesty's navy freighted with a sizable contingent of Hessian auxiliaries and their officers and disabled by storm—all these received the same cavalier treatment, and the personal baggage of protesting German officers was ransacked as ruthlessly for valuables as the belongings of any petty trader.[4]

Little Egg Harbor, with some thirty armed sloops operating from it,[5] was perhaps the chief base for privateering activity; but Toms River, which then enjoyed easy access to the ocean through Island Beach by way of Cranberry Inlet, almost opposite the mouth of the river, was also a thriving center.[6] After a visit there in May 1779, one active sponsor of privateering ventures wrote to his partner to inform him that no work had been done on a vessel of theirs laid up in the harbor. "The Busy season," he explained, "for the People on the Shore since the late Captures has made

[3] *Am. Arch.*, 5th S., Vol. I, pp. 741, 742; *N.J.A.*, 2nd S., Vol. I, pp. 110-11; Abraham Clark to James Caldwell, Aug. 2, 1776, in Sparks MSS., 49, Vol. II, p. 170.

[4] *N.J.A.*, 2nd S., Vol. I, p. 486, Vol. II, pp. 137, 189; Von Jungkenn MSS., Vol. 7:8, No. 8.

[5] Heston, *op. cit.*, Vol. I, p. 142.

[6] Edwin Salter, *A History of Monmouth and Ocean Counties* (Bayonne, N.J., 1890), pp. 193-4.

them Negligent of any thing but dividing & determining their Shares in prizes."[7]

Other places shared in a lesser degree the profitable though risky activities of Toms River and Little Egg Harbor. Cape May had its privateers,[8] and so did Chestnut Neck on the Mullica River;[9] even from New Brunswick a daring free-booter could snatch a prize in Prince's Bay from under the very noses of the British.[10] All along the Jersey shore the militia were prompt to confiscate the cargo of any luckless British vessel driven upon the beach by storm.[11]

Naturally, the British did what they could to punish these "nests of pirates." Any royal man-of-war passing by was happy to capture or destroy whatever craft, peaceable or predatory, it might find heading to or from one of the inlets.[12] The first deliberate act of vengeance took place in October 1778, when the neighboring hamlets at Chestnut Neck and Bass River were attacked from the sea by an overwhelming force, plundered, and laid waste—houses, barns, storehouse, shipping, salt works and sawmill.[13]

Some years later, in 1782, another privateering center, Toms River, was destroyed. By this time the war was obviously over, and military operations had reached a virtual standstill; yet in March of that year, Clinton, as one of his last acts before being superseded by Sir Guy Carleton, permitted over a hundred Loyalists to attack and overwhelm the little settlement, burn down houses, the gristmill, and

[7] John Van Emburgh to Col. John Neilson, May 20, 1779, in James Neilson Papers.

[8] Maurice Beesley, in *Geology of . . . Cape May* (Trenton, 1857), p. 196.

[9] Heston, *op. cit.*, p. 138.

[10] Capt. John Burrowes to Stirling, Feb. 3, 1779, in Washington Papers, Vol. 97.

[11] Letter of Col. N. Gist, March 31, 1779, Washington Papers, Vol. 101; *N.J.A.*, 2nd S., Vol. I, pp. 434, 439, 443-4, 449; Lewis T. Stevens, *The History of Cape May County, New Jersey* (Cape May City, 1897), pp. 209-10.

[12] *N.J.A.*, 2nd S., Vol. I, pp. 354, 400, 429-30, 434-5.

[13] Heston, *op. cit.*, pp. 138-46; Livingston to Stirling, Oct. 11, 1778, Washington Papers, Vol. 87.

the sawmill, and take away the only two boats in port at the time. Thus Toms River, too, paid a price, though a belated one, for its war boom.[14]

The frenzy of privateering was accompanied by a sharp increase in peaceful commerce and industry. While many of the great American ports were more or less under surveillance by prowling royal men-of-war, and particularly while both New York and Philadelphia were in British hands, smaller harbors reaped the benefits of obscurity. Goods from the West Indies and Europe, acquired by normal means of exchange, joined the spoils of captured prizes to be loaded aboard wagons at Mays Landing on the Great Egg Harbor River, at Chestnut Neck, or at the Forks of the Mullica and hauled overland to the Delaware valley.[15] Another item in this trade was the salt made from sea water in the numerous evaporating works which sprang up all along the shore as war scarcity raised the price of this essential commodity.[16] Labor for the salt works was hard to get, since there were more alluring occupations for the natives of the shore than being sun-broiled and mosquito-bitten while tending the vats; storms and Tories frequently destroyed the equipment; but the promise of gain was so great that the industry persisted.[17]

Opportunities for profit in the new and feverish trade from the shore were enormous. Substantial businessmen repeatedly braved the heat, the mosquitoes, and the poor roads of eastern New Jersey to bid for the cargoes of incoming ships, to arrange privateering ventures, and to acquire salt for resale inland, where it was at some times and places

[14] N.J.H.S.P., N.S., Vol. XIV, pp. 430-1.

[15] Heston, op. cit., Vol. I, pp. 138, 256; Vol. II, p. 248.

[16] ibid., Vol. I, p. 218; Stevens, op. cit., pp. 201-2; Salter, op. cit., pp. 240-1; N.J.A., 2nd S., Vol. II, p. 6; Journal of the New Jersey Convention, pp. 73-4; Wilson, Acts of New Jersey, pp. 6, 41; Votes and Proceedings of the General Assembly, Sept. 11, 1776.

[17] Major John Van Emburgh to Col. John Neilson, July 12, Nov. 17, 18, 21, Dec. 27, 30, 1778, May 20, 1779, in James Neilson Papers.

as good as money, or better.[18] Their gains were handsome. Committees of Congress might deplore profiteering; legislatures might pass bill after bill against "the evil Practice of Engrossing and Forestalling";[19] but no one was in a position to clip the wings of the shrewd traders. Washington wrote with unwonted bitterness at the end of 1778 of "those murderers of our cause (the monopolizers, forestallers, & engrossers) . . . the pests of society, & the greatest Enemy we have to the happiness of America"; and added, "I wish to God that one of the most attrocious of each State was hung high in Gibbets upon a gallows five times as high as the one prepared by Haman."[20] At that very moment, one of the most prominent and respected delegates of New Jersey to the Continental Congress was John Neilson of New Brunswick, whose military activities in the war had been tireless, and who was to become deputy quartermaster general for the state of New Jersey in 1780. In May 1779, Neilson profited from a deal by which his business partner, Major John Van Emburgh, bought salt at Toms River for fifteen dollars a bushel and sold it at Morristown for thirty-five. The letter in which Van Emburgh announces the sale adds that he has found nothing else in the past few days "Worth Speculating in, If I had shou'd have Interested you therein. If anything offers with you expect you'll think of me."[21]

When such pillars of the new state felt free to speculate upon the necessities of their fellow countrymen, it is not surprising that many lesser men saw no harm in filling their pocketbooks by a trade one degree more unpatriotic—that with the British occupants of New York. The correspondence of Washington and Livingston and the records of

[18] Same to same, July 12, Sept. 13, 1778, and other dates, *ibid.*; Thacher, *op. cit.*, p. 220.

[19] *N.J. Exec. Corr.*, pp. 132-4; *N.J.A.*, 2nd S., Vol. I, pp. 519-20; Acts of General Assembly, Dec. 15 and 21, 1779.

[20] Washington to Joseph Reed, Dec. 12, 1778, Washington Papers, Vol. 94.

[21] Van Emburgh to Neilson, May 5 and 20, 1779; in James Neilson Papers.

the New Jersey legislature throughout the war years are full of complaints concerning this illicit commerce, and of projects for stopping it. The Shrewsbury district was reported by one of Washington's spies in New York to have supplied the city in 1778 with "not less than One Thousand Sheep, five Hundred Hogs, and Eight Hundred Quart^r. or up-wards of good Beef, a large Parcel of cheese—besides Poultry."[22] This particular branch of the trade received a severe blow in June 1780, when an American privateer, disguised under British colors, ran among fifteen Shrewsbury traders fishing off Long Island, and captured eleven or twelve of them.[23]

No measure taken, however, could put an end to the steady influx of provisions into New York and the corresponding outward flow of the manufactured and exotic articles for which Americans were so eager. The reason is not far to seek. Elisha Boudinot, an outstandingly Revolutionary Whig of Elizabeth-Town, had some wedding garments imported from the city for his bride in 1778—though, by an unusual display of official zeal, they were confiscated "and the poor Bride put under the Mortification of being Married in her old Cloaths."[24] Not all violators of the law were so unfortunate. The officer in charge of checking illegal importations under cover of flags of truce felt obliged to ask Washington, in 1779, for instructions as to how rigorously he should carry out his duty. "I have Reason," he explained, "to expect some Effects sent to my Superior Officers may fall into my Hands & perhaps some of the first Families in the State may have dealt to a small amount at different Times with their Friends in New York."[25] It is hardly a matter for wonder, then, that as late as December 1782 the

22 Report from "X", Dec. 7, 1778, Washington Papers, Vol. 94.
23 Forman to Washington, June 17, 1780, in Washington Papers, Vol. 138.
24 Stirling to Washington, Nov. 24, 1778, ibid., Vol. 93.
25 Samuel H. Parsons to Washington, Dec. 16, 1779, ibid., Vol. 123.

state legislature was still vainly seeking to check commerce with the enemy.[26]

Aside from these varied and somewhat feverish manifestations of the business instinct, the life of New Jersey in the years after Monmouth shows some effort to rebuild normal civil relationships. In May 1778, two educational institutions, Queen's College and the Elizabeth-Town Academy, followed the example of the college at Princeton by making preparations for reopening. The cautious authorities of Queen's transferred their school from New Brunswick to a new and safer site on the North Branch of the Raritan.[27] The Academy, however, resumed activity in its old location, where, separated only by a short stretch of water from the ravaging armies of the King, young ladies and gentlemen might again be taught "reading with propriety and gracefulness, oratory, writing, arithmetic, surveying, navigation and mathematical branches in general; also geography and philosophy, besides the Greek and Latin languages."[28] The will to maintain for the next generation such advantages of education as could be salvaged from the turmoil of war also found expression in an act passed by the legislature in December 1778, which aimed at securing continuity of instruction by exempting school teachers from militia service.[29]

Nevertheless, despite such occasional examples of constructive forces at work, the life of the people in general during the years after Monmouth was scarcely brighter than it had been before. More than one ravaged community bore witness by its desolation or squalor to the degradation of war. Perth Amboy, which had never recovered from the British occupation, was reported in December 1778 to be so "destitute of Meat bread & all the &c that you can imagine" that two of Washington's staff worried over the problem of finding subsistence there during a short confer-

[26] Wilson, *Acts of New Jersey*, Chap. CCCXLV.   [28] *ibid.*, p. 229.
[27] *N.J.A.*, 2nd S., Vol. II, p. 215.
[29] Wilson, *Acts of New Jersey*, Chap. CXX (Dec. 10, 1778).

ence to be held with a couple of British officers.[30] Bound
Brook, which during the years of the struggle played host
willy-nilly to a succession of British and American detachments, became, with its dirt and its dramshops, a byword
for slovenliness.[31] The two armies which departed from New
Jersey in the summer of 1778 left behind them whole districts stripped so bare of food and forage that some of the
inhabitants were perilously close to actual starvation; and,
since the crops proved to be a partial failure, more than one
family faced a winter of hunger.[32]

To distress the people further, a few minor military operations took place before the advent of cold weather. In the
chief of these, during the closing days of September and the
first two weeks of October, the British swept the lower part
of Bergen County clean of hay, corn, wheat and rye. While
their fleet of sloops, schooners, gondolas and small water
craft plied busily up and down the Hackensack, carrying
their booty to larger vessels anchored in the Kills or directly
to landings on British territory, two Continental brigades
under Lord Stirling watched helplessly, and bodies of hastily summoned, halfhearted militia, in whom Stirling said
"the Spirit of going home" was universal, looked on gloomily
day after day and pestered their officers with clamor to
return to their hungry, neglected families. The ineffectiveness and feebleness of American resistance seemed most
humiliatingly demonstrated when on the night of September 27 a regiment of Continental light dragoons under
Colonel Baylor was surprised in its sleep at Herringtown near
Tappan, by a prowling corps of Clinton's regulars, and all

[30] Col. Robert Hanson Harrison to Nathanael Greene, Dec. 5, 1777, in Washington Papers, Vol. 94.
[31] Col. Israel Shreve, about to march with his troops from Elizabeth-Town
to Easton, begs leave of Washington, May 28, 1779, to halt at the forks of
the Raritan instead of Bound Brook "on account of that place being so very
dirty and Such a Number of Dram Shops."—Washington Papers, Vol. 108.
[32] James Caldwell to Lord Stirling, Oct. 11, 1778, in Washington Papers, Vol.
87; Greene to Washington, Oct. 19, Oct. 27, and Nov. 30, 1778, *ibid.*, Vols. 88, 90
and 93 respectively.

but a few were put to the bayonet or taken prisoners.[33] This exploit was more embarrassing to the Americans than creditable to the British, whose excess was deprecated in their own camp and gave the Americans opportunity to accuse them of a "horrid massacre."[34]

Towards the end of the year, Washington once more moved his headquarters to New Jersey, to stay there until the opening of the next campaign. He was late in putting the army into winter quarters, since he felt it unwise to withdraw the major part of his forces from the Hudson until the "Convention troops," captured at Saratoga, were safely in New England on their way to Boston from Virginia, and until he had satisfied himself that the rumors of British military preparations in New York, brought him by spies, boded no offensive move of importance.[35]

By the latter part of December, the American troops were settled for the winter in an irregular semicircle of cantonments stretching from Danbury in Connecticut to Burlington on the Delaware. Washington's headquarters were in the Wallace house, a comfortable dwelling a short distance from the village of Raritan, and the majority of his officers and men were quartered within a few miles of that spot, with the greatest concentration in the Middlebrook valley, with which the army had become familiar during the spring of 1777.[36] In order to avoid a repetition of some of the needless discomforts suffered at Valley Forge the preceding winter,

[33] The best source of information about the whole expedition consists of the numerous letters scattered through the Washington Papers, Vols. 85-8, covering the period from Sept. 23 to Oct. 19. Briefer accounts are to be found in Clark, *Diary*, pp. 108-9; Kemble, *Journal*, p. 163; André, *Journal*, pp. 97-9; Von Jungkenn MSS., 7:6; Caldwell to James Abeel, Oct. 6, 1778 (typewritten copy in Rutgers University Library).

[34] Kemble, *Journal*, p. 163; Baylor to Washington, Oct. 19, 1778, in Washington Papers, Vol. 88.

[35] Washington Papers, Vol. 79, *passim*.

[36] Mills, *Historic Houses of New Jersey*, p. 241; Thomas G. Frothingham, *Washington, Commander in Chief* (Boston and New York, 1930), p. 276; Major Henry Lee to Tench Tilghman, Dec. 30, 1778, Washington Papers, Vol. 95.

the commander-in-chief issued strict and detailed orders for the proper construction of huts and the plan of the camp.[37] Eventually, the soldiers found themselves far more comfortably housed than they had been a twelvemonth earlier; but the cutting of logs and the building of huts took time; January had passed before the last of the men were freed of the necessity of sleeping under canvas, and meanwhile they had shivered in the bitterest weather of the winter and, indeed, of many years.[38]

Although Washington was able to affirm with satisfaction in March that the troops were "better clad and more healthy than they have ever been since the formation of the army,"[39] the winter had not passed without its troubles. Provisions for man and beast ran short from time to time, as usual.[40] Friction with the local inhabitants developed in innumerable ways: soldiers resumed their old habits of burning fences for firewood and committing petty or occasionally serious depredations; at moments of need the army impressed grain from stingy and irascible farmers; officers whose manners and tempers had not been improved by years of army life, quartered on terms of enforced intimacy in the homes of substantial citizens accustomed to deference, did

[37] Orders of Dec. 14 and 24, 1778, and Jan. 4, 1779, in orderly book in the possession of the Hon. H. E. Pickersgill, Perth Amboy.

[38] Thacher, *Military Journal*, pp. 188-90, 192; Clark, *Diary*, pp. 109-10; Stirling to Washington, Dec. 28, Washington Papers, Vol. 95; Maxwell to Washington, Dec. 28, *ibid.*

[39] Washington to Lafayette, March 8, 1779, Washington Papers, Vol. 99.

[40] *N.J. Exec. Corr.*, pp. 125-8, 130-1, 139-40; Stirling to Washington, Dec. 28 and 29, Washington Papers, Vol. 95; Major Henry Lee to Tilghman, Dec. 30, *ibid.* Inefficiency and petty graft in the foraging service were, as always, partially responsible for the troubles. Captain John Burrowes complained to Stirling on Feb. 3 of one forage master who "has been down in Monmouth with Eleven waggons these Eight days & how much longer I cant tell—but in the Eight days he has been at two farms about two miles apart and not one mile further. he has had to the amount of five loads of forage at these two farms the first two days, and he would not send them forward with it but staid without looking for more till he has feed it all to the waggon horses—it seems his father owns four or five of the teams which I suppose are better of there than at Camp."—Washington Papers, Vol. 97.

not invariably display perfect tact.[41] As the dull winter months drew to a close, discontent among the soldiers became very noticeable, and by spring considerable numbers were deserting from outlying posts whence escape was fairly easy.[42]

Yet the season of inactivity had not been entirely without its accomplishments. General von Steuben, who had been appointed inspector-general of the army in 1778, found time in those months to drill the troops according to Prussian methods. So gratifying were the results of von Steuben's tireless activity that in April Washington was able to hold a gala review of the army for the French minister and the semiofficial Spanish representative, which passed off with great éclat.[43]

To the people living in the exposed sections of New Jersey, this improvement in the discipline and smartness of the soldiers was of little help. Washington's army, however improved, was still not strong enough to seek out and defeat the enemy; and so long as the King's henchmen lay snug on Staten and Manhattan Islands, the war remained for Jerseymen a hovering threat from the northeast which might at any moment be translated into the reality of fire and sword. When the commander-in-chief wrote to Livingston with some impatience in June 1779 of "the desultory kind of war which the enemy seem determined to pursue,"[44] many of the governor's constituents could have furnished, if necessary, full illustration from their recent experiences.

[41] Orders of Dec. 29 and Jan. 4, 15 and 25 in orderly book in possession of Judge Pickersgill; Livingston to Washington, March 9, 1779, Washington Papers, Vol. 100; Washington to Wayne, March 16, *ibid.*; H. W. Archer to Washington, March 23, *ibid.*, Vol. 101; Wayne to Washington, March 23, *ibid.*; letter of Col. P. Adams, May 25, *ibid.*, Vol. 108; depositions of Benjamin Lindsley, Dec. 31, 1778, *ibid.*, Vol. 95, and of Peter Davis, March 9, 1779, *ibid.*, Vol. 100.

[42] Orders of Feb. 10 and 12 in Judge Pickersgill's orderly book, cited; see reports of various officers in late March and early April, Washington Papers, Vols. 102 and 103.

[43] Thacher, *op. cit.*, pp. 193-5.   [44] *N.J. Exec. Corr.*, p. 173.

Bergen County had been scourged by roving bands throughout the winter and spring.[45] Elizabeth-Town had seen its barracks burned down in the small hours of a February morning, and some of its houses plundered, when regulars making a surprise descent avenged their failure to trap General Maxwell's little corps there.[46] Sleepy Tinton Falls, in Monmouth County, had learned the meaning of British fury on April 26, when a nocturnal landing expedition, again frustrated in its hope of cutting off an American detachment, fired the houses of two militia officers and gutted all the other dwellings in the little hamlet. Having demolished the furniture of the homes and left not one windowpane intact in the village, the marauders made off with the horses and cattle of the neighborhood, though they were obliged to leave behind a good many of the stolen animals along their line of retirement.[47] Within a few weeks, the same community had suffered a second and much more daring raid, effected this time by fewer than two dozen Loyalist refugees under the command of the Jerseyman James Moody. The visitors destroyed a magazine of powder and arms and carried off public stores which later sold in New York for more than five hundred pounds sterling; pursued by militiamen, they inflicted nearly a dozen casualties and made good their retreat.[48]

Such a policy of trifling annoyances can scarcely be called serious campaigning. Lord George Germain, however, was

[45] Livingston to Washington, Nov. 7, 1778, Washington Papers, Vol. 91; Washington to Livingston, Nov. 18, *ibid.*; Col. Christian Febiger to Washington, Nov. 29, 1778, *ibid.*, Vol. 93; Nathanael Greene to Washington, Nov. 30, *ibid.*; Sir Henry Clinton to Washington, Jan. 23, 1779, *ibid.*, Vol. 97; Maxwell to Washington, Jan. 27, *ibid.*, and April 6, *ibid.*, Vol. 102; Col. T. Clark to Washington, May 17, *ibid.*, Vol. 107; Shreve to Washington, May 28, *ibid.*, Vol. 108.

[46] Kemble, *op. cit.*, pp. 173-4; Washington to Livingston, March 8, Washington Papers, Vol. 99.

[47] Lt. Col. Benjamin Ford to Washington, April 26, in Washington Papers, Vol. 104; Capt. John Burrowes to Stirling, April 26, *ibid.*

[48] Moody, *op. cit.*, pp. 18-19.

not above recommending to the King the officers who had directed the first Tinton Falls raid, and writing approvingly to Clinton: "The enterprise . . . appears to have been conducted by Colonel Hyde with much spirit and judgment, and must have its share in keeping up the apprehensions of the rebels, and preventing the militia of the country exposed to such attacks from sending draughts to Mr. Washington's army."[49]

To retaliate for these many unimportant but more or less successful depredations on the part of the British, the Americans made one bold stroke in New Jersey on August 19, quite in the spirit of Wayne's capture of Stony Point up the Hudson during the preceding month. Major Henry Lee— the impetuous "Light Horse Harry"—made a characteristically daring assault just before dawn upon the British port at Powles Hook. Despite the strong position of the fort, protected on three sides by water and on the fourth by salt marshes and a ditch, besides the fortifications built by the Americans and strengthened by the British, Lee's force of some four hundred men was able to carry the post by storm before the sleepy garrison had had time to rally for effective defense. A handful of the defenders, under their commander, Major Sutherland, took refuge in a central redoubt, whence the attackers had no time to dislodge them. Anxious to avoid being cut off in this isolated spot, and aware that his men's ammunition had been ruined by the plunge through the ditch, Lee hastily gathered up his prisoners—a hundred fifty-nine of them—and retired without setting fire to the barracks, blowing up the powder magazine, or spiking the cannon. By one of the typical mischances with which inefficiency and poor coordination so often imperilled the American army, the major found, on arriving at the Hackensack River, that the boats which he had arranged to have waiting to transport his weary force to Newark were not to be seen. The only

[49] Historical MSS. Commission, *Report on Stopford-Sackville MSS.*, Vol. II, p. 130.

alternative route of withdrawal was the long and dangerous road to the New Bridge, exposed to attack from the enemy; and along this road Lee's men, worn out from hours of marching and fighting, and encumbered with their captives, set off. Twice they were threatened by pursuing detachments of British, but fresh and timely reinforcements had met them, and, strong enough now to stave off attack, they safely completed their retirement into the hills.[50]

Although the storming of Powles Hook was a *tour de force* which could under no circumstances have led to important results, it was at least a clean-cut military enterprise. Sutherland's men were not massacred, as Baylor's had been at Tappan; nor did any of the Tory civilians in the neighborhood of the Hook suffer the fate of the Whigs at Tinton Falls. The British answer, nevertheless, was quite in keeping with the Clinton technique. On the night of October 25, a party of some eighty cavalrymen from the Queen's Rangers, under the leadership of Lieutenant Colonel Simcoe, crossed from Staten Island and moved swiftly up the left bank of the Raritan. At Van Vechten's Bridge, above Bound Brook, they burned a number of flatboats, mounted on carriages, en route from the Delaware to Washington's camp on the Hudson. The raiders also set fire to the Dutch meeting house, in which some forage for the army was stored, and made prisoners of the commissary and his subordinates. Returning on the opposite side of the Raritan, they passed through Hillsborough, where they stopped long enough to release three Loyalist prisoners, and, of course, to burn the courthouse of Somerset County. (Officers of Simcoe's type seemed to feel a peculiar hatred for courthouses, as physical symbols of American self-government.) By now, the alarm was beginning to spread through the country, and an occa-

[50] Winfield, *History of Hudson County*, pp. 154-9; Washington to Lee, Aug. 10 and Sept. 1, 1779, Washington Papers, Vols. 114 and 116; Washington to Stirling, Aug. 12, *ibid.*, Vol. 115; Col. Christian Febiger to Washington, Nov. 29, 1778, *ibid.*, Vol. 93.

sional shot from the rear warned the colonel that the militia were gathering at his heels. His reaction was characteristic: let him tell it in his own words:

"Passing by some houses, Lieut. Col. Simcoe told the women to inform four or five people who were pursuing the rear, 'that if they fired another shot he would burn every house which he passed.' "[51] Evidently the British sense of sportsmanship had its limitations: the colonel was daring enough to make a hazardous incursion into the heart of the country, but not chivalrous enough to let the aroused inhabitants have their chance of revenge, if he could frighten them off. Although the threat was not put into execution— possibly because the retreat was too precipitate—the mere utterance of it is reminiscent of the bullying ultimatum to Elijah Hand during the Salem County foray in 1778—in which, incidentally, Simcoe had participated.

The colonel's attempt to intimidate the militia is surprising in view of the fact that one object of his raid was to entice pursuing militiamen into an ambush of British infantry which he had arranged near the South River Bridge. By an ironical twist of fate, the tables were turned. Simcoe himself fell into an ambush because he failed to turn off the New Brunswick road at the intersection he had in mind—and the reason for the error, it was later discovered, was his guide's unawareness that the house by which he remembered the crossroads had been one of those wantonly burned by Howe's army in the spring of 1777![52] Surprised by a score or more of militiamen hidden in the woods, the Rangers lost four prisoners, including their commander, to the enemy. Though they avenged themselves by mortally wounding Captain Voorhees, leader of the attacking party, they were obliged to make their escape, without recapturing Simcoe, to their supporting party at South Amboy, where they reembarked. The outing had not been so cheap as most of the Clinton-

[51] Simcoe, *op. cit.*, pp. 109-16. [52] *ibid.*, p. 116.

sponsored rural excursions; several of the participants had been killed and some wounded, and the colonel himself was forced to submit to the indignity of being taken as a prisoner by the insurgent rabble to Bordentown. It is a testimonial to the quality of the British military mind that Simcoe, after his repeated not-overly-gracious dealings with Jerseymen, seems to have been genuinely surprised and hurt that the inhabitants of Bordentown showed "umbrage" at seeing him walk about the streets.[53]

With the coming of the winter of 1779, the American army, which had left New Jersey for the north in June, once more returned to spend the winter. As on previous occasions, this move was determined by considerations of economic and strategic geography. Washington's force, a horde of benevolent locusts, had consumed nearly all the supplies and forage available in the rugged Hudson valley during its five-months stay there; and replenishments through the hills of Connecticut or the wild country to the west would be difficult under winter conditions of transportation.[54] Most of the provisions for the army must come from the south and west, and the farther it went in that direction without leaving the Hudson fortifications too unsupported, the less would be the cost and trouble of carriage. Furthermore, northern New Jersey had already proved itself well suited for winter cantonments—conveniently near New York City, but well protected by nature from sudden incursions. Accordingly, after a few small detachments had been stationed at and near Danbury and enough New Englanders left at the strongly fortified West Point to resist a possible surprise attack, the rest of the army was marched off to Morristown. There it could be safe from assault even when weakened by the detachment of considerable numbers sent to hamper Clin-

[53] Simcoe, *op. cit.*, pp. 116-18, 265-7 ; Robert Hanson Harrison to Heath, Oct. 28, 1779, Washington Papers, Vol. 119.
[54] Greene to Washington, Nov. 14, 1779, Washington Papers, Vol. 121.

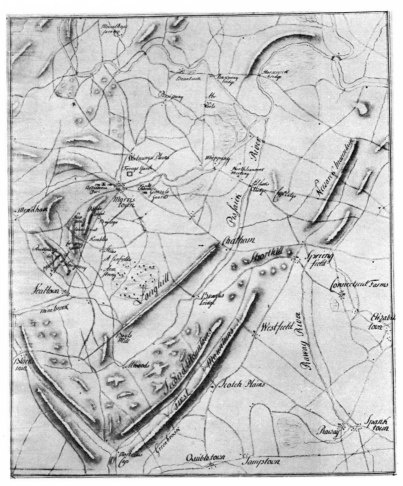

Washington's position at Morristown, 1780. Headquarters at Ford's House, shown in left center of map. Reproduced by permission of the William L. Clements Library.

ton's campaign in the Carolinas. A few outposts were established in such places as Paramus, Basking Ridge, Springfield, Pluckemin, and Monmouth County, to cover the country as well as might be from Clinton's raiders.[55]

The winter in Morristown proved to be a second Valley Forge. When the last soldiers arrived in the middle of December, they found two feet of snow on the ground, and no shelter prepared. The bitterest winter in decades was setting in, and the men, without tents or blankets, some of them "actually barefooted and almost naked," had to huddle for protection under flimsy structures of brushwood. Officers with horses were considered lucky, for they could use the horseblankets to keep themselves warm. In the course of time, tents were provided, but they offered little effective shelter, and were torn apart by such storms as the great blizzard of January 3, which piled the snow from four to six feet deep and buried some of the soldiers "like sheep" during the night. Construction was begun at once on log cabins, but it was the beginning of February before they were ready for occupancy.[56]

The higher officers did not have to sleep outdoors, but only because Washington took it upon himself to requisition quarters from the reluctant inhabitants.[57] Nathanael Greene, the new quartermaster general, was overwhelmed with demands for the use of his inadequate supply of lumber and carpenters. "Every officer," he lamented, "feels the peculiar inconveniences of his own situation, and is proportionably urgent for assistance." In consequence, even the commander-in-chief was unable for some time to obtain the new log kitchen imperatively required for his headquarters.[58]

[55] Washington to Gates, Nov. 17, *ibid.*; to Greene, Nov. 23 and 30, *ibid.*, Vol. 122; to Lt. Col. DeHart, Dec. 22, *ibid.*, Vol. 123; to Col. Armand, Dec. 23, *ibid.*; to Brig. Gen. Parsons, Dec. 13, *ibid.*; McClintock, *op. cit.*, p. 21.

[56] Thacher, *op. cit.*, pp. 215-28; Wayne to Washington, Dec. 9, Washington Papers, Vol. 122.

[57] Washington to Greene, Dec. 22, Washington Papers, Vol. 123.

[58] Greene to Washington, Jan. 21, 1780, *ibid.*, Vol. 126; Fitzpatrick, *op. cit.*, p. 369.

The tourist of today, visiting the stately Ford House in which Washington lived or the pleasant, admirably reconstructed campsite in the National Historical Park, finds it hard to recreate in his mind these scenes of discomfort and suffering. Even more difficult to imagine, in the solid ease of present-day Morristown, is the hunger which for weeks threatened the army with dissolution. By the end of 1779, the catastrophic depreciation of Continental currency had reached such a point that New Jersey farmers were unwilling to accept it in payment for their hay, grain, and livestock; and the credit of Congress and its agencies had utterly disappeared. The countryside abounded in all things needed by the famished soldiers; but "poverty in the midst of plenty" was the humiliating lot of the Continental defenders. The usual inefficiency among the auxiliary services played its part: while the men at Morristown went hungry, forty or fifty head of cattle belonging to the army were allowed to remain at Princeton, and over a hundred in the vicinity of Woodbury, long since purchased, were left to pursue the even tenor of their ways untroubled by the drover or the butcher.[59]

Whatever the reasons for the emergency,[60] the shivering Continentals working with numbed hands to raise their cabins on the hills outside Morristown were enfeebled by a starvation diet. "The whole army," one officer reports in December, "has been for seven or eight days entirely destitute of the staff of life; our only food is miserable fresh beef,

[59] Letter of Col. Francis Barber, Jan. 14, 1780, Washington Papers, Vol. 125.
[60] Nathanael Greene, quartermaster general, enumerated them in May: "The universal commotion among the people respecting the money, the heavy demands against the Department and the rage for oeconomy without regard to the service or the circumstances of the Army, the confusion the Department has been thrown into, the poverty of the treasury as well as the acknowledged want of activity from a defect of powers in Congress to draw forth the resources of the Country for the support of the Army."—Greene to Washington, May 21, 1780, Washington Papers, Vol. 136.

without bread, salt, or vegetables."[61] Another period might find a scanty supply of bread on hand, but no meat for a week. As early as December 16, Washington was writing: "The situation of the army with respect to supplies is beyond description alarming. . . . We have never experienced a like extremity at any period of the war. We have often felt temporary want from accidental delay in forwarding supplies; but we always had something in our magazines and the means of procuring more—Neither one nor the other is at present the case. . . . Unless some extraordinary and immediate exertions be made by the states from which we draw our supplies; there is every appearance that the army will infallibly disband in a fortnight."[62]

By January 8, when the soldiers had been reduced to robbing the inhabitants to save their lives,[63] Washington was forced to take drastic measures. He impressed supplies from each of the counties of New Jersey, enlisting the support of the local magistrates in the process by sending out a circular letter to them, explaining the emergency and requesting their assistance. The response to the appeal was universally gratifying. By the end of the month, the commander-in-chief was able to report to Congress:

"The situation of the Army for the present, is and has been for some days past, comfortable and easy on the score of provision. . . . I was obliged to call upon the Magistrates of every County in the State. . . . I should be wanting in justice to their zeal and attachment to that of the Inhabitants of the state in general, were I not to inform Congress, that they gave the earliest & most cheerful attention to my requisitions and exerted themselves for the Army's relief in a manner that did them the highest honor. They more than complied with the requisitions in many instances

[61] Thacher, *op. cit.*, p. 216.
[62] Washington to Livingston, Dec. 16, Washington Papers, Vol. 123.
[63] Quartermaster Joseph Lewis to Moore Furman, Jan. 8, 1780, in Ford House, Morristown.

and owing to their exertions in a great measure the Army has been kept together."[64]

The immediate crisis was over, but the basic problem was not solved: for the rest of the winter and spring the army lived from hand to mouth, and as late as the last week in April there were on hand in Morristown supplies of flour for only a week and of meat for two days.[65]

Not only the physical condition but the morale of the army was seriously impaired by the weeks of privation. The clothier general might declare: "The manly perseverance & virtuous resignation of the Soldiery under the compound Calamity of Starvation and Nakedness transcends past examples & exceeds credibility";[66] the inhabitants of Morristown and vicinity would have subscribed to no such eulogy without extensive reservations. During the height of the emergency, desperate soldiers had plundered civilians openly; and, once restraint had been broken, some of them continued the agreeable practice even when the worst of the stringency was over. A real grievance motivated much of this violence, for some inhabitants had not been above selling food to their defenders during the crisis at extortionate prices. It took several weeks and severe punitive measures on Washington's part to restore discipline to its normal level.[67] Under the surface, discontent continued to smolder within the ranks, and at the end of May, an abortive mutiny of two Connecticut regiments, though quickly suppressed,

[64] Washington to Huntington, Jan. 27, 1780, Washington Papers, Vol. 126. Scattered through Vols. 125 and 126 are the reports of the emissaries sent to the various neighborhoods. On the back of the draft of the circular letter of Jan. 8 (Vol. 124) is a table of the exact quantities of provisions to be collected from each county.

[65] N.J.H.S.P., 3rd S., Vol. III, p. 121. The Washington Papers for these months abound with references to the problem, and so do the letters of Quartermaster Joseph Lewis of Morristown (in Ford House, Morristown).

[66] Wilkinson to the Board of War, Jan. 4, Washington Papers, Vol. 124.

[67] Addresses of Morris County magistrates to Washington, Jan. 25 and Feb. 29, ibid., Vols. 126 and 129; Washington's reply, Jan. 27, ibid., Vol. 126; John Cleves Symmes to Washington, March 6, and Washington's reply, March 7, ibid., Vol. 129; Thacher, op. cit., pp. 222-4.

foreshadowed the much more serious outbursts which were to occur within less than a year.[68]

The uneasy monotony of camp life was broken in January by a raid on that perpetual temptation to unoccupied American forces in New Jersey, Staten Island. The moment seemed particularly opportune, since the uncommonly cold weather had frozen the Sound into a passable highway, at the same time that New York Upper Bay, over which any

[68] Thacher, *op. cit.*, pp. 235-6; Col. R. F. Meigs to Washington, May 26, Washington Papers, Vol. 136; John Henderson to Mr. Nicholson, May 27, in Ford House, Morristown. Gloomy though this winter was for the most part, it had its agreeable hours for the higher officers. Washington knew how to lighten the monotony of camp life by cheerful dinners and suppers, and the presence in Morristown of officers' wives and frequently of distinguished civilian guests permitted considerable social gaiety. An engaging and little known facet in the personality of the austere Father of His Country appears when we catch a glimpse of him at a large dinner given by Colonel Biddle. In the course of a hilarious evening, the commander-in-chief cast aside his dignity long enough to engage in a "scuffle" with Mrs. George Olney of Rhode Island, with the result that before long gossipy tongues were spreading a highly colored tale to the effect that "Mrs· Olney, in a violent rage, told him, if he did not let go her hand, she would tear out his Eyes, or the hair from his Head; and that tho' he was a General, he was but a Man." (Contemporary certified copies of letter from George Olney to Tilghman, March 11, 1781, and reply, March 14, in possession of Judge Pickersgill, Perth Amboy.) The climax of the social season came in April, when the French Minister, the Chevalier de la Luzerne, and the Spanish agent in Philadelphia, Don Juan de Miralles, visited camp. The army paraded smartly before the distinguished guests, to general admiration; a grand ball followed the review; and the officers of the artillery topped off the occasion with a display of fireworks. The most spectacular event of the visit, however, had not been scheduled. Don Juan de Miralles was stricken with pneumonia and died. He was given a state funeral, and the local rustics were dazzled with the sumptuousness of the coffin, the magnificence of the corpse, tricked out in scarlet full-dress with a profusion of gold lace, bejeweled shoe and knee buckles, diamond rings, and other knick knacks, and the impressiveness of the mile-long funeral procession. Don Juan provided Morristown with a fine spectacle indeed, and the enjoyment of it was enhanced by the consideration that, for all his wealth and splendor, he was dead. As one New England officer wrote in his journal, with relish: "Here we behold the end of all earthly riches, pomp, and dignity. The ashes of Don Miralles mingle with the remains of those who are clothed in humble shrouds, and whose career in life was marked with sordid poverty and wretchedness." It was necessary to set a guard over the grave, lest the soldiers dig up the valuable contents. (Thacher, *op. cit.*, pp. 228-31.)

reinforcements for the island would have to come from Manhattan, was shut off by floating ice.

The expedition was prepared in all secrecy, and some three thousand troops under Lord Stirling, having sped over the snow from Morristown in several hundred sleighs, crossed the Sound early in the moning of January 15. As always, however, the attempt at a surprise was a failure. The British, who were on their guard, retired into their fortifications, where they could defy attack; and Stirling could bring off only a handful of prisoners and some blankets and stores.[69]

Much more disturbing than the failure of the raid was the revelation it gave of the deterioration of civilian morale. Hordes of persons from the New Jersey side of the Sound, exasperated by the depredations they had suffered for years at the hands of the British, accompanied the expedition across the ice in the guise of militiamen and avenged themselves by plundering with marked brutality not the redcoats themselves, who had little of value to lose, but the helpless inhabitants of the island. Stirling and his men did their best to check the looters and deprive them of their swag, and all that could be recovered was returned to the British authorities a few days later, but, as one prominent citizen of Elizabeth-Town wrote: "From the vast multitude who greedily rushed to plunder, our Country has rec\u1d48. such disgrace as will not be easily, I may say possibly, wiped off."[70] Furthermore, the royal authorities now could justify their depredations in New Jersey under pretext of retaliation, and the outraged farmers of Staten Island were clamoring to join the regulars in punitive measures.[71]

[69] Thacher, *op. cit.*, p. 225; Simcoe, *op. cit.*, pp. 120-9; circular letter of Joseph Lewis, Jan. 12, 1780, in Ford House, Morristown; Lewis to Moore Furman, Jan. 15 and 22, *ibid.*; following letters in Washington Papers, Vol. 125: Wm. Irvine to Washington, Jan. 12; Stirling to Washington, Jan. 13, 14 and 16; Washington to Stirling, Jan. 13 and 14; Hamilton to Stirling, Jan. 14.

[70] James Caldwell to Washington, Jan. 19, 1780, Washington Papers, Vol. 125; Stirling to Washington, Jan. 16, *ibid.*

[71] Col. Moses Hazen to Washington, Jan. 19, *ibid.*; Charles Cameron to Caldwell, Jan. 25, *ibid.*, Vol. 126.

It was, indeed, less than two weeks before the British struck back. On the night of January 25, they surprised both Newark and Elizabeth-Town, captured a number of soldiers and kidnapped several prominent Whigs. At Newark, the Academy was burned; at Elizabeth-Town, the courthouse and the pride of the town, the meeting house.[72] As one local bard put it:

> Their first attempt in vain they try,
> The reluctant fire seems to die,
> But soon they try the other end,
> And lo! the kindled flames ascend.

> Alas! the building all has fell,
> The pulpit, pinnacle, and bell,
> And rows of beauteous windows round,
> Are melted and lie on the ground.[73]

This exploit marked the opening of a new series of raids in Essex and Bergen Counties, which kept those districts in a state of uneasiness during the rest of the winter and spring.[74] The vernal season, indeed, brought little joy. The hard winter, which had killed fruit trees, timber, and winter wheat, was followed by a cold and backward spring. Hundreds of cattle were reported to have perished for want of fodder. "The prospect of Scarcity," wrote one mournful Quaker, "of Cleanness of teeth and want of Bread more and

[72] Col. Moses Hazen to Washington, Jan. 26 and 29, Washington Papers, Vol. 126; Washington to Congress, Jan. 27, *ibid.*; minutes of court of inquiry, Jan. 30, *ibid.*, Vol. 127; Joseph Lewis to Moore Furman, Jan. 27, in Ford House, Morristown.

[73] David Chandler, "Verses composed on the burning of the Meeting-House in Elizabeth-town," quoted in *N.J.H.S.P.*, 3rd S., Vol. IX, p. 16.

[74] St. Clair to Washington, Feb. 11 and 20, 1780, Washington Papers, Vols. 127 and 128; James Abeel to Col. Mead, Feb. 13, *ibid.*, Vol. 128; letter of Thunis Dey *et al.*, March 24, Livingston Papers, Box 2; Simcoe, *op. cit.*, pp. 140-2; Jonathan Hallet to Washington, April 16, Washington Papers, Vol. 133; Maxwell to Washington, May 15, 26 and 28, *ibid.*, Vols. 135 and 136; Caldwell to Washington, May 18, *ibid.*, Vol. 135; Washington to Stirling, May 19, and to Maxwell, May 28, *ibid.*, Vols. 135 and 136; Major Thomas Moore to Washington, May 22, *ibid.*, Vol. 136; Thacher, *op. cit.*, p. 228.

more appeared, & the Crys of the poor began to be heard in our once plentyful & peaceful Land."[75] At Morristown, there was especial reason for gloom. "Public business is in a wretched train," wrote General Greene, "all things at a stand."[76] National finances were still disorganized; and "the great departments of the army," as Washington informed a friend, "are now in total confusion."[77] The commander-in-chief was more despondent than he had been since 1777, as he saw repeated before his eyes the old story of a dwindling army. "It is to be lamented," he confided to his brother, "—bitterly lamented—and in the anguish of Soul I do lament, that our fatal & accursed policy should bring the 6ᵗʰ. of June upon us and not a single recruit to the army. . . . Thus it is, one year rolls over another—and without some change—we are hastening to our ruin."[78] A committee of the Continental Congress, visiting Morristown to consider reforms in the military organization, fully shared these dismal convictions. Unless changes were adopted with a celerity equal to the occasion, they declared, "the period which is to end our Liberty, and commence the most disgraceful State of Slavery which human nature has ever experienced is not far distant."[79]

These reasons for disquietude were intensified when news arrived from the south at the beginning of June 1780 that Charleston had fallen and that General Lincoln and the entire Southern army had been taken prisoners by Clinton. At this dark moment General Knyphausen, commanding in New York, struck the last heavy blow which New Jersey was to suffer in the war, the strange expedition in the direction of Morristown, which got no farther than Springfield. What the purpose of this movement may have been it is still

75 John Hunt, Diary, in *N.J.H.S.P.*, Vol. LII, pp. 237-8.
76 Greene to Washington, Washington Papers, Vol. 132.
77 Washington to Laurens, April 26, *ibid.*, Vol. 134.
78 Washington to John Augustine Washington, June 6, *ibid.*, Vol. 137.
79 Circular letter, June 12, *ibid.*, Vol. 138.

impossible to determine with certainty today, as it was at the time. Two officers who were compatriots of the general and ought to have known as well as anyone what was in his mind assert, one tentatively and one positively, that his aim was to test the rumors constantly reaching headquarters that war-weariness among the Americans had reached the danger point. According to these reports, the militia would not rise again to resist an invasion, and the Connecticut regiments, which had recently mutinied, and perhaps other troops as well, would desert to the enemy if given a favorable opportunity. One of these officers adds, "with certainty," that had dispatches from Clinton arrived before the expedition got under way, instead of just afterwards, the entire enterprise would have been cancelled.[80]

Among the Americans, various explanations were current. One suggested that Knyphausen had struck to divert Washington from an expected move in the direction of White Plains, until reinforcements should arrive from Clinton.[81] Another, based on secret news from New York, supposed that control of the Hudson was involved: the raid was

[80] Letter of Johann Friedrich von Cochenhausen, June 30, 1780, in Von Jungkenn MSS., 3:34, and letter of Carl Leopold von Baurmeister, *ibid.*, 3:38.

[81] Anonymous communication endorsed "June 1780. Intelligence," mistakenly filed under date of June 4 in Washington Papers, Vol. 137. It is true that the arrival in American waters of a French naval squadron commanded by the Chevalier de Ternay had briefly revived Washington's perennial dream of a joint attack on New York by land and sea. During the month of May he had hoped that quick and energetic action by the French fleet and the American army might lead to a spectacular success while the British garrison was still weakened by the absence of Clinton's expeditionary force, and he had gone so far as to arrange for pilots to be in readiness at Black Point to guide the French into New York harbor. (See abstract of letter from Lafayette to de Ternay, May 19, 1780, in catalogue of the Destouches Papers sold by the American Art Association, Dec. 1, 1926.) Like most of Washington's more ambitious military schemes, however, this project failed to materialize, through no fault of his. By June 1, when a spy in New York warned him of an impending operation in New Jersey (message in secret ink, Washington Papers, Vol. 137), he was already thinking in the familiar terms of defensive action only. (Washington to Major Talbot, June 4, to Gov. Trumbull, June 1, and to Dayton, June 3, *ibid.*)

intended either to put the American army to flight and seize
its artillery and stores in and about Morristown, after which
an attack upon West Point would present few difficulties, or
else to keep Washington occupied until Clinton's force,
returning from South Carolina, should have time to proceed
directly up the Hudson and seize the American fortifications.[82]

Whatever aims Knyphausen may have had in view, so
indefinite were the reports which reached Morristown that
when the invading force of some three thousand men—British regulars, German auxiliaries, and Loyalists, including
some from New Jersey—crossed over from Staten Island on
the night of June 6, they caught the Americans unprepared.
A few hundred militiamen and New Jersey Continentals
stationed at Elizabeth-Town under General Maxwell fell
back from their post, though not without offering energetic
resistance. General Sterling, who had been put in command
of the expedition by Knyphausen, was so badly wounded
almost at once that he had to be replaced by a German
officer; and as the invaders proceeded to the village of Connecticut Farms they were under a constant fire from the
retiring Americans. From that hamlet on, the advance became increasingly difficult, as the militiamen began to collect
from the surrounding countryside and to supplement the
defense by a galling fire from every thicket and woodland.
By mid-afternoon, Maxwell's force had received a further
stiffening from the Continental army, and was fighting so
stubbornly that Knyphausen, arriving to take personal charge
of the attack, was obliged to withdraw his men some distance
from their most advanced position only a half mile from
Springfield.

As darkness came on, the unwelcome visitors encamped
for the night, presumably in the expectation of pressing on

[82] General Robert Howe to Washington, July 16, Washington Papers,
Vol. 138.

through Springfield in the morning and seizing control of the Short Hills which dominate the nearby pass through the double mountain range. Disquieting reports brought in by American deserters altered these plans. General Washington, said the informants, was advancing with his army, and was expected in Springfield in the course of the evening; furthermore, he had detached Lord Stirling to outflank the expedition and cut it off from the water. Knyphausen wasted no time. His tired men were set in motion again, and reached Elizabeth-Town Point in the early morning hours.[83]

So far, the enterprise had brought the British and Hessians neither glory nor advantage; but it had, as usual, left sorrow and devastation in its wake. The pleasant hamlet of Connecticut Farms had been plundered and laid waste. It was necessary to set fire to some houses, says the one Hessian officer who seems to have considered the matter worthy of record, because the militia were shooting from them; but that explanation hardly accounts adequately for the burning of ten dwelling houses, the meeting house, the parsonage, the schoolhouse, and numerous barns, shops, sheds, bee houses, milk houses, and cow houses; or for the destruction of the Widow Clark's four hundred apple trees; or for the extensive looting; or for the wanton murder of Mrs. Caldwell, wife of the Presbyterian minister, as she sat quietly with her children indoors.[84] These outrages stirred up the flagging zeal of Jerseymen, and brought them out in furious swarms when Knyphausen next ventured inland.

[83] The best account I have found of this stage of the Springfield offensive is in the journal of the Jäger Corps, Von Jungkenn MSS., 7:13. Other pertinent sources are letters from Cochenhausen and Baurmeister, Von Jungkenn MSS., 3:34 and 3:38 respectively (diagram of Knyphausen's order of battle in former); extract of another Hessian journal, *ibid.*, 7:14; Washington to Talbot and Dayton to Washington, June 7, both in Washington Papers, Vol. 137; Washington to President Huntington, June 10, *ibid.*, Vol. 138; Maxwell to Livingston, June 14, copy in Sparks MSS., 49, Vol. III.

[84] MS. book, *Damages by the British in New Jersey, 1776-1782. Essex County*, in State Library, Trenton. The murder of Mrs. Caldwell is described in numerous works, *e.g.* Thacher, *op. cit.*, pp. 236-7; Quincy, *op. cit.*, p. 31.

For more than two weeks after this initial fiasco, Knyphausen's force remained quiet, part of it withdrawn to the
security of Staten Island, part of it entrenched at Elizabeth-
Town Point. Well over a thousand of the militia remained
embodied, and, with some of the Continentals, plagued the
enemy as best they could. From time to time, advanced posts
on both sides were shifted; and Elizabeth-Town was for a
while on the front lines, with the stone bridge over its creek
a no-man's land between the pickets of the hostile forces on
opposite banks.[85]

Washington, meanwhile, was on tenterhooks. That some
sinister purpose must lie behind this incursion he felt almost
certain, and more and more he inclined to suspect that it was
a ruse to keep him from moving to defend West Point
against a sudden blow up the Hudson. Yet could he be sure
enough to move his army away from the passage through the
hills at Springfield, which it was now guarding? In order
to strengthen the river fortresses, would he be justified in
exposing to capture or destruction the provisions, baggage,
and stores of his army in and about Morristown?[86]

While the commander-in-chief thus fretted, sharp-eyed
lookouts, posted at intervals for over fifty miles along the
New Jersey shore, scanned the horizon vigilantly. Peering
through the haze, some of them dimly made out at last, on
June 17, what Washington was most dreading: the sails of
a great fleet standing in for Sandy Hook. General Clinton
was back from South Carolina with his victorious army.[87]

[85] "Return of the several Regiments &.ᶜ of Militia now doing duty on the
Lines . . . June 19th 1780" in box labelled "New Jersey Miscellaneous, 1664-
1853," MSS. Division, Library of Congress; Von Jungkenn MSS., 7:13; Wash-
ington to Dickinson, June 13, Washington Papers, Vol. 138; Washington to
Stirling, June 8, original in Ford House, Morristown; Green, *Life of Ashbel
Green*, pp. 110-14.

[86] Washington to Howe, June 15, and to Heath, June 20, Washington Papers,
Vol. 138.

[87] Forman to Washington, June 17, John Stillman to Forman, June 16, 17, 18,
ibid.

Washington's hesitation was over. On June 18, the same day the news reached headquarters, an order was sent to Morristown to engage all available means of transport to move from northern New Jersey to Pennsylvania, with the utmost dispatch, all army stores not immediately needed.[88] General Greene, the quartermaster general, was instructed to hurry seventeen hundred barrels of flour from Trenton to the North River fortresses, "and to get this army in a moving condition." All officers at Morristown were commanded to be in camp at Springfield by afternoon, without fail. To the governors of New York and Connecticut went urgent pleas to assemble their militia; to the Council of Massachusetts, an entreaty to send reinforcements. "Ride night and day!" was the admonition to those who bore the messages. "There is no time to be lost," declared the general. "The movements of the enemy will probably be rapid and a correspondent spirit of energy should animate our efforts."[89]

Every new report seemed to justify this frantic activity. From the Highlands of the Hudson on June 18 came news that six enemy vessels had hove in sight of Verplanck's Point. Major Lee declared to Washington the next day, on the strength of reports coming in from behind the British lines: "I am privily of opinion you will hear of General Clintons being before West Point in less than 48 hours."[90] By the twenty-first of the month, the commander-in-chief was off to meet the danger with a sizable portion of his army, leaving Greene to hold the pass at Springfield with the rest.[91]

Clinton acted as promptly as if this were just what he had been waiting for. He had already personally inspected his troops in New Jersey, and early in the morning of June 23, with considerable additions from Staten Island, they

[88] Joseph Lewis to Major William Stevens, June 18 (two letters) and Major Claibourne, June 20, in Ford House, Morristown.

[89] Washington to Forman, to Greene, to Howe, to Congress, June 18, Washington Papers, Vol. 138.

[90] *ibid*.   [91] Various orders, June 21, *ibid.,* Vol. 139.

began a rapid advance northward from Elizabeth-Town. The entire corps did not amount to more than four or five thousand; but even so it was stronger than the total number of Continentals Washington would have been able to muster in opposition before his departure with the reinforcement for West Point. Greene had received ample warning from spies—possibly because Clinton intended he should[92]—and had made such poor preparations for defense as lay in his power. Just beyond Connecticut Farms, Colonel Dayton's New Jersey regiment held up the advance of greatly superior numbers for a short time; then all the Americans retreated to the vicinity of Springfield, where the Rahway River offered a defensible barrier. The attackers now divided into two columns. The right, commanded by Major General Mathews, headed by the Queen's Rangers under Colonel Simcoe, the old friend of the Jerseyman, and including some of Skinner's New Jersey Volunteers, forced a way across the river at Vauxhall, some distance above Springfield, despite the stiff opposition of a corps under Major Lee. Meanwhile, the left and principal column, under Knyphausen, met even more stubborn resistance at the bridge leading directly into Springfield. The flooring of the structure had been torn up, and for forty minutes Colonel Angell's Rhode Island regiment, with some other small detachments and one piece of artillery, frustrated the attempts of the Jägers to rush across on the string-pieces. Eventually the Hessians made their way to the other side of the river—not over the bridge, but by fording the waist-high stream. By this time General Mathew's column was approaching down the road from Vauxhall, and Greene, afraid lest part of his scanty force be trapped between two enemies, abandoned the village and withdrew all his men to heights some distance away which commanded the approaches to the pass.

[92] Dickinson to Washington, June 20; Greene to Washington, June 22, *ibid.*, Vol. 139.

Knyphausen, however, showed no inclination to push farther. The opposition he had met had been wholehearted but inadequate; it may well be that despite the increasing numbers of the militia and the greater difficulties of the terrain, he could have forced his way through the pass and on to Morristown. Such a course of action he did not attempt, and the fact that his corps had brought no baggage indicates that no such ambitious *coup* had been contemplated. After resting his men an hour and a half in Springfield, while the Americans cannonaded him briskly but ineffectively, he set the village afire and started home. The militia, who were hastening in from the entire countryside, pursued and did some execution, but Knyphausen moved swiftly, and by one o'clock the next morning the last of his men had passed by a pontoon bridge to the safety of Staten Island.[93]

Greene and other Americans professed complete mystification as to the purpose of this apparently senseless foray. Knyphausen's subordinates were no wiser. The commander of the Jägers, the troops who had borne the brunt of the militia's vengeance during the retreat, wrote home to Kassel: "I regret from the depths of my heart that the great loss of the Jägers took place to no greater purpose."[94] If the first raid at the beginning of the month had really been intended to test the morale of Washington's army and of the people of New Jersey, Knyphausen had received his answer on the way home from Connecticut Farms. The only explanation of this second attack which seems to make sense, if Clinton's actions are to be regarded as those of a rational being, is that it was an unsuccessful attempt to lure Washington back while another expedition from New York should strike

[93] The most useful accounts of the Springfield affair are to be found in Simcoe, *op. cit.*, pp. 143-7; Green, *Life of Ashbel Green*, pp. 117-21; Stirling to Washington, June 23, Washington Papers, Vol. 139; Greene to Washington, June 24, *ibid.*; Von Jungkenn MSS., 7:13; *Damages by the British in . . . Essex County.*

[94] Ludwig Adolph Johann von Wurmb (to von Jungkenn?), July 1, Von Jungkenn MSS., 3:35.

swiftly at the weakly held river fortresses. At any rate, Washington was not lured back, and no expedition up the river was made.

Whatever Clinton's purpose, the burning of almost the entire village of Springfield, a larger community than Connecticut Farms, was an act of wanton cruelty. To some Jerseymen it seemed that their cup of sorrows and indignities was running over. In the words of one militiaman who made his way home over the scene of battle:

"The whole scene was one of gloomy horror—a dead horse, a broken carriage of a fieldpiece, a town laid in ashes, the former inhabitants standing over the ruins of their dwellings, and the unburied dead, covered with blood and with the flies that were devouring it, filled me with melancholy feelings, till I was ready to say—Is the contest worth all this?"[95]

It would have comforted such despondent citizens to know that New Jersey had seen the last military engagement of any consequence to be fought on its soil during the war. The long and harrowing drama was nearing its close. One more spectacular episode, however, had still to be played before the curtain finally fell. At the opening of the year 1781, a double mutiny broke out in the army among troops which had reached the limit of their endurance.

Of all the sad aspects of the war, one of the most distressing and most unnecessary was the constant suffering of the army from lack of the provision which the reasonably prosperous country could well have afforded. The absence of any centralized authority, the jealous anxiety among the states lest one might be called upon to do more than its proportional share in the common cause, the rudimentary degree of development of national consciousness, the selfish unwillingness of solid citizens to be taxed in support of a war to which many were indifferent or secretly opposed, the in-

[95] Green, *op. cit.*, pp. 120-1.

efficiency of politicians to whom personal ambition was more important than the common weal, and above all, the catastrophic depreciation of currency attributable largely to these other factors—such conditions reacted disastrously upon the welfare of the army. The extent to which the winter at Valley Forge has been dramatized in American tradition as a spectacular incident has tended to obscure the fact that that episode represents a normal rather than an exceptional state of affairs. As we have seen, the second winter at Morristown yielded little to Valley Forge in point of misery, and the underlying causes of such horrors were never removed as long as the war lasted.

Most of the responsibility for the sufferings of the soldiers lies at the doors of the various states, which neglected to clothe or pay their troops at all adequately; and in this respect it is clear that New Jersey was no better than the rest, and probably worse than some. From October 1776, when Richard Stockton, visiting Dayton's "barefooted and barelegged" regiment at Ticonderoga, appealed to friends at home for clothing,[96] there was scarcely a time when the men from New Jersey were well clad.[97] in the spring of 1780, complaints of the inefficiency of Enos Kelsey, clothier general for the state, were so strong and so detailed that the legislature authorized an investigation which seems to have brought incriminating facts to light. So far as the records show, however, nothing was done to remedy the situation thus revealed, and one more potential political scandal was hushed up by the lethargy or the dishonesty of the conscript fathers.[98]

Another source of complaint, common among both officers and men, was the failure of the legislature to readjust the

[96] *Am. Arch.*, 5th S., Vol. II, pp. 1274-5.
[97] See for example *Votes and Proceedings* of the Assembly, Sept. 21 and Nov. 6, 1777; communication of New Jersey officers to Council of Safety, July 30, 1778 (Room 118, State Library).
[98] Votes of Assembly, May 15, 24, 26, 27, and 30, 1780.

pay of its soldiers to keep pace with the depreciation of the currency. Time and again the matter was brought to the attention of the legislature, but nothing was done. By the spring of 1779, the officers of the New Jersey Brigade were desperate, and addressed their employers in no ambiguous terms:

"The Legislature need not be informed that our pay is now only *nominal*, not real, that four Months pay of a Private will not procure his Wretched Wife and Children a *single* bushel of wheat.—The situation of your officers is worse—The pay of a Colonel of *your* Regiment will not purchase the Oats for his Horse, nor will his whole days pay procure him a single Dinner. . . . Congress seeing the enormous rise of the Necessaries of life, so long ago as Decemb^r. 1777 recommended it to the several States to provide all necessary Clothing for their officers and Soldiers at prices proportioned to their pay—We had examples of the States both to the Southard and Eastward complying with this Resolution, and in many instances, exceeding it,—

"That your Troops are less Brave, or have done less duty than any Troops in the Union, is a position, that none have been hardy enough to Advance; and why they should be so long neglected, is a problem in politics hard to be explained."[99]

General Maxwell strongly seconded this remonstrance:

"I have wrote or waited on you at every time of your sitting for two years past, or permitted officers to wait on you, that a close attention to my Duty would permit me, with a design to draw your attention to the distresses of the Officers, or Soldiers of your Brigade. . . . With respect to the distresses of your Troops, I have no doubt they are visible to the meanest capacity in the country. They have been so shamefully neglected by the Legislature of the State that I am now at a Loss how to address on the Subject. . . .

[99] Address of officers to Council and Assembly, April 17, 1779, Washington Papers, Vol. 103.

"It is useless for you to say you are not able to pay in full value I ask pardon I know better, your Merchants and Farmers never were so rich in this World before I cannot say what provision they have laid up for the other World but if We are to judge by the old rules 'To lay up Treasures in Heaven such as Charity Virtue Public spiritedness &cᵃ. &cᵃ. I think they have not put much in that Bank lately it is likely they intend it when the Hard Money comes in use. The Farmer as well as the Merchant is come to knowledge that everything is worth what it will bring and not withstanding he knows that the Security of his Property & Privileges has cost the Soldier dear in Heats Colds Thirsting Hunger & Watchings yet they will make no scruple to strip him of his Month's pittance one for a days Subsistence and the other for a Toy; Charity will not carry any of them further than a drink of coldwater which shews the absolute necessity of the Officers and Soldiers having a decent subsistence to support them according to the Custom of the Times without trusting to Charity."[100]

When nearly a month had elapsed and the legislature had indicated no intention of acting upon these pleas, but had instead referred the matter to Congress, twenty-one officers of the First Regiment sent in a collective resignation on May 6, to take effect unless they should be afforded relief within three days.[101] Their action precipitated a crisis. Washington interceded to urge reconsideration, since the wholesale withdrawal would cripple Sullivan's impending expedition against the Indians;[102] but the officers remained firm. "We have lost all confidence in our Legislature," they insisted; "Reason and Experience forbid that we should have any."[103] As for that august body, it was unwilling to yield anything under duress, "and some of the Obstinate Members

---

[100] Maxwell to Governor, Council and Assembly, April 25, 1779, Room 118, State Library.

[101] *N.J. Exec. Corr.*, pp. 156-7.   [102] *ibid.*, pp. 161-4.

[103] Jonathan Forman to Washington, Washington Papers, Vol. 106.

talked of rather seeing the Brigade disbanded than Submit to the appearance of being bullyed."[104]

The impasse was broken by Lord Stirling, who happened to be in Trenton. "As I saw that the Appearance was now the Chief Obstacle in the Way," he reports, "I proposed to some of the leading Members the expedient of withdrawing the Memorial and the Legislature takeing the Matter up (to all appearance) of their own meer Motion this was Instantly agreed to on all sides, and in a few hours pretty ample resolves were made by both houses, among the rest it was ordered that £200 be paid to each Commissioned Officer & 40 dollars to each Soldier to enable them to pay their debts & to fit them for the Campaign."[105]

One immediate crisis had been surmounted by last-minute concessions, and within a few weeks further legislation which temporarily removed some of the grievances was passed;[106] but the lawmakers still showed a strong tendency to saddle upon Congress all responsibility for sweeping improvements,[107] and discontent persisted.

Before another year had passed, a further source of contention appeared in the case of the common soldier. Enlisting for the army had long been conducted in haphazard fashion, and many of the troops now insisted that they were being held beyond the term of service to which they had agreed. Those who had signed up "for three years or for the war" considered themselves at liberty at the expiration of the third year; their officers sometimes gave the words a different interpretation. Furthermore, there were often inconsistencies between muster-rolls and enlistment certificates as to the length of service, and records were not infrequently lost, with the result that officers and men disagreed as to what had been in them. A special incitement to restlessness, particularly among early recruits from Pennsylvania and

[104] Stirling to Washington, May 10, 1781, *ibid.*   [105] *ibid.*
[106] Wilson, *Acts of New Jersey*, Chap. CL.
[107] Votes of Assembly, Dec. 7, 1779.

New Jersey, was the disparity between their poverty-stricken condition and the prosperity of late comers, especially from New England, who had been lured into service for short periods by generous bounties. The natural effect was to increase desertions and to raise a clamor, among all those who had any shadow of claim, for a discharge in order that they might reenlist under more favorable conditions.[108]

As early as the beginning of 1780 these difficulties were giving the commander-in-chief considerable worry, and a year later they precipitated the most acute internal crisis the army had faced since the end of 1776. Washington's headquarters for the winter of 1780-1781 were at New Windsor, near the Hudson in the state of New York; but the Pennsylvania regiments were encamped again at Morristown, and those of New Jersey at Pompton and Chatham. Life was none too pleasant for the troops. Those from Pennsylvania, in particular, were in a pitiable state for want of clothes and blankets, and, what seemed an equal hardship for them, they were compelled to go for weeks with hardly a drop of liquor to revive their "drooping spirits."[109] It was inevitable that the men should contrast their privations with the luxury of Philadelphia, known to them by report, and with the prosperity of the countryside about Morristown, flowing with milk and honey, or, more pertinently, hard cider and applejack.[110]

On the evening of New Year's Day, 1781, almost the entire Pennsylvania Line suddenly turned out by prearrangement, seized the ammunition and artillery, spiked two of the fieldpieces, and prepared to march off with the other four. Efforts of the officers to restore discipline were unavailing; one of them was killed, two were mortally wounded, and

---

[108] Thacher, *op. cit.*, pp. 295-6; John Cleves Symmes to Caleb Camp, Feb. 14, 1780, Washington Papers, Vol. 128; Washington to Livingston, Feb. 19, *ibid.*

[109] Wayne to John Moylan, Dec. 30, 1780, in Wayne MSS., Vol. XI, p. 89, Historical Society of Pennsylvania; same to Col. Azariah Dunham, Dec. 7, and reply Dec. 9, *ibid.*, Vol. XI, pp. 27, 30.

[110] *ibid.*, Heath, *op. cit.*, pp. 284-5.

others were injured by blows from muskets, bayonets and stones. Even General Wayne, who was very popular in the ranks, failed to persuade the mutineers to lay down their arms; and at eleven at night they marched off to Princeton. The alarmed inhabitants of that village received them with generous if nervous hospitality, and the troops for their part behaved "with the greatest decorum." They promised to turn and fight the British if the latter should attempt to take advantage of the situation by making an incursion into the state, and they handed over to Wayne two emissaries whom Clinton had sent to lure them into his lines by lavish promises. Nevertheless, the mutineers made it clear that their intentions were firm: they were going on to Philadelphia to demand justice from Congress in respect to overdue discharges and arrears of pay.

It was one of the strangest mutinies in history. General Wayne, the commanding officer against whom the men had risen, accompanied them voluntarily to Princeton and Trenton, haranguing, pleading, and negotiating; and the soldiers, after the initial skirmish, offered violence to neither officers nor inhabitants. Since the revolters had so much justice on their side, Congress and the state of Pennsylvania soon capitulated. It was agreed that enlistments for three years or the duration of the war were to be considered as expiring at the end of the third year. Commissioners appointed by Congress went to work at once to put the decision into effect, and so urgent was the situation that they did not wait even for the officers to produce the enlistment papers in question, with the result, it was later discovered, that many who had enlisted expressly for the duration of the war received discharges. In consequence of the settlement, somewhat more than half the men were released from the army, and the rest were furloughed for a couple of months. Once this grievance had been removed, considerable numbers showed themselves anxious to reenlist for new bounties, so that the total decrease

of men in the Pennsylvania Line in consequence of the
January rising was probably slight.[111]

By the end of the month, the difficulties were over, so far
as the Pennsylvania troops were concerned, and in all probability their regiments were more reliable with a dangerous
source of friction removed; but an example had been set for
soldiers from other states. It was followed with little delay
by the discontented Jerseymen. Shaken out of its inaction
by the alarming events of early January, the legislature at
Trenton had hastily appointed a committee of three "for
the purpose of liquidating & settling deficiencies of pay of
troops of the state, occasioned by depreciation of Cont. currency."[112] The commissioners were also authorized to investigate "any Uneasiness . . . among the Soldiers respecting
their being detained beyond the Term for which they engaged"; but, upon inquiring of the officers at camp, they were
assured "that they knew of no Uneasiness then in the
Brigade; that very few had ever complained of being un-
justly detained; and that therefore they conceived it unnecessary then to go into any Examination on the Subject."[113]

Never was complacency less justified. Some two or three
hundred of the soldiers, unaware that the commissioners who
were in camp computing and disbursing back pay were also
empowered to explore the problem of enlistments, left their
huts near Pompton on the evening of January 20 and
advanced upon the headquarters of the brigade at Chatham.
Although the recklessness of the mutineers may well have
been stimulated by the quantities of liquor they had been
able to buy with their back pay, their behavior was in no way

111 Thacher, *op. cit.*, pp. 295-300; Wayne to Washington, Jan. 2, 8, 21 and
29, 1781, Wayne MSS., Vol. XI; proclamation by Wayne, Jan. 2, *ibid.*; "Proposals from a Committee of Serjeants," Jan. 4, *ibid.*; Wayne to Gov. Reed,
Jan. 8, *ibid.*; Elias Boudinot to Livingston, Jan. 2, Sparks MSS., 49, Vol. III;
Samuel Smith to Livingston, Jan. 3, *ibid.*; James Burnside to Livingston,
Jan. 11, *ibid.*
112 Wilson, *Acts of New Jersey*, Chap. CCXL.
113 Votes of Assembly, June 5, 1781.

violent. "They left the Camp with great Decency," reports Commissioner Frelinghuysen, "& discovered a great Affection for their Officers."[114] Deaf to the pleadings of the latter, however, they continued rebellious until the next day, when they returned to their quarters upon being promised a pardon by the officers and a hearing of their complaints by the commissioners.[115]

It had been a rising of the mildest sort, but General Washington, as soon as he heard of it, determined to put an end to such dangerous insubordination. Five hundred men under the command of Major General Robert Howe were sent out from New Windsor to restore order at Pompton, and, after having struggled through deep snow for several days, they arrived at dawn on January 27 outside the huts of the insurgents. The buildings were soon surrounded, two fieldpieces were trained upon them, and the occupants were ordered to parade in line without arms. The startled troops complied meekly with the order, whereupon three of their ringleaders were given a summary trial on the spot and condemned to be shot. "Twelve of the most guilty mutineers," says an eyewitness, "were next selected to be their executioners. This was a most painful task; being themselves guilty, they were greatly distressed with the duty imposed on them, and when ordered to load, some of them shed tears. The wretched victims, overwhelmed by the terrors of death, had neither time nor . . . power to implore the mercy and forgiveness of their God, and such was their agonizing condition, that no heart could refrain from emotions of sympathy and compassion." After two had been shot, the third was pardoned.

"Never were men more completely humbled and penitent; tears of sorrow, and of joy, rushed from their eyes, and each one appeared to congratulate himself, that his forfeited life

[114] Frederick Frelinghuysen to Washington, Jan. 20, 1781, in Gratz MSS., Historical Society of Pennsylvania.
[115] Draft letter, unsigned, Jan. 26, in Sparks MSS., 49, Vol. III.

had been spared. The executions being finished, General Howe ordered the former officers to take their stations, and assume their respective commands; he then, in a very pathetic and affecting manner, addressed the whole line by platoons, endeavoring to impress their minds with a sense of the enormity of their crime, and the dreadful consequences that might have resulted. He then commanded them to ask pardon of their officers, and promise to devote themselves to the faithful discharge of their duty as soldiers in the future."[116]

The dangerous spark of mutiny appeared to have been safely extinguished before it had had time to kindle a blaze that might have destroyed the rickety American army. To prevent its flaring again, Washington was anxious for an improvement in the lot of the soldiers. "Without this," he declared, "it may be smothered for a while, but it must again break out with greater violence.—It is not to be expected that an Army can be permanently held together by those ties on which we have too long depended."[117]

The committee of the New Jersey legislature belatedly set to work to remove its troops' grievances in the matter of enlistments, but soon found itself faced by almost insuperable problems and irreconcilable contradictions. "In a number of instances," it reported, "positive Enlistments were produced by the Officers, for the Term of the War; where the Soldiers produced as positive Evidences that they had engaged only for three Years."[118] Little could be accomplished to unsnarl these tangles before a considerable part of the brigade was withdrawn from the state in February to participate in Lafayette's Virginia campaign.

After the first shock of the January fiasco had worn off, the discontent of the New Jersey troops began to revive. It was impossible for any body of normal men to remain long

[116] Thacher, *op. cit.*, pp. 301-4.
[117] Washington to Gov. Clinton, Jan. 29 (photostat in Princeton University Library MSS., AM 1008, from original in Armstrong Collection).
[118] Votes of Assembly, June 5, 1781.

so "heartily penitent & perfectly subdued & subordinate" as one of their colonels found them at the end of January.[119] A bitter resentment filled their minds against the New Englanders who had helped repress the mutiny, and their suspicions of the legislature at Trenton did not lessen. When part of the brigade was on its way to Philadelphia at the end of February to embark for Virginia, one of the officers reported in great vexation the change which had come over a formerly well disciplined corps:

"The Jersey troops have behaved scandalously thus far. Last night, when at Princeton, they created a small riot with the Eastern troops. The grudge occasioned by the late sub-duction was the leading motive. After a little tumult they were dispersed to their quarters and all quiet after. This night many of them were drunk & very turbulent. They are clamorous about their money, meaning the fourth part of their depreciation, which they say is due tomorrow, the first of March. Several threaten not to march unless they receive it. This is the effect of liquor, and I hope when that is evaporated, they will be quiet. Our men I think are exceedingly altered for worse; from being almost the most orderly & subordinate soldiers in the army, they are become a set of drunken, and unworthy fellows. The situation of an officer among them is rendered more disagreeable than any other calling in life, even the most menial, can possibly be. . . . Nothing but the highest severity will reclaim them, and whether or not that will be effectual while they receive such countenance from the public, is very uncertain."[120]

That part of the brigade which remained in the North was fully as demoralized. Regimental orders for the rest of 1781 are full of despairing complaints about soldiers who sit down or even go to sleep while on sentry duty, disobey orders, desert, stay away from camp after dark, steal or

---

[119] Shreve to Dayton, Jan. 27, Sparks MSS., 49, Vol. III.

[120] Francis Barber to Dayton, Feb. 28, 1781, Gratz MSS., Historical Society of Pennsylvania.

destroy the property of the inhabitants, appear on parade without arms, make so much noise when assembled that orders cannot be heard or commands executed, fire their guns unnecessarily, and brawl with one another.[121]

Within the army and without, indeed, all Jerseymen, like all Americans, were feeling a thorough disrelish for the war. An atmosphere of drabness and bleak exhaustion lay heavy over the country during most of the twenty-six long months between the Pompton mutiny and the news that peace had been signed. After the capitulation of Cornwallis at York-town in October 1781, which left no doubt as to the outcome of the struggle, military operations virtually ceased. Only the refugee Tories still had the energy to carry on sporadic depredations from New York; and even these were checked when the conciliatory Sir Guy Carleton succeeded Clinton as supreme commander of the King's forces in America in May 1782.

Life in New Jersey coursed sluggishly in a channel that was neither war nor peace. The state finances were ailing, though perhaps less alarmingly so than they had been a few years earlier. New Jersey paper currency fluctuated erratically in value; the ratio of paper to specie seems to have varied between 2½ : 1 and 4 : 1 in the years 1781 and 1782.[122] If it did not collapse so catastrophically as the emissions of the Continental Congress, the reason is that the state had the power of taxation and used it, though none too cheerfully.[123] Taxes were invariably late in coming in. By 1781, Essex,

---

121 *N.J.H.S.P.*, N.S., Vol. I, pp. 130-42.

122 See various receipts to John Neilson for these years, in James Neilson Papers.

123 From the time the Revolution broke out, the New Jersey legislature imposed no taxes until March and December 1778, and then very inadequate ones. "The Majority [of the legislators] are influenced by I know not what unaccountable timidity of disobliging their constituents in laying a larger assessment," wrote Livingston, who had long been urging the necessity of meeting expenses through taxation. (Livingston to Scudder, Dec. 9, 1778, Livingston Papers, Box 2; Votes of Assembly, Sept. 8, 1777, and March 5, 19, and 26, and Dec. 5, 1778; Wilson, *Laws of New Jersey*, Chap. LXXVI.)

Monmouth, and Gloucester Counties were just completing their quotas for the year 1775; Somerset and Gloucester were still paying their shares of the sinking-fund contribution for 1776; on nearly every tax that had been voted in subsequent years one county or more had fallen into arrears; and on a levy which had been payable on March 1, only Cape May had met its quota by November, while six counties had turned in nothing.[124] The most common excuse for delinquency offered by the inhabitants was that they had been obliged to surrender the products of their labor to the army in return for commissary's certificates of doubtful value, and so had no money to pay taxes.[125] Many who could not offer this excuse sincerely nevertheless used it as a pretext for avoiding their obligations to the state, and the effects upon public finance were baneful.

One group of persons in New Jersey had particularly good reason for worry over unsettled conditions—the East Jersey Proprietors, or such of them as still remained in the state on reasonably good terms with the Revolutionary authorities. At the beginning of the war, a majority of the board had sought refuge with the British—among them the vice-president, Cortlandt Skinner, and the registrar, John Smyth, who took with him all the records. By 1778, the handful of Proprietors left in New Jersey were alarmed to find that the commercial and industrial boom along the seacoast was leading to encroachments on their jointly owned lands in that vicinity which had formerly had little value and had attracted few buyers. Salt works were being set up, and great tracts of woodland were being cut over to supply fuel for the vats. The managers of the new establishments, justifying their actions by the national emergency, disavowed any intention of cheating the Proprietors: they would be glad to purchase legal title, they said, if given the oppor-

[124] Votes of Assembly, Nov. 22, 1781.
[125] Votes of Assembly, March 14, 1780; William Houston to Livingston, May 26, 1780, Sparks MSS., 49, Vol. III.

tunity. In the summer of 1778, the president of the board, James Parker, scraped together ten members, who held a meeting, authorized the sale of some tracts in Monmouth County to such enterprising citizens as Kenneth Hankinson and Samuel Forman, and ordered the proceeds invested in Continental Loan Office certificates for the benefit of the Proprietors.[126]

The legality of such action by a rump Council was highly questionable, particularly since the records and surveys upon which new allotments must be based were in New York. As the years passed, the situation became intolerable, and in the spring of 1782, when fighting was over and communication across the lines was not too difficult, young John Rutherfurd was sent to New York, with the permission of Governor Livingston, to get possession of the records. John Smyth, the registrar, who still had the books in his possession, professed a willingness to do whatever his fellow Proprietors in New York should determine; but men like Stephen Skinner and Oliver DeLancey were so violently opposed to surrendering anything that they converted even Cortlandt Skinner, who had at first been sympathetic. "They appeared so Blinded by passion and actuated by a Reflection on their own Situation," reports Rutherfurd, "that they seemed rivitted to their first opinion and would not hearken to any Thing that was said to them—the Chief Argument made use of by them was that their Estates by Law were already Confiscated, and all that could be discovered was Sold, that their Shares of Propriety were alone untouched, because the Particular Parts were unknown and that the delivery of the Books would tend to designate their Shares, and also a Number of Surveys in such a Manner as to occasion their Confiscation and Sale and that it would be ridiculous in them to Assist others in the security of their Estates, who had done

[126] *Minutes of the Council of Proprietors of the Eastern Division of New Jersey No B*, in office of Surveyor-General, Perth Amboy, pp. 195-200.

all in their power to deprive them of theirs—Arguments and answers were given in Return but very little attended to."[127]

Rutherfurd then played his trump card. Regarding Smyth as a man "actuated entirely by a rectitude of intention divested of passion or Resentment," he sought him out alone and produced a letter signed by nine of the Proprietors in New Jersey, making requisition of the books.

"This I shewed him as the Act of a Board of Proprietors . . . which he as a sworn Officer was bound to obey, after Considering it for sometime, I was happy to find that he conceived it his duty to comply with it—I was for hurrying them from Town immediately, but M[r]. Smyth thinking it incumbent on him to mention it to the other Gentlemen, they applied to Governor Franklin and got him to go with them to Sir Guy Carlton's and General Robertson's, where they formally protested against the Measure, and made a very unjust and false Representation of the Negotiation, of the tendency of the papers, and the purport in sending for them.

"General Robertson sent for me and said that he was informed of the Order of the Proprietors in New Jersey and that I had acted in a very Extraordinary and imprudent manner, in Carrying on a secret Negotiation between Persons in Rebellion and others within the British Lines, and ordered me to desist from any further proceedings—I then had some intention of presenting a Memorial to Sir Guy Carleton, but found it would have no Effect against so powerful an opposition, and might only occasion the removal of the Papers from the Hands of M[r]. Smyth, which was studiously to be avoided, as it might perhaps injure their authenticity as Records."[128]

Thus Rutherfurd was obliged to return home empty-handed, and though the Proprietors in New Jersey reorganized the same summer, with John Stevens as president, they had to do business without their records until 1785.[129]

[127] *ibid.*, pp. 205-6.
[128] *ibid.*, p. 207.
[129] *ibid.*, pp. 201*ff*.

Wherever one turned his eyes in New Jersey, then, the maladjustments produced by the war continued to be painfully evident. The college at Princeton was nominally functioning, but only part of its building had been repaired and kept in repair after the ravages of the British, Continentals, and militiamen who had successively occupied it. Its library had been pillaged—some of the books found their way to North Carolina with the literary-minded but light-fingered officers of Lord Cornwallis. Its famous orrery, the pride of the institution, had been ruined, and most of the rest of its meager scientific equipment destroyed.[130] Its finances were so deranged that the trustees were obliged to appeal to the state Assembly in 1781 for special favorable legislation,[131] and its president had to be dunned by a carpenter for payment of a small bill.[132] What was worse, rumors had spread around—though they were vigorously denied—that during the years when President Witherspoon was spending most of his time in Congress, "Nassau Hall was become a nursery of Vice and irreligion rather than an institution of Virtue and morality."[133]

Such was the condition of long-suffering New Jersey when rumors began to spread at the beginning of March

[130] Green, *Life of Ashbel Green*, pp. 136-7.
[131] Princeton University Library MSS., AM 527 and AM 8685.
[132] *ibid.*, AM 7454:

> Sir be pleas to let me hef the monny of meyn firts acount next weeck ey must hefit hevit ey want to le in meyn winter store
> Ballans Due to me   2550 Daller Conten
> wichs is hard 42½ Dallers pray sir Dont fail
> from jur humbel Servant
>   Philip Hartman

[133] *ibid.*, AM 8804. In view of the gloomy realities of the time which no one at Princeton could overlook, one is a little surprised at the nature of what seems, from a student's description, to have been the outstanding social event of campus life in February 1782, "the acting of a tragedy called that of Ormisinda and Alonzo, never were people better pleased, than with our performance, our dress was rich and elegant and every circumstance to render it noble was strictly attended to, it was so affecting that it caused the tears to flow from many a compassionate mind [and] made them feel for the characters in distress."—*ibid.*, AM 8796.

1783, that peace was imminent. A constant trickle of deserters from the army passed through the state bound from the encampment on the Hudson to their homes farther south, and they were insistent that the official end of hostilities was in sight. Jerseymen shrugged skeptical shoulders. "We have heard that story so often and so long," remarked one, "that it seems to sound rather dull than lively to me, and I imagine it does to most other People by this time. I believe the best way is to think nothing about it, and then perhaps it may come all at once, which if it does will be a very happy alarm."[134]

Confirmation of the rumors was published in the press before the end of the month, and in mid-April the entire state officially celebrated the end of war. Trenton held a solemn ceremony in which governor, the legislature and the town dignitaries participated; and almost every town in the state had its church service of thanksgiving, its banquet, its festive illumination at night, its bonfire, or its grand ball. The seemingly endless ordeal was over, and a new era of independence was to be the reward of the years of suffering and perseverance. "In the day of prosperity be joyful," intoned the minister conducting the service at New Brunswick, and his listeners heartily concurred in the sentiment from Ecclesiastes.[135]

Yet the war was not so simply disposed of as that. It had left deep scars on New Jersey—physical scars which anyone could see; psychic scars which were more painful and more pitiful. Burnt villages could be rebuilt; desolate farms could be made to flourish again; peaceful industry and trade could gradually be restored to a normal state; but the hatred and the bitterness accumulated through feverish years could not be wiped away by the signing of a treaty. In communities of fierce party division, like Swedesboro, some people

---

[134] Princeton University Library MSS., AM 9511.   [135] Salter, *op. cit.*, pp. 309-11

"would not go to church, because, as they pretended, the sight of their enemies aroused the memory of the evils they had suffered and filled their minds with anger and sorrow, so that they were unable to worship."[136] Petitions poured in upon the legislature, especially from Monmouth County, urging the governor not to permit refugee Tories—"Bloodthirsty Robbers" and "Atrocious monsters"—to return to their former homes. The greed of commercial competitors was sometimes but thinly covered by a veneer of vengeful and somewhat incoherent patriotism, as in this passage from one of the addresses:

"To Explicate to your honours the aggrievances this State Doth & will Sustain by their abiding here is this, their impeading & taking the profits of the good subjects of this State in Sundry things which may be innumerated. first, their flocking inn in Different classis, some of one trad, & some of an other takeing the Bread out of the mouths of our good Subjects who has Risked their lives against them for the Support of our libertys against unconstitutional, & arbitrary laws. Their occupations may be many & Each in their measure Retard the living of our good subjects. Some may open shops of goods & undersell our good Subjects by reason of two things, namely, they can purchase goods at prime cost; 2^d.ly, they have got their welth to purchase goods by Robing us of our welth. . . . We shall have them flocking in to the impoverishing of grateren part of the townships of this state, in paying taxis for the support of the poorer Sort, who has spent their Substence in the land of Noviscotia, & coming Back will gain a Residence in Each town ship where they Reside."[137]

[136] Collin, *Journal*, p. 253.
[137] Petition to New Jersey Legislature, April 10, 1787, from 76 inhabitants of Monmouth County (P.R.O., Trenton). There are other petitions of similar tenor dating back to 1781 in the same office. See also Honeyman, "Concerning the New Jersey Loyalists in the Revolution," in *N.J.H.S.P.*, Vol. LI, pp. 123-4.

The persistence of pre-war class antagonisms is clearly indicated in the demand of more than a hundred Middlesex petitioners:

"There is many Internal Enemies living among us, formerly of the first class of people, when called upon to any duty, either in the field or Cabinet State or Church, they would say they had Nothing to do with the Dispute, and would do Nothing but what they were Compelled to do, for their Country, but we have Reason to believe they have done all they could against us, and no doubt would again, whenever they Should have it in their power, the Lawyers is one set of Men that we are pointing at, or that part of them that did not do business under the New Constitution from the first declaration of Independence, or aided or Assisted in the Support of the Country—

"We your petitioners do most Earnestly pray that your honours will please to pass a Law to Exempt for ever all that Class of Lawyers that did not take a Desided part in favour of their Country and Strictly adheard to it ever since the Declaration of Independence from ever coming to the barr of Justice in this State in the Character of a Lawyer— and that no Writ of any kind Issued by any of that Class, to be Valued in any Court in this State."[138]

Obviously, then, all was not serenity and comradely love in the little state of New Jersey as it stood for the first time acknowledged as independent by the entire world. Great transformations had indeed taken place in eight years. The power of the Perth Amboy Group had been forever shattered, and its members dispersed. The pleasant little town where their wealth, prestige, and self-assurance had been so long displayed was now a desolate and deserted village, its primacy usurped by rising Trenton, where men of a new political generation and a new political vocabulary were filling the places of the Skinners, Johnstons, Smyths and

[138] Petition of May 3, 1783, P.R.O., Trenton.

Kearnys. Yet in the war-battered New Jersey in 1783 there was probably more relentless hatred between different groups than there had been in 1775, and fully as much social discontent. What the state would make of its new-found freedom and democracy was a question that remained to be answered; and he would have been an optimist indeed who could have given a cheerful answer without reservations or misgivings.

INDEX OF PERSONS

(Names of unimportant individuals or persons casually mentioned are frequently omitted from this list. Moreover, no attempt is made to direct the reader's attention to any but the more significant references in the text to such prominent figures as George Washington, William Livingston, and General Howe.)

INDEX OF SUBJECTS

DATE DUE

Jul 29 '75			
Aug 12 '75			
Aug 14 '75			
Oct 13 '75			
Oct 13 '75			
Nov 18 '76			
Sep 9 '81			
Nov 26			
SEP 1 7 1996			
OCT 0 7 1996			
JUN 1 7 2004			
MAR 1 3 2010			
JUL 2 4 2010			
AUG 1 4 2010			